AMERICA AT WAR
1917 ——————— 1918

AMERICAN DEMOCRACY and the WORLD WAR

★ ★

AMERICA AT WAR

1917 ——— 1918

FREDERIC L. PAXSON

COOPER SQUARE PUBLISHERS, INC.
NEW YORK
1966

TO
J., E., and P.
COMRADES

PREFACE

DEMOCRACY is a vehicle so lumbering that a part of the world has come to doubt whether it is a dependable carrier for a national interest. As a consequence of its basic principle a little less than half of any democratic nation is commonly engaged in partisan struggle to prevent the little more than half, which constitutes the majority of the moment, from achieving a purpose. Yet the behavior of the United States in its war years, 1917–18, should be a reminder to Americans and a warning to the world that when emotion whittles the minority down to nearly nothing and makes citizens agree among themselves, even a democracy may act with speed, directness, efficiency, and weight. One kind of victory, at least, was blocked by the American intervention in the World War; and for once in history a great nation went whole-heartedly to combat, shared in the labor to defeat an enemy, and marched its men home carrying no plunder and asking none.

The war years of the United States are a necessary chapter in the history of the World War. They constitute an even more important chapter in the history of democracy in action.

FREDERIC L. PAXSON

Margaret Byrne Professor of United States History in the University of California

BERKELEY, CALIFORNIA
December, 1938

CONTENTS

MAPS AND TABLES

I. THE WAR OF 1917

A BRIEF period of twenty hectic months was long enough to cover the experiences of the American democracy as a participant in the War of 1917. With its mind at last made up, the United States entered the World War, designed its weapons, created them, stabilized its doctrine, forwarded its men to France, used them at the end of a line of communications whose three thousand miles or more in length connected every American household with the remote trenches, and delivered a military blow without which it is hard to believe that a German victory could have been avoided.

The people of the United States, in these twenty months, passed through all the mental phases from a chamber-of-commerce 'business as usual' to an avid 'work or fight.' They discarded the reservations with which a domestic order had been built up inside the framework of the Constitution and revealed the driving capacity of democracy in the rare moments when democrats agree among themselves. They stopped their war with the enemy defeated; and their withdrawal affected the world as greatly as their entry. They saw, or their effective majority saw, nothing grotesque in the substitution of 'back to normalcy' for the exaltation of 'safe for democracy.' Their retreat was as much a part of democracy as was the hesitation with which the United States watched its interests for three years before April 6, 1917, or the one-mindedness with which it helped to win the war.

The story of this war must at least be three-dimensional. The narrative of events, from which no historian may long dissociate himself, is packed with episode; and it should never be forgotten that each episode depends as much upon the atmosphere in which it happens as upon those of its causes that run directly back into the past. Cross-purposes and traffic jams become in themselves new causes to complicate the story.

In the second place, the institutions of the war, created for the purpose or expanded from existing agencies, were events when they emerged, each representing a crystallization of the opinion of the moment; but as institutions they kept on growing; and the description of their enlargement, their structure, and their overlaps, not to mention their success or failure, gives another dimension to any picture of the war.

A third dimension has to do with intangibles — ideas of democracy, of world order, of war aims, of reform to be squeezed out of life because of the crisis. Like the institutions of the war, these grew. Not the same in any two consecutive months, their impact affected at all times the institutions of the war, the civic experiences at the rear, and the military operations at the front. The American mind that looked into war in April, 1917, was not the mind that looked back upon it in December, 1918. Whatever the War of 1917 may display respecting war, it affords impressive exhibits illustrating the functioning of democracy.

The Congress, voting war on April 6, 1917, signed a blank check upon the future. Ignorant of American resources, of the need to use them, and of the mechanisms that might bring them into operation, it did not know the war that was and could not foresee the demands upon its strength. The most effective members of Congress had been trained in the Progressive decade, whose philosophy found more social advantage to be gained through the restriction of combination than through the development of centralized and efficient authority.

Better than the Congress or the Administration, the Allies were aware of the completeness of American inexperience. They knew their own man-power was weary and their young-man-power was exhausted. They knew how near they were to the limit of their financial resources. They knew what private national aims lay screened behind their slogan of a war of democratic governments. They knew that not only their objectives but perhaps their existence depended upon the power of the American reinforcement, and each of them knew what form it would prefer to have that reinforcement take. When Congress passed the war resolution, they hurried their War Missions out upon the Atlantic to proceed to Washington to welcome the United States as an associate. Missions these were with impressive figures at their head — Balfour for England, Joffre and Viviani (who was mortified because Americans did not know how important he was) for France. Behind the heads of Mission limped lesser men, broken in action, perhaps, but mentally acute to the need, ready to explain to those who were at work upon the American program what war meant, how the United States might avoid the errors the Allies had made, how American democracy might co-operate so as to permit the Allies to win the war.

A fortnight after the passage of the war resolution the earliest of the congratulatory War Missions were nearing the Atlantic ports of their destination. The lesser Allies followed the greater, with delegations whose receptions were spread into the summer weeks. But those of England and France alone captured the American imagination; and among the members of these, Joffre stole the show. Enthusiasm for the France whose Lafayette had been friend and associate of Washington could be poured without stint. Joffre, at the Marne, was believed to have turned the Germans back, and this belief was as effective as though it were entirely based on fact; it fully justified 'une mission, plus sentimentale et exceptionnellement decorative,' to carry greetings. It was even more useful because enthusiasm for England was not everywhere negotiable.

The available documents do not yet reveal how fully calculated was the indiscretion of Joffre, who turned American attention to an angle of the war that had been generally outside the picture in the weeks of entry. On the day of his arrival at Hampton Roads, it was permitted to be said that he was prepared 'to discuss the sending of an American expeditionary force to France.' He proceeded to Washington, to be the guest of the nation in the home of Henry White, and talked to the waiting correspondents. He asked for troops when he met the President in the White House, suggesting in his appeal the French sense for concrete reality, the sense that would recognize assistance in the form of goods and cash, but that would know it to be real only when men and flags were visible in Paris. France was bled and tired. The Nivelle drive was a greater failure than had been disclosed. French morale needed every support, and if the gaps in the French armies could not be filled with Americans in uniform, they could not be filled at all. 'Let the American soldier come now,' he pleaded.

To the Congress, wrestling with its third week of war legislation, the new idea was disturbing. That an army must be organized was obvious; but participation with an army heavy enough to weight its side was not part of the first intention. It could not be floated, for there were not ships enough. It could not be supplied, even if it could be floated; for transporting a soldier was only the first step in a long process of provisioning him, outfitting him, and providing him with the heavy tonnage of war goods that could not be interrupted while he lived. Every new increment of troops to be sent to France would add to the permanent burden on a tonnage already inadequate to the minimum needs of the Allies themselves. Indeed Joffre did not ask for a great army at once nor had he any idea as to how it should cross the ocean, but he wanted troops to be seen in France.

The Administration Army bill was already under consideration before the Allied War Missions made their appearance, and involved as much shock to established notions as Congress could well stand, for it was based upon a draft. Conscription was odious among Americans; among even those who were less emphatic than Speaker Clark, who declared that 'in the estimation of Missourians there is precious little difference between a conscript and a convict.'

The experience of England provided the talking point for the advocates of compulsory service, for England in the early years of war had filled the ranks with volunteers, only to learn too late the dire consequences of promiscuous volunteering. Worst of these was the injury done to war industries which must not be crippled if the armies were to survive. Many men were of greater use in the shops than in the trenches, and when their enthusiasm and patriotism took them to the front as volunteers, industry was disorganized behind the lines. Victory in a war like this depended upon the even development of all parts of the national effort. Government could know little enough of how to plan for a proper equilibrium; but the results when it selected its servants were more useful than when each citizen chose his own duty after emotional appeals made in a campaign to swell enlistments. The next dire consequence had to do with officer material. At least one man in every twenty, fifty thousand in the million, must be an officer; and to learn the simplest duties of the officer, so that his men might not be murdered through his ignorance, called for an aptitude at lessons that was most commonly shown in lads of college age, with formal education. But these very lads rushed first to the colors in 1914, and so many of them were dead after two years of war that England lost a generation of its normal leaders, and was crippled immediately by a lack of material for junior officers. England, with an inhibition as great as that of the United States, had come reluctantly to the draft. The War Department followed suit, and set itself to establish the principle of selective service in the face of a history of consistent volunteering practice. The Civil War draft was a device to stimulate volunteering rather than a means of filling ranks. War was no longer amply served by professional officers and patriotic volunteers; it called for the whole of national strength, with men at their best jobs, not those that they preferred.

The Selective Service Act, as it was finally called, came into the two houses simultaneously and just as the English Mission reached American soil. It had been ready for introduction early in April, but the committee had to digest its novelties before they could defend it in open debate. The chairman of the Senate committee, Chamberlain of Oregon, was for it. His counterpart in the House committee, Dent of Alabama, was so sure that a draft ought not to be used until after an attempt to raise an army of volunteers that the management of the measure passed out of his hands and into those of Julius Kahn of California, a German-born Republican. The measure was under violent argument in both houses during the week of public entertainment of the Missions, with its purpose becoming more concrete as the idea of an expeditionary force seeped into public consciousness. The two bills, simultaneously discussed, passed by great majorities on the same day, April 28; but they were different bills, and original passage was only the prelude to a long struggle in conference for three weeks more. The size of the minorities voting No — eight in the Senate, twenty-four in the House — gives no indication of the bitterness of the opposition, but shows only that in the prevailing American state of mind the more courageous alone, or the more obstinate, were willing to be counted as opposing basic measures of the war.

The principle of the draft was accepted, as unbeatable. The final fight turned upon the age limits for registrants, the negation of volunteering (apart from enlistment in Army or in National Guard), and the attempt of prohibition profiteers to get something for their reform out of the emergency. The last succeeded. The final bill forbade the sale of liquor in the vicinity of army camps or to soldiers in uniform.

The other last controversies became matters of compromise after conference reports had shuttled back and forth. The age limits within which citizens should be liable for service were fought throughout the whole debate. The War Department preferred that these should range from nineteen to twenty-five, but Dent declared from the beginning that he, and those who agreed with him, 'would never vote for a bill . . . to conscript a boy nineteen or twenty years of age . . . who did not have the right to vote.' The adjustment in conference was between the House demand that the ages should be twenty-one to forty so that mature citizens should bear their share, and the Senate preference for twenty-one to twenty-seven because as men pass out of their twenties their usefulness as private soldiers lessens rapidly. It was not proposed to use the physically unfit, or certain classes of constitutional objectors, or to call at once men with heavy domestic responsibilities. All great armies have been built on boys, and professional opinion regarded boys of nineteen as mature enough. The conflict of principle and opinion finally came to rest in a compromise at twenty-one to thirty.

The issue of volunteering threatened to wreck the whole debate and increased in intensity when it appeared that some troops at least would go at once. It was a sentimental issue, congressmen believing that their constituents would resent conscription. It was hardly justified by actual failure to accept the volunteer, for the armed forces, Army, National Guard, Navy, and Marine Corps, were all actively recruiting, and could absorb nearly a million men before they reached their maximum authorized limits. New recruits were being enlisted and trained in existing units more quickly than they could be turned into soldiers in any training camps; and this sort of volunteering was not discontinued until the Selective Service Act was passed and put into operation. Volunteers for officer duty were welcomed, too. Under the National Defense Act of 1916 training camps for junior officers were arranged as soon as war became a fact. On May 15 some fourteen of these were opened to give an intensive three months' course to the second lieutenants, who would in turn train the first half-million drafted men. But the issue between the houses was more than a conflict between sentiment and efficiency; it contained its measure of politics, and in this it revolved around the ambition of Theodore Roosevelt to lead an army.

Roosevelt, devoted to a sound Army as he had shown himself to be as President, died unconvinced that a volunteer army raised around his name would have been inconsistent with either efficiency or the principle of selective service. He supported the draft, always believing in it; but having raised one volunteer unit in the war with Spain he wanted now to raise another. He was afraid the United States would fight a war with no troops at all upon the line. There were plenty of officers ready to accompany him, anywhere, on any basis. His name would undoubtedly have attracted private enlistments in sufficient number. He allowed a preliminary enrollment to be made; and on April 10, the 'most eminent and able, if not most bitter critic' of the President (Longworth's words), he called at the White House to urge the acceptance of his force. Said Gardner in the House: 'The people want the Stars and Stripes waving over those trenches... [and] if Roosevelt or any other Pied Piper can whistle 25,000 fanatics after him, for Heaven's sake give him the chance. He may whistle his division into the trenches half trained, of course; but I will wager that they will make up in nerve what they lack in drill. Roosevelt is no fool.' In his enthusiasm Roosevelt, who had already before 1914 described himself as 'a stout, rheumatic, elderly gentleman,' brushed aside the objection that he was fifty-eight years old and without the training of a general. He did not advertise the fact that he was blind of one eye (lost through a boxing accident while President) and intermittently slowed down 'due to the poisoning of his system by the equatorial fever that he had incurred while on his Brazilian trip.' His chosen biographer, Joseph Bucklin Bishop, made these matters public when he died, in *Theodore Roosevelt and his Time* (1920). Roosevelt approached his old enemy with a packet of letters from Europe, welcoming him as a companion in arms. Clemenceau volunteered advice that he should be allowed to come.

But for once a war of the United States was being fought as war, with plans drafted by professional soldiers (of whom the best owed their chance for training largely to Roosevelt). The evils resulting from the use of political commanders had been sufficiently displayed in the Civil War. The casualties due to ignorance of untrained line officers had been a scandal during mobilization for the war with Spain, and quite as scandalous, though less well advertised, in the war of 1861. The War Department had decided to resist the admission of young men to commissions until they had been selected after stern competition in the officers' camps. These schools gave little enough of training, but it was better than nothing, and vastly superior to any previous American practice. The President supported the Department in this determination and fought for freedom to avoid the necessity to accept any but trained commanders at the top.

The friends of Roosevelt held out in the Senate through a long debate as they sought to make the acceptance of volunteer units mandatory upon the President. Rooseveltians supported it, and Republicans, and some who opposed any draft, and a few who were ready to press for anything they were sure the Administration did not want. Three weeks after the separate bills passed their respective houses the conferees were still in deadlock. 'The delay in Congress is becoming a scandal,' wrote one of the Washington correspondents, as this earliest controversy over war policy reached its crisis. Other measures, nearly as necessary as the army act, were held back until the friends of Theodore Roosevelt surrendered.

By the terms of the surrender that freed the Army from the menace of political commanders, the President was left at liberty to accept volunteer units or to refrain from accepting them. The President signed the Selective Service Act on May 18, 1917, releasing at once a statement settling the matter: 'It would be very agreeable to me to pay Mr. Roosevelt this compliment.... But this is not the time or the occasion for compliment or for any action not calculated to contribute to the immediate success of the war.' He announced, as well, that on June 5 men over twenty-one but not yet thirty-one would be called upon to register near their homes and that 'at as early a date as practicable' a force of Regulars would be sent to France under the command of Major-General John J. Pershing.

Pershing had surmised that something of this sort was about to happen. On May 3, he had received from his father-in-law Warren, stalwart Republican Senator from Wyoming, a cryptic telegram: 'Wire me today whether and how much you speak, read, and write French.' He wrote this hint into the opening paragraph of his *My Experiences in the World War* (1931). Roosevelt, who had made *My Experiences* possible when he promoted Pershing from captain to brigadier-general in 1906, accepted the adverse decision. He disbanded his division on May 20, published his correspondence with the War Department in the *Metropolitan* in August, and plunged into an oratorical co-operation with the war that was interrupted only by sickness and ended only by his death.

Even the announcement that an American expeditionary force was to be sent to France did not convince the Government or the people that the American reinforcement was to be military in character. The ocean tonnage at the disposition of the United

States was too small to make this possible. The hope of Joffre for a fighting army was a dream, on whose coming true no military realist could rely. The new commander, who likewise had no right to dream that his command was for the first time in American experience to be free from political hobbies, was already quietly back in Washington and at work upon the details of organization. Common opinion held it that the force was to be sent to France chiefly for the purpose of parade, yet the orders being formulated treated it as though it might become an army. The War Department set to work to draft and train a National Army. Congress plunged into other business. And the Administration kept to its course of preparing a program that should be largely material and economic.

Only one measure of consequence for the conduct of the war reached the White House earlier than the Selective Service Act. This was a loan act, passed without effort, which was signed on April 24.

The financial basis of the war had been under discussion during the weeks preceding the declaration, for, however the United States should participate, it was certain that the cost of American effort would be great, and that the supply of materials to the Allies must not be stopped. The public knew less well than the Treasury how nearly the Allies had reached the end of their own financial resources. They had bought supplies in the United States since 1914; paying in credit and gold, commandeering American securities held by their citizens and sending them to the United States for sale to pay the bills, and borrowing in loans floated in America by the Morgans and their associates. The Missions arriving in Washington in April spoke their congratulations in public, and in private asked for cash. They would have been glad to be placed on regular monthly allowances suited to their own statements of their needs.

Wilson recognized the need for 'adequate credits' in his war message and the 'very practical duty . . . of supplying the nations already at war with Germany' with the things they could use. But when Professor E. R. A. Seligman of Columbia, perhaps the most distinguished of the financial economists, suggested that the war would cost at least ten billion dollars in its first year, he was 'greeted with a smile of incredulity.' The Treasury was accustomed to a scale of operations far below this. During the three preceding fiscal years, 1914–16, it had averaged 737 millions in receipts and 718 millions in disbursements. It was hard driven to find sufficient revenue to enable it to avoid deficit finance. War had interfered with the flow of trade and with the revenue derived from trade through the tariff. Only the new income tax, increasing in productivity since its first assessment against incomes of 1913, had enabled McAdoo to meet Federal obligations out of taxation. In the next three fiscal years, 1918–20, expenditures were to be stepped up to an average of 12, 538 millions, against taxes of 41 per cent of the amount, 5170 millions a year. The readiness of the United States to cast its fortunes by the side of those of the Allies was not accompanied by any realization of the cost in dollars or by any plan to meet the deficit.

Economists had studied the financial aspect of war as they watched it after 1914. In England there had been made the most vigorous effort to pay a large fraction of its cost out of current taxes. On either side of the Western Front the Central Powers as well as their enemies had preferred to rely upon loans rather than upon taxes; for the latter would mean immediate burdens upon their citizenry, while it might be hoped, as each side hoped, that the defeated adversary could be compelled to assume and pay the loans as war indemnity. And the cynical observed that, in the event of defeat, repudiation would not add greatly to the other unavoidable burdens.

Discussion of the ways and means of war broke out in the United States not as a part of war preparation, but as one of the fighting fronts of the opponents of American entry. It was Socialist doctrine, in which most pacifists and many Progressives concurred, that wars were fomented by capitalists for their own advantage; and that one of the ways of dissuading capitalists from this was to make war costly. As the new Congress convened for its war session, the American Committee on War Finance, self-nominated, advertised its demand for a 'pay-as-you-go' war that should have the advantage of throwing the cost upon the wealthy who provoked it, of redistributing some of their too-large accumulations, and of freeing posterity from an enduring burden of taxation. The connotations implicit to this found acceptance among many to whom the very word Socialist was anathema; even among many in the Government. 'I hope,' said the President on April 2, that the necessary credits may be sustained, 'so far as they can equitably be sustained by the present generation, by well-conceived taxation.' The demand that the whole cost of the war be borne out of current taxes was impracticable with all, sincere with some, and a convenient method of obstruction with a few. The fiscal proposals brought in at once were based on an assumption that about one dollar out of three could be raised as spent. The Secretary of the Treasury says, in *Crowded Years: The Reminiscences of William G. McAdoo* (1931), that he gave up the idea of taxing half the costs out of the people because he thought 'such a scale would be excessive, and perhaps destructive ... of the capitalized energy which keeps the wheels turning.' During the Civil War the proportion was approximately one to five.

Three aspects of immediate finance, as distinguished from permanent policy, confronted Treasury officials and the congressional leaders before Kitchin opened the brief debate on an emergency loan measure on April 13. Perhaps first in importance of these was the requirement of the Allies for funds. They were about drained dry. They did not expect, much as they might desire, immediate military aid; but the United States was an untouched storehouse of supplies if only the Government would contribute the financial key. Second was the certainty that Treasury requirements would run ahead of tax collections under existing laws. The Committee on Ways and Means was busy with proposals for a new revenue law, written in the language of war necessity, but until this should be worked through (six months it took), there could be no revenues except those to be collected from the operation of pre-war laws. No one yet knows how far commitments by the Government ran in advance of appropriations, but everyone then knew that tax receipts would be both insufficient and slow. The Treasury must have authority for short-term borrowing in anticipation of taxes and the proceeds of bond sales.

And third, there were the needs of the immediate future in excess of anything that taxes could be speeded up to provide. However the war was to be financed after new legislation should become productive, it would entail spending of great sums in excess of taxes. Bonds were to be authorized; and with a sharp recollection of the obloquy incurred by Cleveland because of his marketing of bonds through bankers' syndicates, both Administration and Congress were aware that these bonds must be placed through the mechanics of popular subscription.

With a unanimity unscratched by any single adverse vote in either Senate or House, the loan act was passed in less than two weeks from the date of its introduction. The House accepted it, upon report from the Committee on Ways and Means, on April 14, the day after the debate opened. The Senate passed it three days later. The slight matters of difference between Senate and House were ironed out in time for conference reports to be accepted April 23, two days after the British Mission rolled into the United States. And the President signed it April 24. The very next morning Baron Cunliffe of Headley, Governor of the Bank of England and one of Balfour's associates on the Mission, was at the Treasury for the signing of British notes to the amount of 200 million dollars against the credits voted in the bill. And shortly after him came Jusserand, borrowing for France, but so piqued that he declined the proffer of the pen with which his check was signed. He received but 100 millions at the start and, like the Italian Ambassador, thought that, all being first-class powers, 'all should be treated alike.' 'Mr. McAdoo is the most active and enterprising member of the Cabinet,' the British Ambassador, Spring Rice, wrote to Balfour: 'It is he who distributes proceeds in the forms of loans to the Allies.' The American reinforcement was in operation.

The loan act authorized the addition of five billions to the debt of the United States, in the form of bonds drawing three and one-half per cent interest. Two of the five billions were earmarked for the use of the Treasury, for the costs of war. Three billions were pledged for loans at the same rate to nations 'engaged in war with the enemies of the United States.' The comments made upon the proposal for financial support to the Allies did not challenge the underlying idea. It was accepted that this was to be the nature of American aid. 'The Supreme need of our own Nation and of the nations with which we are co-operating,' declared the President while the bill was in the Senate, 'is an abundance of supplies.' The critics of the bill expected to vote for it, and did; but they wanted to make sure that the loans would be offered directly to the public, without the intervention of bankers or bankers' percentages, and that the advances would be made only to the associated enemies of Germany. To associated enemies, not to Allies of the United States; for it was made clear that the United States would not attach itself to that Pact of London whereby Britain, France, and Russia, in the first instance, pledged themselves to common war and common peace. Balfour was explicit in assuring the United States that his country had no desire to entrap the United States or to detach it from its traditional policy of avoiding alliances. There came into being a clumsy title for the enemies of Germany — the Allied and Associated Powers. When inquirers invited Kitchin to explain the nature of the security that could be pledged to the United States for the repayment of the loans, he replied simply: 'We have to trust the Governments to whom we loan the money,' and his answer was accepted as sufficient. Administration, Congress, and the people adhered to the policy of loans throughout the war. The upper limit was raised as later loan acts authorized more borrowing. Nearly all of the ten billions thus made available was before the Armistice converted into obligations of the enemies of Germany.

The provision permitting the Treasury to sell short-term notes as needed, with an upper limit of two billions to be outstanding at any time, was sometimes erroneously interpreted as making the loan act one of seven billions rather than of five. This was, however, only a device for flexibility in finance, vital in its effectiveness and less well understood than its importance called for. There was no need for paper money, and no legacy of greenbacks was left for adjustment after the war. As the commitments of the Government reached the moment of necessary payment, the Treasury, under this and later acts, thirty-one times before the Armistice, sold its certificates of debt, to run for not more than twelve months. It sold them to the banks which took their quotas automatically, knowing that the funds in payment would stay on their books to the credit of the United States until the cash was actually disbursed. As the inflow of receipts, whether from taxes or loans, built up the Government deposits, certificates were retired. Whatever inflation the war produced was an inflation of credit, less visible than if in paper money, but quite as real. When the time came to buy back the certificates out of the proceeds of the great war loans, it was only the form of the obligation that was changed. A large share of the money for the purchase of war bonds was raised by buyers who borrowed from the banks up to the face value of the bonds, with the bonds as collateral and the interest rate the same. But as the financial burden of the war was spread, much of what began as Government debt to the banks was converted into private debts to the same banks, secured by the evidences of public credit as collateral. How far this constituted in fact a money inflation tending to raise the level of prices is a matter for nice measurement.

The requirement that the bonds, when sold, should be disposed of by popular subscription taxed the inventiveness of the Treasury, and gave another opening to its ingenious and driving Secretary. The loan act left to his discretion the dates of issues, and the amounts to be called for at each loan. He consulted banking opinion as to the capacity of the people to absorb the bonds. Every adviser thought it impracticable to get as much as three billions upon a single call; and McAdoo quotes Morgan as believing one billion to be enough, and one dollar in five enough of the total cost to be borne by taxes. It was guesswork at best. The Spanish War had not caused a ripple in financial circles. The Civil War, a desperate business, had baffled Chase until he discovered Jay Cooke and paid him well. McAdoo, with a keen sense for slogans and before he revealed its dimensions, named his loan 'The Liberty Loan of 1917 ... because the money will be spent to the last dollar in the fight which democracy is waging against autocracy.'

On May 2 the Secretary of the Treasury announced that two billions would be required, to be subscribed through the gratuitous services of financial institutions, to be paid for by subscribers in installments, and to run from June 15 for thirty years, though callable sooner. He announced as well that he would himself go on the stump, beginning with Chicago, to explain in the Middle West the need for the money, connecting it always with the purpose of the war. As he did this, says Mary Synon (the author of what might have been his campaign biography in 1920), 'to hundreds of little communities ... the tall, thin, hollow-cheeked, blazing-eyed man on the rear platform ... symbolized the Government of the United States.'

A director of publicity in the Treasury represented the Secretary at the head of the war loan organization; and beneath him the Federal Reserve Banks adapted their structure to the new sort of business. The paper work passed through the banks. Local committees to promote sales were instituted in every region and local talent provided the speaking at public meetings except upon the occasions when McAdoo, or another with a known name, was passing that way. The stock and bond men served willingly as private solicitors, with the energetic assistance of local volunteers. Subscribers wore on their lapels the buttons indicating that they had done their part. Newspapers gave space to report the progress of the campaign, with regional rivalries built up by quotas allotted, and with daily diagrams showing progress in meeting quotas.

Bankers had told McAdoo that his task would be made difficult because not over 350,000 Americans were in the habit of investing in bonds. He and his coadjutors, however, when the books of the first loan were closed on June 15, had persuaded more than four million subscribers to offer to take 3035 million dollars' worth of Liberty Bonds. The doctrine of the salesmen, reiterating the phrases and sentiments of Wilson and his Secretary, permeated every backwoods of the United States. Participators in the work acquired the interest that came from participation and responsibility. The citizen who had supported the war when it was voted, without always knowing why, began to have a rationalization of it satisfactory to himself as the loan drive brought it home. And the popular *War Message and the Facts Behind It*, issued and annotated by the Committee on Public Information, was in circulation as a reference text. Before it had gone far, the President reinforced its argument when he spoke at Arlington Cemetery on Memorial Day; and colloquies in the Senate bore a warning to obstructionists and critics.

Not all the orators on Memorial Day were as confident or as emphatic as the President. The junior Senator from Ohio, Harding, allowed himself to tell an audience in Columbus that he regarded the Liberty Loan campaign as 'hysterical and unseemly.' James Hamilton Lewis, Senator from Illinois, descended upon him for partisanry when the report of the address reached Washington. James A. Reed of Missouri, far from unswerving as a follower of Wilson, belabored him with sarcasm. And Harding, outmatched in forensics, slipped out of the discussion, to the final words of Reed taunting him with ambition 'to preside as Chief Executive.'

The day before the drive was ended, on Flag Day, June 14, the President spoke again, at the foot of the Washington Monument in a driving rain. Pershing was received in Paris that day, after a brief pause in London. Root was in Petrograd, where Russia had a few days before declared against annexations and indemnities. Northcliffe was in Washington, directing a permanent British War Mission there. And Wilson explained again the aims of the United States. He drove farther in the wedge between the German people and their Government. He set another wedge among the Central Allies by describing Austria-Hungary as the dupe of Germany. House had urged him to clarify the issues in the absence of 'intelligent or co-ordinate direction of Allied policy'; and Wilson responded so effectively that Creel, now his publicity manager, could dispose of 6,813,340 copies of the address in the United

States. The President avoided statements to which the Associates of the United States might object (as he had avoided discussing war aims with the Missions lest argument defer victory), and directed the American effort against 'the military masters' of Germany: 'if they succeed, America will fall within the menace. We and all the rest of the world must remain armed . . . if they fail, the world may unite for peace and Germany may be of the union.' The subscription to the Liberty Loan closed a first phase of the War of 1917.

II. THE CIVILIANS' TASK

LORD DEVONPORT, whose title gilded a successful tea merchant, set up an office as British food controller in the Ministry of Lloyd George in December, 1916. He was engaged in the task of adjusting public need to scant supply of food during the months through which the United States prepared its mind for war. England was slower in the regimentation of its citizens than the Central Powers had been. Yet the necessity to see that all be fed, and that visible supply be rationed fairly, grew with the war. No country could escape it. Lloyd George urged it in vain until as Prime Minister he was in a position to have his way. The fact that modern war and regimentation go hand in hand impressed itself slowly upon the United States, but not too slowly for it to receive consideration while the preparedness measures hung in Congress in the summer of 1916.

War had become a national effort in which no citizen was too unimportant to have a part. Success was a matter of armed forces, to direct which there was adequate professional skill in every country. It takes training and experience to make a soldier, but the raw material is everywhere as extensive as manhood, and there are more potential marshals in every army than there are batons to be distributed. Success was a matter, too, of material supplies, in which the combatants differed widely and of which none had enough. But success was, even more, a matter — and here the World War provided new tests of human adaptability — of the ingenuity and effectiveness with which resources of men and things were conserved, rationed, and delivered against the enemy. This process was civilian at one end and military at the other. In 1914, in neither civil nor military life, were there many men who were competent to plan and administer the process. As the United States watched the warring nations experiment with conservation and procurement, those who knew what was happening could appreciate how completely the success of American performance would depend upon American handling of similar experiments.

The Council of National Defense emerged among the preparedness measures of 1916 as a war agency to bridge the gap between what the armies needed and what the civilians possessed. Some of its powers had been anticipated in clauses of the National Defense Act which enlarged the discretion of the President in matters of procurement. He was authorized to commandeer plants in the national interest and to create an industrial mobilization board. The Council was designed to be a latent arm of the Government, and while there was no war there was no pressure to hurry its activities. There was, indeed, no one who could hurry them until the President was ready; and he was slow to fight. A modest sum of $200,000 was appropriated, and the Council was empowered 'to supervise and direct investigations and make recommendations to the President and the heads of executive departments ... for the co-ordination of industries and resources for the national security and welfare.' The Council, embracing six members of the Cabinet, organized formally in the autumn of 1916, named its operating agent which was described in the law as its Advisory Commission, and met with the Commission a few times to discuss procedure. But neither Council nor Advisory Commission set to work upon war plans until a week after the dismissal of von Bernstorff. In the eight weeks thereafter, until war became a fact, the civilian specialists of the Advisory Commission heard much of what they must learn to do and of what they could do only at their peril.

Regimentation by the Federal Government was a novelty that must be based upon principles hostile to the American trend. For a generation the best political thought of the United States had been devising means to give fuller effect to the prohibition of 'conspiracies in restraint of trade.' Regimentation would reverse much of this policy as the citizen should be called upon to co-operate, not compete, and to accept the decisions of bureaucracy in place of individual free choice. It could not be foreseen how readily Americans would adopt the principle of selective service in the field of military duty, or how completely their approval of the war brought with it a desire to be told how best to be of use. Not foreknowing the answers that were apparent only after the Selective Service Act had been passed and the Liberty Loan had been absorbed, the Advisory Commission faced a war, aware that controls must be set up along every walk of life, and that these controls would be unworkable if they were not welcomed by so many of their victims that the minorities could be ignored. It was quite another matter to devise controls that would produce the ends desired.

Hard as it was to chart a course, it was just as hard to fit the existing frame of government into its requirements; to make the Commission supplement, not block, the military effort; to avoid the jealousies of professional soldiers certain that they knew all there was to know about war. Civilians had to blunder because of their ignorance of simple military fundamentals. Military men, competent and devoted as soldiers, were rarely possessed of the training or imagination to enable them to organize and manage production in the field of manufacture. They were hampered, too, by snarls of the red tape of peace time and by that fear of mistakes that keeps junior officers silent in the presence of their seniors. It was only Theodore Roosevelt, a temporary colonel with no military future, who could engineer the 'round robin' in the trenches before Santiago; regular officers knew its need but dare not be insubordinate.

In bridging the gap between civil production and military procurement, there was no established competence. The pick of the military men could not be spared to learn a new trade. As in the other countries at war, so now in the United States, business and professional men must be detached from their jobs and converted into public servants in an unfamiliar field.

The seven specialists of the Advisory Commission — 'each of whom shall have some special knowledge,' said the law — opened their minds to the task. They learned its dimensions, realized the thin legal foundation upon which they must operate, and experienced the reluctance with which military opinion accepted civilian intrusion. They were hampered, also, by lack of funds and by the unreadiness of the Administration to permit them to make definite commitments until war had been declared. For two months they made tentative arrangements, waiting for the declaration to give them definition. They waited even longer before the departments had money with which to do the things they recommended. Still longer they waited for Congress to adjust law to necessity and to empower the Government to break away from conventional methods. Daniel Willard, president of the Baltimore and Ohio Railroad, was elected chairman of the Commission. Walter S. Gifford, of the American Telephone and Telegraph Company, as its director, opened and organized its temporary offices in the Munsey Building. Grosvenor B. Clarkson, who was to turn historian in his *Industrial America and the World War: The Strategy Behind the Lines, 1917–1919* (1923), was installed as secretary.

Even before the Advisory Commission decided to set up and to function through as many grand committees as it had members, it recognized the dependence of any military program upon railway transport. Willard was armed with knowledge and at his own suggestion was set to work. The Adamson Act was in the courts, with both roads and men exasperated. And even if the hazard of a strike during mobilization should be avoided, there remained the question of the capacity of the railroad net to bear its load.

Operating in legalized mandatory competition, the American railroads were uneven in their ability to serve the peace needs of the United States, let alone the requirements of war. Thirty-two systems, no two organized alike, operated 201,000 of the 261,000 miles of 'first main track' in the United States, and collected seven-eighths of the operating revenues. They provided a steady market for a third of the soft coal and for even a larger share of the output of iron and lumber. Among them were competing lines, dividing without profit what was too little traffic to justify a single line. Regions were not evenly served with reference to area, population, or produce; some were over-built, some under-built. The rolling stock was watched jealously by parent lines lest it be appropriated by their rivals. Some of the older railroad servants could remember a time when gauge was not standard and when a road built deliberately to a gauge different from that of connecting lines in order to keep its rolling stock on its own tracks. There resulted yards of empty cars, kept empty by the owner when a neighbor line could have used them. There were trains of empties rolling past freight crying for a carrier. War business was already congesting some of the Eastern terminals, with others nearly bare. The two and a quarter million freight cars of the United States were insufficient for the cargoes war would crowd into them, yet were lessened in their capacity by private control, regional demand, and lack of plan.

The Interstate Commerce Commission had complained of this inadequacy, and Congress had endeavored to correct it by granting the President power to take over the railroads in an emergency; but there was no existing organization through which he could act. The railroads themselves, nervous before the threat, were eager to avoid Government ownership. In the autumn of 1915 the American Railway Association, at the request of Garrison, created a special committee to advise the Secretary of War on troop movements; for troops have a habit of needing to be moved along unanticipated routes to unexpected destinations. No railroad man would willingly have picked Tampa, with its single-track line, as a suitable place for the mobilization of the force destined for Cuba in 1898; and the traffic mess at Tampa became a horrible example. After experience with the small-scale activities of Pershing's campaign in Mexico, a car-service committee was created on February 2, 1917, three days before Pershing moved his column back into the United States on its own legs. The Interstate Commerce Commission was pressing on Congress for an act permitting it to pool and control the use of cars without reference to their ownership. It received this addition to its authority, May 29, 1917, but the emergency had already carried the railway lines several steps farther toward unity and system.

Willard, by direction of the Council of National Defense, began in January his conferences with the officers of the American Railway Association. This was some weeks before his Committee on Transportation and Communication was formally authorized. While the Council and the Advisory Commission were still feeling out their theory of operation, he got action. The Railway Association named Fairfax Harrison, president of the Southern Railway, as chairman of a committee which, it was hoped, might both be adequate in the crisis and prove that voluntary co-operation could keep ahead of public control. From the Attorney-General assurances were asked and received that the members would not be rewarded for their effort by being prosecuted under the Sherman Act for illegal conspiracy. Harrison proceeded during March to work out the details of what became on April 11 the Railroads War Board.

The executive officers of the railroads approved the action of the Association. The railroad corporations ratified it, to 'co-ordinate the operations of the railroads in a continental railway system in aid of the Government during the war.' Harrison, with the assistance of four other presidents as an executive committee, operated the Railroads War Board for eight months, until at the end of the year the President exercised his power to take over the railroads and substitute national administration for that of private ownership. The Board had a hand in the troop movements to more than thirty camps and cantonments. Each of the new cities of 40,000 or more had itself to be hauled into position, piece by piece, before it could be occupied.

The Board co-ordinated the troop trains moving men from their camps to the Atlantic ports of embarkation. It assembled construction material and workmen at the camp sites and hauled an increasing tonnage into war plants for manufacture and out of them for shipment to France. It did its best against the natural inhibitions of the solvent railroads which stood to suffer by divergence of rolling stock or traffic to the lines of less successful rivals. Whatever the larger men of the Railroads War Board recommended on the basis of national advantage had to be filtered through the minds of others, less well-informed than they, but immediately responsible to stockholders and balance sheets. No voluntary agency could quite forget the fact that operating officers were bound to show the greatest possible profit to their corporations.

But it was not the fault of the Board that war traffic jammed the yards at Atlantic ports, that cars ran east full and west empty, that Nature froze the congested terminals in December, or that the users of transportation complained because the service was not better than it was. Through the long summer of trial-and-error approach to a policy, the Railroads War Board was among the busiest of the new organizations for the advancement of the war. It had an advantage over other war organizations in that it possessed a plant ready to be operated. It did not have simultaneously to construct and to produce. Before its internal organization was complete, the Advisory Commission had paralleled the Committee on Transportation with six other topical committees and a miscellaneous group of specialized boards and bureaus.

Quite as important to the business in hand as was the attitude of railway managers was the disposition of railway employees and of all Americans who worked for wages: 'my boys,' Gompers called them, as he begged the Council to be patient with their attitude. Samuel Gompers went upon the Advisory Commission as ambassador for labor, and as such he was accepted even by the railway men who held aloof from the American Federation of Labor. He sat under Willard, with whom he had been in bitter conflict during 1916, until the latter said to Commissioner Martin, who kept a diary; 'If anyone had told me that my personal antagonism toward Samuel Gompers would change within one week to ardent admiration and real affection, I would have pronounced that individual a fit candidate for an insane asylum.'

The close association Gompers had had with the Democratic Party since 1908 (when he was peddling his anti-injunction plank), and the protection that party had extended to his 'boys' in the Clayton Act and the Adamson Act, made it easier for him to work with the Administration than it might otherwise have been. His task, and that of his Committee on Labor, was to keep labor behind the war and in agreement that though war was bad a German victory would be worse. As early as March 12 he had arranged and sat in a conference with the leaders of the Federation and the railway unions, and with them he had adopted a labor platform for the war. The Government recognized the principle of unionization and the right of labor to be protected against disastrous changes in the price level. In return, union men agreed that work should proceed, uninterrupted by basic strikes.

After the war was over, the Department of Labor made a list of some six thousand strikes occurring during the nineteen months of hostilities; most of the interruptions were brief, many were the outgrowth of no more than misunderstandings arising from emergency changes, and nearly all were ended on terms acceptable to labor. The Government increasingly became the ultimate customer. It could and did press its contractors to settle with their men, and was willing to allow a price out of which labor could be paid. As the draft came into operation, the principle of deferred classification protected workmen who were indispensable on their jobs. Pay, allotments from pay, family allowances, and insurance took care of the dependents of those who were called to the colors. The American Federation, inspired by Gompers, made it its business to fight labor radicals and to meet propaganda with counter-propaganda. And in every Government venture in war production the labor side of the business was managed by labor men, drawn into the Government, but not forgetting that the crushing of labor was not to be a consequence of the war.

Out of the experiences of 1917 there emerged a more formal arrangement of labor relationships in 1918. But through the formative months, as policies were maturing, the Advisory Commission kept labor willingly in step with the great body of citizens.

Deliberating and resolving through March into April and May, the agencies of the Commission were commonly well ahead of enabling laws. Their full powers were not released for war until actual war was declared. The Congress had the unfinished duties of the preceding session to perform before it could give its undivided attention to new business, and the loan and the draft took precedence of all else that was new. The various boards concentrated their efforts on matters that could be reached without law, upon the shaping of the American mind, and upon the suggestion of tasks for Congress.

In its first *Annual Report*, the Council of National Defense covered its activities through June 30, 1917, listing the long series of committees, boards, and sections through which it began its task 'of mobilizing the national resources.' It had 408 persons on its staff, only 168 of whom drew compensation. Two of its seven major committees were largely educational, as were many of its special groups. Godfrey and Martin, of the Commission, presided over such activities, working chiefly in the field of national morale. The Commercial Economy Board, the Food Committee, and the State network operated in the same field, partly because that was the field in which they could operate best, partly because the controls they advocated must await the assent of Congress.

Godfrey's Committee on Engineering and Education made it its business to act as liaison between the Government and the professional specialists. Beside it stood the National Research Council, created in 1916 by the National Academy of Sciences on request of the President, to put scientific research at the disposal of the Government. The National Research Council moved its offices into the Munsey Building, next to the Advisory Commission, and at its beck a procession of chemists, physicists, and engineers moved out of their college jobs; sometimes into uniform, sometimes into laboratories, but always into war duty. The Committee on Education reached out toward the colleges and universities to bring them into the line of co-operation, but found them already so much better organized than it was itself, and so eager to work, that this remained perhaps the least significant of the subdivisions of the Advisory Commission. Even so non-military a group as the historians organized on its own initiative, borrowed a Washington office, installed a National Board for Historical Service, and asked for work to do. Its members helped to shape Creel's course.

Medical preparedness came within the scope of the Committee

on Medicine and Sanitation. Doctor Franklin H. Martin, chairman of this committee, was a Chicago surgeon, something of
a medical statesman with a gift for organization already revealed
and so successful in his practice that when the press thought at all
of his politics it assumed, erroneously, that he must be a Republican. He soon became a colonel in the Medical Corps and directed
his professional efforts into the General Medical Board, created as
an official body to correlate the work of the medical divisions of
Army and Navy, the Public Health Service, and the body of medical practitioners. He remained an active member of the Advisory
Commission, but his committee was overshadowed by his board.
There was an abundance of medical work to be done — sanitation
for the civilian population, procurement of medical officers for the
service, maintenance of medical education in spite of war. He
found the Surgeon-General of the Army, Major-General William
C. Gorgas, ready and eager for co-operation, and his professional
associates were already so well organized that his committee only
had to point the way.

Throughout its career the Council of National Defense had no
interest in administering the services that it conceived. It sought
to launch them, to see that someone was attending to them, and
to turn to the next job not yet being done. It was a civilian parallel
to the military general staff except that it gladly abandoned all
control of its creations once they were at work.

The Commercial Economy Board was born on March 24, in anticipation of the moment when the war program would demand
more raw materials and supplies than could be provided; a moment when civilian industry must economize and learn to do
without. The word 'conservation' was applied at a later date to
the realm within which this board sought to operate, but it was
early recognized that war would compel a curtailment of many
peace activities, an abandonment of others, and a conversion of
non-essential branches of production to the novel requirements of
war. Arch Wilkinson Shaw of Chicago, an enthusiast for office
'system' as well as a publisher, was enlisted for this work, 'to guide
and co-operate with business men in this planning and in making

the necessary readjustments.' The aim of the Commercial Economy Board was to draw a line which might separate essential from non-essential activity. The line once found — and few manufacturers who found themselves near it were happy in the discovery — it was the business of the Board to eliminate the non-essential or to convert it to useful work.

The Board began modestly with a campaign to stop the waste involved in the return to bakeries after each day of some four per cent of their bread, unsold and stale. It went on to a survey of duplicating deliveries by retail stores and losses involved in the return and money-back privilege after retail sales. Before many weeks it was studying the conservation of wool and leather, and destroying the notion of the early weeks of war that 'business as usual' could be a guiding maxim. By its side another committee which the Council of National Defense did not even list in its first *Report* was applying similar philosophies of conservation in the field of food.

Herbert Hoover, fresh from Belgian experience, was in Washington to inform the Council of National Defense as it made its first chart in February and to insist upon the importance of food production and food conservation. If feeding the Allies was to be a major part of the American reinforcement, it was necessary to know what could be shipped, what would be left for consumption in the United States, and what could be done to stimulate production. Hoover returned to Belgium in March to transfer the Commission for Relief in Belgium to the control of neutrals, and he declared from London in April that 'the foremost duty of America toward the Allies in this war is to see that they are supplied with food.' The Council of National Defense had already resolved to set up a food committee, inviting him to be its director. Back in Washington in May, Hoover became chairman of that committee. He appears to have been the whole committee, too, for it is not evident that the membership was named. Events were moving rapidly. All that a committee of the Council could have done was limited to those things that could be accomplished by exhortation. There was no statutory basis for either stimulation or control or for the moderation of gamblers' prices: and nothing was more foreign to the American habit than a bureau in Washington with power to control the farm or to restrict the breakfast table. Hoover took the problem directly to the White House, food was detached from the jurisdiction of the Council, and Congress was importuned for an adequate grant of powers. While the President waited for Congress to confer authority, he installed Hoover at the head of a voluntary Food Administration on May 19.

But between those things that the Council of National Defense had no right to do, and those that it knew not how to do, lay a wide range for co-operative activity. Every one of its active committees projected itself throughout the United States with a maze of sub-committees, by region, by craft, or by theme. And as it built its network, the States undertook to erect, of their own authority, State councils of defense. Sometimes by direction of the law, sometimes without its explicit sanction, the governors began to appoint committees headed with impressive names. It was uncertain what authority these might have, or grasp, but every community was bustling with citizens who desired in some way to serve. On the day of the declaration of war, the Council established a Section on Co-operation with States, as a staff agency of the director rather than as one of the ordinary committees. The several State councils, already created on paper, were asking what to do and besieging the Council with requests for tasks.

Baker, Secretary of War and chairman of the Council of National Defense, recognized the benefit, moral if not concrete, to be derived from this co-operation. He invited all of the States to do what some had already done, and called their representatives to conference in Washington on May 2, 1917. Twelve governors came in person, every State sent some representative, and for two days officers of the Government outlined the work accomplished and the work ahead. Before the end of June the 'national chain of State councils' was complete; and each in turn penetrated with its committees into even the voting precincts. In these the draft boards had already set an example of decentralized participation as they arranged for the registration under the Selective Service

Act; and the local committees soliciting subscriptions in the Liberty Loan Drive had not only knocked at every door, but had given average citizens a chance to show good-will. There were now added county councils of defense, city councils, speakers' committees, and women's committees. Those whose local standing required it were given place and title; those who could organize were given work; those who could talk were given audiences; and all looked back to Washington, to be told just what to do and what to say. A Woman's Committee of the Council of National Defense was created only a few days after the States' Co-operation Section to affiliate with the women's clubs and to tighten the local organization so that recommendations as to individual conduct emanating from Washington might with little loss of time reach the citizen in his home. Home-known women were to be connected with every step. Nationally known names were at the head of the list, with that of Doctor Anna Howard Shaw at the top.

The wide publicity earned by the women who had led the suffrage fight was harnessed into the Government. The list, crowned by Doctor Shaw, included Ida M. Tarbell, Carrie Chapman Catt, Maude Wetmore, and various women whose official position already gave them leverage. On June 19 delegates from sixty of the women's organizations met in Washington with the Woman's Committee. The agreement at home with the effort in Washington was profound: so profound that what distrust there was acquired painful prominence. The anti-war minority suffered an isolation and unpopularity, and even danger, unknown to the objectors during earlier American wars.

But at least three members of the Advisory Commission with their committees found immediate duties whose connection with matters of general morale was less intimate than their connection with actual services. The Committee on Raw Materials, organized by Bernard M. Baruch, knew from the beginning that the success of a procurement program would hang upon the ability of the United States to obtain somewhere the specific commodities not to be found at home. The Committee on Supplies, under Julius Rosenwald, knew that an army must use nearly every commodity that its individual members would require as civilians, and that someone must do its buying. Both committees knew that, of all supplies called for, the munitions of war came first. Howard E. Coffin, an automotive engineer from Detroit, was the specialist on the Advisory Commission charged with munitions, but as the dimensions of this program outgrew all power of imagination, he soon found himself assigned to one of its essential elements.

'Here in America mechanical flight had been born,' wrote Benedict Crowell in his report as Director of Munitions in the War Department, whither he had been advanced by the end of 1917, after service with the munitions committees. But when the war came, American feet had not learned to leave the ground, however far the American head may have been projected into the clouds. Few officers of the Army could fly, and flying was still largely an acrobatic stunt for display at county fairs. There was no important airplane industry in the United States. There were not even designs and patterns upon which such an industry could be erected. The aviation engineers, who were to conceive and produce the Liberty Motor after twenty-four days of drafting in June, were engaged until then working as rivals under a system in which each producer guarded his secrets from his competitor.

Yet the military planners issued a call for 22,000 planes to be delivered for use in the twelve months after June 30, 1917; men who knew manufacture knew also that such a program would entail in fact the 'securing of the equivalent of 40,000 airplanes in twelve brief months.' The National Advisory Committee for Aeronautics, a creation of Congress in 1915, working in close contact with the Signal Corps of the Army, the Bureau of Standards, and the aviation industry, recommended that the Council of National Defense give aid. A new quantity industry was to be set up; and it must be built upon automobile foundations, as nearest to its needs. The Council asked Coffin to undertake the task a few days after war was declared, and on May 16 the Aircraft Production Board was in existence under his chairmanship. This was another of the concrete things that soon slipped away from the control of the Council. While Coffin remained one of the members of the Advisory Commission the functions of his Committee on Munitions passed largely into other hands and under another name.

Raw materials, supplies, and munitions were basic. And the Advisory Commission would have been less than American if its members had not believed that in approaching the problems of supply they should approach them in the American fashion. Nothing in manufacture was more American than the principle of interchangeable parts. This had brought out of Connecticut cheap watches for the million. It had spread agricultural machinery designed for the American prairies over the plains of Russia and the Argentine. It had more recently made of Henry Ford's assembly line a symbol of a new principle in quantity production.

In this spirit the Council of National Defense acted in March, creating the Munitions Standards Board to aid in speedy production by standardizing munitions specifications. There is a large chapter that might be written around the task later assigned to a National Screw Thread Commission, whose mission was to discover whether every screw and bolt ought to have an identity of its own, or whether types might be so simplified that any machine might be repaired by parts taken from another. So far as the work of the Munitions Standards Board was concerned, there was a better legal basis than in other of the projects of the Council of National Defense. The National Defense Act of 1916 had specifically authorized the Secretary of War to provide for the manufacture of arms and munitions a full equipment of specifications, plans, gauges, jigs, and tools. He had only to decide what weapons he wanted, to bring these powers into life. The War Department had ideas of its own on the processes of manufacture, for as recently as January 4, 1917, Colonel Francis J. Kernan had presented an elaborate report on 'Government Manufacture of Arms' to which the Senate had given publicity as a public document. The Munitions Standards Board proposed to supplement and advise and to bring into the departments in Washington the accumulated experience of those American manufacturers who had for more than two years been working on Allied account.

A Cleveland manufacturer of instruments of precision, Frank A. Scott, was called in as chairman of the new board, and was surrounded by a group of similar manufacturers, only to learn before the Board had begun to function that the task called for broad powers and wide representation which his committee lacked. There could not be much useful work in the standardizing of specifications until it could be known what was to be procured. There could be no knowledge of this until the fighting agencies had decided what they wanted. And there could be no decision upon the size of orders until it had been learned what were the full resources of the United States. The Scott board could not standardize production unless it could persuade the fighting forces to accept the standards. Rapidly and inevitably the technical problems beginning with so abstruse a matter as the pitch of screw threads expanded into the whole problem of war industry; and war industry, growing in its demands, became before long the whole of national industry in war time.

A second phase of the activities of Scott began on April 9, when his establishment was renamed the General Munitions Board and his membership was enlarged by officers from Army and Navy appointed to serve with it. His efforts were now directed 'toward co-ordinating the making of purchases by the Army and Navy, and assisting in the acquisition of raw materials, and establishing precedence of orders between the Departments of War and of the Navy, and between the military and industrial needs of the country.'

In the set-up that emerged in April there was such intimate correlation among the parts of the General Munitions Board and the Committees on Raw Materials and Supplies that the respective chairmen could not be certain where the boundaries of their authority began and stopped. Industry that had to do business with them had difficulty in discovering where final power lay. Each of the military departments had its own system of procurement and pride in its own departmental efficiency. The Navy, with an always simpler problem and incapable of revolutionary expansion, gave what co-operation it must to the new machinery of survey and control, but escaped the unsettlement to which the Army had to submit. The Army, due at the first estimates for a fivefold increase, and destined to cope with further increases that came more rapidly than the War Department could estimate them, lacked personnel and plans.

In spite of the real advance in control following the creation of the General Staff of the Army, no satisfactory balance had ever been established between the General Staff as adviser of the Secretary of War and the permanent bureaus of the War Department through which the peace Army was actually governed, fed, clothed, and armed. There was a perpetual feud between the Chief of Staff and the Adjutant-General, and competition among the several supply bureaus of the Army, each of which bought for itself. Procurement in the Civil War was a costly mess, less hampering than it might have been because most of the supplies of the Army in 1861 did not differ greatly from commodities of ordinary manufacture and use. The war with Spain lasted only long enough to indicate how complete would have been the defects of management had it lasted longer. Neither war presented the necessity to convert to military use the maximum power of the nation, or to create for this use elaborate machines and weapons unknown to peace. War manufacture in 1861–65 was peace manufacture expanded; in 1917–18 it was new manufacture upon an unknown scale.

Until the spring was well advanced there was not even agreement upon the supplies to be required. In so simple a matter as the uniforms of troops there was but a loose knowledge of the sizes that must be ordered, and the proportion of each. The tables of sizes, based on experience with soldiers in the old Regular Army, broke down. The uniform prescribed in existing regulations was so close-fitting that the better it fitted the less was it suited for field service; yet to maintain military smartness it must fit. The quartermasters carried coats in eighteen sizes, breeches in thirty-two, and protested in vain that the adoption of a more suitable and comfortable uniform would reduce the number of sizes to six or eight. Not until the draft men began to come to camp was it

learned that their distribution of sizes was different from expectation. Small men were enrolled, whom the old Army would have
rejected as undersize; the Granger States sent large men in such
numbers as to leave many of them for a time unclad. Even had
there been agreement as to the type of shoe best suited to field
service there was no experience that would have brought into the
depots the extremes of sizes necessary for the comfort of patriotic
feet. It was equally undesirable to leave a soldier out of uniform,
or to interrupt manufacture to make his clothes to order.

There was no foreknowledge of the rapidity of the consumption
of uniforms. The War Department knew how rapidly uniforms
wore out in time of peace, but had no means of estimating their
deterioration and loss in time of war, or the size of the reserve that
must be maintained. When Pershing cabled back from G.H.Q.
in France that uniforms disappeared four times as fast as in the old
Army, the news was slow in reaching the Quartermaster-General,
whom Army regulations made responsible for their procurement.
Even the number of men in France from day to day was kept back
from him, as a military secret, until his task became next to impossible.

The specialized needs that the United States was unready to
meet produced the Aircraft Production Board, an Automotive
Transport Committee, and an Emergency Construction Committee to advise upon the building of nearly two score new cities to
house the recruits. All of these originated in actions of the Council
of National Defense, as did a Storage Facilities Committee to
house the supplies. But the procurement of the supplies themselves
had in many cases to wait until Army boards had agreed upon the
types of weapons to be used, and until chemists, who were in time
to become the Chemical Warfare Service, had determined what
gases to use for offense and for defense. The organizations created
for purposes in connection with these supplies run to nearly five
thousand titles in the *Handbook of Economic Agencies* (1919), prepared when most of them had become only historical. While they
operated, they got in each other's way, experimented and blundered, showed all the weaknesses of emergency organizations

manned by the willing but inexpert; but they performed an unavoidable service as the Army prepared for war.

In the end, the preparation of the Army depended upon raw materials and their use. This was foreseen in the committees of the Advisory Commission as Baruch and Rosenwald mobilized their assistants to supply the General Munitions Board with knowledge and to speed the letting of contracts for the Army and Navy.

Bernard M. Baruch had no special fitness for the task assigned him except a devotion to Woodrow Wilson, a long experience in building his own fortune on the treacherous bottoms of Wall Street, and an uncanny set of hunches that had served him well when he bought a mine or sold its stock. He talked the language of business so that men who must adjust themselves to new conditions could get his meaning. And he had no respect for the red tape with which conventional government must ordinarily surround itself to protect the public interest.

But his was a new kind of task for which there did not exist the kind of specialist called for in the statute. His Committee on Raw Materials utilized the machinery of the Bureau of Mines and of the Department of Commerce as it studied available resources in nitrates, rubber, tin, manganese, and those other key materials without which the production of munitions must stand still. He discovered what had been thus far only an academic fact — that many of these lay outside the United States, and could be procured only through a control of trade for which no legal authority existed. Ocean tonnage was still as scarce as though the United States had remained at peace. Allied merchant ships carried only the cargoes acceptable to Allied interests. Until Congress should make it legal for the Government to bargain for bottoms and to exercise the power to stop trade unless conducted on American terms, the United States program must remain secondary to that of the Allies in the war against Germany.

Baruch was aware that steel and coal would shape the program, and that the requirements of the Government for munitions would immediately produce a clash between the fighting needs of the United States and the operating needs of the factories and railroads that must supply the people as well as equip the forces. He learned, if he did not know it already, that the price level would have much to do with the volume of possible output. Industry could not produce and sell below the rising costs of production. If Government conceded reasonable wage increases to workers, it must allow reasonable price increases to those who paid the wages. With the total supply of raw materials insufficient for all the demands (and the Government was soon demanding for its exclusive use more steel than all the furnaces could produce), some must come first, some last, and some not at all. This involved priority.

As the Committee on Raw Materials brought forth its organization, its sub-committees were manned with men drawn from the industries and set to serve the Government. Before the end of June there were co-operative committees in nearly forty basic industries working under Baruch. They ranged from alcohol and aluminum to wool and zinc. Their rosters carried key names. By their very completeness they raised new problems, for the Government must buy from the firms whose employees were the only persons who knew enough to advise the Government whence to buy. In many cases Baruch's men, working for a dollar a year and planning to frame their pay checks, were still carried on the payroll of the firms that lent them to him. It was, indeed, possible to detach some of them from their old jobs, and eventually this was done. But in the early stages in procurement the Government was always subject to embarrassment. It could be charged that such men as these could not serve two masters and that contracts went by favoritism. Yet as experience produced a completer understanding it could not be dodged that the program in hand compelled the Government to reach down into every basic industry, to learn its resources and methods, and to devise means for securing uncolored advice that would be good enough to act on.

The Committee on Supplies had at least the advantage of a chairman who already knew his trade. President of Sears, Roebuck and Company, Julius Rosenwald had felt the intense unpopularity with which retail trade regarded the mail-order house. But he knew, as perhaps no other American knew, the whole range of requirements of ordinary life: where to get the goods, where quickly, where cheaply. For nearly forty years, after the depression of 1873 brought the agricultural machinery makers into such disrepute that mail-order houses got a toe-hold, his firm and a few others had studied the market. The Bible might be lacking on the rural table, or the photograph album, or the county history, but the fat mail-order catalogues were almost certain to be there, embellished with picture and price of everything from nutmeg graters to gas engines. And shopping by lamplight had become a major indoor sport after rural free deliveries made it easy for the Post Office to serve these firms.

Baruch concentrated on raw materials. The finished products over whose purchase Rosenwald set up a supervision did not include actual munitions of war, but ran to food, textiles, leather, and the multitude of little gadgets with which life operates. The Rosenwald committees, less numerous than those of Baruch, could operate promptly, for the Army needed much of many things already under production. Orders here need not await long technical discussions about jigs and gauges. Nevertheless these committees were formed under conditions that brought them under the same suspicion that embarrassed those of Baruch. No chief of a sub-committee was of use to Rosenwald unless he knew his trade. If he knew this, he had an attachment to some one of the producers anxious for contracts. And this made him suspect.

But the Army had no unified buying system, no trained personnel to be spared to build one; and each of its bureaus had a long series of unimportant specifications for simple items to which it clung. The items had so wide a range as to call for reinforcement by specialists; whether in the name of Sergeant Irving Berlin to oversee the equipment of sheet music for 390 bands in the A.E.F., or in that of the unknown aide who designed the 9,224,210 brushes with which the Army fought the enemy and which had to be extracted from fifty-nine factories in the United States. As costly as this variation in specifications was the competitive buying that brought different bureaus into the market for the same inadequate supply.

Charles Eisenman, vice-chairman of the Committee on Supplies, became at once the shadow of the Quartermaster-General, and took on so much substance that it became difficult to differentiate him from his chief. Under ordinary circumstances each contract for supply would have been required by law to be advertised, subjected to competitive bidding, and awarded to the lowest bidder. There had grown up around the Army bureaus a shoal of middlemen, bidding for contracts that they could not fill, and that they intended to sublet when and if their bids were accepted. These were in opposition at once to any scheme by which the Government should buy directly from the producer; they told their tale of disappointment, suggesting favoritism, to every ear that would listen under the dome of the Capitol. Their criticism became more plausible when, on April 12, as the law allowed in the emergency, the Secretary of War permitted contracts to be let without competitive bids. Henry G. Sharpe, the Quartermaster-General, appreciated help and needed it. But in the rush of business the contractor hardly knew whether he was bound to the Government of the United States or to a volunteer official of no legal standing. At times he delivered his goods subject to adjustment of price when someone had time to get around to it. In theory the Committee on Supplies advised, in practice Eisenman determined, in the early weeks of war.

While Congress authorized loans and enacted the draft, and its committees deliberated upon next steps in war policy, the Council of National Defense presided as best it could over a patriotic madhouse. Honest devotion and hard work were the redeeming features in a job that had no precedents. In 1919 and after, a multitude of Republican-controlled investigating committees, hopeful of the worst, scrutinized the performance. They uncovered ignorance and error, but found few and unimportant evidences of malfeasance. Every day brought the announcement of new war organizations and more committees. The managers of fresh ventures, virgin to the ways of Washington, worked each as though he were the only bearer of responsibility. The permanent employees of the Government, slowed to the easy stride of civil service, often could not understand new colleagues who did not know there was a time-clock. When the new enthusiasts failed, no one had time to eliminate the wreckage. When they succeeded, batteries of desks crowded their gorged offices, overflowed into the corridors, shifted into apartment houses whose occupants were turned into the streets between dawn and bedtime, and migrated soon to mushroom buildings on vacant lots. Men who had lived their business lives in bitter competition and worked for money learned to love the thrills that came when working on an unpaid job for the sake of the job. And the members of the Advisory Commission, responsible for much, and watching it all, fed Congress with so many proposals for helpful legislation that a bewildered Congress wondered whether they or it bore the responsibility.

But the effective work of the civilian volunteers, like that of the Government itself, had its limits. These were set at the frontier where legal authority was necessary for further action. The morale work of the committees, operating among intangibles, had an importance to be guessed at but never measured. Their administrative powers, as the law stood, were unimportant. Neither they nor the Government could go safely far beyond the law.

Upon the return of Herbert Hoover to the United States in May, it took but a fortnight for him to work out of the Food Committee of the Council of National Defense and to receive status as voluntary Food Commissioner under the President. The powers needed before he could work with the sanction of the law behind him were asked of Congress and began to be discussed as soon as the Selective Service Act was passed. But the discussion was long and tedious, continuing until the planting season had given way to the harvest. The first important addition to the powers of the President, in the field in which Baruch, Rosenwald, Scott, and Hoover were operating, was attached as an amendment to a law that happened to be passing — the Espionage Act, signed on June 15. By this enactment exports were brought under the control of the Government.

There were various reasons for the control of exports by the United States. One of these was the continuance, in spite of

American entry, of the trade restrictions by which the Allies endeavored to conserve tonnage and to narrow the opportunity of the enemy to derive advantage from trade borne in Allied or neutral bottoms. Until the United States should assume similar responsibility with reference to its own exports, the Allies were unwilling to lift the vexatious hand which their control of the seas had enabled them to lay upon all American trade.

Another of the reasons was the American need for the home-rule of native tonnage, for the procurement of raw materials obtainable only outside the United States, and for the control of the destination of American-produced supplies. Under the new empowering act an Exports Council was at once created, with Vance C. Mc-Cormick as its agent. McCormick had been chairman of the Democratic National Committee in 1916; he now turned his organizing ability to the management of a Bureau of Export Licenses, with law behind him.

The date of the Espionage Act marks the end of another of the chapters of American preparation. Just a month earlier Nivelle had been relieved of his command on the Western Front where his drive had broken down. Pétain replaced him, and in his turn was succeeded as French Chief of Staff by Foch. France needed help more bitterly than was revealed or than has been remembered with victory won. On the day of the passage of the act, in the Picpus Cemetery in Paris, Pershing laid his wreath at the tomb of Lafayette. He might have uttered, had he thought of them, in his French that Harbord has described as 'not exactly God-given . . . but never misunderstood,' the famous words 'Lafayette, we are here.' They were, indeed, uttered in his behalf by one of his colonels after a parade battalion of the Sixteenth Infantry had marched to the same cemetery on July 4. But such words, on either occasion, were a reckless promise for whose fulfillment the means had only just begun to be devised.

III. THE MIND OF THE CITIZEN

THE keen wits of Secretary Baker were not deceived as to the reality that lay behind the 'physical manifestations' accompanying the American preparations for war. 'There is nothing great in the world but man,' he has said; 'and nothing great in man but mind.' He foresaw that 'the future historian' would find a 'mental cause' behind the material consequence, and that 'the thing which ultimately brought about the victory of the Allied forces . . . was not wholly the strength of the soldier . . . but . . . was rather the mental forces that were at work . . . producing . . . that unconquerable determination that this war should have but one end.' The minds of the citizens of the United States, working for the moment in close harmony, were assisted in maintaining that harmony by the activities of a Committee on Public Information.

It would have been possible to let the military mind prevail; to clamp down the lid of a tight censorship upon all news and opinion lest some of it, released, give aid and comfort to the enemy. It would have been equally possible to erect a propaganda agency to speak as dogmatic truth the doctrine most acceptable to the Government. For nearly three years the United States had been flooded with documents emanating from every Government at war, telling, each of them, the story of official wish, attacking the good faith of the enemy, and shading off at the margins into lies too clumsy for belief except where the will to believe had doped the conscience and stupefied the intellect. The President had been blamed as obtuse; but there was deep irony in the sentence of his peace circular of December 18, 1916: 'The objects which the statesmen of the belligerents on both sides have in mind in this war

are virtually the same, as stated in general terms to their own
people and to the world.'

It was not possible for the United States to escape the danger
that the leakage of military secrets might be disastrous, or the
necessity to inform the mind that asked for facts and reasons.
The United States lacks that condition of parliamentary governments, in which the ministers of the moment sit with the lawmakers,
able to challenge the irresponsible, and subject to interrogation
every day. It has no official mouthpiece except as the President,
from time to time and on occasions of his own choice, may address
the people. Possessing a written Constitution with a mandatory
statement that 'Congress shall make no law . . . abridging the
freedom of speech, or of the press,' it was impracticable to prevent
the utterance of statements and opinions such as snarl the processes
of government, misinform the public mind, and confuse the issue
on every public question. Less misleading than propaganda, more
liberal than censorship, there was need for a channel through
which facts might be used to wash away the foundations of false-
hood or misconception and to establish liaison between the Government and the citizens upon whose minds democratic government
must stand or fall.

Seven days after the declaration of a state of war, the Secretaries
of State, War, and Navy addressed to the President a letter urging
him to erect an 'authoritative agency' for the publication and
dissemination of facts about the war. Wilson acted the next day,
April 14, naming the same secretaries as a Committee on Public
Information, for which a contentious journalist, George Creel,
was appointed executive. 'A man of primitive violence,' as *Collier's*
described him somewhat aptly in the autumn, Creel had been an
editor and free-lance writer for nearly half of his forty years. His
literary urge was to range from *Quatrains of Christ* (1907) to *Ireland's
Fight for Freedom* (1919). He gloried in the duty he now undertook
and when it was done he described it in *How We Advertised America*
(1920). In his journalistic career Creel had trod on many political
toes; he continued so to tread, and not always discreetly. His
tongue was too restive for easy control. Men whose plans he had

impeded sat too numerously in Congress for his comfort in the months to come. But he could act quickly. Within a few days of his appointment he took over an old-fashioned dwelling on Jackson Place, opposite the White House. His warrant gave him easy access to all the departments, and in the White House he could always reach the President. He sent his fellow craftsmen everywhere, searching for news.

The appointment of Creel was described as that of a censor by newspapers afraid their freedom to print would be curtailed. Censor he was not, in any exact sense; for censorship implies scrutiny and control in advance of publication or utterance. At no time during the war was such a censorship in existence except as military commanders prevented release of news from within their lines, and as the foreign-language press was required to submit translations. At no time was there an antecedent barrier to utterance and publication for the individual ready to risk the legal consequences in case his action became the cause of injury. The right of Congress to punish military crime is quite as complete as is the freedom of the citizen in speech and in press; and there is no reason for supposing that the latter freedom carries with it release from the consequences of publication. Libel and slander remain actionable even under the First Amendment to the Constitution; sedition comes about when the free tongue and pen do damage to the State. In a unanimous opinion of the Supreme Court, Justice Oliver Wendell Holmes (whose opinions even in dissent have come to be treated as inspired) declared:

> It is a question of proximity and degree. When a nation is at war many things that might be said in time of peace are such a hindrance to its effort that their utterance will not be endured so long as men fight, and that no court could regard them as protected by any constitutional right.

Under a censorship an anonymous censor determines in advance what shall be printed; under the First Amendment it becomes the duty of the courts to determine whether damage has been done. There is a difference.

It was the view of Creel, and of the group of journalists who

made up his staff, that their business was to release the news.
Every department of the Government was nervous, fearful lest a
slip should give information to the enemy, and disposed to treat
innocent news as vital military secrets. Creel conceived that full
news of the American effort would add another to the weapons of
offensive war. He entered into a prolonged campaign to lift the
lid, to compel the departments to give his men the news, and to
procure for this news the widest publicity. His offices were open
twenty-four hours of the day. As rapidly as his staff assembled
material, the piles of mimeographed releases were made ready for
distribution to the newsmen for whom access to the bureaus was
generally barred. Correspondents used the releases in their
stories. A 'country editor' was brought to Jackson Place to prepare a weekly digest of the news for rural papers, whose mailing list
soon reached 12,000 offices. It became desirable to keep track of
the news released, so on May 10 appeared the first number of the
Official Bulletin, in which the items were printed the day after the
correspondents had used them and which reached a daily circulation of 118,000 in the summer of 1918.

Much led to more; as men came to the C.P.I. with plans to help
disseminate fact and argument, Creel took them on. A volunteer
from Chicago brought him the idea of a brigade of speakers; men
with self-restraint enough to stop in four minutes, who should be
briefed with appropriate material from Washington, and who
should slip to the stage in front of the screen in movie theaters.
Creel thought, when he summarized the work of the Four-Minute
Men, that 75,000 such had addressed 7,555,190 audiences carrying
their message. A speaking division was created to send more
formal orators on tour. Advertising men were mobilized to contribute their technique. Artists were tied into the organization to
draw posters and cartoons. Films were prepared showing the
nature of the American effort. Far from suppressing the foreign-
tongued as though they were a class apart, Creel turned his
material into as many dialects as he could find, fed the foreign-
language press, and found it as anxious as any to co-operate. He
sent his agents abroad to advertise the United States and to force

through the close lines of the enemy an explanation of the American cause and a picture of the preparation. He pressed everywhere the wedge that Wilson had started between the enemy peoples and their Governments, and among the allies of the Central Powers.

From Jackson Place his staff assembled the raw materials of news, publicity, and propaganda. Pamphlets soon began to appear, explaining and interpreting with more good conscience than men are apt to keep in time of war: *How the War Came to America; The War Message and the Facts Behind It; Why Working Men Support the War; War Cyclopedia;* and a multitude of others until the C.P.I. could count 75,099,023 pieces of printed matter that it circulated. An extra-legal agency, created without authority and supported out of the President's special fund, the Committee on Public Information invited criticism and received much of it. Creel became 'whipping boy' for the President, his every utterance searched hopefully for flaws, his every slip — and all journalism is full of these — treated as of the heart. Once or twice his overconfidence in the accuracy of offices describing their own work betrayed him when the performance did not come up to promise. But the *Official Bulletin* became not only an experiment in government journalism, but also the best of single sources upon the flow of daily events.

Apart from the work of the C.P.I. as publicity bureau and as impresario, the doctrine that it held and spoke, and offered for the adherence of the citizen, was a weapon of the war. This was freed at the start from one of the adulterations most deadly to European propagandas. The United States had none of what was commonly described as 'ulterior aim.' The defeat of the enemy was the single objective: and this only in order that an American vision of a world without war might be raised to reality. No belligerent on either side of the European contest, except perhaps Belgium, could be entirely sincere in its statements of war aims. Each had national cravings dressed up as though their satisfaction were in the interest of the world. Until the Czarist régime crashed in Russia there was incongruity in arguing that the war was one of democratic governments against autocracy. Russia and Italy, at least, had received promises of ultimate compensation inconsistent with the claim that they were fighting for peace alone. The complaint of the Central Powers that the war was forced upon them by an encirclement by their enemies was as inconsistent with the aggressive mood of Austria-Hungary when invading Serbia, as it was with the speed of Germany when grasping a military initiative at the expense of Belgium. Before the entry of the United States it was equally possible to think of the Allies as determined to eliminate Germany from the map, and of the Central Powers as inspired by deliberate lust for conquest. Each was in error in describing the motive of its enemies: neither was entirely frank in stating its own. The temper of the century compelled every Government to speak the language of a nation loving peace. This war lacked the simplicity of motive that makes earlier wars more easy of historical explanation.

The United States craved no dominion and asked no indemnity. Its aim was freed from the taint of earthly desire, however it might be inflated with impracticable vision. The Wilson doctrine was the doctrine of his C.P.I. It was elaborated in the war of pamphlets and was explained out of the history of the United States and of the world. It was rationalized as a reasonable outgrowth of United States experience. It was grounded in the ideas implicit in the phrase, 'a world safe for democracy.'

Neither picture as presented to the people was entirely fair. The antithesis of democratic governments and autocracies was less than complete. The assumption that went with each was less than warranted. It was lacking in historicity to assert that the aims of democracies had habitually been those of peace and useful to the world, or that the aims of autocracies were of necessity those of conquest. It is hardly likely that historians can ever drag from the record of the past material sufficient to provide adequate sailing charts for the future. Most causes briefed out of history have only rationalizations behind them; and even when it is done with more than average sincerity, as it was in the C.P.I., there still runs through all of it the distorting influence of a state of mind. The historians who saw in the United States a democracy of peace were hopeful rather than authoritative. They were helpful, however, for it was possible to pick out of the American story validated events with which to construct the sort of picture that Americans wanted to believe; and that, believed, made firmer their willingness to carry out the war.

The main thesis of the Allies, hardly challenged in the United States except by those who were discredited as pro-German before they spoke, was that Germany, a military nation, 'Prussianized' by a ruling class, was ready for war and craving it was a means of increasing national glory. It was easier to overlook flaws in the argument of the Allies than to argue away the implications of compulsory military training, the 'goose-step,' and the Junker officer caste, which indeed were facts. Upon the American devotion to a theory of peace and upon the positive aversion to conscription or rule by an army, the ideal of a world 'safe for democracy' could be built, and was. War became less distasteful when it was believed to be a war to end war. Victory by Germany might be the first phase of a menace to American safety. Gerard, back from Berlin, threw his recollections as ambassador first into *My Four Years in Germany* (1917), and then into *Face to Face with Kaiserism* (1918). He told of an Emperor waiting only to finish with European enemies before dealing with the Monroe Doctrine and the United States. A peace that would last formed the positive side of the American doctrine; the reverse displayed a United States which, to be safe, must live armed to the teeth.

The reasons for American entry, the validity of the picture sketched by Wilson and disseminated by Creel, came in due time to be challenged by a younger generation and disputed in the interest of the doctrines of the American minority. C. Hartley Grattan inquired into the matter, delivering a verdict hostile to the official view in *Why We Fought* (1929). Walter Millis, in *Road to War* (1935), discarded much of Grattan, but found reasons of his own for believing the United States to have been misled. Charles C. Tansill, first to make careful use of the great mass of manuscript already available, brought all students into his debt in *America Goes to War* (1938), yet failed to see eye to eye with either of his predecessors as he displayed his grounds for distrust of the intelligence or sincerity of much of the American war leadership. It remained for Secretary Baker to make a documented restatement of what Americans of the war generation thought to be the American case in *Why We Went to War* (1936).

With every medium at his disposal Creel displayed the American case. His staff elaborated it. As an hypothesis it was as close-knit and coherent as most political hypotheses are, and it was largely true.

Perhaps as convincing for the moment as any of the illustrative material brought forward to support the major theses of the war was the material believed to bear upon the 'war guilt' of 1914. Georg Michaelis had much to say about it. Speaking as new Imperial Chancellor in the summer of 1917 (for von Bethmann-Hollweg was retired in July), Michaelis repudiated 'war guilt' and clung to the official German story that the war had been forced upon his country. Subsequent investigations by the horde of historians who tried in the next two decades to fix the matter of guilt have made it reasonable to believe that Germany did not 'will the war' to occur when and as it happened. Berlin slipped when it underwrote an arrogant Austria-Hungary in the demands on Serbia. But at the last minute, in the fatal days of July, 1914, the German Government made great efforts to prevent the local struggle from spreading across the map. The subsequent investigations are far from establishing the fact that Germany was victim of a plot to destroy its power. This, however, was official doctrine among the Central Powers as was the opposite among the Allies.

As the first flurries of bewilderment subsided in the autumn of 1914, the Allies built upon the obvious truth of German readiness to fight and presented a picture of unnecessary war, precipitated deliberately by a military caste, and threatening the world. None of the immediate diplomatic publications of the various combatants was inclusive enough to prove the truth of this. Many of the official collections published on both sides sinned by omission, part statement, and even fraud. All suffered from lack of full knowledge. But the Allied picture helped make up the American mind. Wilson eventually accepted it and after the breach presented its details in his public utterances. Henry Morgenthau, his ambassador at Constantinople, sustained it by recalling utterances quoting the Kaiser as saying in May, 1914, that war was inevitable. He made this more specific by recalling details passed to him at his post; details of a conference at Potsdam, July 5, 1914, only a few days after the funeral of the archduke and the opening of the rebuilt Kiel Canal, at which it was said to have been decided that *der Tag* had come. The elaboration of this conspiracy, with Germany in the leading rôle, had propaganda values whether true or not. And elaborated it was. The *War Cyclopedia* fell for it, though cautiously prefacing its summary with the caveat 'it is asserted.' How far a belief in the conspiracy cooked up at Potsdam turned men's minds can only be guessed at. But it was unsound. The events recalled by Morgenthau had not occurred as he related them.

Much sounder and as useful was the proof of the intrigue by German officials in the United States; to destroy plants, to deceive labor, and to do sabotage. Here there were official records and cross-examined facts. And as useful, too, informing the mind that sought to know why democracy and autocracy were in clash were descriptive pamphlets of the C.P.I., such as *German War Practices; The German War Code; The Government of Germany*, in which was brought out the undemocratic character of the German Government. The war-practice booklets showed the degree to which the modern German officer had carried war away from the wise moderation of the earlier German, Francis Lieber, who prepared for the use of Union armies in the Civil War the first rule book of its kind: *Instructions for the Government of Armies in the Field*. This had been published as General Orders 100, in 1862.

The American hypothesis of democracy *versus* autocracy had its considerable, if incomplete, basis in fact. It was, however, an affair of the intellect, and like most structures of the intellect it had less influence than fear or hate upon men's minds. The hate mills set to work. Not often did their output bear the imprint of the C.P.I., but private names and private organizations were enthusiastic sponsors. The National Security League, founded in 1914 to advance preparedness, loaded itself now with the duty to keep America loyal, saw traitors behind Teutonic names, and suspected dangerous liberalism when Creel and his men were moderate in their denunciations. It launched a campaign for 'Patriotism through Education,' published a *Handbook of the War for Public Speakers* (1917), and hardly concealed a deep Republican suspicion that a Democratic Administration could not be loyal. The Wilson distinction between the enemy peoples and their Governments was disruptive as it worked across the lines. At home, by its very moderation, it ran counter to a human tendency to hate an enemy and to distrust those who were moderate in their hates.

At one point the C.P.I. paused and by the pause it established itself as different from many of the propaganda agencies whose pages had been thrust before American eyes since 1914. It did almost nothing with 'atrocities.' The *War Cyclopedia*, prepared for the use of speakers, referred in general terms to these and spoke, indeed, more than it knew, but it refrained from citation of specific cases, although it referred the reader to the Bryce report on Belgium. Nothing in the war argument worried the American German more than the allegations of murder and maltreatment done by his relatives in Belgium and France. A documented proof of these would have had superlative value as a propaganda document, and to prepare this Creel set a distinguished historian to work. It was supposed that the material would be easy to find, but no 'atrocities' were discovered sufficiently documented to be used and nothing was faked. The matter was dropped to the lower temperature of a technical study of military illegalities. It was neither hatred of Germany that did most of the work as binder of minds, nor affection for the Allies. As involvement in the war progressed a conviction grew that somehow or other a better world was within reach once victory was won.

Alongside the positive doctrines of the war, the C.P.I. worked to resolve doubts, and at particular points to counteract and combat specific oppositions. Before the war session of Congress met, most of the groups opposing participation had dwindled, because

[handwritten margin note: Abstain from Atrocity except Bryce]

they were convinced, or were in hopeless minority, or were unwilling to incur popular hostility. The organized Socialists, however, had issued an anti-war manifesto in the spring, and called an
extraordinary national convention that met in St. Louis the day
after the declaration. Here Morris Hillquit advised some two
hundred delegates that 'the country has been violently, needlessly, and criminally involved in war.'

The nature of the Socialist Party, based upon dues-paying
members, was such as to make it uncertain how much weight
ought to be ascribed to party pronouncement. Its voting strength,
always much in excess of its registered membership, had never
been large enough to influence a national election. Beginning
with some 94,000 in 1900, at the first candidacy of Eugene V.
Debs, this was built up to 897,000 at his fourth candicacy in 1912.
There was no reason to suppose that so many voters espoused his
doctrine. His totals were increased by protest votes of persons dissatisfied with trends or candidates of the major parties, as the
totals of the Prohibition Party had sometimes been. In 1916, behind a candidate less inspiring than Debs, and after many Progressive protest votes had dropped away, the Socialists polled but
585,000. Socialist doctrines had never spread greatly in the United
States. Labor held itself aloof. Socialist leaders were so often of
foreign birth — German, Austrian, or Russian — that the party
hardly appeared to be an American body. Not pacifist by conviction, the Socialist Party was against all wars but its own, Hillquit
describing it as a 'militant, revolutionary organization.' In the
weeks before its anti-war convention many of its supporters
dropped out, making public explanations why they could not oppose this war. After the St. Louis convention more retired. Upton
Sinclair and John Spargo left it voluntarily. Charles Edward Russell was expelled. A. M. Simons denounced it as scuttled by 'German nationalistic jingoes and anarchistic impossibilities.' Debs
and Victor L. Berger stood by their doctrine and faced the growing
unpopularity of their position.

Socialists nowhere had held generally to their avowed determination not to fight for their countries. In Europe they marched

off with their regiments at mobilization with rank and file hardly depleted by conviction. Some of their leaders had in all countries stood out longer, forming even in Germany an opposition critical of national aims and methods. The utterances of these brought to many of them quick punishment as seditious; and to all of them wide publicity, as quotations leaked across the borders to be handled as though they were expressions of responsible minorities.

The events in Russia, from the deposition of the Czar until the Bolshevik triumph in November, 1917, were inspiring to Socialists wherever they found themselves. As the succession of Russian provisional governments side-stepped to the left through the summer, the Russian radicals claimed to speak for all common people who bore the burden of capitalist and imperialist war, and called upon proletarians of the world to unite with them for revolution and peace. In May, a few days after Kerensky had taken over the ministries of War and Justice, their Council of Workmen's and Soldiers' Deputies came out for peace based upon twin doctrines: 'no annexations, no indemnities,' and 'the right of all nations to determine their own destiny.' Leaders as far apart as President Wilson and the German Socialists could accept these. The latter, for the moment allowed to get out of hand in the Reichstag, put through a resolution, July 19, demanding the former of the aims.

It was inevitable that in the United States those who stayed Socialist should desire to co-operate in this, and that many who had been reluctant to enter war were ready to accept these utterances as made in good faith. A People's Council for Democracy and Terms of Peace was born in Madison Square Garden at a Memorial Day conference, shortly after the Russian plea was heard. Hillquit and Berger were there; as were Lochner, who had steered the Ford peace mission in 1915 and who now thought this was a 'ground swell,' and Oswald G. Villard, whose *Nation* was now out of sympathy with most of the group who had been its mainstay. Tumulty refused to procure an audience with the President for the committee of the conference: but headquarters appeared, and its propaganda stayed in the limelight until the autumn.

The immediate objective of the People's Council was representation of the United States at a Stockholm Conference, called by Russian Socialists for September, at which plans were to be formulated for the people to take over their governments and end the war. It had been announced, even before the People's Council was formed, that the United States would send no agents, and that the State Department would withhold passports from persons desiring to go as delegates from private organizations. The London *Saturday Review* opined that the conference would doubtless be attended by 'a considerable number of tricksters and traitors.' When the German Government gave support to the conference, as though in sympathy with its proponents, the project was denounced as a plot for a German peace. Lincoln Steffens was reported as convinced that Germany desired it not for peace but to save kaiserism.

The Stockholm Conference was postponed from time to time, because its international character was blocked by general passport trouble. But the People's Council continued its advocacy of terms of peace as urged by Russia and endorsed by the Reichstag, and determined to hold its own convention in the Middle West about the time the conference at Stockholm ought to have met. It was easier to call such a convention than to find hosts who would welcome it. North Dakota was considered, whither Governor Lynn J. Frazier was said to have invited it, and thither a special train, jeered at as the 'rabbit special,' departed August 30 from New York. Ex-Senator John D. Works held a meeting in its favor in Los Angeles, but he resigned from the Council when he became convinced that it was a Socialist annex. Fargo, the North Dakota destination, was abandoned as a meeting place in favor of Minneapolis, whose mayor extended an invitation without reckoning with the Governor of Minnesota, who forbade the Council to assemble in his State. Two Wisconsin towns, Hudson and Milwaukee, were suggested and abandoned, until at last Mayor William Hale Thompson permitted it to come to rest in Chicago. Here it met and passed its resolutions, surrounded by a hostile publicity that defeated its purpose and challenged by another organization launched by Gompers with the aid of Creel for the specific purpose of combating radical movements.

The American Alliance of Labor and Democracy was put together in New York before the end of August to be a militant flying squadron, with a mission to challenge every statement that labor did not support the war. Gompers knew much about the left-wing movements within the American Federation of Labor. These had long sought to turn labor into a political party, a movement that he distrusted and despised. He had opposed them successfully in his annual conventions. He now fought the People's Council when it attempted to detach labor from the war. When the 'rabbit special' left New York on its devious search for a place to meet, the 'red, white, and blue' special of the American Alliance followed it on September 2, with a welcome assured. Invited to Minneapolis, there it went. The President wrote Gompers a letter of congratulation upon the effort: and the Minneapolis resolutions were drafted as though the authors had the war speeches of the President under their eye. The American Federation of Labor, at its annual meeting in November, sustained the policy of Gompers by a vote of 21,579 to 402, and listened to Wilson expound his own ideas in person. There was no room for pacifism in the American Federation: to avow one's self interested in peace as immediately obtainable was to invite denunciation as pro-German.

The intensity of the fight to keep the American mind behind the war was out of proportion to the importance of the various minority movements that were either critical or in open opposition. Ready to accept war in April, convinced that it knew why it was right to accept war in midsummer, American loyalty was exasperated by opposition however slight. Toward the end of the war session of Congress, and soon after the collapse of the demonstration of the People's Council, Senator La Follette spoke before another of the out-of-step brigades and fell victim to the burdens of opprobrium.

The Nonpartisan League, a Western offshoot of the Progressive movement, flared up in North Dakota in 1915. Capturing its State with the ease with which any angry electorate can always capture its State, it was proceeding upon its course of economic self-help when war broke out. It was not greatly interested in the war. It was willing to suspect that any policy approved by finance and business in the East was wrong. It readily absorbed a part of the doctrine preached by La Follette and his associates in the Senate that the war was one of big business in which the United States ought not to be involved. Having fought big business the North Dakota voters liked to believe the worst about it. But when the People's Council tried to bring the Nonpartisan League into its organization, the leaders of the latter stayed out. When La Follette addressed the annual convention of the Nonpartisan League in St. Paul, September 20, the *Nonpartisan Leader* endorsed his utterances upon free speech, but declined to accept him when 'he speaks of the causes of the war and gives his interpretation of the events leading up to it.'

There was no concealment of La Follette's bitter opposition to American entry. He had used in his remarks upon the war resolution the words: 'Germany has been patient with us.' And he had made the words even more deliberate by withholding the draft of the speech from immediate publication in the *Congressional Record*, and by leaving the words in the copy finally provided for the public printer. He now repeated at St. Paul what every reader of the *Congressional Record* knew by heart; but he did not say what the Associated Press attributed to him: 'We had *no* grievances.' Too late for it to do him any good, the Associated Press acknowledged its interpolation of the word 'no,' and made apology. Another of the storms of denunciation to which La Follette was accustomed broke about him. His constituents passed resolutions repudiating him. There was a movement in the Senate to expel him. *Viereck's* was doing his reputation no good by declaring that the 'stars seem to point to Robert M. La Follette as the leader in the fight to make democracy safe at home'; a distinguished historian wrote to the *New York Times* that only Aaron Burr was 'more ready to betray democracy for his own selfish ends'; Roosevelt was quoted as saying that La Follette was 'loyally and efficiently serving one country — Germany.' La Follette kept his head up through the storm.

The Senate, for once getting good out of its stubborn insistence on its privilege, postponed action upon the demand for his expulsion until the wave of emotion changed its course. But the extreme isolation into which he and those who thought more or less like him were thrown became a measure of the unanimity of thought, in the directing of which the C.P.I. had a hand.

Aversion to the necessity for war was one of the American moods from which could be evoked a willingness to sustain the 'war to end wars.' Along with this marched a desire to relieve suffering, which helped to harden the morale.

From the beginning of combat in Europe relief movements of a sort had grown in popularity in the United States. The German efforts to send food and milk back home were only in part a device to bring about an embargo by embroiling the United States with Britain. They received the sympathetic co-operation of many who had no sympathy with the German Government. A similar sympathy created ambulance services and hospitals and efforts to reconstruct the desolated areas that began to rebuild almost before the echoes of the guns were silenced. The American Society of the Red Cross took advantage of this emotion to extend its chapters and strengthen its organization before 1917.

Congress had not incorporated the American Society of the Red Cross until 1905, although it had been privately chartered since 1881. Saint Camillus de Lellis, founder of the Agonizants, whose sixteenth-century badge it used, had been designated as patron saint of nurses by Leo XIII in 1886. It pushed its membership on war emotion and raised funds for Washington headquarters, a memorial to the women of the Civil War. The President spoke at the dedication of its building, May 10, 1917. Plans were already afoot to make the Red Cross an auxiliary of the armed services.

As he looked back upon the war, Secretary Baker avowed that were it to be done by him again he would not permit auxiliaries under independent management to take the part assumed in 1917 by the Red Cross, the Young Men's Christian Association, the Knights of Columbus, the Young Men's Hebrew Association, and the Salvation Army. He would instead perform these services as a part of the military organization. But in this reflection Baker was thinking as administrator of the Army and not in connection with the contribution of these volunteer associations to the morale behind the lines. The overworked Army in 1917 was ready to take aid where it could get it. Before long Baker accepted as an Assistant Secretary of War Frederick P. Keppel, a dean from Columbia University, who knew about social workers, college professors, and the sorts of people who could work better in the auxiliaries than in the regular service. Looking after these became a large part of his duty. The citizens whose boys must go to war let them go the more contentedly when they themselves had a chance at home to advance the Army welfare.

Himself honorary president of the Red Cross, Wilson announced on May 10 the erection of a Red Cross War Council, to take over large responsibilities, human and financial. He borrowed a Morgan partner, Henry P. Davison, to direct the work. Davison, used to thinking in millions, announced that during the week June 18–25, on the heels of registration and the floating of the First Liberty Loan, they would raise by voluntary contribution $100,000,000 to enable the Red Cross to be in fact what its charter stated: 'a medium of communication between the people of the United States of America and their Army and Navy.'

The Red Cross drive was a financial success. It overshot its mark by three millions. It accumulated at once five million enrolled members whose Red Cross buttons joined the Liberty Loan buttons and the Service Stars as badges of co-operation. At the end of the war it claimed twenty million members organized in 17,186 branches. The speakers in the drive, the new members, the local officers of local chapters, added another layer to the mesh of patriotic organizations. The other auxiliaries followed with their own drives, until the Salvation Army doughnuts, hot from the sizzling kettles just behind the trenches, became a symbol of service.

The statutes of the United States did not grant enough authority even to dig out and restrain sabotage and conspiracy while the neutral status lasted. Conspiracy to obstruct the operation of law was indeed forbidden, but there was lack of power to differentiate among those acts which, done in time of peace as no more than bad manners or misdemeanors, became threatening in their possibility of evil in time of war. Other nations at war had found it necessary to revise their criminal statutes in order to reach war crimes. DORA, the English Defense of the Realm Act, was already a widely known intrusion upon the affairs of private citizens. Congress conceived that there would be need for such law. No one in the United States had foreseen that public opinion, so nearly unanimous, would do most of its own policing. This was not visible as fact until Congress had ended its own debate upon what to do about it.

In the preceding Congress the Senate had considered and passed a revision of the neutrality act, carrying new provisions for a better prevention of espionage and sedition, and for a control of the dissemination of such military information as might be useful to an enemy. The attempt had lapsed with the end of the session in March. The fighting departments, and the Attorney-General, continued to lament the inadequacy of the law and made new drafts of their desires for the consideration of the new Congress. In the letter of the three secretaries urging upon the President the creation of the Committee on Public Information, it was suggested that the two functions of censorship and publicity might be combined in one body, without any legal authority beyond that of the commander-in-chief. The censorship functions were thought of as involving a restraint upon 'premature or ill-advised announcements.' The President went on record, in a letter to Arthur Brisbane, against a 'system of censorship that would deny to the people of a free republic like our own their indisputable right to criticize their own public officials.' But he needed a law to expand the existing provisions of the criminal code so as to cover sedition in its various forms, and he did not interpose objection to the projected censorship and sedition law presented to the judiciary committees by the Department of Justice.

Debate upon the project was under way even before the declaration of war. It took much of the time of Congress in the fortnight

after the completion of the loan act. It did not end until the
Espionage Act received the approval of the President on June 15.
In the early days of May both houses were hard at it, giving simultaneous consideration to the Administration proposals, as modified
by their committees before introduction. The rider to the measure,
granting a power to control exports, was discussed as a risky concentration of discretion in the hands of the President, but the real
fight was upon a group of sections vesting in him the equivalent of
a censorship.

The offensive words, upon which debate turned, came in 'Title
I, Section 4,' which the House reached on May 3. In these, during
war or a threat of war, as declared by the President, the latter was
empowered to 'prohibit the publishing or communicating of . . .
any information relating to the national defense which, in his
judgment, is of such character that it is or might be useful to the
enemy.' There was a proviso that nothing should be construed as
restricting criticism of the Government or its agents; but there was
a violent opposition to even so much of a restriction of a free press
as the words contained. Republicans in the House, and some
Democrats, attacked it as inconsistent with the guaranty of the
First Amendment. The Hearst papers gathered and presented a
petition of a million and a half signers against it. The American
Newspaper Publishers' Association opposed it. And editorial
writers went back to the sad history of the Sedition Act of 1798 to
show how contrary it was to the spirit of American institutions.

In this, they were in harmony with American preference. The
Sedition Act, passed by the harassed Federalist Administration
during the naval war with France, had expired in 1801, by a limitation stated in itself. It had never been repeated. There were
none to defend the right of any newspaper to sell for its profit the
military news upon whose secrecy national safety depended; but
the arguments decrying any grant of authority to restrict the press
carried far. Much was made of the useful exposures of British
military incompetence by the Northcliffe papers, and of the
injury to public interest inherent in the military desire to repress
criticism of military performance. It could be shown with con-

siderable soundness that the President already, as commander-in-
chief, possessed large authority to control the dissemination of
military secrets. George S. Graham, a Republican member from
Philadelphia, moved to strike out the offending section, and had in
this the support of Speaker Clark. The House sustained the
motion by vote of 221 to 167, with most of the consistent supporters
of the Administration in the minority. The evidence hardly bears
out the assertion of Josephus Daniels: 'Woodrow Wilson saw to it
that there was no censorship of the press in the United States during the World War.'

It was one thing for the House of Representatives to kill the
censorship, and quite another thing to keep it killed. The Senate
liked it and had its own bill with censorship intact, completed at
the moment when the House bill was brought to it on May 9. In
the interest of simplicity and speed the Senate struck out all of the
House bill but the enacting clause, substituted its own measure,
passed it and sent it to conference on May 14. There were only six
dissenting Senators (three had been 'willful men' and had voted
'no' on the war resolution — Gronna, La Follette, and Vardaman)
to oppose the seventy-seven who advanced the measure. It came
from conference with censorship modified, but kept alive by
insistence of Senate conferees; and it went back to conference upon
a House refusal, 184 to 44, to accept the Senate amendment. At
the second conference the Senate surrendered, yielding to House
determination not to vote a censorship. The Espionage Act as
passed gave much new authority to the Government, but not this.

In addition to power to control exports, and a revision of
neutrality details, now unimportant, the Espionage Act gave a new
definition of crimes against the public interest in time of war, and
enlarged the power of the Postmaster-General to see to it that
enemies of the Government did not make use of the mails in advancing their arguments.

Under its heading 'Title I, Espionage,' it not only defined
espionage and provided penalties for those convicted of being
spies, but also defined crimes of obstruction or conspiracy that were
likely to interfere with the execution by the Administration of the

acts of Congress. To most of these no serious objection was raised in either house. The sections granting power to control enemy aliens and to punish for industrial sabotage, desired by the Department of Justice, were not included, and the Attorney-General lamented this omission for several more months. But the operations of such as might oppose the war were made more difficult by a section on false reports and false statements, made willfully, 'with intent to interfere with the operation or success of the military or naval forces'; and by penalties running to ten thousand dollars' fine and twenty years' imprisonment for those who should 'willfully cause or attempt to cause insubordination, mutiny, or refusal of duty . . . or shall willfully obstruct the recruiting or enlistment service.'

A remote equivalent of a censorship made its appearance in 'Title XII. Use of the Mails.' It was no new thing for the United States to get at offenses otherwise, perhaps, outside its jurisdiction, by exercising its power to control the character of material passing through the mails. Lotteries had been attacked by this technique. Obscene literature was similarly banned. The definition of 'unmailable matter' was now enlarged to include every 'letter, writing, circular, postal card, . . . newspaper, pamphlet, book . . . in violation of any of the provisions of this act.' It was made also to include material of any kind 'advocating or urging treason, insurrection, or forcible resistance to any law of the United States.' Attempts to use the mails for these forbidden purposes were awarded penalties up to five thousand dollars and five years; and the duty devolved upon the Postmaster-General and his staff to apply the rule to matter offered to the mails.

Critics of the measure urged as an objection to it the necessity to open and examine first-class mail matter in order to determine whether the law was being violated. This innovation struck at a cherished right, based upon the sanctity of the mails. Printed matter, sent unsealed, offered no difficulty to enforcing officers except the great labor of examination, but letters were sacred. Under existing laws there was no right to open a sealed letter without a search warrant; and while there was some doubt whether this matter was covered by the constitutional guaranty of the 'right of the people to be secure . . . against unreasonable searches and seizures,' it was certain that indiscriminate examination of sealed first-class mail would be so unpopular as to defeat its purpose. The law made it clear that only a duly authorized 'employee of the Dead Letter Office' or 'other person upon a search warrant authorized by law' might 'open any letter not addressed to himself.'

The Post Office was not the best place in which to conduct the filtration of material called for by Title XII. In nearly every case the determination upon the character of the material called for information, judgment, and poise not certain to be part of the equipment of postal inspectors. As the summer advanced, Burleson was in increasing controversy with the owners of periodicals in which he found matter apparently in violation of the law. When he ruled that a given issue was unmailable, his action prevented its distribution and the regularity of issue upon which second-class mailing privilege was based was broken. The next number could not exercise the privilege thus lapsed, and the owner was forced again to make application for admission to it. This involved great loss to the owners and increased the penalty. The *American Socialist* was out of the mails immediately upon passage of the law. Jeremiah A. O'Leary's *Bull* lost its privilege in July. Max Eastman's *Masses* followed it in August, and Victor Berger's *Milwaukee Leader* in October. None of the journals barred under the law was of wide circulation or influence, but such censorship by indirection gained them sympathizers in circles that disapproved their policy.

In spite of the complaint of the Attorney-General that the powers to protect the Government were inadequate, the evidence of the cases rising under either the exclusion powers of the Postmaster-General or the new definitions of sedition indicates that sedition was uncommon. Whether it was in fact necessary to proceed against it is open to debate. The sharp criticism of Government and courts by those who disliked any legal coercion was out of proportion to either the extent of the dislike or the burden of the coercion. Public opinion settled the matter, for public opinion supported the war and the effort of the Government to carry it to a successful end. The Espionage Act, as applied, went further than the words on the statute book, for it was administered by officials earnest in the war. The powers conferred were extended by another law, the Trading with the Enemy Act, in October, 1917. And the Sedition Act, May 16, 1918, incorporated in the statutes something of the growing impatience with dissent. But the Espionage Act became a tool to trim the margins of public opinion. Arrests were made by patriots irritated by any opposition. Juries, and the panels from which they were selected, had their ideas about proper behavior in war time, as their indictments and verdicts proved. Attorneys and judges had too little of that dispassion that should go with law enforcement. And before final judgments could be obtained from the Supreme Court upon the propriety of verdicts, the war was over. Zechariah Chafee, a professor of law at Harvard, brought out his *Freedom of Speech* (1920), lamenting the damage done to the spirit of the First Amendment. But it was a damage in which neither the Congress nor the Administration had the first responsibility. The personnel of bench, bar, and jury were moved; and being moved they gave to law a scope that those who drafted it had hardly had in mind.

IV. THE WAY TO WIN: SHIPS AND FOOD

In the early days of war, between the delivery of the war message and the passage of the loan act, while it was still not to be expected that American armies would fight in France, and before the Allied Missions arrived with brief-cases bulging with good advice, the most absorbing question in the United States was how to win. Woodrow Wilson had recited in his message the matters he could think of as involved in war. He had indeed mentioned military participation on the battle front; but he dedicated 'our lives and our fortunes' to victory without more than a guess at the drafts that were to be drawn upon both. In the war message he signed a blank check, to be paid by the United States. He stood ready to write in upon it whatever amount the necessities of the Allies might call for and already some of the Allies were prepared to tell him what to do.

David Lloyd George, Prime Minister of England, was one of these. George had come into Downing Street at the head of his own Cabinet after his successful dislodgment of Asquith in December, 1916. He had already made his name a synonym for action and his tongue one for blunt speech. His six fat volumes, *War Memoirs of David Lloyd George* (1933–36), bristling with criticisms of the incompetence of others, have caused more than one reviewer to inquire: 'Can any statesman in the fog of war have been so often right?' On the Thursday after the declaration he ate with the American Luncheon Club in London, welcomed his hosts as comrades in arms, and told them the duty of the United States: 'The road to victory, the guaranty of victory, the absolute assurance of victory, has to be found in one word, ships, in a second word, ships, and a third word, ships.' He was at least explicit. Even at this, however, he did not reveal to his hearers the terrible damage done to Allied shipping by the German submarines. Had the Imperial Government been a little more careful and much less arrogant in the matter of neutral right and life there is good reason to suppose that it might have carried its maritime campaign to success against its enemies. Its blunders brought the United States into the war. Yet its submarines sunk their millions of tons with only occasional loss to non-resistant crews. There need not have been any loss; or at least no more than by prompt avowal and indemnity would have prevented neutral anger from rising into war spirit.

In the quarter in which Lloyd George spoke, the second quarter of 1917, the merchant marine of England alone lost 1,360,000 tons of ships, making a total of 5,360,000 lost since the beginning of the war. Every day — for the Allied shipyards could not launch new keels as rapidly as the enemy could sink them — the deficit in tonnage was growing worse. In the very fortnight of the address, 'one out of every four ships leaving the United Kingdom for overseas' never came back, wrote Edward N. Hurley in *The Bridge to France* (1927).

Even before Lloyd George pointed the duty, the United States had seen an opportunity to win the war by building ships faster than the U-boats could sink them. The 'bridge of ships' became one of the slogans of the war, gratifying to those who could feel a good slogan to be half the victory, and there were few in the United States to doubt the national capacity for large-scale production. The existing shipyards did not promise this, for the sixty-odd yards with some 215 ways had room for an occasional new way, but no elasticity sufficient to enable them to get beneath the load. Edward A. Filene was not far wrong when he stated, somewhat later, that it would take four tons of shipping in continuous operation for every American soldier in France.

It was not easy for Filene, or anyone else, to speak with precision of the carrying capacity of ships. World practice had not reduced ship dimension to a numerical notation intelligible to laymen, or revealing clearly the capacity of a vessel to carry freight or men.

This was the only thing that mattered: the number of actual net tons of freight that could be packed away in holds. But even tons could not tell the whole story, for light and bulky freight takes ship space, and the trick the loader must learn is to fill his hull with as many tons as his ship can carry, filling at the same time its cubic capacity so as to waste no space. The men in charge of the American effort soon learned that little was on record about 'stowage factors' — the weight-space requirement of each type of freight — except as seamen by rule of thumb had mastered them. Locomotives, shipped fully assembled, had one factor; steel rails another; fodder another; even sausage casings were important; and no yarn of the war had more pertinence than that of the yardmaster with wooden piles to ship to France who cut them into short lengths so that they would go neatly into the hold. Existing usage spoke of ships' capacity in four ways, all misleading, as Hurley had later to explain to Senator Hiram Johnson.

In the United States marine men preferred to talk of 'dead-weight' tonnage, or the weight of cargo, coal, and supplies carried in a fully loaded ship. This was a figure much less than 'displacement' — used chiefly for ships of war — in which the total weight of ship, stores, and cargo was given. British usage clung to 'gross tonnage,' a maritime fiction ascertained by dividing the cubic space of a ship by an arbitrary 100, on the assumption that 100 cubic feet of freight weighed a ton; but since the cubic space included superstructure as well as hold, and there was no uniformity in the measurement of space, the gross tonnage was an inaccurate estimate of the capacity of a ship. The term 'net tonnage' meant the pay-cargo space divided by 100. Net, gross, and deadweight tonnage were related to each other, only approximately, as 3:5:8.

Ten days after the declaration of war the Emergency Fleet Corporation took a charter from the District of Columbia and faced its task. 'A separate corporation was formed and I am it,' wrote Major-General George W. Goethals, builder of the canal at Panama, to whom the President assigned the post of general manager. Good-will and a readiness to accept ship contracts spread far beyond the fences of the existing yards. Construction companies, with the demand for office buildings checked, were prepared to turn to ships and build new yards. The timber in the South and West, with 'birds still nesting in their tops,' stood ready to be logged and fabricated. If ship carpenters had passed out with the shift from wood to steel, house carpenters might learn the work. Ingenuity was ready to prove that it was possible to make a ship of concrete, and have it float. Steelmakers, in the interior of the country where no navigable water ran, saw no difficulty in standardizing a type, making the parts wherever there were steel and factories and labor, and shipping all to assembly yards along the coast. And Henry Ford, no longer pacifist, conceived an assembly line at River Rouge from whose ways an endless procession of light vessels should slide to sea.

The organization of this industrial enterprise, the preparation of plans, and the operation of the ships when built fell to the duty of the United States Shipping Board, one of the creations of the preparedness movement. The Administration had not been blind to the condition in which the advent of war in 1914 had left the United States. For a generation, since the steel merchant ship became the type tool of maritime trade, the United States had permitted the carriage of its exports to be generally in foreign bottoms. War kept the vessels of the Central Powers locked in port. Submarine excesses lessened the number of neutral carriers that dared to go to sea. Insurance rates became prohibitive, until the United States set up war-risk insurance of its own. The Allies needed most of their own tonnage for their own business, and hired it to American shippers on their own terms or not at all. They carried what they pleased, whither they pleased, and were able to make their 'blacklists' a death warrant to neutral firms. In 1914 Wilson urged the creation of a shipping board to build and operate a merchant fleet under the United States flag, thus to lessen the painful dependence upon the ships of others. In 1915 this was made a party measure, but could not be pushed through Congress. More successful, in September, 1916, when the wave of willingness to prepare for emergencies pressed upon the constituents of congressmen, his bill went through.

It was in late December that Wilson named to the Senate the five members who were to compose the Shipping Board. He could hardly have named them much earlier since the law was signed only on September 7, the day before the session adjourned, while the new session did not meet until December 4. He named as chairman William Denman, of San Francisco. It took tact to get confirmations from the Senate. The Board had a fund of $50,000,000 with which it was authorized to buy the stock in a corporation to be formed to build the ships, and it had large powers in the control of their operation.

The use of the corporation, as a means of avoiding the red tape incident to construction by the United States, was a novelty whose advantage had been revealed at Panama where the Government had had to acquire the stock of the Panama Railroad. A corporation president was vastly more agile than any bureau chief could be, for Congress was solicitous to guard against misappropriation of funds expended by a branch of the Government. American law surrounded every operation of a financial character with specifications and accounting rules which slowed it down. Here, speed was needed: a speed and flexibility comparable to that with which a United States Steel Corporation or a Pennsylvania Railroad could meet emergencies and get results.

The Emergency Fleet Corporation was owned by the United States through the Shipping Board which could control its policy by voting its stock. Its officers were much the same as those of the Board; but when they acted as agents of the Emergency Fleet they acted, not under the restrictive laws of Congress, but under the general incorporation laws of the State of their incorporation. What any private corporation could do, they might do. Denman was president of both Board and Emergency Fleet at the start. Goethals was general manager of the Fleet, less 'it' than he anticipated; and before the end of May he was telling the Iron and Steel Institute in New York that he regarded 'all boards as long, narrow, and wooden.' In July both he and Denman were thrust aside and the ship program passed to other hands which could take advantage of the spade-work the first crew had done in preparing for a fleet. Wilson delegated Edward N. Hurley, a Chicago Democrat, to disentangle the snarl. Hurley had been a go-between for the Wilson proponents and the machine of Roger C. Sullivan, as well as chairman of the Federal Trade Commission and one of Davison's co-workers on the Red Cross Board. He remained at the head of both Shipping Board and Emergency Fleet throughout the war.

Hurley readjusted the relations between the governing Shipping Board and the operating Fleet Corporation so that a deadlock like that of Denman and Goethals could not recur. He provided himself with the beginnings of a merchant fleet by commandeering on August 3 for the use of the United States all hulls of twenty-five hundred tons under construction in American yards. There were 431 of these, aggregating three million deadweight tons, that might carry cargoes when once they were completed. So far as the immediate moving of freights was concerned this was no more than a bookkeeping order. It transferred the ships from the owners who would have operated them to the United States which would only slightly modify their use. Many of the hulls were under contract for foreign owners, so that the commandeering became an international matter in which the Shipping Board stood fast to its right. Of a different international slant was the use of the ninety-seven interned German merchant ships, running in size from the gigantic *Vaterland* which was soon to figure in the news as the *Leviathan*. These had to be repaired before they could be sent to sea, for Bernstorff had attempted their disablement.

Yet another international complication was developed in March, 1918, upon the seizure of eighty-seven Dutch ships, of some 533,746 tons, which were at the moment within the jurisdiction of the United States. Holland, between two deadly belligerents, was in a jam. The freight the Dutch ships might carry had been dictated to them for many months by the Netherlands Overseas Trust. Now the very ships were taken from their owners. There had been tedious negotiations conducted by England and the United States in a hope that a way might be found whereby the inactive Dutch tonnage could be utilized, for the owners had preferred loss of revenue while keeping them in port to loss or damage to ships in the war zone. The negotiations were dragged-out and futile since Germany made it clear that voluntary compliance by the Dutch, whereby the ships should be used for Allied advantage, would be followed by German retaliation. And the Netherlands lived throughout the war in fear of a violation similar to that of Belgium. The ships concerned, tied to dock in British and American ports, were now seized. Those within the United States were operated thereafter by the Shipping Board, and since the Dutch had not been a voluntary part to the seizure the provocation given thereby to Germany was softened. They were taken subject to compensation to the Dutch owners for hire and damage, and the transaction was justified under an old principle of international law, the right of *angaria*, whereby in time of war a nation may turn to its own use such of the physical property of neutrals as may be within its jurisdiction. The Dutch Government complained loudly of the seizure, largely for the German ear. The owners were fully compensated, even for damage done by Germans which Germany would have been unlikely to reimburse. Even the insurance liabilities for the dispossessed Dutch crews, under Dutch law, were assumed by the Shipping Board.

The bookkeeping by which an American merchant fleet was put on paper counted as part of the fleet the ships not yet completed, those of the enemy, those taken under *angaria*, and also those requisitioned from private American operators and placed at the control of the Shipping Board. In October all American ships of over twenty-five hundred tons, fit for use, were taken over for the account of the Emergency Fleet, to be operated under charters by the owners. Even a few steamers from the Great Lakes runs, ore boats and grain boats, too long to pass the locks of the Welland Canal, were cut in two, brought through in halves, reunited, and sent to sea.

Beginning in April with 'three small rented rooms,' the Emergency Fleet Corporation had within a year a score of buildings in Washington alone. In June, 1918, the Army Quartermaster moved two hundred truckloads of office material and the personal equipment of the twenty-four hundred central office employees to new working space in Philadelphia, where there was room to grow. But as yet it had chiefly a paper fleet, without adding many tons to the available supply of ships.

The real task of the Emergency Fleet was to enlarge this supply, and upon this problem Denman and Goethals had concentrated before they parted. To add the fifteen million tons their program called for (seventeen hundred steel ships, one thousand wood) they must build an industry up from vacant lots, get steel from the mine and lumber from the forest, find labor where they could, and let their contracts to men whose pre-war business had been something else than building ships. The chief novelty of the program, beyond a few fantastic experimental types, was the designing of a 'fabricated' steel ship — a standard vessel whose parts need not be built upon the ways in crowded yards, but could be manufactured to specifications anywhere in the United States and put together at tidewater. Weeks ran to months before the designers could agree upon shape, type, and engines for the standard ships, so that the specifications and blueprints could go to fabricating plants. A straight-line, flat-plate ship, largely the design of Theodore Ferris, set a new type of which the seven seas knew nothing. It was not good enough to survive the war in competition with vessels more deliberately put together, but it was capable of freight service and could be constructed quickly.

While wooden shipyards were budding on Southern and Western waterfronts the Emergency Fleet Corporation prepared the assembly yards for the new steel ships. Under its contracts, at Wilmington, North Carolina, at Newark, New Jersey, at Bristol, Pennsylvania, and on the unoccupied mud flats of the Delaware River below Philadelphia which the early settlers called Hog Island, ninety-four new shipways were built. Fifty of these were at Hog Island alone. The Shipping Board had its vision of a continuous stream of bottoms slipping into the water, if only the war should last long enough for the builders to get into their stride. The engineering and human difficulties of building the yards through a hard winter made them costly. But the Hog Island yard, out of a contract let September 13, 1917, laid its first keel five months later, February 12, 1918. It had eighty miles of new railroad track to serve its two hundred and fifty buildings, and through its telephone central passed the calls of a 'city of 140,000' people. Before the peace stopped its operation, it was laying six keels a week. Yet it did not launch its first ship, the *Quistconk*, until August 5, or deliver it until December 3, 1918, the day before Wilson sailed for Paris to make a peace. Much was made of the fact that from the several American yards nearly one hundred ships were launched simultaneously on July 4, 1918; but few of these carried cargoes to help win the war. As an heroic effort to create an industry, the shipping venture was a great success, expensive as it was; but had the war waited to be won by these ships it must have lasted longer. The intriguing melody of George Cohan's 'Over There,' sung when the *Costigan*, first of the Newark brood and named by Cohan for his grandfather, took the water, had little reference to the matter in hand. By this time the 'Yanks' were indeed coming, but in other bottoms.

But the hand of the United States had been laid upon what shipping there was, or what might come into being, and the Shipping Board was soon forced to determine upon what principle to operate the fleet so as to conserve tonnage and help win the war. Its experiments with the chartering of ships, whether its own or those of neutrals that could be hired, built up experience. It worked in co-operation with the War Department, as principal shipper, and with the British agencies of ship control. Early in 1918 it brought into command of its Shipping Control Committee the president of the International Mercantile Marine Company, P. A. S. Franklin, and gave him a free hand. Franklin worked for a 'liquid fleet' — one whose units should be detached from exclusive control by any single agency of the Government and, being pooled, should be available as needed. This was what the Car Service Bureau of the Interstate Commerce Commission was trying to do with railroad rolling stock. The Shipping Control Committee attacked the 'turn around' as the weak spot in the use of ships, for vessels lay too long in port while waiting for their cargoes. By shortening this to half its duration they multiplied their tonnage.

They studied economical packing, giving weight to stowage factors, and cut the time while saving space. In April, 1918, they loaded thirty-three locomotives, 'practically ready for steam,' into the hold of the *Feltore*; jammed them tight between bales of hay; and delivered them at St. Nazaire ready to be lifted bodily from hold to track.

In the reorganization of the Shipping Control Committee under Franklin a new type of office was set up in Washington, full of implication for a future when government should be called upon to plan. Professor Edwin F. Gay, economic historian and dean of the Graduate School of Business Administration at Harvard, became director of a Division of Planning and Statistics. In his office figures were analyzed, upon which the decisions of Franklin ought to be made. Independent development based upon enthusiastic effort had gone the limit, and the men responsible for results were getting time to think about co-ordinating their efforts. Divisions similar to that of Gay made their appearance in departments other than the Shipping Board and they interchanged their figures and interlocked their effort. They conceived as a goal a work-sheet showing program and performance. If they could manage to get the gist of it on a daily sheet for scrutiny at the White House, so much the better. Planning to win a war was in a way a simple matter, for all knew the nature of the enemy and the common aim. Planning to run a government was to be a more complex affair, as was later to be seen; for aims are overlapping and inconsistent in periods of prosperity and may become murderously antagonistic during the dark days of a depression. The economic planners, with their wits whetted, never quite left Washington, and never forgot the days when war gave them their earliest chance. 'Gay ... was our economic mentor,' wrote Hurley; 'the work of restricting unessentials and allocating ships was centered in a single body.'

All tasks in the preparation of the war machine were interlocked, as the Emergency Fleet Corporation learned while pushing the construction of its new yards, and as every maker of munitions discovered as he speeded up his plant. The working gangs were assembled with difficulty, and to the Draft Boards it had to be made clear how important it was to leave key workers on their jobs. Every enlistment and every draft took potential workers from the labor market at a moment when the market needed more rather than fewer. The Four-Minute Men were put to the task of drumming up industrial recruits. Girls began to slip into the jobs their brothers vacated; some of them even into overalls beside the lathes. But when workers reported to new factories and yards they found no beds. Housing was none too good in well-established industrial communities. Around the new projects there were no dwellings for executives, no small houses for workmen, no boarding-houses and restaurants, no garages. And to this problem the Council of National Defense turned its attention early in the spring of 1917. It foresaw housing scarcity, and that the hiring of labor to build residences for war workers would add still another difficulty to the task of getting men to work.

Conceiving it as a welfare matter, and before the several production establishments had created their own housing sections, the Council of National Defense had a sub-committee studying the problem before the end of June. It held open hearings in October to prove by figures how greatly war work was being held up by lack of housing; and it recommended to the Government action on a scale larger than it could start itself. The Department of Labor, through a new bureau under Otto Eidlitz, took charge in February, 1918. As the various appropriation bills came along, funds were allotted for industrial housing and transportation work.

The Fleet Corporation was allowed ninety-five millions for this before the spring was gone. It had twelve thousand workmen to crowd into Bristol alone. It was soon drafting a program to house 56,296 of its workers with their families near its various plants, and it included in this scheme 8774 dwellings and nearly one thousand apartments, not to mention dormitories, cafeterias, and stores.

New snarls in the law and new concepts of public policy came to view with reference to the taxation of this sort of Government property; for each new venture placed a burden upon the community near which it was erected. There were streets to be built, and schools; and police and fire protection must be provided. Yet Government property, as such, was untaxable by local authority, and if left untaxable the cost of serving it might smother the community concerned. In July, 1918, the Secretary of Labor was allowed to incorporate in New York a Housing Corporation in which as agent for the Government he held the whole of its hundred million of stock. Red tape was cut again, and the corporation as a tool of government took on a larger significance. New houses called for new designs, new city plans, new architectural and engineering efforts by the United States, as well as new standards of living for the working folk. Before peace rang the bell another field for public planning had been reconnoitered.

Before Denman and Goethals had explored the woodenness of boards, and before experience with Liberty Loan and registration and the Red Cross drive had demonstrated that public opinion was abundantly able to enforce itself, the solvency of Lloyd George's formula to win the war had been challenged from another quarter. Herbert Hoover had come into the picture. Acting in front of the vast prestige of the Commission for Relief in Belgium, a prestige too great to be forgiven when the Post Office delivered to him a letter addressed to 'Miracle Man, Washington,' he demanded calories as the first of the munitions. 'Food will win the war' became a slogan. It had a drive whose force was equal to that for ships, and one whose consequences pushed farther down to the grass roots. Ships could be built only by captains of industry, with huge yards and plants, vast capital resources, and throngs of workmen. But every citizen could appreciate the need for food and do his bit. Wherever he was he could do it: whether at the breakfast table with bran muffins and a trifling pat of butter, or in his garden as he nursed a potato patch, or on a local committee of the Food Administration, explaining and exhorting, or in the mails, writing his congressman to let the food bill pass.

It was service of a sort for the Treasury to lend the Allies cash to pay for what they needed to buy in the United States. It was another to hurry ships to carry the necessities to Europe. But at the bottom, the food must be raised, the right sorts saved and shipped, and the rest eaten with patriotic zest. Spinach and cabbage, as they appeared at dinner, could be made into symbols of patriotic co-operation. 'Wheatless' and 'meatless' days tested devotion.

The President had anticipated that Hoover should do what must be done about food and that the Department of Agriculture, instead of being expanded into a war administration, should stick largely to its peace-time activities. He had called Hoover home even before the declaration and named him commissioner in charge of a voluntary body on May 19, since Congress was not ready for immediate action upon a food bill. Hoover accepted 'on the condition that he is to receive no payment for his services and that the whole of the force under him, exclusive of clerical assist-ance, shall be employed as far as possible upon the same volunteer basis.' Three days later, Lever presented to the House a bill that was described as an Administration measure to encourage agri-culture and to regulate the marketing of food and other necessaries.

Hoover gathered about him a staff recruited from among the men who came back with him from Belgium, from the agricultural colleges, and from where he could find them, and set about to make the United States food-conscious. In the absence of legal authority it was for nearly three months a matter of advertising, the only addition to the power of the Government being in the control of exports attached to the Espionage Act. The Allies buy-ing food with part of the loans extended through the Treasury were willing to act in co-operation with him, law or no law. A fear of rising prices, injurious to both war finance and to the standard of living, was one of the chief reasons for an effective food control. The matters to be impressed upon the public mind were the need of the Allied countries for huge food exports from the United States, the necessity upon the people to increase the yield of crops, the importance of consuming at home the food unsuitable for shipment, and the iniquity of profiteering. Even the Commis-sioner of Indian Affairs was brought into the campaign, advising his wards 'that the careless paring of potatoes' was wasteful and that 'every spoonful of left-over gravy can be used in soups.' And the Bureau of Fisheries was inspired to advocate 'the use of the meat of whales, porpoises, and dolphins . . . for food.'

The rapid progress in organizing the localities made it possible to use the State councils of defense and the Woman's Committees under the Council of National Defense in spreading the food message. The *Official Bulletin*, at the end of June, made public a circular from Anna Howard Shaw, as chairman of the Woman's Committee, advising the local groups: 'If you have not already extended the organization of your State to the counties, cities, and towns, will you undertake to do so at once?' she asked. She advised a house-to-house canvass to secure signatures to food pledges, and the posting in front windows of a sign to indicate compliance. The Blue Eagle of N.R.A. in 1933 had a technique already completely worked out before it left the egg. Hoover issued bulletins preaching the 'Gospel of the clean plate' and warning that 'full garbage pails' mean 'empty dinner pails.' More fruit and vegetables, he urged, 'less wheat, meat, milk, fats, sugar, and fuel.'

In sober vein the Food Commissioner addressed the President on July 10 'with regard to wheat.' He believed that his conservation measures were taking hold and that they had saved for export some eighty million bushels that would ordinarily have been eaten in the United States. He was alarmed, however, at the prospect of only 678,000,000 bushels in the 1917 harvest — and others were distressed at labor troubles in the wheat harvest and found there a ground for deep suspicion of the loyalty of the I.W.W. Should the American diet not be checked, Americans would consume all but seventy-eight millions of the new harvest. If they had saved the eighty, these, with the seventy-eight, would make only 158,000,000 bushels, too little for the export need. The harvest had been bad in 1916, leaving less than a normal carry-over. It was 'absolutely vital' to stimulate an enlarged planting for 1918 and at the same time to insure the farmer who broke new ground for wheat against a slump in price in case there should be a glut. It was as important to keep the crop out of the hands of speculators. But Hoover had no powers. 'We are practically helpless to safeguard either the farmer or the consumer until the pending legislation is passed.' Congress was genuinely busy, but it had many doubts to overcome before it was willing to ask the free American farmer to accept regimentation.

With the Espionage Act out of the way, the House Committee on Agriculture, of which Asbury F. Lever of South Carolina was chairman, was free to claim the attention of Congress. The committee had received Lever's own proposal and had worked out of it and other proposals and the testimony given at its hearings a bill for food control. The House settled down to consider this June 18. 'In the short space of a few months,' said Lever, opening the debate, 'the foundation of a great army has been laid, the expenditure of $7,000,000,000 has been authorized, and the machinery for the mobilization of this stupendous sum is well under way. . . . That a democracy can be organized . . . is being demonstrated.' His bill proposed to erect 'a governmental control of necessaries which shall extend to and include all the processes, methods, activities of, and for the production, manufacture, procurement, storage, distribution, sale, marketing, pledging, financing, and consumption of necessaries, which shall be exercised and administered by the President.' It was hardly necessary for the bill to have gone further, though it did to the extent of twenty-one sections. In this one sentence lay a grant of power unknown to American experience and so generous as to need no elaboration. The other sections were admittedly no more than explanatory and designed to limit the exercise of the powers to the period of the war with Germany and one year thereafter. 'To delay,' said Lever, 'is but to stay temporarily the day of wrath. . . . The wrath . . . is not going to be appeased by the screams and squalls about conferring autocratic powers upon the President.'

Lever was no sooner back in his seat than another Democratic member, Young of Texas, was on his feet to challenge the whole proposal and to denounce a dictatorship 'that will go to the remotest precincts . . . And take charge of the little, humble farmer who is seeking to eke out an existence for himself and his hungry children.' And the parliamentary fight was on.

It was not a long fight so far as the House was concerned. With its representation based on population, and giving full weight to urban and Eastern groups, it was easier for the House to rule the farmer than for the Senate, which received the bill six days later. Through these six days the Representatives talked about shortage and price, about constitutionality and the sins of profiteers and the war powers of the President; but they did not fundamentally change the grant. The term 'necessaries' was indeed brought down to earth by the enumeration of the chief commodities concerned; and a prohibition of the use of food for the manufacture of alcoholic liquors was accepted. But the measure passed the House by a vote of 365 to 5. Few were prepared to test the reality of the 'day of wrath.'

The Senate received the Lever Bill from the Committee on Agriculture and Forestry on June 25, and three days later entered a debate that ran intermittently for twenty-four days. Chamberlain of Oregon had it in hand, hurrying it as best he could, but even with the possibility of a cloture at his hand he could neither expedite action nor prevent fundamental amendment. He used the threat of cloture, in order to force on July 10 a unanimous-consent agreement that the Senate should vote on July 21. He could do no more. The fiscal year ended and a new year began, there was inconvenience for the Administration and uncertainty for the people, an abnormal share of the wheat crop was held on the farm in hope of higher prices; but the Senate could not be hurried. Most of the matters that Senators talked about were worth discussing, peace or war, but the delay was heart-breaking to those with an immediate responsibility for victory. The urban East was content with regulation and fearful of rise in prices. The farmer West and South wanted the farmer to get his price, wanted no regulation unless it be applied to industry as well as to agriculture, feared a dictator who might restrict freedom and save the cities or the Allies at the cost of him who raised the crop.

The fight against a food dictator brought into the debate the personality of the Food Commissioner, who was by common consent to be designated Food Administrator when the bill should pass. This was Herbert Clark Hoover, whose self-made life, out of his origin on an Iowa farm, had been the theme of a multitude of writers since he first broke into the news in connection with an American relief committee in London in 1914. An enthusiastic article by Will Irwin, in the *Saturday Evening Post*, brought the matter to a head. Reed of Missouri, a distinguished jury lawyer and a parliamentarian of ingenuity and persistence, found reason to dislike Hoover, as he called to the attention of the Senate the details of the Food Commissioner's career. What he wanted (and the Senate was with him) was to amend the Lever proposal by throwing the control of food and fuel into the hands of a commission of three instead of leaving it to the discretion of the President, which meant Hoover.

Reed took the floor, on a question of personal privilege, to deny the truth of a charge that he was treating Hoover 'as if he had been up before a police court for stealing chickens in Kansas City'; but the testimony of the *Congressional Record* hardly clears him of the bad manners that Senators have too often shown to inconvenient outsiders. He sought to discredit Hoover by doubting his status as American voter, if not citizen. Johnson of California, however, regarded his fellow Californian as 'a distinguished world figure... particularly fitted for the task.' But to Reed, Hoover was quite too much of a 'world figure.' In the forty-three years that Hoover had lived, most of the last twenty had been lived outside the United States. His work as mining operator and promoter had carried him whither mineral or capital could be found. He had a house in London. He had even been talked of as a possible cog in the English war machine; and there were some to say that had he been a British subject he might have hoped to end his days as Sir Herbert. It was nonsense to talk of him as English, but it was true that he had no special knowledge of food in advance of the studies thrust upon him by the German occupation of Belgium. He was, as he admitted, 'very much of a stranger in my own country, as I have been away since the war began.' The Senate added the commission of three as one of its amendments.

If the farmer felt safer to have the food control vested in a commission, he was encouraged, too, by Senate insistence upon a price for wheat. Hoover, in Belgium, was said to have used his food stocks not only to feed the hungry but also to break the speculator. He felt free, the story ran, and if true it was to his credit, to throw part of the Belgian food back into the market when speculating bulls forced it to an artificial rise. He knew as much about markets as the speculators did, and was said to have made a tidy profit for the Commission for Relief in Belgium out of the transactions. Fear was in the air that, with control unchecked in his hands, he might whittle down the price the farmer received. The Senate added another amendment guaranteeing a minimum price of two dollars a bushel for 1918 wheat. The price of the current crop, that of 1917, was stabilized by the President at $2.20, upon recommendation of a commission headed by President Garfield of Williams College.

Republican Senators were ready to exalt Congress at the expense of Wilson, and found Democrats ready to co-operate. Restrained by the pressure of their own constituents from too open obstruction, they were yet loath to leave the war in presidential hands. They had been quite willing to let the last Congress expire, March 4, with appropriations unvoted, for this made a special session necessary. Now, through Weeks of Massachusetts, they asked for the creation of a committee on the conduct of the war.

Such a committee as Weeks proposed had watched and bothered Lincoln through the Civil War. It had been a joint committee, created in December, 1861, and sitting long enough to turn in eight great volumes of testimony and report. Benjamin Franklin Wade, a fire-eating Republican Senator from Ohio, had directed its affairs. Its earnestness in prosecuting the war had been too clear to doubt, but its deep fear that Lincoln did not know enough to prosecute the war provides full testimony to prove that the fame of Lincoln was less than complete while he lived. Wade came to know so much more about the war than Lincoln did, and so much more about reconstruction, that by the summer of 1864 he led a coalition against a too-moderate peace. While Lincoln was candidate for re-election, Wade, in his own party, denounced him for a 'studied outrage on the legislative authority' and asserted a duty

to 'check the encroachments of the Executive.' The Committee on
the Conduct of the War had pretty generally escaped the attention
of the historians, of even so thorough a student as James Ford
Rhodes or so charming a writer as Professor Wilson. But Lincoln
had known how difficult it had made his work, and Wilson as
President had no doubt about it. It will 'make my task of conducting the war practically impossible,' he declared when the Senate
added the suggestion of Senator Weeks to the Lever Act. The committee which it was now proposed to revive had more than the
support of critical Republicans. There were fifty-three Senators
who voted aye when the 'joint committee on expenditures in the
conduct of the war' was added as a rider to the act for food control.
Five Senators and five Representatives (three to be Democrats in
each case), constituting the committee, were to keep themselves
informed, to confer with all departments and voluntary boards, to
take testimony as needed, and to advise Congress upon 'expenditures and contracts.'

The amended Lever Act, with only six negative votes on its final
passage in the Senate, went back to the House. It was nearly three
more weeks before it could become a law. A food-survey bill
directing the Secretary of Agriculture to make a food census, which
passed by both houses and was sent to conference earlier in the
session, was now brought out of conference and offered as a part of
the food program. The conferees on the Lever Act wrestled with
the Senate amendments until the House members of the conference
committee had their way and forced the adoption of a report from
which had been stricken both the commission to have charge of
food and the joint committee to watch expenditures. But this took
time. When the report came back in August, the House accepted
it without a recorded 'no'; it passed the Senate with but an ill-
assorted seven voting in the negative: France, Gronna, Hardwick,
Hollis, La Follette, Penrose, and Reed. The dissenters were acri-
monious as they protested the necessity to accept the bill, leading
Oscar S. Straus, Republican though he was, to declare that there
was 'no politics in this country now except on Capitol Hill.'

Signed by the President on August 10, 1917, the Lever Act gave him authority to erect controls over foods, feeds, fuel, and fertilizers, and the machinery and equipment for producing them. It prohibited the use of food in the manufacture of 'distilled spirits for beverage purposes,' and authorized the President to forbid such use for 'malt or vinous liquors.' It fixed the base price for the 1918 wheat crop at two dollars a bushel and empowered the President to set in advance a minimum price for succeeding years.

There was no news in the announcement coming immediately from the White House that Herbert Hoover had been appointed Food Administrator. His volunteer organization was complete, and ready to be regularized with law behind it. He was already in agreement with the assistants through whom he was to throw an additional network of public service across the United States. War industries, without specific law, had been reorganized a fortnight earlier, and with the new War Industries Board he could set up intimate co-operation. A Purchasing Commission for the Allies was nearly ready to be launched. Foreign trade, imports, and exports were heading into an organization of their own. The President was in agreement, too, upon the technical method of managing wheat, most important of the food commodities.

Four days after the signature of the Lever Act an executive order directed the incorporation in Delaware of a fifty-million-dollar structure, to be known as the United States Food Administration Grain Corporation. Under the presidency and direction of Julius H. Barnes the business of the Grain Corporation was to build up stocks of grain, to facilitate the export of flour, and to stabilize the price. When the time came to fix the price for the 1919 harvest, the Grain Corporation did not do it, or Hoover, although the latter received the odium of it when it proved unpopular. The President entrusted it to a special group selected for the purpose. A corporation similar to the Grain Corporation, and also subsidiary to the Food Administration, was created in 1918 to buy, hold, and allocate raw and refined sugar, under the name of the Sugar Equalization Board. By this time Government-owned corporations were so common as to attract no considerable attention.

Part of the mandate of the Lever Act dealt with fuel, which was described in some detail. Coal and oil, produced under conditions far different from those of agriculture and having different connections with labor, capital, and transportation, were not suitable for handling in the Food Administration, even if the work of that body were not already as complex as one man could hope to master. The Council of National Defense had in the spring gone farther than the law allowed in the effort to stabilize the price of coal. Here was a commodity in which price was closely connected with volume of production. The coal deposits, whether hard or soft, range from great veins of high-grade fuel cheaply mined to thin and inaccessible deposits of low-grade coal. The normal price, set by normal consumption, always kept low-grade mines out of production. Yet these inferior mines could be worked if the output could be sold. The anti-trust laws had made it difficult if not impossible for the coal companies to adjust production to demand, and there were not, when the war began, adequate figures to indicate the rate at which coal moved to mine mouth and was shipped to market. The Federal Trade Commission, set to many studies of price in connection with war supply, had been assigned coal as a subject for investigation. The Lever Act vested in the President power to fix a price that would bring coal into the market. He did this in August, and followed the action by erecting a Fuel Administration parallel to the Food Administration on August 23. Harry A. Garfield, son of a former President of the United States, and President of Williams College, was made Fuel Administrator. And oil, as a type of fuel requiring special treatment, became the business of a new division of the Fuel Administration under Mark L. Requa in January, 1918. Petroleum products had become one of the most important of the munitions of war.

In the closing stages of the debate over the Food Administration it was an added argument for a one-man direction that the division of authority in shipbuilding had broken down. The clash of personalities between Denman and Goethals brought about the elimination of both. On the very day that the Lever Act went to conference, Hurley was placed in full authority over Shipping Board and Fleet Corporation. What Goethals thought of boards

was true, when there was work to do; and for the next eight months
the trend of war work was in the direction of assignment of key
tasks to powerful personalities, each, under the President, in
charge of his own job, and with boards and committees mostly
engaged in clearing the ground so that their chiefs could act.

V. THE YANKS ARE COMING

THE Baltic Society, one of the most exclusive organizations of military reminiscence, one that differs from the Cincinnati or the Aztecs, which took shape when the job was done, still holds its occasional reunions. Its membership is limited to the little group, fifty-nine officers and twice as many more field clerks and enlisted men, who sailed as inconspicuously as possible on the White Star *Baltic*, May 28, 1917, headed for London, Paris, and the uncertain future. Those who were to be its members sailed not too perfectly disguised as civilians. In London they put on their uniforms, including the side arms that had nearly disappeared from the Western Front. They were so far behind the times that they had as yet no Sam Browne belts. They had no army, and hardly a promise of one. Yet when they paused in England to be received by royalty, and crossed to Boulogne where the welcoming French tongue wrestled with what sounded most like 'Puerchigne,' they were hailed as though they were a host.

The major-general in command of the American Expeditionary Forces had a more intimate experience with troops in the field than any of his several seniors on the active list of the Army. It is interesting to conjecture who would have been in his place if the Administration had anticipated the full dimensions to which his military adventure would grow. Perhaps it would still have been John J. Pershing, for the only other major-general flexible enough to be considered was Leonard Wood. But Wood had himself destroyed the possibility that Wilson could work happily through him. Pershing, indeed, did not desire him to come to France in even a subordinate command. Baker thought he had been 'very indiscreet'; the President thought him, in spite of great attainments, a trouble-maker. Wood stayed at home, bitterly disappointed, to have Hermann Hagedorn, fighting friend of both him and Roosevelt, record his great services to the army Pershing led, in *Leonard Wood: A Biography* (1931).

But that army was non-existent when Pershing arrived in France; and the best military opinion, whether behind him or at the front, did not see any way in which a considerable army (conceding that the United States was competent to assemble it) could ever be transported. The English and French Missions had not even suggested a co-operation in which American troops should play a large part. Later, when the A.E.F. had become a fact, some of their leaders imagined that they had expected it from the first, and had counted on it. Joffre had desired marching units, to display the flag to doubting Frenchmen. Pershing was followed by these. Their first regiments, under the immediate command of William L. Sibert, an engineer officer who had done well at Panama, began to disembark on June 26. Their landfall was at the mouth of the River Loire, at St. Nazaire. The appearance of a few of them in Paris on Independence Day was an emotional success. Already tentative names were preparing for them, for *poilu*, *Boche*, and Tommy were convenient short cuts to a new vocabulary. 'Sammies' was tried, perhaps from a free rendering of *les amies*, perhaps a derivative from Uncle Sam, but only 'Yanks' stuck, after George Cohan set the word to music.

There is nothing in the prosaic but enlightening pages of *My Experiences in the World War* (1931) to indicate that the commander of the A.E.F. believed in fairies; but within a few days of his arrival at his headquarters in the Rue Constantine Pershing had convinced himself that he was to command a fighting army and win the war if it should last long enough to be won. There was doubt of this. The Missions had not revealed all that he now learned in Paris: the collapse of the Nivelle drive, the mutinous weariness of some of the French divisions, the exhaustion of manpower, and the prevalence of defensive tactics in both French and British armies. They were holding on; none could guess how long. Pershing built his policy upon the assumption — incapable of proof today, but not proved wrong — that the Allies were bankrupt in a military sense. They might postpone exhaustion or defeat, but in his judgment they were too tired to win, and the long necessity for economical defense had destroyed the capacity of either high command to turn the armies out of the trenches and by military maneuver destroy the power of the enemy.

It was his mission, as he saw it in the intervals between state entertainments, to prepare to receive and operate an army; an army large enough for its weight to turn the tide, an army trained for other than trench warfare and not exhausted or blunted by a long defense, an army that could win the war only by keeping its method and its morale apart from anything he found in France. This was an army that none but he anticipated, and only a capacity to believe in fairies could have let him believe in it. But he formulated the idea, stuck to it through thick and thin, and being a stubborn man had his way to the extent that the Allies gave lip service to the project. Three weeks after his arrival in Paris he upset the forecasts of Washington by a calm notification that his requisitions would begin with the requirements of his first million men, with additional millions to follow as needed and with the first million to be ready to take the field within a year. His training directions contained the mandate that 'all instruction must contemplate the assumption of a vigorous offensive.' While Washington gasped at his determination to make up the mind of the War Department, the Allies gasped at his inquiry where he should begin and at what spot along the front he should prepare to launch his non-existent army.

His orders warranted his assumption, although there is still some mystery about the drafting of a paragraph that read as though someone at home had anticipated his conclusion. James G. Harbord, his chief of staff, doubts whether he ever read it, and has told much of the story sensibly in *The American Army in France, 1917–1919* (1936); but the words were there. Pershing, while in Washington picking his associates and making preliminary arrangements, had among other things foreseen the necessity for orders to himself. He had them drafted. Tasker H. Bliss, then

acting Chief of Staff in the absence of Hugh Scott who was with
the Mission in Russia, signed where he was told, for no one desired
to obstruct the commander. Baker had not heard of this, yet he
had the same idea and confided to Brigadier-General Francis J.
Kernan the duty of drafting an order for the A.E.F. Kernan discarded the suggestion filed in a memorandum by Hoover recom-
mending that Americans going to France should go simply as
'man-power.' He made some study of the problems of earlier
expeditionary forces, recalled the way in which the armies sent to
the relief of Peking had wrestled with the question of command,
and was aware that each of the Missions then in Washington
wished there were some way in which American manhood might
fill the gaps in its own battalions. As a safeguard against seizure,
rather than as a chart for combat, Kernan penned the words:

> In military operations against the Imperial German Government
> you are directed to co-operate with the forces of the other countries
> employed against that enemy; but in so doing the underlying idea
> must be kept in view that the forces of the United States are a dis-
> tinct and separate component of the combined forces, the identity
> of which must be preserved.

As Pershing said farewell to the Secretary, with the orders he
had himself prepared properly approved by the Chief of Staff,
Baker surprised him with the other set, bearing an endorsement of
the President, and ranking into oblivion his own. It was as well
that it should be thus, for Pershing had been less explicit than
Kernan. But the fundamental relationship was hardly embodied
in either of the drafts. It was contained in what Baker later told
his biographer, Frederick Palmer. 'I said ... that I would ...
give him only two orders, one to go to France and the other to
come home. ... If you make good, the people will forgive almost
any mistake. If you do not make good, they will probably hang us
both from the first lamppost they can find.'

The demand for an American front was annoying to the military
authorities of both France and England, who wanted no such
front and who did not believe there would be an army, or, if it
existed, that it could be trusted. They had seen fighting and

thought they knew this war. But they were in no position to meet the demand with blunt refusal, for already the action of Congress had insured a steady flow of those supplies which they expected were to be the real American reinforcement. They could not dam good-will by refusing to tolerate what, after all, was unlikely to happen. They discussed the front.

It was by a sharp and obvious course of elimination that the front was found. Ever since the first battle of the Marne in 1914 marked the failure of the German plan to rush France off its feet, the trenches of the Western Front had stretched unbroken from an anchorage at the Swiss border to a point some 466 miles away, on the Strait of Dover midway between Calais and Ostend. The chain of trenches had been often deflected, swinging a little either way, but it had been unbreakable. From the Swiss border, running west of north to the French fortresses around Verdun, it lay close to the pre-war boundaries of France and Germany. This was a region made nearly impassable for large armies by act of nature, and impregnably fortified since the Franco-Prussian War by the hand of man. The war had not been fought here.

West of Verdun the trenches cut across the roads leading into France, the lines of invasion and attack used by armies since the days of Rome. To get an easier terrain than that of the Franco-German frontier, Germany violated Belgian neutrality. The Imperial armies entered France in 1914 north of the Belgian Highlands (unfriendly to large-scale operations) and followed the more moderate grades between the Meuse and the Somme. Nivelle's drive failed to break the German line in 1917, as Germany had failed to break the French at Verdun in 1916; the English, nearer the Channel, had advanced and fallen back with the tides of battle; and no unit on this front could sleep in certainty that attack was not impending.

The English forces, by obvious right, held the end of the Western Front next the Strait. By this route might come an attempt to invade England, which Britain must always be in a position to forestall. Here, too, the services of an army from an English base ran over the shortest routes. The Channel had been kept swept clear

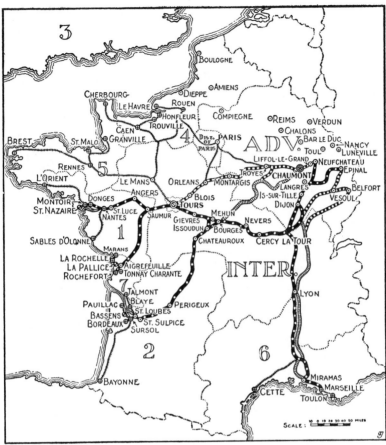

PRINCIPAL FRENCH PORTS AND RAILROADS
USED BY AMERICAN EXPEDITIONARY FORCES

⊕ GENERAL HEADQUARTERS   ⊛ H.Q. SERVICES OF SUPPLY
⊘ PRINCIPAL PORTS   ⊕ SECONDARY PORTS   ⊙ IMPORTANT TOWNS
▬ MAIN LINES   ▨ SECOND LINES   ▤ THIRD LINES   ∿ OTHER LINES
NOTE: LARGE NUMBERS INDICATE SUBDIVISIONS OF THE BASE SECTION
INTER.•INTERMEDIATE SECTION   ADV.•ADVANCE SECTION

Map drawn from Pershing, *Final Report* (1919), Plate 8

of mines, and pretty free of submarines, and was still a highway of the Allies. It was so certain that England could not surrender any part of this sector to Pershing that it was not even asked.

East of its junction with the British right lay the French left, with such acute problems of liaison brought to a focus at the place of meeting as to give to this word a new definition and a new importance in the English tongue. The soldiers of the two great Allies did not always fraternize easily; their officers were often embarrassed by difference in language, temperament, and point of view. Wherever the weld was at the moment, there was the weak spot on the line. This was somewhere above Amiens, near the basin of the Somme, and east of this the French armies guarded the roads into Paris. It was unthinkable that this position of importance and sentiment should be entrusted to an ambitious new general with an untried army.

By elimination, the American front was pushed to the east of Verdun, where war was expected to be quiescent, where an army as incompetent as the A.E.F. was expected to be, if it should be at all, could do no damage too bad to be repaired before it wrecked the enterprise. By a quaint coincidence this sector may have been the one portion of the front of which some of the American officers had a detailed knowledge. It is said that in the 'war games' played at Leavenworth, and in the Army War College, the only good military maps that could be procured for purposes of instruction were maps of the Toul sector. Here Pershing was permitted to aspire to independent operations.

Acting relentlessly upon his own judgment, Pershing accepted cheerfully what was offered with reluctance, and published in July the basic orders for the concentration and training of an army east of Verdun, and for its continuous supply. As obvious as the place where he might operate were the conditions of his operation. Europe was short of goods. It was never so short as legend made it out, but only American prices could tempt supplies into the market. It was accepted in the undertaking that the A.E.F. must fetch its own supplies. The railroads north of Paris were too vital to the French war to be clogged by these, or by the troops to use them. Both must find entry into France by lines running to the south of Paris and through ports not already working to a full capacity with English business.

But France is so organized that Paris is the heart and head. All of the great railroad systems radiate from the capital of the country to the borders. There did not exist any main lines of railroad running where the Americans and their supplies must travel. There were local and branch lines over which it was physically possible to move trains from Brest and seaports farther south to the Toul sector: but none was equipped for heavy through service, none could carry the locomotives and rolling stock that the A.E.F. must bring to France to move its goods.

The ports themselves, south of Brest, had been allowed to fall behind as French commerce concentrated at Marseilles or in the Channel ports. St. Nazaire, La Pallice, and Bordeaux were ill-equipped to carry modern traffic, but they were at least available for use, not being underfoot. The Toul sector was nearly as remote from the seacoast as Louisville is from Washington, and to bring reality to Pershing's dream of 'a distinct and separate component' there was work to be done along every mile of the intervening country. The call went home for engineer regiments, railroad regiments, forestry regiments: not as yet for men to fight, but for technicians to get ready for men to fight. The cables were soon crowded with requisitions, not always harmonious, but all indicative of a scheme of activity that Washington had not anticipated. There were harbors to be dredged, docks to be built, piles to be cut to build the docks, unloading cranes, dredges, freight yards, storage sheds, refrigeration plants, and all the equipment to be provided without which a million Americans, not to mention the second or third million, could not operate. Frederick Palmer, seasoned as a war correspondent and wise beyond most, crossed with Pershing on the *Baltic*. Here he renewed an acquaintance as old as the Russo-Japanese War, in which he had been a reporter while Pershing was a military observer. He was soon in uniform and a colonel, and mouthpiece for G.H.Q., which came to be heard of as 'somewhere in France.' He reversed his mechanisms

of a journalist to become something of a military censor, learned
what not to tell, dealt with visitors (for he knew everyone) and
guided their footsteps, and wrote of the vision while memory was
fresh. The story has not been better saved than in his *America in
France* (1918), and *Our Greatest Battle* (1919). With war over, he
turned to more deliberate things as he arranged the papers of the
Secretary of War in *Newton D. Baker, America at War* (1931).

With the keen eye of the reporter, Palmer saw not only what
was in building, but in what the character of the preparation for
the A.E.F. differed from French ways of doing things. There were
many miles of land travel before any American could be floated;
the first contingent averaged 2392 miles per man. There were
three thousand miles of ocean and after this a journey. All other
American armies, operating in the field, and drawing their supplies
out of the War Department, had learned to hate the bureaus in
Washington. Pershing's orders set up an equivalent for the War
Department under his own command in France. He could not
control actions in the United States, but he managed to maintain
his authority once men and supplies had been landed in Europe.

Kernan was before long made chief of what was called the Line
of Communications, which was a heavy responsibility after the
goal had been set of ninety days' supply in France (forty-five days'
at the base, thirty at intermediate stations, fifteen in the hands of
the fighting army at the very front). The War Department hunted
for a railroad man to manage the specialized activities of the lines
between the ports and the front, and found one in a vice-president
of the Pennsylvania Railroad, William Wallace Atterbury, who
was given rank as a general. Atterbury was not the man Pershing
had decided upon, but he was accepted for the sake of peace, and
soon learned to live in the Army, while the Army eventually became aware of his unusual capacity. Out of one of the engineer
regiments Pershing picked an old Nebraska friend, Charles G.
Dawes, made of him as unmilitary a brigadier-general as ever was,
and used him as buyer in the Army and as financial negotiator
with the Allied supply services. And Dawes found in war-starved
France so much of value that A.E.F. funds could bring to market

that he nearly cut in two the freight that the crowded sea lanes would otherwise have had to carry.

The first plan for the organization of the A.E.F. was drawn up in Paris in July. But Pershing had no intention of staying in Paris. He accepted the Toul sector, prospected the region, received assignment of the barracks in a garrison town in eastern France, Chaumont, and on September 1 he moved his G.H.Q. thither. Thereafter until the end of the war his place of residence was hardly named in the United States. Much of the time he was personally on the move in his general's special train or in his motor car. But the name of Chaumont was the kind of military secret that was kept secret from everyone except all Europe and the enemy. The initial force of about 14,500 men grew gradually, less than a thousand men a day, and in nine months still had too few men trained to arms to matter. But the technical troops kept at their work of building the matrix for an army as though their commander expected the Allies to hold the line until he and it were ready; and the Allies kept nagging at his idea that he was to have and lead an army. The 'black spot' of the American reinforcement, Clemenceau thought and said was 'the fanatical determination of the great chiefs of the American army to delay the arrival of the Star-Spangled Banner on the battlefield.' Had Germany won the war, Pershing's vision would have made him the scapegoat of the military historian.

It was on September 1 that G.H.Q. was moved to Chaumont, in the heart of what was to be the training and operations area for the A.E.F. This was five months after American entry; but it was four days before the first of the young men selected for the National Army were due to report to camp to begin their study of the duties of the soldier. The War Department had received and read, without entirely grasping its implication, the bombardment of cables and dispatches in which Pershing had sent home tables for this and specifications for that. It was quite as much as it could manage to expand rapidly enough to carry the load of the Regular Army and the National Guard, as these grew by enlistment.

No military personality, with a drive equal to that of John J.

Pershing, had yet appeared to bring into order the chaos of the War Department. Scott and Bliss, who in turn performed the duties of Chief of Staff, were fine old officers. They had shown adaptability in understanding the meaning of the change in Army theory that was basic in the Root reforms. Since the erection of the General Staff and the opening of the Army War College, professional study had become the channel to military advancement. But many of the older officers, too stiff to change (some of them too fat to ride a horse, as Theodore Roosevelt had discovered), had resisted the new order, only to find themselves far from the center of things when war came. The younger men, eager for professional study, set a new pace. In Army circles they were regarded as self-admiring. Since much of their work was done in the schools at Fort Leavenworth, the epithet 'Leavenworth clique' was attached to them by their seniors and by the lazy, who poured too many tales of woe into the ears of friendly congressmen for the General Staff to have an easy life. The National Guard interests, with much State politics in reserve, were equally hostile to the Leavenworth professionals.

Although the organization of the Army had advanced far from its status of 1898, it was still uncertain whether the heads of the permanent bureaus of the War Department would be able to run the war, or the untested General Staff. The law forced Army purchases to follow 'channels' different from those the General Staff would have liked. The post of Chief of Staff was still so lightly regarded that Scott was lent to Root's Russian Mission. Bliss was detached in October for other work abroad. The desk was occupied by an acting Chief of Staff until Pershing reluctantly sent back to Washington in 1918 a tested officer, Peyton C. March, son of a distinguished lexicographer, organizer of the artillery for the A.E.F., and a man with a backbone as rigid as Pershing's own.

It was not until March took office, March 4, 1918, that Baker had the advantage of a military adviser who was part of the new adventure and capable of rising with its demands. He spent his time thereafter, he lamented, soothing the souls in Washington that March had brusquely bruised. He had continuously to mediate between two strong men who served him — Pershing, who could never forget that it was the chief business of the War Department to meet his every need, and March, who felt that the Chief of Staff because he was Chief of Staff had temporary rank superior to that of the officers to whom he transmitted the orders of the Secretary of War. March took his temporary rank overseriously, regarded Pershing as a subordinate to be upheld 'as long as we kept him in command in France,' acquired grievances against the A.E.F., and poured out many of them in *The Nation at War* (1932). But with him the War Department caught its stride. It was still stumbling when in September the drafted men were due in camp.

In Enoch H. Crowder's office, that of the Judge-Advocate-General of the Army, the draft provisions of the Selective Service Act were born. The General Staff had worked with the idea for many months, sending forward memoranda in favor of the only principle of recruiting in which military men had confidence; but it could not break from the notion that as in the Civil War draft the Army itself was the agency to select the men. Crowder, a bureau chief, did a truer job, using for the purpose a young captain of cavalry, Hugh S. Johnson. Johnson, who took a law degree (1916) while on duty at his post in San Francisco, could be used in the law department of the Army and was assigned as a judge-advocate with Pershing's column. Back from Mexico in February, he was shifted to Washington where Crowder worked him hard. He had shown himself to be a handy man with Funston at the Presidio, caring for the aftermath of the San Francisco earthquake and fire. He was handy now. His draft became the basis upon which the law was written, and he outlined the memorandum issued by the President when he signed it.

The law threw the draft out of Washington and outside the Army to be administered by committees of the neighborhood in which the draftees lived. This was done partly because centralization in Washington would crowd the Capital, which was already too crowded. A more compelling motive was that the people should select themselves, through registration at their voting places, under the eye and understanding of their neighbors. The classification of the registration cards was to be carried out in 4557 local boards. June 5 was set as the day for registration, with the War Department less nervous than Reed of Missouri, who said, 'Baker, you will have the streets of our American cities running with blood on Registration Day.'

Johnson had cut red tape, too. Before the law was signed, he persuaded his immediate chief and talked the public printer into the illegal preparation of the millions of forms and questionnaires needed for enrollment. When Baker, after signature, took up the ways and means of administering the act he could be informed that through a courageous breach of discipline it had been administered. The bales of blanks, already printed, were also already in the sheriffs' offices throughout the United States, only awaiting the organization of the draft boards to be opened and put to use.

Four days after signing the Selective Service Act, Wilson gave Crowder a new desk, reviving the Civil War office of Provost-Marshal-General to look after recruiting and enlistment. Crowder kept Johnson with him until the episode of registration was passed, when the bubbling energy of his junior procured for him a different field in which to operate. This was not the combat field which Johnson hoped for and intrigued to get and the lack of which he bewailed in his *Blue Eagle, from Egg to Earth* (1935). But on any job he helped to make things move.

The registration on June 5 was more than a step in building an army. It was a test of public opinion, proving that obstruction was not to add to the difficulties of war administration. In the debates over the Selective Service Act, the Civil War experience with draft riots was cited to suggest how hard it would be to enforce the draft. But the draft, harmonizing with a state of mind that was impatient of even vocal opposition to the war, enforced itself. The bloodshed anticipated at the registration places did not occur. There was some crowding, to get through with it. There was some bewilderment, because the forms were too hard for many of the boys to understand at first reading. There was later some waste motion because of unnecessary medical examination of men who would not have been used, whether fit or not.

General Crowder could state, in his *Spirit of the Selective Service* (1920), that 9,586,508 men, over twenty-one but not yet thirty-one, filed their blanks. There was no important group that evaded because of affection for the enemy. There were few who resisted duty because of conscience; and fewer like the Rhodes scholar, Haessler, who went the whole way with conscience because to accept ' "bombproof" service on my part would give the lie to my sincerity.' Out of 2,810,296 men inducted into service, only 3989 claimed exemption on the ground of 'conscientious objection'; and of these only 450 failed to find 'some form of service, satisfactory to the Government.' Norman Thomas had sympathy for them, but in his *Conscientious Objector in America* (1923) he stated that their objection 'created a stir . . . entirely out of proportion to the number of objectors.' How many disapproved this war, without rejecting all war, is beyond proof. But they did not impede the operation of the draft.

The steps in the process of selection advanced in a routine after June 5. Once filed, the registration papers went to the draft boards, receiving serial numbers in the order of filing. The longest list of any board ran to 10,319. When this was known, as many numbers were sealed in capsules, mixed in a large bowl, and drawn in a careful lottery. On July 20, Baker drew out the capsule containing the number 258, giving first place in the order of calling to every registration card bearing that number. In a few days the checked official lists were in the papers. The calls for men to go to camp were apportioned among the States according to population after the number of registrants in each State had been enlarged by the addition to it of the number of citizens from each State already in military service. Until his serial number, established by the lottery, was called, the registrant remained at liberty as yet to anticipate the call and enlist directly. Both Regular Army and National Guard were swelled by this free choice, as well as the Navy and the Marine Corps. It was contemplated that the Regulars should be allowed to grow to 488,000, and the Guard to 470,000, and that troops in excess of these numbers should be provided through the draft. As it worked out, neither Guard nor

Regular Army was filled in this fashion, but both were raised to final strength by troops transferred to their divisions from the National Army camps. The first contingent called to the National Army included 687,000 names.

Selective Service was new to the United States, but it was not more novel than the principle of organization which was announced in July. Previous wars had generally been fought by military units whose titles bore at the moment of entry and of discharge an ascription to the States of their origin. There had indeed been troops of the Continental Line in the Revolution, and of the Regular Army in later wars, but most of the fighting men had been organized in regiments of the States and State pride had been touched by the success of State units. But State grief had been aroused when the accident of combat brought into murderous action several regiments from a single State with casualty lists that wiped them out, appearing back home to indicate an unfair distribution of the loss of war.

The Army weighed the alternatives of localized units supported by State pride and interchangeable units trained alike and as nearly uniform in quality as facts permitted. It overrode sentiment, searching for efficiency. The new notation accepted the division as the unit in place of the regiment. Pershing soon fixed the strength of the division at 979 officers and 27,082 enlisted men, upsetting thereby the estimates of the War Department, for his divisions were twice the size of those of the enemy or of his associates. But he gained his point. And back of each fighting division he hoped to have at least half its number of officers and men to operate the lines of communication and the indispensable services of the rear.

The lowest numbers in the serial of divisions were set aside for those to be formed around Regular Army units, distended by enlistment or transfer. Sibert's force was organized in France as First; the Second was built around other Regulars likewise with the A.E.F. It was never practicable to use all of the numbers reserved for Regulars. Divisions whose original components were National Guard units drafted into the service of the United States (and the whole National Guard had been so drafted by August 5) began with the Twenty-Sixth. This was composed of New England Guardsmen. Fifteen other divisions, running through the numbers to forty-one, received the Guardsmen of the other States, each on a regional basis at the start. The first of the divisions of drafted men, constituting the National Army, was the Seventy-Sixth and received registrants from New England. Sixteen of these were contemplated in the beginning, but it was understood that the number would be added to as war might require.

The State ascription was abandoned, although neither the Guard divisions nor those of the National Army ever quite forgot the locality of their origin; and their regions continued to claim them. Men were transferred and officers were interchanged as the War Department worked for uniformity of quality and took advantage of transport space. In France some of the divisions were assigned to depots. The Forty-First was grounded near Le Mans, had 227,000 men pass through its roster, yet never saw the enemy. Others retained a considerable degree of individuality until the Armistice. But when this came, the handful of Regular officers was spread through the whole army, leavening it all, while newcomers from civil life swamped the enlisted men who had been trained before April, 1917. In August, 1918, the distinctions among the divisions, always irritating, had become unreal, and all troops were merged in one Army of the United States. There was hardly one chance in twenty that a soldier on the rolls at the Armistice had seen duty before the declaration of war.

Around nuclei of Regulars and Guardsmen new troops made fastest progress. These were the units likely to be sent first to France. The National Guard divisions were sent for training to cantonments in the South, whence, it was hoped, transportation might be available to move them abroad before winter. Pershing had asked for a million before the end of June, 1918; the War Department saw no way of getting to him more than two-thirds that many, and these only if new tonnage should be discovered.

The sites chosen for the cantonments were commonly near Army posts already in existence, none of which had housing capac-

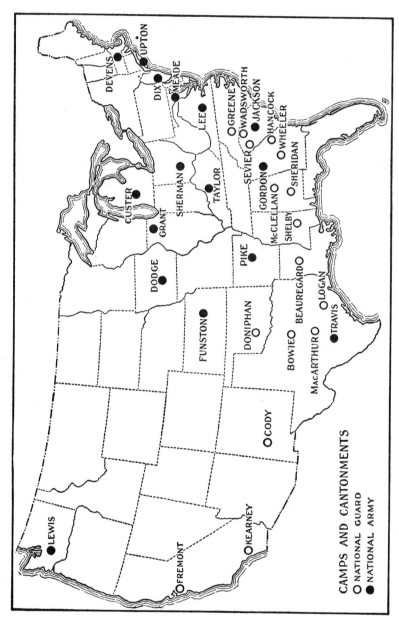

CAMPS AND CANTONMENTS IN THE UNITED STATES

From L. P. Ayres, *The War With Germany* (1919), page 28

CAMPS AND CANTONMENTS
○ NATIONAL GUARD
● NATIONAL ARMY

ity for a complete division. There was an abundance of hurried work in new construction, complicated by shortage of labor and of tentage, and difficult to manage even on the assumption that the troops would soon be moved to France. There was political pressure, too, for many States were eager to know that their troops had gone. Only the Twenty-Sixth (Yankee) Division was ready for early shipment, and there was political trouble to anticipate if any one region was to be singled out to lead the reinforcement. The Twenty-Sixth became the third division to arrive in France; but an additional division of Guardsmen was improvised, to be built out of units selected from the Guard at large. This was the Forty-Second, bearing the appropriate name of 'Rainbow,' and concentrated at Camp Mills on Long Island, near the 'Atlantic port' of embarkation. It paraded in its first review September 30, and then dropped out of the news until it could be announced that it was with the A.E.F. in France. By Thanksgiving it was proceeding to its training area. The First, Second, Twenty-Sixth, and Forty-Second were all the combat divisions Pershing had that were reasonably ready for the field when activities were resumed in the spring of 1918. His dream was still a dream. He had, in all, less than a third of his million, and of these half were service troops.

It was not the immediate duty of the War Department to get the troops to France. That duty fell between the Navy, convoying the transports, and the Shipping Board, mobilizing tonnage. But it was imperative to the Army that the troops be moved. For this purpose an Embarkation Service was created in August. Kernan had charge of this for the first few weeks, before he went to France and was assigned the Line of Communications between the ports and the A.E.F. Created as a General Staff agency to 'supervise' and to co-ordinate, the Embarkation Service actually operated the United States end of the long trip. It was bad theory for the General Staff to operate it, for the *raison d'être* of that body is to advise. But there was no organization in the old Army fitted to the work, emergency pressed, and high co-ordination was imperative. The *Washington Post*, near enough to the center of co-ordination to know something of its problems, feared that 'It will be humanly impossible to get 250,000 men on French territory within a year.' Hoboken and Newport News became the 'Atlantic ports' of mystery whence the Embarkation Service shipped the men, 45,000 by the end of August, and 142,000 more before January. The Navy protected the transports once at sea: 'superbly efficient,' Baker described the protection. But the Navy could as readily have protected more had there been transports to carry them. Seven hundred men a day made a depressing record between the declaration and the end of 1917.

The sixteen camps, designed to receive the first increments of the National Army and subsequent drafts as they might be called, were expected to be as permanent as the war itself. In them the recruits were to receive the general training of the soldier, leaving for France the final polishing. Additional training in the specialized camps of the A.E.F. was in the scheme, to be followed by duty on quiet sectors of the front before going into the line of battle.

In ordinary Army practice, the erection of the camps would have been the duty of the Quartermaster Corps, one of the permanent service bureaus of the War Department. But it was clear to the Council of National Defense in April that this bureau, already overburdened with more explicitly military work, would have difficulty in handling as lavish a building program as the war would make necessary. An Emergency Construction Committee, Council of National Defense, began to function, drawing its executives from the ranks of large contractors. If these men knew their business well enough to be of use, they were so closely interlocked with the contractors who would build the camps that they were open to attack as being improperly involved. It was a matter for shrewd guesswork to sketch the unavoidable equipment of each of the cities of 48,000 to be built for the training of National Army divisions. There were barracks and mess halls, service offices, recreation places, water systems, sewage, and telephones to be provided. Before these could be spread upon any blueprint the War Department was forced to a hurried examination of sites as offered, and to an annoying struggle with local interests each craving a camp near home.

The Quartermaster Corps permitted the Emergency Construction Committee to select contractors to build the camps, awarding each camp to a single well-established firm. By the end of May it was ready to inaugurate its own Construction Division to sign contracts and take legal responsibility for the work. Since speed was of the essence of the contract, and work must begin before plans were completed, contracts were let on a cost-plus basis, whereby the contractor was allowed a profit of seven per cent, but not over $250,000 on any one camp. Every contractor entered into competition with shipbuilders and munition-makers for labor and for materials. Construction could not be begun until near the end of June, 1917, which was too soon for accuracy and too late for the military need. Rushing the work as best they could, the contractors were not completely ready for troops when the day of mobilization arrived, September 5. Not all of the 687,000 drafted men were in camp before Christmas. It was never necessary to build the fullest estimated capacity into the camps, for troop shipments in 1918 left room for new recruits.

With small prospect of shipment, the War Department built up an army and the camps to house it. Of the sixteen National Army camps, only one was on the West Coast, Camp Lewis in Washington. Only four others were west of the Mississippi: Dodge in Iowa, Funston in Kansas, Pike in Arkansas, Travis in Texas. Four were in the Middle West: Grant in Illinois, Custer in Michigan, Sherman in Ohio, and Taylor in Kentucky. The remaining seven were lined up near the Atlantic Coast: Devens in Massachusetts, Upton in New York, Dix in New Jersey, Meade in Maryland, Lee in Virginia, Jackson in South Carolina, and Gordon in Georgia. It was a triumph of skill and energy to have the camps as nearly ready as they were: a triumph for W. A. Starrett of the Emergency Construction Committee and Brigadier-General I. W. Littell of the Quartermaster Corps. It would not have been unreasonable for Congress to have foreseen that war would entail such work, or to have profited from the sad experience of the training camps in the war with Spain. Congress might have learned from the record of the Civil War that disease is more deadly than bullets, and have made provision for an accumulation of foreknowledge about camp sites.

The need for the equipment of the soldier was as pressing as that for his housing, and would have been hard to meet even if the nature of the equipment had been determined in advance. Food, clothing, bedding, and all the ordinary requirements of a million men were to be procured, a process in which the Rosenwald committees did their share. These things did not in most cases call for commodities unknown to trade, such as would require the erection of new factories to make new kinds of goods. They could be bought, and the Quartermaster Corps welcomed the aid of the committees. The usual provision of the *Revised Statutes*, forbidding any servant of the United States to let a contract if he had any financial interest in the commodity concerned, got in the road of the process. The provision was made more specific during the summer, and much of the debate on the Lever Act was in criticism of members of voluntary committees who passed contracts to their own firms. It was possible to make the technical point that the voluntary committees did not legally let the contracts, but merely passed upon their suitability so that officers in the Army might act more quickly and with better judgment. But the Council of National Defense found it necessary to revise its whole committee structure, under the new prohibition, and to require its agents to cut themselves away from their former business connections. The difficulty was transitory since, once the flurry of the first six months of war was over, the structure of the Army grew up to its task. In this Goethals found his final job. Out of the Emergency Fleet in July, he was back in the War Department in December, as acting Quartermaster-General, solidifying a buying organization that was competent enough to dispense with the services of the committees that had helped it at the beginning. The men who did the work were often the same, but they were encased in uniforms and detached from business.

The tools of the soldier were another matter. New weapons

had made their appearance since 1914, old weapons had changed in relative importance, and none could be manufactured in quantity until military opinion had approved the plans. Pershing was not convinced that war had so changed as to lessen the need for infantry. He still thought of the individual rifleman as the backbone of an army. Not blind to aviation or to machine-gunnery, or to the changes due to the use of gas and gas defense, he made the rifleman who could both shoot and use the bayonet his indispensable unit. He called for such, and the stress his requisitions placed upon bayonet drill emphasized his notion that the A.E.F. must be trained to fight close to the enemy, in the open. Trench warfare was inescapable, but the trench was not a weapon of aggression.

The old Army was equipped with the Springfield (1903) rifle, made in United States arsenals, and believed to be as good a gun as was; but it was one for which no factories existed capable of turning it out by the million. There was a stock on hand sufficient for the first million men, a total soon passed by the Regular Army, the National Guard, and the first increment of the National Army. At this point Congress had not been completely blind to necessity. But as the Pershing vision permeated the War Department, and his estimates suggested second, third, and even fourth millions of men in arms, the question rose whether it would be quicker to build new factories for Springfields, or to make use of American plants that had, since 1914, been engaged in quantity production of the British Enfields. England had passed the crest of man-power, which meant that some of the capacity of the Enfield factories was available for the use of the United States. The decision was to modify the Enfield, so that it could use Springfield shells whose large-scale manufacture was relatively simple. Without abandoning the American guns, all of which were put to use, the American Enfields were put into production in August, 1917, so that two and a half million of them were available at the Armistice and the supply was ahead of the requirement. When the draft men came to camp there were not enough rifles for all of them and, until the factories had speeded up, this absence of weapons made mobilization appear to be less effective than in fact it was.

Machine guns had been used with such success in the European armies that there was no difference of opinion about their lavish issue to an American force. The only question was one of type. The allowance of machine guns per regiment, fixed at four in 1912, was 336 in 1919. The selection of types, accelerated by the war, had been made possible by a large appropriation for machine guns, voted by Congress in 1916. The various boards of officers, sitting to determine type, had to consider not only absolute efficiency but ease of manufacture, for the machine gun is a complicated weapon. Unless it could be put easily into quantity production it was not suitable for adoption. Officers of equal intelligence and experience were capable of violent partisanship for different guns, and laymen had no opinion worth notice. The friends of an American inventor, Colonel Isaac N. Lewis, could not understand why his guns did not become the standard for the A.E.F. The Allied armies were using them in thousands. But the War Department thought them not dependable. It bought whatever guns it could get for temporary use, but deferred final decision until it was convinced. 'We added the Browning gun in May, 1917,' testified Baker, during an investigation of the War Department after the war was over. Two models of this gun, light and heavy, were put into production as soon as factories could handle them; a slow process, since before guns could be made, machines to make them must be designed and made, and machines to make the machines, and factories to house them. Not until 1918 were Brownings available in large numbers. And even then their use was retarded because of their superiority. Not until several divisions had been fully equipped with Brownings did Pershing want to risk the chance that a captured gun might reach the enemy and give away its secret. Brownings were not in use until the last three months of war. Whether this was speed or sloth depends largely upon the temperament of the inquirer.

Artillery was vital, and was the subject of a battle of its own, once war was over. The first program of divisions called for 2100 field guns of standard type, not to mention many specialized varieties. There were some 554 of these on hand; not enough for the training of the artillery brigades. What there were were kept at home for this use. A program of American manufacture was launched, but was not pressed to the injury of other programs, since there was plenty of artillery in sight. Both France and England were prepared, in their own factories, to turn out more batteries than their own armies could use. There was double economy in buying these: it relieved the United States of a degree of congestion and saved some cargo space. The Allies were ready to guarantee guns for American artillery as it might arrive, in return for American assurance that steel and other raw materials for their manufacture should come to them in steady flow. Before the Armistice the American factories were turning out complete artillery units of 75 mm. guns as rapidly as needed; but the A.E.F. in action used foreign guns. This was a condition to be approved, not blamed.

The provision of aircraft was a matter not of question, but of creation. The industry did not exist in the United States. At the declaration the Army had two air fields and fifty-five 'serviceable planes' (of which, however, the National Advisory Committee on Aeronautics said fifty-one were obsolete and four were obsolescent). The supply of aviators was no better than that of planes. But after this start from scratch there were, at the Armistice, 11,000 flying officers in the Army, with 4300 of them in France.

The program for aviation would not have been American if it had not been expressed in large numbers and quantity production of standard types. It could not, like artillery, be worked up gradually, in confidence that the Allies could carry it until the American factories were in operation. France, not inviting an army to fight as such, demanded planes and aviators as soon as the United States entered the war. The aircraft factories of the Allies could not build planes as rapidly as they cracked up in use, and had no reserve strength with which to build squadrons to overwhelm the enemy. Carrying a part of this load was part of the reinforcement, but no organized industry was ready for it. There was plenty of clean spruce in the forests of the Northwest, but it had to be logged and fabricated. There were plenty of skilled woodworkers, who could be diverted from billiard tables and barroom equipment to the manufacture of planes. But this would take time, even were there plans available. There were no plans or models. There was not even a known engine adapted to quantity production. Aviation was everywhere so new that it was still true that each new model launched against the enemy was obsolete in the designing-room before it took the air. Yet the vision of a bridge of ships had hardly faded before another vision of swarms of airplanes took its place.

A joint Army-Navy board agreed easily that 22,000 planes were needed for the year, and the press took up the announcement of intent and need as though it were one of promise and fulfillment. Congress was willing, voting $640,000,000 for the purpose, July 24, 1917, and the Aeronautical Division of the Signal Corps went hard to work. 'The Liberty Engine,' says Crowell in his *America's Munitions, 1917–1918* (1919), 'was America's distinctive contribution to the war in the air, and her chief one.' England was working with thirty-seven types of engines, France with forty-six. It was determined that the United States should design a standard type. In a few days in May, 1917, in a private suite of the Willard Hotel, a handful of aviation designers blocked it out. It was adopted June 4. The first engine was delivered in Washington just a month later. It proved to be a great engine, was hurried into production, and deliveries of 31,814 were made before the Armistice. But it could not be delivered in quantity for a year after the first experimental model had been made, and the engines shipped were too few for the equipment of the A.E.F. Until the end, the eyes of the Army went aloft in foreign planes. Here, too, it is a question of temperament whether the program was a huge achievement or a failure. The Aircraft Production Board gave its advice in the early days of the program, but full responsibility rested upon the shoulders of Brigadier-General George O. Squier, chief of the Signal Corps.

The eighteen months of war fall easily into three periods of about six months, in each of which a special phase of the work that was to be done was dominant. For six months after Congress convened in

April, 1917, *program* was in the air — the large planning for the kind of war that could be guessed, and the ways to win it. It was a war in which the United States might never get to fight in France, but it might be necessary to carry on the struggle if the Allies cracked. By the time Congress ended its session in October the larger plans had been made; overlapping, some of them, and often inconsistent and impracticable, but on large scale and indicating a determination that had no limit. For the next six months, the problem was *administration* — making plans work, eliminating deadlock, and constructing the physical and human machines needed for victory. Such schemes as ships and planes, too complex for improvisation in an age in which miracles were rare, absorbed money and good-will. But the struggle was over before their weight was on the line. By the spring of 1918 most of the plans were working, and the *operation* of the American war machines became the striking feature of the picture. The war lasted long enough for Pershing to figure in the victory, and for the army of his dream to become reality. But at the moment in September, 1917, when the earliest of the drafted men were sent to their uncompleted camps, and when Pershing established G.H.Q. in eastern France, the first phase of war was only just changing into the second. There was room at every part of the program to wonder if it was sound.

When the men arrived at camp they found that the army they were in was such as the United States had not seen before.

A distinctive feature of the National Defense Act of 1916 had been its emphasis upon the Officers' Reserve Corps, and the principle that thereafter the line commands in the Army (the commands that had to do with fighting men) should not be assigned through politics or influence, but should go to officers who at least knew more of the duties of the soldier than the recruits they commanded. The propriety of this had always been obvious; the practice, the reverse. Volunteers had been allowed to choose their own officers. Politicians had been given line commands. The need for a reform in this direction had been emphasized by what had been heard of the struggle of the English to procure trained officers. Leonard Wood, while Chief of Staff, had utilized interest and apprehension to launch his series of civilian camps. The military requirements in the land-grant colleges had taken on a new seriousness, once young men felt themselves under the shadow of impending war. The President indicated his adherence to the new principle when he declined to make Theodore Roosevelt the greatest possible of political generals.

The War Department acted upon the new principle in advance of the passage of the Selective Service Act. On May 15 it assembled at some sixteen army posts a series of training camps whose graduates might hope three months later to be qualified to receive officers' commissions in the National Army. Nearly 40,000 students contested for the chance to be tested and trained. They came from the upper groups in the university regiments and from private life, and 27,341 of them received commissions.

The first camps, graduating their classes in time for the mobilization of September 5, were followed by a second series August 27, and by a third and fourth. The process of officer training thereupon became continuous. At every divisional camp it was the intent to maintain an officers' training unit, whose candidates were selected by merit from among the drafted men — to create both a democratic army and a competent command. A camp for Negro officers was conducted at Des Moines. It was not possible in ninety days to make a finished officer out of a civilian, but the young lieutenants into whose hands were entrusted the drafted men in September had learned more in their three months than officers old in the service believed young men could learn. Planning of program was transmuted into execution when the men reported and the drill began.

VI. THE UNARMED FORCES

THE Yanks were indeed coming. But no one who was not in the know knew the painfully small figures of their embarkation. What was happening in France, as the Pershing program took definite shape, was screened from view. Not even the newspapers knew much about it, and that which they knew was withheld from publication. The voluntary censorship, agreed to without a law, worked well. The news releases from the Government were deliberately vague, full of preparations for great things, but not revealing detailed events.

Men were moving to camp. One could see the trains. Red Cross women met them at the stations and distributed cigarettes. Letters home told of camp experiences. Large numbers of troops were shifted from camp to camp without apparent reason. The public was aware of the numbers of the divisions as originally assigned to cantonments and camps, but no great comment was made when it was discovered that a shift had occurred. The Forty-First (Sunset) Division of Western National Guard was first assembled in Camp Fremont near Palo Alto, but was taken away after the War Department had quarreled with the local powers over the cost of a necessary sewer. Hunter Liggett, detached from his Presidio command, escorted it to a new location at Camp Greene, near Charlotte, North Carolina. In October, Baker addressed the division, which was noted without comment, though it was significant enough for comment. Next came the news that the tents at Greene were occupied by a newly organized Third Division and that Joseph T. Dickman was in command. But when and how Liggett took the Forty-First to France, no one was told. When the Eighth Division, successor at Camp Fremont to the Forty-First, was moved east its men were carried in forty-two special trains spread over six days.

Even the War Department did not know too much. When the drafted men began to move in September, the camps were too uneven in their advancement for an exact schedule to be maintained. Much, however, was made of the ceremony of mobilization. On Tuesday the fourth, the day after Labor Day, Wilson marched again, this time at the head of a Washington procession escorting the draftees from the District to the railroad. In a Western State the group of draftees entertained their whole neighborhood in recognition of the honor conferred upon them. Civic celebrations and parades were the order of the day. Yet it was impossible to predict the numbers made available or how the 687,000 of the first draft would be assigned. The adoption of the Pershing division of 28,000 as the American type compelled a revision of War Department tables and made necessary the assignment of drafted men to fill the Regular and Guard divisions. Great numbers were detached for the specialized services — air, forest, medical, engineer, and the rest. What were left after all the drains upon them became the nuclei of National Army divisions whose commanding officers could not know from day to day what men or officers they were to have.

In spite of hesitant beginnings the preparation of the armed forces was in motion with men in charge whose whole professional life had had to do with troops. The War Department was competent to convert its civilian recruits into soldiers, given time. It was now ready to raise an army of maximum size and to think of Europe as a destination, although the new Embarkation Service was ever short of ships. What worried most in the seclusion of the council chamber was the growing problem of procurement, and the necessity to add to the fighting equipment of the United States a proper quota of those unarmed forces whose utilization by the Allies had in three years brought the Central Powers into a tight investment and state of siege. Procurement passed into a new phase in July, with the creation of a War Industries Board. Congress, at the end of the war session, provided the last legislation necessary as a preliminary to the erection of a War Trade Board. Through the whole session the legislative brain was racked as it sought to devise means to pay the bills. And, uninformed of much that was going on in Europe, it could not keep away from the intriguing question of war aims. As more and more was being authorized, and more and more had to be taken on faith, the need increased to make it clear why the United States was fighting.

The hard-pressed Sixty-Fifth Congress deserved more sympathy than it received. For one hundred and ninety-two days it labored, as no other Congress had worked. Nearly every aspect of war legislation was novel; most of the methods urged by the Administration were 'un-American' if judged by any pre-war experience in the United States. The great laws, without which the United States could not have fought a war, were ground out with what seemed under the dome of the Capitol to be surprising swiftness. Looked at from Main Street, the deliberation with which they came resembled culpable delay.

The acquiescence of Congress in the needs of war lagged behind the need. Unavoidable as this was, it aroused acid comment. Congressmen, working without let-up and in a fog, became acid themselves when called upon to solve the unsolvable and when the proportions of a war measure kept growing while the measure was under consideration. The war was in its forty-seventh day before an army was authorized; and in its one hundred and fifty-seventh day before the drafted men were due in camp. And it was only three days before adjournment on October 6 that the revenue bill was passed.

Behind the protective wall of the Allied armies and the British Navy the United States remained safe while it deliberated and took the steps in the conversion of a peaceful democracy into a war machine. Yet in thirty-seven days in 1914 most of Europe had sprung to arms, Belgium had been overrun, and the invader had been turned back from the gates of Paris with his Schlieffen plan a failure.

No aspect of the process of preparation is more interesting than the way in which the people crowded the Government. They were the most effective of the unarmed forces of the war. The official mind was hesitant as it faced the crisis. The non-official, not knowing enough of red tape to be bound by it, stumbled over what it ignored, yet became a continuous prod upon Government action. All conceded that a democratic war could not be fought without popular approval, but none had guessed how much more popular desire would ask than the Government could accomplish.

The civilians' task at the beginning was to advise and to do odd jobs; to supplement the efforts of the Government; to assist in planning things for the Administration to carry out. In this work the Council of National Defense had no difficulty in enlisting whom it wanted. The busiest of men, called to Washington at their own expense, came at the call, many to remain until the Armistice. The committee system, hurriedly assembled, crowded some of the Government offices so as to impede their work. In others it reinforced the effort and provided the fresh point of view that bureaucracy tends to lose. As Congress approached the end of the session many of the committees had done all they could do, and were ready to be thrust aside because the departments concerned had caught up. In any event they would have had to be shoved aside, since they lacked legal authority and Congress was properly critical of their interlock with business. The post-war investigations of their behavior produced no important testimony to indicate either favoritism or malfeasance, but they did not represent an orderly procedure. As its committees receded from the picture the Council of National Defense itself lost some of its prominence. Conceived as a sort of civilian general staff, to advise and launch but not to execute, the Council had done its work when its advice had been taken or declined. Its large proposals came quickest in the first three months of war. Thereafter, its planning refined the margins of the war program or was brought to focus upon unexpected developments in the execution of it. Many of the committees 'seem to have had but short life, but in reality they were governmental creations in the process of integration.' Gifford remained director of the Council until the war was over, but he never sought or received the prominence adhering to the quasi-dictators of the war administrations.

The Emergency Fleet Corporation, operating agency of the Shipping Board, was the earliest of these war administrations to take shape by the side of the pre-war Government. Next came the Food Administration in its voluntary phase, before Congress legalized it in the Lever Act. Before this legal benediction was bestowed the third war administration arose, never to have status in law, but to become in fact the greatest of them all. This was the War Industries Board, conceived in the Council of National Defense and erected with the approval of the President, July 28, 1917.

The sequence of problems to whose solution the War Industries Board was assigned went back at least to Kernan's report upon the manufacture of arms, made early in the year. The Council of National Defense first attacked this with its Munitions Standards Board; and Scott, who was drafted as its chairman, stayed by the problem and grew with it until his health gave way under the strain. In the second phase of the problem the General Munitions Board took on a list of military and naval associates and broadened its vision to the 'equipping and arming' of whatever forces might be raised; bound to bear in mind at the same time the need of general industry to carry on. It endeavored to co-ordinate the needs of the Army and Navy with the industrial requirements of the country, and learned each day how broad these were and how far down they penetrated into the ordinary life of the United States.

It was easier to comprehend the ends to be obtained than to devise workable means for reaching them. Priority came first of all. The most elementary of the surveys of procurement revealed probable shortage of materials that could not be done without. It was obligatory to devise a method by which prior needs should be met first, and secondary needs held back. It was impossible to gauge the importance of any demand for material by the vehemence with which it was pressed, since every office believed that the success of the war centered around itself. In the determination of priority it was essential to have a picture of all the needs, of various degrees of intensity, and to consider them dispassionately upon their merits. There was no way in which a volunteer agency could, of itself, possess this knowledge. Some principle of representation had to be worked out whereby each of the war agencies could submit its table of requirements so that these could be appraised by the side of those of industry and normal life. Army and Navy needs were most visible. The Emergency Fleet was insistent. The railroads could not get along without their steel, coal, and timber. And there was always the pressure of the Allies for their supplies. Once priority was determined soundly, it was a simple matter to give clearance to such contracts as were approved and to permit the contract to be fulfilled. It was less simple to persuade industry, deprived of its requirements, to like to live without them. More firms than admitted it agreed with the sharp *Washington Post* that priority was the 'vermiform appendix' of the war machine, and would have been glad to cut it out. The many committees of the Advisory Commission, C.N.D., and in particular its Committee on Raw Materials, were all the eyes the Government possessed through which to glimpse a view of what supplies there were. And these committees, as the weeks wore on, became suspect to war contractors and to Congress.

By the middle of June, Gifford had been assigned the task of devising a reorganization of the committee system that would both work and escape the criticism inherent in the original set-up. He was asked to draft a modification of the General Munitions Board so that it might have an adequate knowledge of requirements. The *Public Ledger* noted that 'a profound change in the civilian conduct of the war' was imminent, and guessed that Baruch, in charge of raw materials, might develop into a general purchasing agent. The unity of management that Wilson was working toward for the Shipping Board and its Emergency Fleet needed to be applied to the problem of procurement. Goethals and Denman could not get along together. It was uncertain whether Scott and Baruch could be made into a team. At the same time, negotiations were proceeding among the Treasury and the Allies in the hope of lessening the competition in buying. McAdoo was restive. Meeting the demands of the Allies, under the loan act, for advances to cover their purchases in the United States, he watched them take the money into the American market and bid against the United States for supplies of which there were not enough for both. The advancing prices resulting from this hurt everyone, and in the end increased the financial burden upon the Treasury. It affected price levels, increasing the cost of living so as to lower real wages and start mutterings of labor trouble in every branch of war work. On July 11 the President announced that price-fixing would become a weapon of the war, and as he made this announcement he had in hand Gifford's proposal for the reorganization. The rearrangements were agreed upon before July was over.

The General Munitions Board disappeared from the organization chart of the Government when its chairman, Scott, became chairman of its successor, the War Industries Board, July 28, 1917. The six men associated with Scott in the new arrangement represented the larger facets of the procurement problem, beginning with Baruch, whose genius for contacts and hunches kept him still in charge of the search for raw materials. Already his people were beginning to survey the world sources of those raw materials essential to manufacture and lacking within the United States. Where these were to be found on Allied soil, it was a matter for bargain, with the Allies indisposed to give anything to the United States without full compensation. Rubber and manganese were among the most necessary of the raw materials. No other country was perhaps as nearly self-sufficient as the United States in its native supply of raw materials, but not even the United States possessed them all. It began to be suspected that world politics in the future would revolve more and more around the necessity of industrial nations to get access to the indispensable supplies that others owned. The Bureau of Mines in the Department of the Interior threw its experts into the search for minerals, and economic geologists began to think that they were to be the coming statesmen.

Robert S. Brookings, who joined the crew as expert in finished products, was a self-made St. Louis business man with a typical 'success' career until he turned in middle life from profits to public

service. His greatest achievement had been the rebuilding of
Washington University; he was, before he died, to erect in Washington an institution bearing his name whose function was to be to
watch and inspect the operation of government and to report upon
it to the people. Hermann Hagedorn has recorded his passion for
facts in *Brookings: A Biography* (1936). When the price-fixing
business was split off to a separate committee, it was under the
direction of Brookings. Robert S. Lovett, who was the new commissioner with special oversight of railroad and priority matters,
was a railroad president who had directed the Union Pacific and
Southern Pacific systems. Lovett had come out of Texas into New
York as a young lawyer without backing. He had caught the
attention of E. H. Harriman, had administered the estate of his
benefactor, and had stepped into the management of the Harriman railroad interests. There were two military commissioners on
the War Industries Board. Colonel Palmer E. Pierce of the
General Staff represented the Army: Rear Admiral William B.
Fletcher, who had commanded at Vera Cruz in 1914, the Navy.
Labor had a spokesman in the person of Hugh Frayne, a veteran of
the American Federation, who had so often been spokesman for
Gompers that the same language came from the lips of each.

The staffs of assistants organized around the seven commissioners were required to separate themselves from business and
industry so that in giving their advice in procurement they might
not fall foul of the law. The third section of the Lever Act was
detailed and mandatory in its prohibition of the dual relationship
that had hampered the old committees. In organizing the many
sub-committees under the new Board the commissioners recognized how fully their policies would depend upon the accuracy of
the knowledge possessed by the various 'commodity' sections.
These sections grew in number and varied in importance as the
need of the moment shifted; but the end — a government advisory
agency whose staff was separate from trade yet was thoroughly
informed about it — was kept in view. The Rosenwald committees,
borrowed from trade in the opening days, were finally dissolved in
November, 1917, with members thanked and either returned to

their jobs or taken wholly into the Government. And industry, now that Government was becoming able to inform itself, undertook a new organization of its resources so as to be able to deal with the Government.

Under the anti-trust laws the proscription of combinations in restraint of trade had effectively prevented frank organization among the American industries. There was undercover agreement, treading so close on the borders of conspiracy that the law officers were ever on its heels. But little had been done to build up, trade by trade, well-informed organization through whose eyes any craft could be looked at as a whole. The new set-up for war industry required the Government to look upon each industry as a unit, and the pressure of necessity brought it about that as Government reached down to control, industry should reach up to serve. The United States Chamber of Commerce, formed in 1912 and maintaining Washington offices close to Lafayette Square, had stuck to generalities and had avoided anything that might be interpreted as illegal conspiracy. It now placed itself at the head of a movement to bring business into line. In a special convention at Atlantic City in September, Gifford told it what the War Industries Board wanted, and resolutions were adopted asking each of the industries to create a Washington bureau, manned by its own people, and able to reveal to the appropriate commodity sections of the War Industries Board the business version of the facts upon which the Government must act. The commodity section members had not been out of business long enough to forget trade secrets that their former business associates might be indisposed to reveal.

There were a few organizations, already in existence and nearly enough what was wanted, able to serve this need. The Chemical Alliance was a Connecticut incorporation. The Iron and Steel Institute was already nearly ten years old. The Textile Alliance (1914) had a mass of information at its disposal respecting fibers and their use. A Tanners' Council was created to meet the call for help. And the rest of industry followed in the train of these. By December, 1917, enough of their bureaus were beyond the original genesis for it to be possible to assemble their chiefs in general conference in Washington. Before the Armistice, under the oversight of the War Service executive committee of the Chamber of Commerce, some four hundred central offices were at work, and the War Service Committees had become a necessary part of business. The titles of many of them revealed a service to be rendered or a sacrifice to be made. Business was either essential, to be nursed, or non-essential, to be stifled. The committees ranged the alphabet from that of the Brewing Industry to that of Wrapping Paper; Sheet Metal Ware had its War Service organization, as did Wooden Boxes. It is not certain what the Brassière War Service Committee contributed to the winning of the war, but the Corset Industry took a steel or two from women's waistlines and claimed credit for releasing many thousand tons of steel for more essential use. A less serviceable contribution was that of one of the 'damned professors' whose duty led him to revise a list of non-essential cotton manufactures. He came to 'corset laces,' and with an innocence unusual in married men disposed of them with the comment: 'Corset laces are certainly not essential. They can just as well wear them without any trimming.'

Before Congress met in December, ready for a new session and vexed by the shroud of secrecy that veiled the field of battle, the War Industries Board was beginning to understand its problem. It had lost Scott and received Willard in his place. The air was full of suggestion of mistake and mismanagement, but the War Department was nearly ready to run itself. A new War Council, created in the War Department on December 15, provided promotion upstairs for certain of the bureau chiefs. In the place of Sharpe, Quartermaster-General, who was thus moved up, Goethals directed the supervision of procurement from an office in the General Staff, and as acting Quartermaster-General saw to it that the Staff advice was followed. The War Industries Board remained a creation of the Council of National Defense and, in theory, was still subordinate to it. Its commissioners were in fact working informally at every place of friction where military need rubbed hard against industrial capacity.

Of the seven original members of the War Industries Board, three were known to be specially concerned with the Allied competition for the output of American farms and factories: Baruch, Brookings, and Lovett. The 'beneficiaries of the huge American loan' were crowding the market. Army and Navy buyers found essential supplies sold out before they could prepare their own specifications. The specialists in raw materials, finished supplies, and priority were the natural members of the War Industries Board to be hampered by the competition and to be called upon to control it; and the greater Allies were working out an agreement with the Treasury while the Council of National Defense was revamping its structure in July. On August 25 an agreement was signed whereby Baruch, Brookings, and Lovett, and Hoover where food was concerned, should constitute a Purchasing Commission for the Allies. Through this agency their needs were to be brought into harmony with those of the American Government at the requirements office of the War Industries Board. There is no earlier step than this in the direction of a single organization among the enemies of Germany. From this beginning the next steps follow in a direct path until in April, 1918, Foch of France came into command of all the armies on the Western Front. But before these steps could be planned or taken, the unarmed forces of the United States had been added to by the creation of other organizations.

To the three major war administrations of ships, food, and industry, that of coal was added before the end of August. Garfield, in fuel, like Hoover, in food, had to meet most of the same problems that confronted industry, and each interlocked his organization with that of Scott. The fifth of the great war administrations received a name when in an Executive Order of October 12 the President created a War Trade Board, assigning its management to Vance McCormick. A sixth was still to come; a Railroad Administration under McAdoo which was not launched until December.

There was power behind the Purchasing Commission for the Allies from the moment of its creation, for the Espionage Act had vested in the President full authority over the flow of exports. Out of this grew the War Trade Board. In the interval between June 15 and the signature of a Trading-with-the-Enemy Act on October 6, the things that were needed to constitute a stranglehold on trade were considered, asked of Congress, and granted, so that McCormick and his Board had a legal status which the War Industries Board always lacked.

The steps in the development of the new policies followed closely upon the law. The President assigned his authority over exports to an Exports Council, whose members were Cabinet officers. The Exports Council entrusted the administration of exports to a Division of Export Licenses in the Department of Commerce, in connection with whose management McCormick learned the requirements of his job. On July 15, by proclamation of the President, the new power was in operation — a 'new weapon against Germany — a noiseless and unseen weapon.'

There was some real danger that uncontrolled exports might have done both of two things: given aid to the enemy and drained from the United States its vital and necessary supplies. The routine figures of foreign trade showed this as they made it possible to compare the pre-war averages of wheat, beef, sugar, and fats with the totals for the first and second quarters of 1917.

Within the United States a consequence of this drainage-off of food was already showing itself in rising prices. There was increasing pinch wherever Americans were living on narrow incomes, and among wage-earners whose continuous and cheerful labor was a necessary part of war the rising cost of living upset the balance of the wage scale. Union labor was uneasy enough as it was asked to accept non-union workers, women, untrained apprentices, and new methods of management. High cost of living made things worse. The Government was daily called upon to mediate in strikes or to avert more strikes. The labor leaders, affiliated with Gompers, were keeping their pledge to hold their followers upon the job, but with increasing difficulty. At many places in the war program events now pointed to the need for a war-labor policy that should be an integrated part of the war administration. The informal agreement made with labor through Gompers meant either this or nothing. Quite apart from this it was desirable that every effort be made to prevent such rises in food prices as might be prevented. The Exports Council prepared to co-operate through the control of sales abroad.

The need to conserve food for home use was balanced by an equal need to prevent enemy use of American food, or neutral use that might indirectly prove to be of enemy advantage. It was only a year since the publication of the British blacklist of American firms had stirred up all the anti-English elements in the United States. It had then seemed to be an unwarrantable interference with American trade for the Allies to forbid their subjects to deal with American firms merely because these were suspected of having a German connection. The United States had traveled a long way in a year. As a belligerent now, it was gripped by the inexorable logic of war in an industrial age. It was bound to defeat its enemy whether in the field or by economic siege. It was bound to use its right over its own ships, ports, markets, and resources so as to prevent indirect aid from passing to the enemy through the neutral and to bargain with the neutral for whatever advantage could be extorted from him through trade restriction. The United States had departed from its status as neutral when the pressure of the belligerents became too great to be borne. The neutrals that were now left lacked the power to resist, without which neutral right is empty. The control of exports was only the beginning of trade pressure.

Before the control of war trade could be converted into a complete and flexible weapon there was need for a grant of additional authority that would, in one direction, bring imports within the scheme, and, in the other, make a clear legal definition of the word 'enemy.' The former was simple enough. It required merely the passage of a law containing the word. Early in July, Andrew J. Montague of Virginia advised the House that 'this is not a war of soldiers so much as a war of economic forces,' and opened a very brief debate upon a Trading-with-the-Enemy Act. What little debate there was did not revolve about the clause conferring power over imports. The House finished with it all in parts of only three days; the Senate in only two. The bill did not become a law until the President signed it at the end of the session, October 6. But the delay was due to crowding occasioned by other bills, and to matters much more complicated than either exports or imports.

The more difficult parts of the act fell under three heads: the definition of the word 'enemy,' so that it might correctly describe those enemies outside the United States with whom all trade was banned; the treatment of such subjects of the enemy as might be resident within the United States; and a rider attached to the bill in the Senate on motion of William H. King of Utah for the purpose of enlarging the powers over opinion that had been voted in the Espionage Act. Even these did not prolong the debate. The Senate adopted the conference report 48 to 42, and the House accepted it without a roll-call.

It was conceded in the discussions that, during war, trade with the enemy became automatically illegal, and that the ordinary war powers of the President authorized its prohibition, with only so much exception as might be for public advantage and conducted under public license. It was conceded, too, that the word 'enemy' included not only the Government of the enemy, but also persons and corporations lying within its control, whether in the enemy country or in regions occupied by its army; and whether the persons or corporations were enemy subjects, or neutrals, or even those of the Allies or the United States. The bill so defined the word, and broadened it to include 'allies-of-enemy,' for the United States was not yet at war with Austria-Hungary, Bulgaria, and Turkey. But the bill did more than this, because the automatic powers of the President did not clearly embrace the right to forbid trade with those in neutral or Allied countries who might be suspected of having an enemy connection. It was this suspect trade that the Allies had sought to strangle. It had brought about the blacklists, the control of bunker coal, and the arbitrary refusal to tolerate trade with neutrals in even innocent matters unless the Allies were assured of a military advantage to themselves.

As the provision came back from conference and was embedded

in the new law, it forbade any person in the United States (except with license from the President)

> to trade, or to attempt to trade, either directly or indirectly, with, to, or from, or for, or on account of, or on behalf of, or for the benefit of, any other person, with knowledge or reasonable cause to believe that such other person is an enemy or ally of enemy, or is conducting or taking part in such trade, directly or indirectly, for, or on account of, or on behalf of, or for the benefit of, an enemy or ally of enemy.

The normal definition of 'enemy,' in its widest form, included enemy subjects and corporations resident in the United States. The policy of the United States in inviting or permitting immigration had brought within the country great numbers of such enemy aliens who had neglected naturalization, kept peacefully at their useful jobs, and were too highly regarded to be proscribed. When these disregarded the hospitality they enjoyed, they were subject to criminal law if they committed crime, or to internment if they threatened danger. But there was no intention of inflicting upon them as a class the full rigor of permissible international law. 'Spy scares' were numerous, and enough intrigue was known to warrant close observance of the behavior of these enemy aliens. But the millions of subjects of Germany and Austria-Hungary in the United States showed no sign of disloyalty as a class. Nervous American neighbors tattled about them in more cases than the Department of Justice has ever been willing to reveal, but when the American Protective League or the Division of Military Intelligence made quiet investigations they found few facts to justify the charges. The law was mitigated with respect to these aliens. They had trouble enough without it, for they were objects of a suspicion that often cost them jobs. The President directed them to keep away from camps and munition factories. They were not permitted to enter or leave the United States without special permission. They were required to register themselves and report their movements. But they were not interned, denied the protection of the law, or generally molested.

One group of enemy aliens possessed a special protection as old

as the earliest treaty made with Prussia in 1785 and continued in
the revisions of that treaty made in 1799 and 1828. These were
Prussian merchants residing in the United States, who were
specifically allowed, in the event of war, 'to remain nine months
to collect their debts and settle their affairs... [and to] depart
freely, carrying all of their effects without molestation or hin-
drance.' And other Prussians, similarly residing, 'whose occupations are for the common subsistence and benefit of mankind,'
were entitled to an unmolested existence.

But the promise of an 'unmolested existence' did not go so far as
to permit them, or other alien enemies, to keep up communication
with the Fatherland, or to send money home, or to engage in
ventures useful to Germany. It did not promise that property
within the United States, owned by enemies outside, should continue to be productive to the owners, and thereby to Germany
itself. The sixth section of the Trading-with-the-Enemy Act
authorized the appointment of an Alien Property Custodian 'to
receive all money and property in the United States due or belonging to an enemy, or ally of enemy... and to hold, administer, and
account for the same.' Germany had already, in the months
before April, 1917, provided for the registration of enemy property
within the Empire, had ordered its sale wherever convenient, and
had brought about the liquidation of British and French firms or
corporations doing business there. Its various decrees were designed to 'prevent the removal of such property from German
jurisdiction.' Its policies had matched and had been matched by
the similar policies of its enemies; and from both sides had come
the claim that what was being done was being done only in retaliation. The claim was not valid enough, wherever advanced, to
receive much consideration. Segregation of enemy property was
too obvious a duty of a belligerent to constitute a special offense or
to need special justification. It was a part of modern war. When
the United States became one of the enemies of Germany the German controls were broadened to embrace American-owned property and the United States of necessity set up similar restrictions.

The new Alien Property Custodian was A. Mitchell Palmer of

Pennsylvania, whose office was launched in an Executive Order of October 12. An 'original Wilson man,' Palmer might have been selected as Secretary of War in 1913 had not his scruples as a Quaker barred this sort of service. He deserved well of his party for having sacrificed his seat in the House in order to contest the seat of Boies Penrose in the Senate in the election of 1914. Defeated in the three-cornered contest with Penrose and Pinchot, he had gone back to his law office after a few weeks as a judge of the Court of Claims. He now undertook as trustee to search out and seize all enemy-owned property in the United States. What was to be done with it in the long run was left to the determination of Congress and to the reciprocal action of Germany after the peace. In the short run, it was to cease to constitute a menace to the war effort. Palmer managed to set up and administer more than 32,000 separate trusts, aggregating in value $502,000,000, and he reminded Congress at the end of his service that he had more than paid the costs of his office by uncovering and collecting for the Government tax obligations that had been evaded.

Different types of property were treated differently. That of Bulgarian and Turkish allies of Germany was generally untouched. That of private persons, some of them Americans caught within German lines, or Allies within occupied areas, was segregated, conserved, and held subject to return when owners could divest themselves of 'their technical enemy character.' But the property of enemy-owned corporations doing business in the United States was made 'a part of America's great fighting machine.' Palmer's scruples against war did not go so far as to prevent vigorous work in co-operation with the armed forces. He found the enemy corporations more numerous than he anticipated, larger, and more penetrating in their industrial character. Their real ownership was often obscured behind false names and faked transfers that compelled 'painstaking investigation.' They owned much actual war material, bought and stored in the United States in absence of means of shipment to Germany. There were factories making magnetos, surgical instruments, chemicals, and drugs. Palmer's explorers uncovered a German penetration of American industry that he regarded as his duty to dissipate. His original powers as public trustee were insufficient for this, but he soon procured an amendment to the law whereby he was enabled to sell such property to new and loyal owners and to convert the proceeds into Liberty Bonds. These he held to the account of the alien owners and subject to action of Congress. He thus avoided the necessity to account for the high war profits that the enemy would have earned within the United States. He was proud 'to make the Trading-with-the-Enemy Act a fighting force in the war.'

No single class of enemy property created more difficulty than the German-owned patents, taken out in the United States before the war, and sometimes operated in the United States, sometimes abroad, and sometimes not operated at all. German industry, like American, had often bought competitive patents to suppress them. American war industry needed the service of all useful inventions to which the protection of the United States patent laws had been extended. Manufacture under them must continue, but without profit to the enemy while war lasted. Where the German owners had elected to manufacture only in Germany the war cut off supplies that could not well be spared: dyes, chemicals, and above all salversan — the famous '606' of Professor Paul Ehrlich which was without rival as a specific against syphilis. The act permitted the President to license the use of German patents by American firms; the President in turn vested the administration of these licenses in the Federal Trade Commission.

Congress was in some doubt, as it debated the Trading-with-the Enemy Act, where to assign the various powers over trade. It discovered that there were jealousies and rivalries among the departments, and here, as in many other cases, it avoided the issue by conferring most of the authority upon the President. On October 12, Wilson made his distribution of duties, giving the largest share to McCormick and a War Trade Board, upon which should sit representatives of the Treasury, State, Agriculture, and Commerce Departments as well as those of the Food Administration and the Shipping Board. The power over the export of 'coin, bullion, or currency' he retained for himself, assigning shares in administration to the Treasury and the Federal Reserve System; it escaped repeal when the war laws had done their work, and a later President found this within his arsenal of powers when panic in 1933 produced a crisis hardly second to that of war. The other powers to license imports and exports and to block enemy trade were administered by McCormick through what became fifth among the war administrations.

The aim of the War Trade Board was to complete the commercial and financial isolation of the enemy, to obtain supplies essential for the United States, and to conserve ocean tonnage. In the last projects it worked in close association with the Shipping Board and the War Industries Board. For the purposes of the others it built up an organization in Washington and sent its agents around the world.

Its bureaus of exports and of imports broadened their control as the war ran on. Beginning with limited lists of commodities and limited areas of origin or destination, their duties and powers were extended until in February, 1918, all imports and exports were required to be licensed. The detailed knowledge of commodities upon which license control was operated was drawn from trade advisers, from the Food and Fuel Administrations, and from the commodity sections of the War Industries Board. The bureaus co-operated with British and French agencies of like character, to dig out knowledge about enemy firms in neutral countries and to make blacklists comprehensive and effective. The 'enemy cloak lists' provide interesting testimony to the efforts of the enemy to hide his hand.

The applicants for licenses had to meet the scrutiny of an intelligence bureau, which exchanged information with the intelligence divisions of Army, Navy, and the Department of Justice. Persons who desired to be permitted to trade were investigated. The investigations were carried into neutral countries by agents, open or under cover, who used their wits to develop devices with which to baffle the efforts of enemy firms to disguise themselves. By November, 1918, the War Trade Board had 2789 employees at work, with its largest units devoting their attention to exports and war trade intelligence.

There was no logical reason for adding to the Trading-with-the-Enemy Act the clauses dealing with opinion and elaborating the powers conferred upon the Government by the Espionage Act. The Senate, however, was worried by expressions of dissent and was driven by constituents whose intolerance grew upon them. Numerous proposals to crack down upon radicals, pacifists, and pro-Germans found their way to the Senate files, and a selection from them was attached as a rider to the bill under consideration. The Senate insisted and the House yielded, with the result that the war powers of the Government were crowded more closely upon the constitutional guaranties of free speech and free press.

The President was authorized, whenever he should 'deem that the public safety demands it,' to operate a censorship over all channels of communication between the United States and other countries. The law forbade (unless under license from the President) any international communication 'except in the regular course of the mail,' and made it unlawful to communicate or attempt to communicate with 'an enemy or ally of the enemy.' The unmailable varieties of communication were defined in detail so complete that a mails, cable, and radio censorship could be operated with whatever rigor appeared desirable. There was no doubt, upon constitutional grounds, of the right of the Government to exercise this power. It was entirely expedient, in time of war, to have a means of blocking disloyal or indiscreet transmission of information. But the result, an outrage in the mind of radicals, was a shock to the feelings of many who gave complete support to the fact and aims of war. In the Executive Order of October 12, Wilson vested in a Censorship Board (representatives of War, Navy, Post Office, War Trade, and the Committee on Public Information) the administration of rules governing communication between the United States and any foreign country by any means.

The last section of the act, section nineteen, was assigned to the Postmaster-General for enforcement, and rounded out the powers to exclude unmailable material that had already been conferred by the Espionage Act. It was in the fourth week of September when the amendment of Myers of Montana (whose State was soon to set a bad example with violent criminal syndicalism and sedition laws) was pressed upon the act in the Senate. The People's Council was in the papers. There were incipient strikes throughout the West. The I.W.W. was responsible for much loose talk and was charged with more. There was still suggestion that the alien enemies in the United States were treacherous. If Myers had had his way it would have become unlawful during the war 'to utter any disloyal, threatening, violent, scurrilous, defamatory, abusive, or seditious language about' the Government, the President, the Constitution, the flag, the Army, the Navy, the soldiers, or the sailors, or any language calculated to bring any of them into 'contempt, scorn, contumely, or disrepute.' The Myers amendment failed now to be adopted (although Congress caught up to it in six months), but in its place King of Utah submitted and secured the adoption of a less sweeping proscription of utterance.

The King amendment struck at the foreign-language press, requiring it to file, in advance of publication, a correct English translation of any material dealing with the countries at war or with their policies. The local postmaster was to receive the translations, and the Postmaster-General was permitted to waive the requirement in the case of such publishers as were not likely to cause 'detriment to the United States in the conduct of the present war.' The new authority over the foreign-language press and the new definition of unmailable communication, added to the powers previously conferred upon him, gave to the Postmaster-General a set of duties incongruous with his principal task. Persons who violated the law did not generally receive the trial and conviction to which even law violators are entitled. They were punished by administrative order without easy redress. Those who needed restraint were enraged, as was to be expected. Those who feared bureaucracy and the loss of reasonable freedom were made nervous. But section nineteen was additional evidence of the solidity of opinion that supported the war effort.

At their worst the various restrictions were less severe than their counterparts prevailing among the other belligerents.

Secretary Daniels was among those cross-examined before committees of Congress, when that body convened for the winter
session. Fred A. Britten of Chicago, with enough Germans
among his constituents to make him responsive to their rights,
heckled the Secretary of the Navy mildly, and evoked from
Daniels the reply: 'The facts are we have no censorship of the
press.... We request the press not to print certain things ...
there is no law or power to compel them to comply ... but that
mere request as to 98 per cent of the newspapers is absolutely as
good as law ... if a paper should be treasonable, it can be denied
the mails ... [but] they are very few.' And to this Britten rejoined:
'Thank God for that.'

VII. THE SINEWS OF WAR

INTEREST on the First Liberty Loan began to run on June 15, 1917, with the Treasury still uncertain how much it could raise during the first year of war or how much it could spend. Both had limits. Wars can be fought only with goods on hand or with goods manufactured while the war is waged. The economic strength that backs armies and produces the sinews of war is an intangible existing at the moment of any declaration, and is certain to be depleted if war is prolonged toward the moment of exhaustion. The fiscal bookkeeping whereby the ownership of this economic strength is transferred from the citizen to the nation becomes a matter of public policy. It may make the rich richer and the poor poorer, or it may wipe out the rich to the disadvantage of the poor. No fiscal system is sound, in the long run, unless it leaves the tax-payer who has paid his tax in a position in which he may hope to earn enough to pay another tax next year. Single cropping, too long indulged in, bankrupts the farmer; unsound taxation defeats its own intent by destroying the very base upon which it is levied. 'The power to tax' is indeed 'the power to destroy.'

If perfect fiscal wisdom were procurable it might conceivably spread the whole profit and loss of war upon the whole population, in precise proportion to the suffering and advantage of every individual and every group. But if there were perfect wisdom in control of governments, there would be no war. In an imperfect world, however, the imperative need to spend, driven by fear of defeat, compels a fiscal policy based more upon the immediate productiveness of measures than upon their ultimate wisdom. There is some small chance of correcting the injustices of war finance by subsequent taxation, whereby unwarrantable profits are recaptured by the nation; but the chance is weakened by the slight political mobility of the small citizens who pay the taxes and the extreme agility of accumulated wealth. There cannot be great accuracy in any laws passed under pressure. There has been no war in which the suffering was ended at the peace.

For the Treasury of the United States, as the scope of war expenditures broadened, it was a matter of guessing how much could be raised, and upon what terms. The people had to pay. It was both right and politic to make them pay as much of current cost out of current taxes as could be accomplished; but no one was so innocent as to believe that debt could be avoided. This debt, owed by the Government to the people, could be got rid of only by shifting it upon the shoulders of the people. There were only two ways of making this shift: those of taxation and of repudiation. And here every interest would pull or push to save itself. McAdoo could not hope to spend more than he could raise.

It was doubtful whether he could spend, during the first year, even this much. The people of the United States had a high standard of life, as standards went, and could tighten the belt many times before exhaustion. The credit of the Government was nearly perfect, reinforced by the policy that restored gold payments in 1879 and by the vote that rejected free silver in 1896. The size of loans that could be raised was limited only by the terms of the contracts and the interest rate. But the expenditure of billions could not start at top speed from scratch. The first six months of war were months of planning how to spend with war producers not yet in quantity production. Not until the second year of war could it be expected to spend as much as was desirable to invest in victory.

The ease with which the first loan was raised testified to the abundant resources of the United States, to the fluidity of its wealth, and to the usefulness of the Federal Reserve System. The banking reforms of 1913 had produced a financial mechanism able to meet the calls of war finance. There was no need for any finance-in-desperation such as Chase had operated in the Civil War; no need to find a twentieth-century Jay Cooke to persuade and bully; no need to fill an empty Treasury with outright fiat money like the greenbacks. The four million buyers of the first loan became as many promoters of the next. The Federal Reserve Banks knew from the first experience how to improve upon it in the second. The volunteers who solicited bond subscriptions put their organization upon a permanent basis, to endure through the war, and got more pleasure from their work than they anticipated.

The short-term loans (Treasury Certificates) authorized in the loan act of April 24 proved their usefulness before it became necessary to make a second drive for bonds. Sold through the Federal Reserve Banks, they simplified the transfer of funds and spread the financial load so as to prevent undue crowding at single dates. They provided a basis for estimate of the amount that must be raised by bonds. Eight times before Congress adjourned in October, the Treasury went to the banks for from two hundred to four hundred millions at an issue, without running over the maximum of two billions permitted to be outstanding at one time. Four of the issues, maturing, had been paid off before Congress on September 24 passed a second loan act in anticipation of a second drive.

No pressure was needed behind this second act. McAdoo held off his request for authority as long as possible, so as to have the fullest picture of his need. The critics of war finance, and those who desired to produce out of revenue legislation something more than sinews of war, raised no serious objections. They withheld their fire for the revenue measure, recognizing that until a tax was voted there was no way of avoiding loans.

The second loan act gave the President authority to borrow at four per cent (raising the rate from the three and one-half per cent of April) and left the bonds tax-free with respect to ordinary taxes. There was no convincing reason why Government bonds should be tax-free, except that they were thereby made more attractive to investors. The exemption had originated at a time when there were so few taxes to be escaped that it had meant little. Now, in an age of income taxes, estate taxes, and progressive surtaxes, the freedom from deduction by either Nation or State gave an advantage to the rich investor that made him a target in politics. The 'bloated bondholder' of Civil War days was bloated because he was paid in gold when other creditors of the Government were forced to accept depreciated greenbacks. The bondholder was now to value his exemption as worth more to him than the gold clause. The bonds of the first loan were free of everything but estate and inheritance taxes. The new bonds were somewhat less desirable and were therefore entitled to a higher rate, since in addition to estate and inheritance taxes they were liable for income surtaxes thereafter to be imposed.

Like those of the first act, the new bonds were made convertible by the holders into bonds of later issues. Congress fixed the authorized total of the new four per cent loan at $7,538,945,460. In addition to this amount, it authorized a new type of loan, in small sums covered by War Savings Certificates, to a total of two billions. It raised the maximum of short-time loans to four billions outstanding at one time. And it authorized the Treasury to continue the policy of loans to those countries 'engaged in war with the enemies of the United States.' Four billions were earmarked for this.

McAdoo was preparing for his second loan while Congress completed the draft of the enabling act. The drive began on October 1, with interest on the loan to run from November 15. Subscriptions were invited for three billions in four per cent bonds, due in twenty-five years but callable earlier. The first loan had been oversubscribed, and the Treasury had rejected oversubscriptions. The Secretary now reserved the right to accept half of the oversubscriptions, and took again to the road to inspire his solicitors and the co-operating committees. Sergeant Arthur Guy Empey, back from service with the British and author of *Over the Top by an American Soldier Who Went* (1917), went on the road also, a thrilling speaker with grewsome descriptions that built up hate. Donald M. Ryerson's Four-Minute Men, under the auspices of the Committee on Public Information, mobilized themselves in the theaters. The speakers' bureaus, whether of the Treasury, the C.P.I., the Food Administration, or the councils of defense, helped in the push. The State Department provided more testimony against the enemy by releasing more intercepted dispatches, among them the famous *spurlos versenkt* advice from Luxburg, German chargé in the Argentine. In this it was suggested that certain merchant ships at sea, whose destruction could not be defended if discovered, be 'sunk without a trace being left.' The Second Liberty Loan was a success, oversubscribed by half, with more than twice as many buyers as the first. To 9,400,000 investors McAdoo finally assigned bonds to the amount of $3,808-766,150.

The War Savings Certificates were launched in December with a drive directed by Frank A. Vanderlip. Like the Liberty Bonds, the certificates had their place in morale as well as in finance. It was Hamiltonian doctrine, and sound doctrine, too, to spread among the citizens a financial interest in the solvency of the State. Every holder of a bond payable, principal and interest, 'in United States gold coin of the present standard of value' (the acts were identical in this), held a stake in the Government. Patriotism and profit were combined. It gave no small stability to opinion when four million creditors were listed. There were well above twice that many now, and more than half as many as had voted for President in 1916.

But even so little as fifty dollars, the minimum amount of any bond, was too much to be swung by every American. Vanderlip undertook to bring the war home to the citizen of petty savings and to inculcate thrift as a by-product. War savings could be accumulated twenty-five cents at a time, in the form of stamps pasted on a card; the same to be turned in at prices ranging from $4.12 to $4.23 for certificates with a face value of five dollars and a maturity of January 1, 1923. Every post office and every rural carrier soon had the stamps for sale. More than $834,000,000 was borrowed by this device in twelve months, leaving the Secretary so happy with the venture as to hope that it might become 'a continuing feature of the Nation's financing even after the restoration of peace.'

At no time was Congress compelled to go slowly on appropriations for fear of lack of funds. The Treasury had closed the fiscal year ending June 30, 1917, with an excess of receipts for the year of $788,000,000 over disbursements. It had paid out in all $2,080,000,000 (of which $932,000,000 went to the Allies), and had taken in $1,118,000,000 from taxes and $1,750,000,000 from loans. But it had not begun to spend. McAdoo made his estimates for the fiscal year 1917–18 a jump at a time, as he learned of new requirements, and ended at about twelve billions, exclusive of foreign loans. The Congress, in its appropriations, gave reality to the estimates. It authorized expenditures or commitments up to twenty-one billions, with the leading items running in millions to 8911 for the Army, 1875 for the Navy, 1889 for the Emergency Fleet, and 7000 for loans to the Allies. The committees concerned, those on Ways and Means in the House and on Finance in the Senate, began early in the session to work upon such a revision of the taxing laws as would be entailed by the expenditures; but the drafting of the measure had to be postponed repeatedly because of the discovery of some huge new cost or some new deficiency in revenue. Their work was not done upon the introduction of the measure. It had to be steered, and rebuilt as steered, until the very end of the session.

From a fiscal standpoint, the greatest uncertainty was alcohol. Long, with tobacco, a heavy contributor to the internal revenue, its standing as a fiscal reliance was threatened from two sides, and shaken from each while the revenue bill was under debate. The advance of prohibition had been persistent and successful for the last decade. From local option to State-wide prohibition, and thence toward national prohibition by constitutional amendment, it had been driven by an organized pressure of dry forces. Every year showed a larger dry area upon the map. War did not stop the drive. On August 1, 1917, the Senate surrendered to the demand, sending to the House the Sheppard amendment. Half the States voted solid delegations for it when it passed the House. Thirty-three States were dry by their own choice when the amendment was ready for submission on December 18. By the terms of the amendment the States had seven years in which to ratify it; it took them only thirteen months. It was far from certain how successful the measure would be as a social reform, but it could be foreseen that upon ratification the Government would lose a source of certain revenue.

The other attack upon alcohol was grounded on the belief that its manufacture was a non-essential use of foodstuffs in time of war. The distilling of alcohol for beverage purposes was forbidden by the Lever Act in August, and the President was authorized to prohibit the use of grain for brewing. Until Congress had shown its hand on these matters it was not possible even to guess at the revenue that might be derived from alcohol. The prohibition upon manufacture did not extend to the sale of alcoholic liquors already made and in bond. These could be taxed, and were. They were made to yield, in the last months before the Eighteenth Amendment went into effect, more revenue than ever before. Spirits and fermented liquors had contributed 283 millions in 1917; they were stepped up to 433 millions in 1918, and to 483 millions in 1919. Behind both attacks upon the manufacture of alcohol was an increasing demand that the consumption as well as manufacture ought to be forbidden as a war measure, even in advance of the adoption of the amendment. But compliance with this was avoided for another year.

The revenue bill came into the House early in May, with Fordney of Michigan opening the debate for the Committee on Ways and Means on the eleventh. It was significant that he opened, rather than Kitchin of North Carolina, the chairman, for Fordney was a Republican. They had a unanimous report to present — unusual in financial legislation. Members of the committee, whether majority Democrats or minority Republicans, went out of their way to praise the patriotism of their normal opponents. They were consciously breaking new gound in American taxation, and labored as diligently and as crudely as pioneers must. When the House finished with the bill May 23 (with a vote of 329 to 21), the Senate Finance Committee worked as resolutely as the Committee on Ways and Means had done, thought as highly of the patriotic diligence of all concerned, but fell short of unanimity

when at last ready to report the measure to the Senate. Yet the
Senate passed the bill September 10, by vote of 69 to 4, the
quartet of dissenters being Borah, Gronna, La Follette, and
Norris.

It was war compulsion rather than a coming together of minds
that produced near unanimity. More than one Republican in
either house made his apology for agreement with Democrats.
Fordney covered his unusual alliance with the story of a lad digging potatoes, of whom a passer-by inquired, ' "My son, what are
you getting for doing this?"' To which replied the boy, ' "I get
nothing for doing it, but I will get hell if I do not do it."' The
House received his confession with laughter, and settled down on
May 11 to a task that was not completed until the President signed
the bill October 3. The bill, as introduced, proposed to raise by
taxation in the next fiscal year the sum of 1800 millions, but there
was no visibility along its ceiling. Within a week McAdoo raised
his requirement to 2245 millions, and all Kitchin could reply to
inquiries as to *maxima* was, 'We can find out as we go along.'
When the Senate Finance Committee was ready to report the bill
(after the passage of the food bill had settled the fate of the alcohol
schedules), Simmons thought the measure would add 2009 millions to the resources of the Government, and it was estimated that
taxes would run alongside loans at about the ratio of 35 to 65.
It passed the Senate estimated at 2416 millions. The conference
report left it at 2535 millions, these in excess of the measures of
internal taxation already in force. When, however, the final
figures for the revenue of 1917–18 were available in the report of
the Secretary of the Treasury at the end of 1918, the fact proved
to be better than the guess. The total receipts from taxation
amounted to 4174 millions, of which 3694 came from the internal
revenue, as against 809 millions from the same source in 1917.
The new law worked an increase of 2885 millions over the internal
revenue total of the previous year.

There was agreement upon the fundamental basis of the tax, an
agreement in which President and Secretary of the Treasury concurred with both parties and all factions in Congress as well as

with vocal comment upon the measure as it was driven along. The war was to cause as small a burden for posterity as was possible. It was to be carried out of current taxes as far as could be done without wrecking the business that must pay the tax. Disagreement began, after the acceptance of the principle, as soon as a place was suggested at which to stop taxing and to begin to borrow. The dissension prevented a unanimous report to the Senate from the Finance Committee. It was best expressed and most effectively led by La Follette, who was never able to be quite convincing as to his motive. There was so much indubitably sound finance in his minority proposals that he commanded respect as he heckled, however greatly he irritated. But he could not persuade either his colleagues or the public of the completeness of his interest in war finance, since there was so much that looked like a hang-over from his prolonged antipathy to big business, its habits, and its social tendencies.

As the debate drew to a close in the Senate his numerous amendments were rejected one by one. At the very end he offered a complete bill, constructed in his office, as a substitute for the project upon which the Senate had been working for a month, and upon which the Finance Committee had worked eleven weeks before the Senate took it up. The fourteen Senators who stood by him when the Senate turned this down, 65 to 15, read like a roster of Progressives and near-Progressives. The speeches they made, rarely as sound as his, contain much to suggest a social rather than a fiscal aim as dominating their minds. They were Borah, Brady, Gore, Gronna, Hardwick, Hollis, Husting, Johnson (California), Jones (Washington), Kenyon, McNary, Norris, Reed, and Vardaman.

La Follette was not content to carry as little of the cost as thirty-five per cent from taxes. He would have paid the whole cost out of current receipts had it been possible. His philosophy was not far from that which Amos Pinchot, through his American Committee on War Finance, had urged upon Congress. If a 'pay-as-you-go' war should make wealth regret that it had helped to make the war — and this both Pinchot and La Follette believed — there would be some satisfaction in voting taxes. If it should prevent the war from increasing the concentration of American wealth in the hands of those to whom the Progressives had already given painful prominence as 'money trust,' it would work some social benefit. The supporters of the La Follette proposals, and those made under his wing, were left cold by the contention of business that a pay-as-you-go war would destroy both it and the power of the United States to carry on the war. They had long since ceased to believe what business said about itself.

Differing with the majority forces upon the ratio between loans and taxes, the opposition differed also upon the subjects for taxation. The House proposal, and the bill as passed, taxed everything in sight. Chewing gum and soft drinks, automobiles and bank checks, postal rate for letters, graphophones, moving-picture films and theater tickets, as well as incomes, war profits, and estates, were made to pay their share. La Follette worked earnestly to avoid the excise and nuisance taxes bearing directly upon the small consumer and to place the whole burden of special war taxation upon incomes, excess profits, alcohol, and tobacco. The most significant debates, becoming sharper as they were prolonged from May into October, turned upon the ratio of loans to taxes, the income tax, the treatment of excess profits, and upon an attempt to take away from the publisher the subsidy he had enjoyed since 1885 in the form of a flat one-cent-per-pound rate on second-class mail.

It was protested in both houses that a reform of the postal system was not properly to be included in a revenue measure. There was no serious objection to an increase in the letter rate from two to three cents, but the attempt to readjust the rate for newspapers and periodicals, in the second-class schedule, aroused concerted opposition that was met by violent advocacy of the change. The project was politically explosive, even in war time. When the matter was under discussion in the first Wilson Administration, the editor of the *American Thresherman* emitted a warning to Democrats: 'If you desire to bring the same fate upon your party which befell the Taft Administration and caused its downfall, increase the second-class postage rates.' It was common gossip that Taft owed many of his misfortunes to his unpopularity with the newspapers, an unpopularity earned by the failure to put print paper on the free list in the Payne-Aldrich Tariff. The newspapers were sensitive to any change in the law likely to cost them money. They were disposed to claim a greater virtue than they had, disavowing self-interest, and to base their arguments upon the importance of an untrammeled press. They were the medium through which the congressman knew his constituency, and his constituency him; and their power to wreck careers made legislators cautious. Their anger at the Payne-Aldrich bill, said Fordney, 'put some of my best friends out of Congress.' But the House bill proposed to take from them the subsidy, repeal the flat rate, and base postal charges on a zone system.

It would be possible to take the one-cent rate as a text, and to write beneath it much of the cultural history of a generation. It was avowedly a subsidy. Except for it, 'Cyclone' Davis once declaimed, the buffalo and the Indian would still be roaming over the West. It was true that the Indian and the buffalo had generally ceased to roam before the subsidy was first voted in 1885, but Davis's statement was perhaps not too inaccurate for oratorical purposes. It belonged to that view of the postal service in which the dissemination of knowledge was a proper national function. When the rate was made, American periodicals dealt in news; now, when it was proposed to change it, they dealt in advertisement, with news in many cases only a side line. The rate was not based on cost of service when voted; in 1917 most of the speeches repeated the charge that it yielded only eleven millions in revenue yet cost one hundred millions to operate. The small-town papers, delivered by carrier, thought it a graft. The small-town merchant resented the advertisements of the great papers and the magazines that lured away his customers.

Trade and life had changed in a generation; business had become national; great corporations assembled incomes that made them targets of jealous fear. The United States was indeed spending large sums to make it easier for big publishing business to get bigger, yet there was some truth in the contention made by the publishers. The subsidy earned an indirect profit, shown in first-class postage receipts as the result of correspondence stimulated by national advertisement. The desire to use the revenue act as a means of correcting an abuse persisted through the debate.

The House passed the bill carrying the new zone rate. The Senate listened to long debate in which the *Saturday Evening Post* was generally the villain, and contented itself with a moderate increase in the flat rate. As the bill came from conference and became a law it carried a compromise unsatisfactory to everyone and timidly deferred its operation until July 1, 1918. Thereafter, a new basis was to be reached gradually through a period of four years. The act placed one rate upon reading matter and a higher rate upon advertising matter, and established a zone system in which the rate increased with the distance. But it permitted the publisher to evade the higher distance rates by shipping his periodical by freight to the town of delivery, and paying only minimum postage to the Government. Burleson objected to 'the use of the postal system for raising war revenue'; Simmons did not believe in it and hoped that before the clumsy scheme became operative a better law would have been enacted as a postal measure.

There was running debate upon the ratio of loans to taxes throughout the whole engagement. The pay-as-you-go war, in which the whole of the extra cost should be raised while the war was being fought, was only an ideal. Its proponents had no expectation that it could be realized. When they alluded to it, as some of them did at every turn of the debate, it was for the purpose of strengthening their argument that the proposed taxes were too light. But probably those who believed it to be a fiscal possibility were more numerous than those who openly advocated leaving taxes as they were and placing the whole burden of war finance upon the loans.

Between the two extremes, the congressional veterans of both parties were in pretty good agreement upon the necessity for heavy new imposts, differing chiefly in their judgment as to how heavy.

The Republican elder statesmen, Penrose, Smoot, Lodge, and the others who had gone through the mill with earlier revenue laws, were unwilling that the business which must pay the tax should be rendered unable to pay it because of the burden of the tax itself. Lodge, who agreed with La Follette in little else, agreed with him that the 'two vital questions' were the proportion to be raised by taxation and the imposition of such taxation 'so as to maintain business in the highest state of productivity and activity.' Said Lodge: 'a just mean must be found . . . between John Trumbull's often-quoted line, "What is posterity to us," and the proposition to raise all the expenditures by taxation.' The Republican Senators made much of the need of industry, expanding to do war business, to retain a large share of the profits for capital investment. They were on firm ground when insisting that unless business could command capital by offering a prospect of earning income on the investment it could not serve the Nation. They resented as demagogic that part of the opposing argument that connected guilt with wealth and treated war taxation as a proper punishment for those who paid the tax.

There were valid questions to be asked which remained unanswered, as to the amounts that could be raised. Before the debate had continued many weeks the minimum requirements of the Treasury had gone beyond all experience. The statisticians who computed probable yields were forced to guess. The British experience with war taxes was studied for the light it might throw upon the problem of the United States, but it threw too little to illumine it. Nowhere else was there to be found quite the same complex of overlapping State and Federal taxes with the result of double taxation for some and possible evasion for others. Upon neither side of the argument did the sensible legislators estimate largely enough the financial strength of the American people or suspect the ease with which the war levies were finally to be paid. They might, perhaps, have drawn more fully from Civil War experience, noting the rapidity with which revenues were built up between 1861 and 1865, the deep penetration of prosperity in spite of war, and the willingness with which their constituents had paid the bills. Fear of what the voters might do to them was as much of a deterrent as fear that they might lay on the people burdens heavier than could be borne. But they could not well know more than they knew, as they blazed new trails through the financial woods. Their pioneer predecessors might have told them that between the squeals of a pinched pig and his actual suffering there is no dependable connection. Not until the taxes they voted now were collected could they have a realization of the full American economic strength. So long as Senators continued to be uncertain about this, they feared to advance beyond popular willingness to accept or financial ability to meet the levy.

The Progressive-minded group, with most of the Administration Democrats at its head, pushed steadily for greater revenues. It believed, beyond its capacity to prove the matter, that business could pay. It was responsive to the idea that, whatever the system or the rate, the small-income American was paying and would continue to pay a larger tax in proportion to his ability to pay than Americans of wealth.

Wages and tables of average prices were studied and quoted. Government had gone a long way toward 'dead reckoning' in finance since the publication of the Aldrich *Report* a quarter-century earlier, even if the law-makers could not agree on the interpretation of the tables of statistics. Amos Pinchot maintained that in the years 1900–14 the wages of 'small people' had advanced some twenty-seven per cent, lagging always behind the cost of living which had risen forty per cent. This was before the war. The cost of living was now advancing even more rapidly, while the mutterings of wage-earners were turning into labor controversy which embarrassed war production in every branch. It was sound finance and policy not to tax business so heavily that it could not pay; it was even sounder to protect the average American in his economic status. The figures were not yet available to measure that status with precision, but in 1921 the National Bureau of Economic Research worked it out that in 1913 the average *per capita* income of Americans was $354, a little less than a dollar a day per person. Out of an income of this dimension citizens must maintain themselves, meet the costs of casualty, and support their Government in peace or war. In the final construction of the revenue act of 1917 the party leaders were pressed by extremists from either side, and the major controversies turned upon the fiscal treatment of profits derived directly from war and upon the income tax. Few things that were taxable were able to escape a share of the tax. La Follette's contention that the whole of the tax must come from income, excess profit, alcohol, and tobacco was rejected.

War profits made an appearance in American legislation before the United States became involved in war. It had been necessary to reconstruct the revenue laws after the outbreak of war in Europe in 1914 because the immediate consequence of the war was a decline in American imports which resulted in a decline in the revenue derived from the tariff. In October, 1914, the internal-revenue schedules were revised upward, and stamp taxes were imposed in a stop-gap measure that remained in operation until the end of 1916.

The income tax was still in the experimental stage, subject to more experiment. Each year that the income tax was collected added to the skill of the Treasury in refining definitions and recovering losses due to fraud or confusion. Each additional annual return made by corporations or individuals made it a little harder next year to evade the imposition. In the Treasury accumulation of annual *dossiers* the history and dimension of every important fortune was written and checked. When in 1916 estate taxation was imposed, the work of the field examiners upon the inventories of estates was made to supplement and support the efforts of the income-tax collectors. No estate could get clearance until it was shown that income-tax requirements had been met. For the fiscal purposes of the United States it made no difference whether the income was honestly procured or came from crime. It was required to be declared, and in due time the Federal penitentiaries opened to welcome, on the charge of tax evasion, criminals whose crimes had been too subtle for grand and petty juries.

The internal-revenue laws were revised again in September,

1916, greatly to the advantage of the Federal income, and estate taxation was built into the system. The individual income tax of a single person, based in 1913 upon one per cent of the net income above three thousand dollars, was raised to two per cent, with graduated surtaxes upon the larger incomes. The corporation income tax, first voted in 1909 at one per cent on net, was doubled to two per cent and the manufacturers of what the law defined as 'munitions' were required to pay in addition a tax of twelve and one-half per cent upon net income derived from such manufacture.

With war business booming and its high prices creating unusual profits, the beneficiaries of war were an easy and appropriate mark. They had quick profits that could be reached. They were in a trade which drew its gains from human misfortune and which had few friends outside its participants. The European belligerents discovered in these war profits a rich source of revenue, and Congress, discovering it in 1916, tapped it again in an amendment to the revenue laws in March, 1917. But it had been discovered also that other industries than those of munitions derived swollen profits from the state of war, and the European effort to seize a share of these was now reflected in the imposition by Congress of an 'excess-profits' tax. It was necessary to assume for the purpose of an excess-profits tax — but it had to be an arbitrary assumption — that a certain amount of income was 'normal' income. Among small corporations managed by their owners the rate earned had little reference to capitalization, yet little or none of it was 'excess.' To protect these small concerns and to establish the arbitrary point at which profits should cease to be 'normal' and should become 'excess,' the act of March defined normal profit substantially as five thousand dollars plus eight per cent on 'the actual capital invested in the property or business.' The new law took, in addition to all other taxes, eight per cent of so much of the net income as was in excess of this amount. The total new revenue to be gathered in by this attack upon excess profits was not yet known when the war Congress debated the revenue act of 1917. But book-keeping and accounting were becoming a skilled and controversial profession as Government was requiring business to know what it was doing well enough to explain its methods and its resources.

As the problem was uncovered through the long summer of 1917, a realization of the gross amount of excess profits and their ripeness for taxation grew upon Congress, but sharp differences developed as to the proper approach. The House, which had managed to force its own proposal upon the Senate in the revenue act of March, adhered to the idea that 'excess' profits were both real and taxable, and asked that an additional eight per cent (making sixteen per cent) be levied upon them.

The Finance Committee rejected the House proposal, holding that while a new surtax was of course to be levied upon incomes there was no place at which a defensible line could be drawn between profits that were normal and those that were excess. Its counter-proposal, in the bill first reported to the Senate July 3, embraced a graduated tax (rising by stages from twelve to fifty per cent) upon net profits in excess, not of an arbitrary eight per cent, but of the average net income for the calendar years 1911, 1912, and 1913.

The final statute was a compromise, reached only after these two bases for taxation had been talked out. The House, and the Progressive critics in the Senate, maintained with reason that an excess-profits tax based upon average earnings in 1911–13 would leave untouched great businesses whose earnings in these years were already unreasonably high. The United States Steel Corporation and Henry Ford were cited, and re-cited. Many concerns like these were not earning in 1917 a higher rate upon their capitalization than they had earned in the three pre-war years, yet their ability to pay was notorious. The Senate majority, with equal reason, insisted that no flat rate of earning, such as five thousand dollars and eight per cent, had logical validity in a tax whose intent was to seize for the Government a part of the excess earnings due to war. No two corporations or individuals earned at the same rate. What would mean prosperity for one might mean poverty for another. The Senate clung to its idea that the only way to measure war excess profits was to measure them against the average earnings shown upon the books in time of peace.

If Senate and House had continued to cling each to its doctrine of war taxation, there could not have been a revenue bill. The conferees, who received the measure after the Senate had rewritten the House provisions and passsed its bill September 10, knew they must find a middle course and compromise. There is little evidence that any of them liked the compromise forced upon the committee and upon the two houses by this necessity. The final law continued the normal two per cent upon net income of corporations and added to this four per cent more similarly assessed. In addition also, a new name was coined out of the discussions: 'war excess-profits taxes.' These were levied at rates running from twenty to sixty per cent. The lower rate was applied when net income did not exceed fifteen per cent upon invested capital; the higher was reached when it exceeded thirty-three per cent. In computing the 'war excess-profits taxes' deductions were allowed, taking into account the profits of the three pre-war years, before assessing the appropriate rate upon the surplus of net income. Business did not know what the new law meant. The Treasury could not be certain. However, a squad of experienced financiers, economists, and business men were hurried into the Treasury as 'excess-profits tax advisers' to draft the forms and regulations, to comfort uneasy industry, and to counsel with the Treasury upon its duty under the law.

The dissenters dissented in part because the high surtaxes were not high enough. None went so far as La Follette in drafting a complete new law, but they filled the *Congressional Record* with tables showing how large incomes would fare under one rate or another and where inequalities in the incidence of the tax would pinch. In the same spirit they entered the debate upon the clauses of the revenue act in which the individual income tax was stepped up to the new necessity.

A vain belief that large incomes were large enough to carry all emergency expenses leaving small folk untouched played its part in income-tax discussions. This belief was to grow in popularity through two decades after the war and was to become a fiscal reliance of financial demagogues. The danger of impoverishing the poor and destroying their willingness to persist in the war was played up as a reason against lowering the minimum net income upon which taxation should begin to operate. The implicit wickedness of large incomes was hinted at — when it was not openly charged — and was made a justification for rates in the higher brackets that should be punitive rather than fiscal. The House finally agreed to lower the minimum from $3000 (in the case of an unmarried person) to $1000 and to leave the normal rate where the act of 1916 had fixed it, at two per cent. But the surtaxes were increased. The act of 1916 had imposed surtaxes advancing from one per cent upon incomes above $20,000 to thirteen per cent on those above $2,000,000. To these were now added new levies, beginning with one per cent on incomes above $5000 and rising to fifty per cent on those above $2,000,000; so that now, in addition to the normal two per cent collected from all taxable incomes, the maximum incomes were required to pay sixty-three per cent into the Treasury.

Whether the rates were too high or too low was beyond proof, but not beyond impassioned argument. They at least set new levels of responsibility upon the citizen and produced revenues that made new records. The Government did not run out of money. Before the revenue act was signed, congressmen were announcing where and how the rates should again be raised. The next session kept revision under running fire, but no new law was passed until February 24, 1919. And when the books were balanced in the summer of 1920 a greater share of war costs had been raised by taxes in three years of war condition than the world had seen before.

VIII. WAR AIMS

The Revenue Bill came into the House in May, supported by a
unanimous Committee on Ways and Means. When it reached the
Senate the unanimity was gone. The favorable report of the
Finance Committee was trailed by a minority report whose signers
fought stubbornly for a different kind of act until they were at last
overridden. While the law was under consideration the aims of the
war thrust themselves into the debate and demands were made
that, as a condition precedent to taxes and appropriations, there
be a clarification of objectives.

Russia raised the question. The first provisional government,
formed in March upon the deposition of the Czar, was of a mind to
continue in the war and to respect the obligations of the secret
treaties as well as to claim their benefits. There was nothing novel
in secret treaties; they were a part of the ordinary implementation
of war. The United States was party to one with England at the
close of the Revolution when the American peace commissioners
deserted the French allies and made a secret treaty containing a
still more secret proviso. The Russian provisional government was
dislodged in May as the mind of the people shifted leftward, and its
successor came to power on a pledge to promote a peace based on
the self-determination of peoples and without annexations or contributions. The manifesto declaring this intent harmonized with
the American desire for a peace that would last, but it embarrassed
the chancery of every nation that either hoped to make conquests
or had made contracts assuming them. Lord Cecil avowed in
Commons that Britain had no imperialistic purpose and desired
only a secure future. The Hearst papers, opposed to entering the
war, immediately demanded that Congress state the aims of the
United States.

Germany took up the cry for terms. The Reichstag resolutions of July 19 supported the Russian demand at a moment when Kerensky barely escaped being overthrown by the embattled Bolsheviki. The text of the resolutions harmonized well enough with the desires of the German Socialists and Liberals, whose coalition put them through the Reichstag, but it was hard to believe that the Imperial Government, allowing the document to pass the censors, accepted its philosophy. It was more reasonable to suppose that trickery in the world of ideals was being used as a war weapon. Yet the language was such as must be welcome to those who wanted to believe that aims of conquest had been abandoned.

The Vatican urged that the war be ended. On August 1 Benedict XV circularized the 'leaders of the belligerent peoples.' The Pope had been Cardinal-Archbishop of Bologna when the war broke out, and was enthroned by his Conclave after the death of Pius X, just as the French Government slipped away from Paris to Bordeaux. He disclaimed 'particular aim' and suggested a basis for a 'just and durable peace.' But before the Papal circular was published on August 16, La Follette had issued a manifesto of his own, asking the Senate to accept a concurrent resolution (which would not require the signature of the President). In his resolution La Follette recited the various hints of a possible peace, reminded his colleagues that these bespoke 'a willingness to adopt the doctrine of "a peace without victory," proclaimed by President Wilson on the 22nd day of January, 1917,' and asserted that Congress had the 'authority to determine and to declare definitely' the objects and purposes of American participation. He wanted Congress to announce that the United States would not aid in any prolongation of the war 'to annex new territory' or to 'enforce the payment of indemnities to recover the expenses of the war' for any of the belligerents. He urged also a 'public restatement of the allied peace terms.'

The La Follette concurrent resolution was allowed to die on the table. A few minutes after its introduction, the Senate took up the revenue bill, which was to have priority for the next month. It was unavoidable that the Senate discussions should embrace both the method of taxation and the motive for it and that those who disliked the former should be the more insistent on being assured upon the latter. Senators, like their constituents, read the papers; and like them, also, they interpreted what was printed in accordance with their hopes. Out-of-doors, the peace feelers were the subject of wide examination. No Government, in the United States or elsewhere, could completely ignore the deep popular hope that the war would stop. So deep was the hope, and so widely was it held, that many who examined the proposals were content to accept the words as uttered, to assume that they fairly represented intentions, and to decide that the war had been won, leaving now only the incorporation of the generous sentiments in a general treaty of peace.

The words of the proposals certainly contained lip service to the doctrine of 'peace without victory.' So far as Russia was concerned it was soon certain that the manifesto of May, not fairly representing the desire of the provisional government, was a price paid by it for support by the councils of soldiers and workers; and that these councils, not permanently content with either the compromise or the leaders in power, were swinging into line behind a revolutionary socialism that disavowed patriotism in the ordinary sense and aimed at a class dictatorship beginning in Russia and extending to the world.

The German endorsement was soon subject to interpretation in the light of German behavior in the treaty negotiations of Brest-Litovsk. It was not in harmony with the quotable parts of German official utterances made since 1914. Unless one could believe that the Empire had experienced a change of heart — which called for a powerful will to believe — it was impossible to see in the Reichstag resolutions much more than a trick, clumsily designed to deceive those whose hope for peace was stronger than their power of discrimination. Those who directed official thought among the Allies insisted that Germany had provoked the war as a deliberate stroke of policy and that the establishment of a German hegemony in Europe was the motive behind it. Obviously since 1914, German opinion had dwelt more and more upon the compensations the Empire was to obtain by conquest and the punishment it was to inflict upon its enemies. The German advance across the Balkans and into Asia Minor was no mere matter of self-defense. Conquest was the object now, whatever had been in the German mind when the war began. Those who believed in German sincerity were regarded as pro-Germans or pacifists and in either capacity as unworthy of trust.

War for its own sake had no party in the United States. Peace had so strong a party that if the proposals were to be disregarded it was necessary that the reasons be explained so that Americans could understand them.

It is impossible, in matters of the mind, for the historian to prove the connection between what is heard and what is thought. It is not often possible to determine what it is that an individual or a group regards as its own best interests, and even with best interests determined the causal relations between interest and action are no more than conjectural. The best the historian can do is to present such a circumstantial case as the facts and events appear to warrant, and judgments upon motivation must remain matters of probability rather than of proof. In spite of the economic determinists the most interesting thing about man is his capacity to ignore what all prudent thought would guess to be his own best interest, and to risk his life, his family, and his nation for no better reason than the grip of an ideal.

Ideal and interest were both imbedded in the utterances of Wilson, and the steps by which opinion in the United States was built up to the near unanimity for war prevailing in the spring are best to be traced in these utterances. He had at least a reasoned doctrine. How well reasoned it was, and how long it had been germinating in his mind, have been abundantly documented in *The Origins of the Foreign Policy of Woodrow Wilson* (1937), in which Harley Notter, one of the few to know the Wilson papers, has analyzed their content. He had, too, the audience. More people, more of the time, in more countries, listened to him with approval through the nineteen months of American participation in the war than listened to any other leader.

He had seen neutrality through to its end. It is still conceivable
that there is no better course for a neutral nation than neutrality,
although it has been demonstrated that if this be not a submissive
neutrality its logical end is war. Acute critics of American neutrality in 1914–17 as at heart unneutral, Edwin Borchard and William
P. Lage, have in *Neutrality for the United States* (1937) developed the
thesis that anything but a stern neutrality is in fact an intervention
friendly to one side or the other. They have shown how hard it is
for Government to dissociate its corporate attitude from the
mental status of its people or its administrators. Yet Wilson's
neutrality, whatever its defects, was so distasteful to both sets of
belligerents as to invite for itself high credit for sincerity.

Wilson had at last accepted war only as an evil less disastrous
than submission. His mind was set to a world of peace and of equal
rights that had seemed to be ripening in the nineteenth century,
only to wither in the twentieth. The two chief aspects of the
dialectic upon which peace had advanced had been the use of
arbitration as a measure in avoidance of war and the insistence by
neutrals upon the enjoyment of normal rights even in time of war.
War itself was a blow to all measures short of war. Belligerent
encroachment upon neutral right was a menace to neutral interest
which, if submitted to, would in a few years destroy the gains of a
century of protest. Wilson went to war, among other things, to
defend his right to stay out of war.

More than this, the President had to fear what the military in-
dices indicated as probable, a victory by the Central Powers and a
post-war militant attitude by the conqueror. Irritated though the
United States was by the excesses of the Allies, there was no wide
fear that the safety of the rest of the world would be endangered
if they won. But the Pan-German extremists talked a doctrine
calculated to encourage suspicion that Germany sought world
domination. As a consequence, the forecast of the future contained for the United States the shadow of still more pressure to be
endured or as an alternative to endurance a fully armed existence.
Within a lifetime the Continental countries had been driven by
their fears to continuous preparation for war and to compulsory

military training for their men in time of peace. The United States revolted at the thought of similar readiness. Paradoxically again, Wilson accepted compulsory selective service in order to defend the privilege of the United States to avoid compulsory service.

It was the easy route of declamation to declare that the United States fought for absolute principles of justice; these were indeed the principles without whose general acceptance by the world the United States could not live the life it wished to live in safety. But behind this abstraction lay the concrete matters of self-defense and national interest that no government may ignore in a world of competitive nations.

The first steps in the formulation of an American doctrine of war aims were taken in the 'peace without victory' speech; but the last steps could not be taken until the war was over, whether the peace should be shaped by the cravings of the victor or not. Successful war was the only way to procure a peace without a master. No public statements more deftly or more soundly assembled the evidence to this than did those of the President. It became his business to prove the obligation upon the United States to defend its kind of existence. The war message of April 2 and the elaboration of it on Flag Day became the common divisor for most American minds. The addresses were weak in historicity where they stressed his belief that Germany had in cold blood provoked the war. But they were strong in realism where they displayed the dangers to the United States from war or from threats of recurrent war.

Whatever other reasons there were for American entry, whatever war-wickedness on the part of munitions-makers who were also making money, whatever solicitude of bankers to save investments, whatever skillful chicanery by the Allies to hypnotize the American Government — all these were minor to the reasons detailed by Woodrow Wilson and accepted with overwhelming concurrence by his people. The consequences of staying out looked to be more deadly than those of going in; and there was room to hope for a better world after peace.

The official copy of the letter of the Pope came to Washington in August by way of London. This was at the request of Cardinal Gasparri, Papal Secretary of State, because the Vatican did not maintain diplomatic relations with the United States. The circular opened with an affirmation of the pacific mission of the Church, its affection for all peoples, and its impartiality toward all belligerents. Citing now the fear of the Church that the civilized world become 'nothing more than a field of death,' it made what it described as 'a concrete and practical proposal' for a 'just and durable peace.' First, was a demand for disarmament, the substitution of arbitration for war, and the establishment of 'true liberty and community of the seas.' It saw no solution for the question of indemnities other than the general principle of 'complete and reciprocal condonation.' Belgium, next, was to be evacuated and to receive guaranty of complete independence. Occupied France, also, was to be evacuated, as well as the German colonies seized by the Allies. The territorial questions of Italy and Austria, of Poland, the Balkans, and Armenia, were to be examined in a 'spirit of equity and justice.' And upon these bases 'the future reorganization of the peoples ought to be built.' 'The whole world recognizes that the honor of the armies of both sides is safe,' said the Pope. 'Incline your ears, therefore, to our prayer.'

For several days before the note was published, it was known in private to the Governments and, according to their respective interests, some feared that Wilson would fail to answer it, others that he would answer it. That it should be answered by any of the Allies was out of the question because the fifteenth article of the Treaty of London, whereby Italy joined the Allies in 1915, contained the specific promise that Great Britain, France, and Russia would 'support such opposition as Italy may make to any proposal in the direction of introducing a representative of the Holy See in any peace negotiations.' It was Italian conviction that the Vatican was an affiliate of Austria.

The immediate disposition of the President, not an Ally or tied by any pact, was to be curt, to give the appeal a mere acknowledgment, and to proceed with the affairs of war administration.

The Allies would have preferred such response (unless they had themselves been permitted to draft the answer), for their leaders were becoming sensitive lest Wilson gain in his growing status as spokesman for their own constituents, and fearful lest he should express a liberalism inconvenient for them to accept. But the Senate had begun to discuss war aims, making it desirable for Wilson to maintain his grip on the American doctrine; and Colonel House pointed out the opportunity to do more wedge work and, by stating the reasons for rejecting the appeal, to strengthen the German Liberals and spread the gap between the enemy peoples and their Governments. The only way to avoid, if it could be avoided, a controversy among the Allies over national ambitions was to build up a picture of the future that should outrank national aspiration in its attractiveness and universal appeal. 'Utopia,' Owen had said in the Senate, 'is better than hell.' 'We are now,' said Lodge after Wilson had transmitted his reply, 'in a war that is purely idealistic.'

The *Official Bulletin* carried the reply August 29, two days after Robert Lansing had signed and transmitted it. House had seen it in draft, had approved it, and had advised an action the President took in substituting 'inexpedient' for 'childish' where he referred to the 'punitive damages, the dismemberment of empires, the establishment of selfish and exclusive economic leagues' that had been suggested among the Allies. The Rathenau plan, so to conduct the war as to delay the revival of Belgium as an economic competitor of Germany, had been matched in an economic conference of the Allies in 1916 by a plan to secure their economic independence of Germany after the war. The word 'childish' appeared to House to be needlessly provocative. He had under his eye, as he suggested the amendment, a note from Jusserand indicating that to France the Vatican appeal was of 'Austro-Germanic inspiration,' and was no more than 'the German note of December last, in a new garb.'

Touched by the appeal of His Holiness for a 'stable and enduring peace,' the President made Lansing say: 'This agony must not be gone through with again.' He noted that the Papal basis of con-

donation would throw the world back to the *status quo ante*, from
which he believed had come the deliberate German attack.
'The object of this war,' he said, 'is to deliver the free peoples of the
world from the menace and the actual power of a vast military
establishment controlled by an irresponsible government.' Not
the 'German people' but the 'ruthless master of the German people'
was the enemy who must not be permitted by the peace of the
Pope to rebuild his strength. He saw, and he spoke for 'responsible
statesmen' as though they admitted him to be their spokesman,
that no peace could rest securely on vindictive restrictions; for the
United States he desired 'no reprisal upon the German people';
peace must be based upon the equal rights of peoples — 'great or
small, weak or powerful' — and the test of peace must be whether
it was based 'upon the word of an ambitious and intriguing
government,' or upon that of free peoples. 'We cannot take the
word of the present rulers of Germany as a guarantee of anything
that is to endure,' he concluded; if peace were now made with the
German Government, 'no man, no nation' could depend on it.
He awaited 'some new evidence of the purposes of the great peoples of the Central Powers.'

This evidence was slow to come; but evidence came promptly
that Wilson's reply had kept his car of doctrine on the track. The
Senate proponents of immediate negotiation could not be kept
from talking, but they talked to empty benches. The People's
Council was shunted from town to town around the Middle West,
with labor's American Alliance upon its heels. Any expression
of opinion that peace was within reach was generally taken as near-
treason or pro-Germanism. Villard noted the wedge work and
his *Nation* detected some measure of success for it: 'President
Wilson put his faith in this liberal Germany when he wrote his
recent answer to the Pope.' The London *Spectator* read it with
interest, and then with admiration: 'A second and longer perusal
of the answer of the United States has shown the document to be
not merely worthy of a great statesman and a great nation, but
one of the most momentous utterances in the History of Mankind.'
But the hard-boiled London *Saturday Review* was annoyed. It was

soon to snap out: 'Instead of twaddling about democracy, if Messrs. Wilson and George would talk the only universal language, viz., £.s.d., the Germans would respond immediately.' It noted ruefully, in the face of Wilson's disclaimer of punitive damages, dismemberment, and economic boycott: 'But these negations bar the war aims of England, France, and Italy, as up to date they have been promulgated by statesmen.'

It was well enough to thrust aside the suggestion that Russia and Germany had between them put forward a sufficient reason for an immediate conference on terms of peace. There had been good reason, too, for the decision reached by the President while the War Missions were in Washington in May. He had then let the aims of the war pass without argument lest, if they were injected into the discussion of the form of American aid, the latter might be disastrously postponed while the aims caused deadlock. From the minute the Missions landed, House advised him 'to avoid a discussion of peace settlements.' Out of his travels as friend of the President in the past four years Colonel House had built up a more extensive acquaintance with practicing statesmen in Europe than any other American possessed. They trusted him; sounded him before they entered the White House; appraised with him their interviews there after they were over. 'If the Allies begin to discuss terms among themselves, they will soon hate one another worse than they hate Germany,' he wrote the President; and he argued out the wisdom of his recommendation with Balfour, discussing with him in private the treaties existing among 'the Allies as to the division of the spoils after the war.' Those who knew anything about the network of secret treaties, whose details the Bolsheviki smeared over the world after the final revolution in November, knew enough to realize the contentious nature of the issue they would some day raise. The United States had even less than an interest in the territorial promises of the treaties; it had a positive aversion to them.

The issue presented by the agreements must be faced. Wilson was emphatic in rejecting the Papal suggestion of an immediate negotiation, yet his mind opened to the importance of preparing for an informed discussion when the time should be ripe. At the end of September, House admitted (and the Department of State confirmed) that the President had asked him to arrange the data that ought to be ready for the peace commissioners when the war should end.

No facts give an unhappier picture of the inadequacy of the foreign service of the United States, a foreign service kept starved by Congress with the approval of the constituents it served, than the facts connected with the organization and work of what was soon informally known as the 'House Inquiry.' The Inquiry had no other name. It was supported by Wilson out of the President's fund. It recruited its workers among journalists and professors. House entrusted its administration to his brother-in-law, Sidney E. Mezes, president of the College of the City of New York, who passed its executive management to Isaiah Bowman, director of the American Geographical Society, in whose New York building its headquarters were housed. Walter Lippmann, who had been doing odd jobs for Baker, and in whose mind was the approach to the world prevailing in the offices of the *New Republic*, became its secretary. Justice Brandeis seems to have breathed doctrine into its ears. Shotwell of Columbia and Haskins of Harvard were right-hand men. And the American specialists in history, geography, economics, and government plunged into the task of doing under pressure what ought already to have been done, digested, and docketed in the files of the Department of State. They reviewed the history of the European and Asiatic world, for nearly every rivalry of the war dated back to the Middle Ages, if not to Rome and Greece. As the Socialist *Call* said, House was 'to prepare a "who's who and what's what" for the use of the American Government.' Lansing made no public protest against this encroachment upon the proper business of his department. It was insisted that the Inquiry had no connection with the notion of immediate peace negotiations, but even though the mere existence of the organization should suggest more than was intended, the study needed to be made, and at once. It began to be gossiped in Washington that the President would himself go to the peace conference when it should be held.

There were, however, many things to be done in the realm of ideas before a peace conference could be more than a dream. The machinery that was to produce an army was in motion and the men who were to constitute it were in camp, although there was no known way of getting them to France. The reorganization of life, industry, and government for the purpose of supporting the army was beginning to produce results. The sinews of war were in sight and were to be adequate. But there was no compulsion behind it all in the United States except the general conviction that the war must be ended in victory before the abolition of war could be undertaken. That conviction needed to be kept firm and unified. Page was quoting Balfour's fear that 'the American energy and earnestness in getting into the war,' might 'cool with the first wave of war-weariness.' Only the President could give the cue to policy or rationalize it.

Before the House Inquiry had got beyond listing the names of men who might be set to work, Wilson added another unit to the structure he was erecting. He had stayed close to his desk in the White House through the spring and summer, since he was busy and his advisers were not anxious for him to incur the risks of unnecessary travel. But in November, after a Tammany mayor, John F. Hylan, had with the support of Hearst been elected in New York, he slipped quietly out of Washington to Buffalo. There he stated the American case to the American Federation of Labor assembled in its thirty-seventh annual convention.

Samuel Gompers was both the figure head of labor in the United States and the actual head of the most important organization of American workmen. He had presided over the American Federation during all but one year of its existence without weakening in his conviction that American labor desired economic rather than political objectives. Labor radicals, who hoped to shift the movement into partisan politics, had short shrift with him between conventions and at the annual gatherings he defeated their motions on the floor. He came with labor into support of the war, although there is no evidence that it needed to be 'brought,' for the workers were as American as any other citizens. Gompers worked out the formulation of the understanding that the Government would keep labor from becoming victim to the war. Behind his leadership the unions accepted as war duty the admission of women apprentices and non-union workers to the shops. What was called 'dilution' advanced under war conditions more rapidly than could otherwise have been the case without war. The trend toward industrial mechanization, obscured though it was by war, was already threatening the integrity of the craft unions. Mechanized factories, with a few skilled workmen in charge and a horde of unskilled, were easily set up for war work.

Gompers did not live to see the open battle in labor ranks between the two union points of view, but the advance skirmishes in their engagement helped to complicate the status of labor in the war. The persistent nagging of Socialist-Labor minorities added to the complications, for some of these were pro-German or pro-Russian, and others looked as though they were. But the status of unions and the workers was most threatened by the rising cost of living which by gradual encroachment nibbled at real wages.

Labor adjustment, necessary if labor was to be protected, raised complicated problems. There were Government factories, factories on Government contract work, and establishments of private industry. What touched one tended to touch all, for all drew their labor from the same reservoir of manhood. It was possible in the first two classes to raise wages as required, either to do justice or to satisfy demands, and to add the cost to the war budget. The cost-plus contracts, such as prevailed in camp construction, made this a simple matter, eliminating employer-objection to increases in the wage scale. But every shift in the wage scale for Government work brought trouble to private business and made the whole labor market uneasy. The disposition on the part of much of the public to regard all labor controversy as traitorous made it worse. The pledge to look after labor had to be implemented.

Bisbee, Arizona, became an inconvenient object lesson in July. Here the I.W.W. was at work in the company towns of the Calumet, Arizona, and Copper Queen mines, whose annual output of some seventeen million pounds of copper was an essential part of the war supply. Wherever the I.W.W. made trouble it was likely to be worse trouble than that of ordinary labor controversy because the I.W.W. even in time of peace was regarded as revolutionary in its objective. Wherever strife broke out in company towns, whether in the anthracite counties of Pennsylvania, or those of the precious metals in the Coeur d'Alene, or here in the copper camps of Arizona, the trouble was worse than normal, since in company towns there was no group of neutral citizens to mediate and act as buffer between contending forces. In the absence of a neutral population labor strife often comes close to civil war. The Bisbee strike was called on June 26, and two weeks later the owners brought about a measure of peace by a forcible deportation of 1186 men. In similar manner Moyer and Haywood of the Western Federation of Miners had in 1906 been kidnaped in Colorado and carried into the jurisdiction of the Idaho courts.

Interned at Columbus, New Mexico, the I.W.W. was a festering spot regardless of the merit of the labor claim. The strike dragged on until in August the Council of National Defense began to think out devices. It announced the creation of its own Labor Adjustment Commission to look after disputes arising under the Federal eight-hour day law, and urged the President to send special missions to terminate such disputes as that at Bisbee. Baker, for the War Department, created a Board of Control of Labor Standards for Army Clothing, to keep clothing from the sweatshops, to remove the causes of strife, and to ensure a continuous flow of goods. Shipyard labor was entrusted to a joint commission representing the Navy, the Emergency Fleet, and the American Federation, headed by V. Everit Macy, president of the National Civic Federation, with Assistant-Secretary Franklin D. Roosevelt sitting for the Navy. The President sent the Secretary of Labor to Bisbee in person. He went at the head of a President's Mediating Commission, whose secretary was Felix Frankfurter, and which brought peace to Bisbee before winter came. In its report to Wilson the Frankfurter Commission dealt sympathetically with the problems of war labor. In January, 1918, it recommended that he set up a 'unified direction of the labor administration of the United States for the period of the war.'

The state of mind of labor was a fundamental charge upon the President, not only because it bore upon the continuous flow of goods from the factories, but also because the American workman preferred status as a citizen to status in an economic class. It was wholesome for democracy that he should continue to prefer it. In both Ally and enemy countries labor was showing a war weariness, strengthening thereby the labor parties and giving an opening to the penetration of revolutionary socialism from Russia. There were two issues before the world: that between the nations, with an alliance endeavoring to prevent domination by a military government, and that between classes, with Russia at the spearhead driving the purpose of an international socialist revolution. Upon those who rejected the latter it was mandatory to convince labor that its interest was tied into the former. Wilson was one of these. Baker, in unity with him, urged him to go to Buffalo: 'I have found labor more willing to keep step than capital,' Baker wrote on November 10.

That same evening it was announced that Wilson would address the Federation. He left Washington the next day, and on Monday, November 12, made his appearance in Buffalo. The visitation was timely, for the papers over the week-end were still wrestling with the interpretation of what had just happened in Petrograd. There, the Navy had joined forces with the Maximilists (who wanted all reforms at once) in the great Bolshevik Revolution. How great it was, was still in doubt. Without entirely believing it, editors ran the story from Kerensky that Russia was still in the war; but few of them would have dared to imagine how completely Russia was lost as an Ally, or how fundamentally the Russian Revolution would shake the world. Trotsky and Lenin had come into their own.

'I want peace, but I know how to get it, and they do not,' said the President, speaking of the pacifist agitators, as he addressed the American Federation on Monday morning. He recited what had become the official story of the origins of the war, and then moved to firmer ground as he described the Pan-German objectives — 'absolute control of Austria-Hungary, practical control of the Balkan States, control of Turkey, control of Asia Minor'—and expressed his revulsion against that 'bulk of German power inserted into the heart of the world.' He thrust aside the idea that peace was near. 'What I am opposed to is not the feeling of the pacifists, but their stupidity. My heart is with them, but my mind had a contempt for them.' What must be done, he said, was to stand together 'until the job is finished,' to make and keep labor free and to keep production uninterrupted. He inquired who could believe 'that any reforms planned in the interest of the people can live in the presence of a Germany powerful enough to undermine or overthrow them by intrigue or force.' He made occasion to cast another hook into the labor interest as he referred to mobs that at Bisbee and elsewhere took law into their own hands. He entered a protest 'against any manifestation of the spirit of lawlessness anywhere or in any cause,' and hurried back to Washington leaving the American Federation to re-elect Gompers, to resolve against strikes on Government jobs, and to continue the part it was playing on the American single front.

Distrust of the adequacy of the basis of peace proposed by the Vatican, and distrust of the honesty of the enemy when talking peace, were enough to justify the rejection of a negotiation then and there. But distrust provided no positive material out of which to build the skeleton of a peace. The time was sure to come when such a skeleton would be required. The world had moved since the end of the preceding January when von Bernstorff had handed to House his confidential memorandum stating the terms Germany would have demanded had its request for a conference, made in December, 1916, been received with favor.

The Vatican terms of condonation, with the evacuation of Belgium and the release of the occupied *départements* of northern France, would have been unacceptable to the Empire in January, 1917, for Germany was then thinking of a peace with victory. The Bernstorff memorandum mentioned special guaranties and compensations before Germany would consider giving up Belgium or returning French territory; it asked for a 'safe' frontier, behind which Germany and Poland might be 'economically and strategically' protected against Russia. It demanded colonies, not only the return of those occupied by the Allies, but colonies enough to be 'adequate to her population and economic interest'; and it wanted also for German business and German subjects compensation for their suffering during the war. Far from revealing the conviction of sin and the repentance that Allied thought demanded as a condition precedent to negotiation, the German memorandum was written in a feeling of just deserts and military success. The gap between the German program and peace without victory was too wide to be bridged by any negotiation. It became wider with the collapse of Russia, the German victories of 1917 along the Eastern Front, and the failure of 'Allied effort to break the Western lines.

Yet rumor had it that Austria-Hungary was tired enough to quit. When Congress met after the autumn recess for the winter session of 1917–18, it gave to the principal ally of Germany additional reason for quitting by declaring war against the 'Imperial and Royal Austro-Hungarian Government.' Wilson had advised against a declaration aimed at Austria-Hungary in April. But now, in his annual address, he asked that such a declaration be adopted. He was not ready to take the same logical action against the other allies of Germany, Turkey and Bulgaria; they were 'also the tools of Germany,' he said, but they were 'mere tools' and not 'in the direct path of our necessary action.' It was embarrassing to be at war with Germany and at peace with Austria-Hungary, for both were fighting along the fronts where some day the A.E.F. would begin to operate. The embarrassment had increased within the weeks immediately previous to the message, as Germany had injected its own divisions among the tired Austrian units, and with new leadership had made possible a drive down the passes of the Alps, around the head of the Adriatic, and almost up to the lines of Venice. Logic and fact forbade further treatment of the Dual Monarchy as a friend.

The Government of Austria-Hungary, Wilson conceded, 'is not

acting upon its own initiative or in response to the wishes and feelings of its own peoples'; but since it had become simply the 'vassal of the German Government' we must 'face the facts as they are and act upon them without sentiment.' Congress responded immediately with a declaration of war that the President signed December 7, 1917.

It had been eight months since Wilson last spoke to Congress, face to face. After his address of April 2 he did not again visit it in person until in December he summed up the progress of the summer and began to be more specific upon the requirements of a peace than had been appropriate at earlier dates.

When in 1916 he gave his adherence to the doctrine upon which the League to Enforce Peace had been founded a year earlier, he endorsed the fundamental idea of his foreign policy of the war, for in his mind the only alternative to self-help and the continuance of war was some sort of league with power to do justice. He took a league for granted now as he had taken it for granted in the January address. His chroniclers, too, took it for granted. Working on *The Foreign Policy of Woodrow Wilson, 1913–1917* (1917), which they had ready for the public at the end of the year, Edgar E. Robinson and Victor J. West found that his papers revealed an articulated structure on the foundations of neutral doctrine and super-league. When the *New York Times* reviewed the book, January 6, 1918, it noted the harmony of the doctrine with the American past, the completeness of it, and the skill with which Wilson the teacher had built up the following of Wilson the politician. Wilson was now taking the difficult step from broad generalization to specific formula. He was catching 'the voices of humanity that are in the air,' as they became articulate in insisting that the peace should not be based on annexations, contributions, or vindictive indemnities. The present task was to 'win the war,' but it would not be won until the German people 'through properly accredited representatives' should right the wrongs 'their rulers have done.'

The President agreed with the Pope that in a fair peace the peoples and land of Belgium and northern France must be delivered from conquest and menace. The peoples of Austria-Hun-

gary, too, and those of the Balkans and Turkey must be delivered
'from the impudent and alien domination of the Prussian military
and commerical autocracy.' But he repelled, as 'grossly and
wantonly false,' the idea that the existence of Germany was at
stake. The worst that could happen to it, in spite of what its leaders
said to scare its people, was a temporary exclusion from the partnership of nations and from the free intercourse that would grow
from that partnership if the German people 'should still, after the
war is over, continue to be obliged to live under ambitious and
intriguing masters.' Here was a clear invitation to the German
people to overthrow the Government of the Empire for the sake of
peace. This was the object of the wedge.

The same forces that brought Wilson from the generalities of
international philosophy down to practical conditions to be attained were playing upon all the statesmen of the war in the
autumn of 1917. In England, only a week before Congress met,
Lord Lansdowne had said his say. In a letter that the London
Daily Telegraph printed on November 29, after the *Times* had
declined it space, this veteran statesman, who had retired from
the Government only with Asquith in 1916, risked his repute to
counsel his people to a negotiated peace. He was afraid that in
crushing Germany with the thoroughness promised by Lloyd
George, the Allies would crush the world. He was willing to do
one thing that Wilson did not make specific in the message: to
consider the matters involved in the freedom of the seas.

The Lansdowne letter was a straw in a gusty wind that might
develop disruptive power. Within a few days the British ministers
were trying to harness the wind and to undo the damage done to
solidarity by a responsible elder statesman talking peace. Clemenceau, who had no illusions, blurted out: 'My war aim is to conquer.'
But across the Channel the leaders were explaining to their audiences that the British aim was still no more imperialistic than it had
been in 1914, and that there could not be peace until after victory.
At Birmingham, Asquith, whose Government had made the
decision for war, defended the decision, defended its necessity,
thought much of the criticism of Lansdowne unfair, but deplored

the letter. Bonar Law condemned its author immediately at a Unionist meeting. Lloyd George embedded his comment in a speech at a dinner of the Gray's Inn Benchers, called a negotiated peace a farce, saw great danger in the Russian truce, and asked how confidence could be put in new treaties until those were vindicated whose violation caused the war.

Within a few days, too, the Bolshevik Government was in conversation with the Germans at Brest-Litovsk, railway center in Russian Poland which Germany had occupied in 1915. Here they were learning by experience how much of a peace without annexations or contributions could be obtained. From temporary cessation of fighting on parts of the Eastern Front, to truce, and from truce to general armistice on December 15, they progressed after they decided on a peace. On December 22 their plenipotentiaries, at a 'solemn sitting,' met the Germans to work it out. They found the Central Powers somewhat divided in their counsels; von Kuehlmann, civil head of the German mission, playing to the moderates, while General von Hoffmann talked the stern language of conquest; but they were not enough divided for the net result in German terms to be recognizable as a compliance with the Bolshevik proposals. One of the Administration Senators a little later played upon the fame of Luther Burbank as an 'assistant secretary to nature': the Germans at Brest-Litovsk, he said, had put him in the shade, for they were able 'to make a large crop of lemons grow on an olive branch.' A doctrine of 'voluntary separations' was devised by the Austro-German negotiators to save them from some of the odium of the dismemberment of Russia which they encompassed.

Poland, overrun in 1915, had already been declared autonomous by Germany in 1916. Finland, just east of whose border ran the Murmansk railway which Germany coveted, had defied Petrograd in July, 1917, and declared its independence. Lithuania and the Ukraine, breaking from Russia, were prepared to make separate treaties (which meant, substantially, annexation) with Germany. Having proclaimed the self-determination of peoples, Russia was caught in its own net. And as to the temper of the peace that the German envoys announced on Christmas Day, it was not misrepresented by the words put into the mouth of William II by an Amsterdam dispatch to the London *Times*: 'The year 1917, with its great battles, has proved that the German people has in the Lord of Creation above an unconditional and avowed ally, on whom it can unconditionally rely.' Leon Trotsky may have said (he was so reported) that the 'German and Austrian Governments have agreed to place themselves in the dock'; but if they had, it was not a dock of Russian making.

'The battle of opinions is in full swing,' wrote one of the correspondents from London as the Russian conversations opened. The battle had the effect of cutting through party lines with no one could tell how much injury to solidarity. Wilson had this in mind when he summarized the aims of the United States to Congress on December 4; House, sitting in Paris with the Allied Conference, tried in vain to procure from the conferees an authoritative statement of aims to close the breach, but he could get nothing that the United States could be expected to endorse. He was back in Washington by December 15, and was at once in conference, persuading the President that only he could command attention or state the case. The Inquiry, still in its swaddling clothes, was called upon to aid in 'remaking the map of the world, as we would have it'; and in a fortnight, helped by the measured data the Inquiry had assembled, the President completed the task.

While all this was progressing in secrecy — a secrecy so secret that the Washington correspondents were writing home that Wilson's utterances of August 27 and December 4 were so comprehensive as to make additional American statements unnecessary — more voices were raised in the 'battle of opinions.' British labor spoke, indicating two things: that it was prepared to fight off war weariness if satisfied as to the aims of the war, and that its ideas concerning war aims were so close to those of President Wilson as to be almost indistinguishable from them.

Arthur Henderson, a Newcastle molder in his early years, bore to British labor somewhat the relationship that Gompers bore to labor in the United States. Henderson was, however, a labor politician rather than an abstainer from politics, and after the arrival of the Labor Party in Commons he was consistently a leader. Not as much of a pacifist as Ramsay MacDonald, he succeeded the latter as the head of the party in 1914 and in 1915 Asquith took him into the Ministry. He looked after labor and its co-operation in the war, surviving the shake-up of 1916 to become one of the little War Cabinet under Lloyd George. His duties took him to Russia after the March Revolution. Here he was impressed by the mutual misunderstandings of new Russia and the Allies and grew to the conviction that the Allies ought to co-operate in the Stockholm Conference of Socialists rather than permit it to fall into German hands. He told this to his British labor associates so effectively at a conference August 10, that he was out of the Cabinet August 11. British opinion was not ready to let British subjects talk with Germans. Out of office, he and the labor group re-aligned their ideas in the light of the various peace suggestions. They began at once the drafting of a labor manifesto, continuing its revision as new proposals came to light and as American leadership began to assert itself.

The resolutions of the American Alliance of Labor and Democracy, based on the doctrine of the reply to the Pope, blazed the way. The address of the President at Buffalo carried it farther. The message to Congress continued its development, until the British labor leaders were ready to submit to a national labor conference called by the parliamentary committee of the trade-union conference the reasons why they should stand by the war rather than accept the Russian leadership, heading into a peace at Brest-Litovsk. Lloyd George regarded the conference as so important as to require a letter emphasizing his position that victory must precede peace, and that the precise terms of a peace must be based upon concurrence among the Allies. 'The Labour Party have from the beginning kept the country to the best of its war aims,' said the London *Nation* a week later. The war aims manifesto adopted in Central Hall, Westminster, on December 28, showed Henderson in its drafting and Wilson in its paternity.

The British Prime Minister, as sensitive to currents of opinion

among his constituents as any politician could be, sensed the aims
of labor and dared not disregard them if he would. Having put
Henderson out of the War Cabinet in August, he now danced to
the tune of labor, with Henderson as leader. He seized the occasion created by a man-power conference with labor on January 5
to harmonize his aims as Prime Minister with those expressed in
the Labor Manifesto. It was as obvious to Lloyd George as to
Woodrow Wilson that there could not be victory unless the aims of
the war could be translated into terms acceptable to the great
masses of working people who did most of the suffering, most of the
dying, and most of the voting in democratic countries. Balfour,
too, and Wilson were alike in understanding this and in appreciat-
ing the need for team-work in such statements as might be made.
They differed chiefly in that Balfour hoped Wilson would stick to
'the lines of the President's previous speeches,' while Wilson hoped
that no British utterance would 'sound a different note or suggest
claims inconsistent with what he proclaims the objects of the
United States to be.' Without detailed knowledge of each other's
doings, Lloyd George said to labor very much what, on the same
day, Wilson was preparing to say as he digested the advice of House
and the memoranda of the Inquiry. This was a Saturday. On
Sunday the President completed his draft. On Monday he
showed it to Lansing for 'verbal corrections.' And on Tuesday
morning he took it to Congress 'at an hour's notice.'

The testimony assembled by Professor Seymour out of House's
diary indicates a more serious than usual preparation of the address, but does not suggest foreknowledge or indeed fore-hunch
that the document in hand was to shake the world. To declare
the general aims of democracy in the war had been a simpler and a
safer matter than it was now to set up heads of business for the
readjustment of the balance of nations and the correction of the
map. But if Wilson regarded this address as of much greater
significance than that of his previous speeches, the evidence does
not as yet display it.

The President reminded Congress as the excuse for his unexpected visit that the Central Powers at Brest-Litovsk had pro-

fessed an interest in a general peace while announcing the terms
upon which they were ready to enter into negotiation with Russia.
But the conditions whose acceptance by Russia was demanded
were not those which Russia had proclaimed in the spring, or even
those voted by the Reichstag liberals in the summer. Not the
proposals of a people craving peace, they were the impositions of a
Government after victory. They raised for Wilson the question:
With whom is Russia treating and for whom are the emissaries of
the Central Powers speaking? He asserted it as his opinion that
the answer was 'the military and imperialistic minority' which had
thus far dominated German policy. He was unwilling to consider
peace with this party, but he saw no reason why the challenge to
state aims should not be responded to in complete candor. He was
not averse to the sound 'instinctive judgment' behind the Russian
doctrine. In December he had declared that Germany was using
this to lead Russia astray, and had asserted that 'the fact that a
wrong use has been made of a just idea is no reason why a right
use should not be made of it.' He now alluded to the need of the
Russian people to know truly what the Allies were about; to the
admirable candor and spirit of Lloyd George three days before;
and to the entry of the United States 'because violations of right
had occurred which touched us to the quick and made the life of
our own people impossible' unless they were corrected and the
world secured. In order that 'the world be made fit and safe to
live in' he proposed 'as the only possible program' of its peace:

1. Open covenants of peace, openly arrived at....
2. Absolute freedom of navigation upon the seas... alike in
   peace and war except as the seas may be closed in whole and
   in part by international action for the enforcement of international covenants.
3. The removal, so far as possible, of all economic barriers and
   the establishment of an equality of trade conditions among all
   the nations consenting to the peace and associating themselves for its maintenance.
4. Adequate guarantees... that national armaments will be
   reduced....
5. A free, open-minded and absolutely impartial adjustment of
   all colonial claims....

6. The evacuation of all Russian territory and... an unhampered and unembarrassed opportunity for the independent
   determination of her own political development and national policy....
7. Belgium, the whole world will agree, must be evacuated and
   restored without any attempt to limit the sovereignty which
   she enjoys....
8. All French territory should be freed and the invaded portions
   restored and the wrong done in France by Prussia in 1871
   in the matter of Alsace-Lorraine... should be righted....
9. A readjustment of the frontiers of Italy should be effected along
   clearly recognizable lines of nationality.
10. The peoples of Austria-Hungary, whose place among the
    nations we wish to see safeguarded and assured, should be
    accorded the freest opportunity of autonomous development.
11. Rumania, Serbia, and Montenegro should be evacuated;
    occupied territories restored; Serbia accorded free and secure
    access to the sea; and the relations of the several Balkan
    states to one another determined by friendly counsel along
    historically established lines of allegiance and nationality....
12. The Turkish portions of the present Ottoman Empire should
    be assured a secure sovereignty [with autonomous oppor-
    tunity for the rest]... and the Dardanelles should be per-
    manently opened as a free passage to the ships and com-
    merce of all nations....
13. An independent Polish state should be erected... which
    should be assured a free and secure access to the sea....
14. A general association of nations must be formed under spe-
    cific covenants for the purpose of affording mutual guaran-
    tees of political independence and territorial integrity to
    the great and small states, alike.

The address of January 8 was hardly on the wires (over which
the Committee on Public Information promptly dispatched it,
securely translated, to foreign lands) before reactions lifted it to
first place among the rationalizations of the war. The London
Spectator saw in it at once 'the minimum terms of the Allies,' but
used the word 'minimum'; while a part of British opinion was
restive at the inclusion of the item on the freedom of the seas.
Colonel House liked all the rest of it better than the paragraph on
the Balkan problem, for, as Seymour put it, 'historically established

lines of allegiance and nationality' did not exist in the Balkans. Republican Senators were uneasy because of implications under the third head that might suggest free trade. But the voices of statesmen and of the press were in a close harmony. Scott Nearing, of the People's Council, approved it. And when a British paper called it a 'great charter,' the *San Francisco Chronicle* (which none could accuse of anything but unrepentant Republicanism) countered: 'Why not the greater or the greatest charter? Magna Charta [sic] was a small-town franchise compared with the proclamation of international liberty and democracy contained in the Presidential deliverance.' Whether the President so designed it or not, his summary contained the texts for the diplomatic discussions of a generation. Viereck, who dealt in superlatives, designated it as 'The most effective piece of propaganda ever designed by any human brain in the history of mankind.' It was read in Germany, as it was intended to be read, as a basis for settlement only after Allied victory. Three days after it was delivered, the *Norddeutsche Allgemeine Zeitung* was quoted as summing it up as 'a real symphony of a will to no peace.' It gave to the content of the address the title thereafter universally ascribed to it: 'The Fourteen Points.'

IX. INTER-ALLY

THE Fourteen Points, by popular acclaim, became the manifesto of the war. In fundamental doctrine they summed up American aspiration so completely that militarist and pacifist alike took them to be obvious. They detoured around the tangle of secret agreements, of which no one could have been ignorant in the summer or oblivious after the Bolshevik Government began to publish them in November, 1917, to smear its Czarist predecessors. Labor and liberal groups found in the Fourteen Points something more attractive to fight for than either national advantage or war indemnities. The manifesto failed in its purpose so far as Russia was concerned because the leaders there had world revolution in view rather than reasonable peace. Wilson's concrete suggestions as to territorial rearrangement were not in every case workable. They developed defects in fact — defects to be embarrassing some day in conference — but at their erroneous worst, the Fourteen Points did not threaten destruction or mutilation to defensible objectives of even the enemy.

The last of the fourteen, promising an association of nations, promised by inference an orderly mechanism for the cure of provable evils. France found in the eighth what it had been eagerly looking for: a clear endorsement of the claim for the return to French sovereignty of Alsace-Lorraine. The wave of approval overflowed Allied boundaries in concentric bands. The doctrine of the freedom of the seas made it easier for neutrals to commend the manifesto. The approval passed even the barriers of the Central Powers. As well as among the Allies, there was war weariness east of the Western Front, where will to war was kept alive by attributing to the Allies a determination to dissolve Austria-

Hungary and to wipe out Germany as an entity. As the reasonableness of the Fourteen Points percolated the censorships and the interpretations of Imperial officials, the common folk of the Central Powers turned their minds toward this sort of peace. Wilson had set a text.

The leaders of the Allies, one by one, gave personal approval to the Wilson doctrine, for its general purpose could not be rejected by one who was unwilling to proclaim himself to be imperialist at heart. Nevertheless, in spite of widening support and wordy admiration it remained the manifesto of only Wilson. It was less than Revolutionary Russia wanted, than the American pacifists called for in the summer, than the Central Powers invited at Brest-Litovsk, than British labor asked from its hall at Westminster. It was not a pledge. The approvals were no more than personal. They could not be national, for the Allies were bound to unity by bond. No statement of endorsement was made under that bond.

The Pact of London, by which the first enemies of Germany became the Allies, involved a pledge by each of them not to talk peace separately. Until the Allies should act in agreement, no statement of the opinion of anyone could bind even the country from which the statement came. Only the President of the United States was a free agent, able to speak with reasonable assurance that what he said was in fact the intention of his Government. Not until the Allies and Associated Powers at last permitted their general in command to receive the German envoys asking peace (and this was when the war was over and Germany had no option but to ask it) was a binding statement given out. Until this moment all expressions of opinion except those of Woodrow Wilson fell short of being binding or dependable. Lloyd George is right in insisting that the Fourteen Points 'constituted no part of the official policies of the Alliance.' Co-operation in the expression of war intent, or, better, victory intent, could not be procured.

The war was a group of wars on the part of the Allies, with freedom of action limited only by the pledge not to talk peace separately. Said Clemenceau, not many days after the statement of the Fourteen Points: 'Since I have fought in coalitions myself,

I have come to think less of Napoleon' — *Depuis qui je pratique les coalitions j'admire moins Bonaparte*. But his recognition that his coalition was weak did not impel him to admit a sacrifice to make it stronger. It was eventually to be vital that the Allies shape their minds to an agreed pattern and adhere to it, else there could never be a peace. But before peace could become more than a philosophic abstraction it was even more vital that the Allies make up their minds to fight a single war. The position of Germany in its alliance gave to the Central Powers what approached a unified command, contributing to the military advantage gained in 1914 and retained since then. The four great Allies had made their drives and defended their trenches, each on its own, and sometimes with as much desire to conceal intent from friends as to hide it from the enemy. Their separateness now broke down, threatening them with defeat. The United States, outside the Allies and outside the net of interest, pressed into their counsels the conviction that unless they united they could not win. Germany, by a master stroke delivered in the late fall of 1917, served notice that unless they unite they must be beaten.

The German blow came out of the Julian Alps on that northeastern frontier of Italy where the ninth of the Fourteen Points was to declare that there should be rectifications 'along clearly recognizable lines of nationality.' Italy was determined that this rectification should bring into the kingdom the region east of the head of the Adriatic known as the Trentino, from Trieste to Fiume, where indeed the 'lines of nationality' appeared to be chiefly German, but where possession of the littoral would give to Italy a control of great strategic value. The Italian armies had been nibbling their way at the eastern end of the Venetian plain until blocked by mountainous country where the Austrian defenses could maintain their line. Cadorna, in charge, had been pressing the Allies for troops and guns to advance his campaign and had been so inadequately supplied as to be unable to do his part when the needs of the Western Front called for him to create diversions on the Italian Front. He started on a new drive eastward immediately after the appeal of Benedict XV. His drive slowed down among the mountains in September, with his armies spread over the upper tributaries of the Isonzo and in possession of the bridgehead at Gorizia. He was, with reason, worried about the morale of his troops, some of whom were too young and some too tired. There were no quick returns to reward Italy for joining the Allies.

Germany, fearful that the Austrian lines would break, was sufficiently fearful to send picked divisions and to lend German commanders for a counter-movement. In a campaign at Riga earlier in the year von Hutier had experimented successfully with a new process of attack calling for specialized troops and precise rehearsals. Preparations were made to apply this method on a larger scale on the Austrian Front. On October 24 the bombardment, overture to the battle of Caporetto, began in a heavy storm. The ensuing attack was successful beyond expectation; so successful as to clog its own mechanism. If, as Pershing feared, the Allies had been driven by trench warfare to forget how to maneuver in the open, Germany remembered how. For the next two weeks every day brought news of the disintegration of Italian defense. Udine, the Italian headquarters, was taken at once; the Austro-German drive crossed the Isonzo, crossed the Tagliamento, and threatened the line of the Piave, until the defenders of Venice hid the bronze horses of St. Mark's, carried the other treasures of art into safe-keeping, and prepared to abandon Venice itself.

As the Italian armies broke, rumors spread that prior to the drive propaganda had done a major stroke among the troops, appealing to the men in the ranks with an assurance that the Central Powers would give an easy peace, and that Italy was being used only for the special interests of the Northern Allies. Coincident with the disaster, making defense more difficult, was the fall of the Italian Ministry October 25, and the entry upon the scene of a new Prime Minister, Vittorio Emanuele Orlando. Orlando brought with him some reputation for defeatism, and was believed, as Minister of the Interior in the fallen Cabinet, to have tolerated the Socialist propaganda that weakened army morale. A few days later Cadorna was removed from his command and Diaz took over and began the reorganization of the Italian Front.

The advance of the enemy around the head of the Adriatic was retarded, and stopped short of success. From Italy to England and France there went cries for help, with the result that divisions and guns were hurried into the new line. Early in November the Prime Ministers of the Allies followed their reinforcements in order to hold counsel with Italy at Rapallo, a resort on the Italian Riviera a little east of Genoa. Here on November 5 the new Prime Minister, Orlando, received Lloyd George whose tenure was now eleven months old, and Paul Painlevé who had for two months presided over the fifth French Ministry since 1914 (and who was due to return to Paris and give way to Clemenceau at the head of the sixth). While the ministers were in conference on the dire necessities of the Italian Front, the news came of the triumph of the Bolsheviki, with the accompanying suggestion of a separate peace by Russia. At Rapallo the question uppermost was whether or not the war was lost.

The near-success of the attack on Italy and the prospect that the Russian lines would soften, if they did not evaporate, contributed to make the military picture at the end of 1917 more favorable to Germany than it had been a year earlier when a peace conference had been asked for. For the fourth year Germany had made gains away from the Western Front to compensate for the failure to conquer there. In the autumn of 1914 Russia had been mired in East Prussia, with crushing losses. In 1915 Serbia was overrun and put out of the war. Rumania entered by the side of the Allies in 1916, only to be eliminated in the autumn and dismembered by a peace at Bucharest. And now Italy had narrowly escaped the same elimination process. While Germany made gains elsewhere than in the West, the Allies, holding in the West, experienced losses in the East. Here the school of Allied strategy that thought to win the war by turning the left of the Central Powers at Constantinople made an attempt at Gallipoli in 1915, from which the unsuccessful forces were withdrawn at the end of the year. The Dardanelles remained closed to the Allies, which opened to Germany a vision of new gains across the Dardanelles, in Asia Minor and beyond. British operations in Mesopotamia in

1915 were not only unsuccessful but resulted in the surrender at Kut-el-Amara of a British army in April, 1915. The 'Berlin to Baghdad' aspiration was too near to realization to be nonsense.

The year 1917 saw German consolidations along the whole length of the Eastern Fronts except at the southern end. In Mesopotamia, after the surrender of Townshend at Kut, the British armies were reorganized and once more taken into the field against the Turk. Baghdad was occupied by Maude in March, 1917, setting a southeastern limit to German hopes. Arabia revolted against Turkey, held on to Mecca, and created a resource for the Allies. In Palestine, too, there were gains which somewhat softened Allied disappointment. Allenby's entry into Jerusalem, December 11, 1917, was the brightest spot in the military vision of the enemies of the Central Powers as winter set in.

The probability of additional German expansion southeast of Asia Minor was slight with Jerusalem and Baghdad taken by the Allies, and with the intervening Arabia in successful revolt. But from the Dardanelles and the Bosphorus north to Finland, the gains were great. The collapse of Russia opened vistas that had not been in prospect until after the deposition of the Czar. Even more than in 1916, if the gains in hand could be consolidated, Germany was in a position to let the West go and yet end the war with profit.

But it was by no means certain, as autumn turned into winter in 1917, that the Central Powers would have to let the West go. The victories in Italy were an inspiration, giving hope that, with the Eastern rear safe, the war might be turned into victory in the West in 1918.

The year 1917 was inconclusive as far as the Western Front was concerned. The trenches had held. Retaining the strategic grip at Verdun in the spring of 1916, the Allies had been unable to break through the line in the Somme campaign in the summer. The great French offensive of Nivelle collapsed in the spring of 1917, leaving the French forces in the confusion Pershing sensed when he reached Paris in June. At the French left and never happy with his liaison, Haig was prepared to co-operate with Nivelle, driving up the valley of the Somme; but the plans of both armies were upset when Ludendorff, anticipating them, made a strategic withdrawal from the front trenches to a new Hindenburg Line, devastating the terrain as he evacuated it. The British offensives of the last half of the year, whether in Flanders or at Cambrai, left the German defenses still intact. The prospect of the Allies for 1918 would have been dark enough without the emergency call from Italy in November. Pershing, just as the Italian line was struck at Caporetto, found it necessary to issue a stern warning to his officers lest they spread to visitors 'an impression that the war is already well along toward defeat for our arms.' He had visitors in shoals — there were newspaper men, whom Palmer could handle, major-generals from the new divisions sent to observe the war, and congressmen whose discretion broke down when they picked up the interesting gossip at officers' messes. When the premiers gathered with their military advisers at Rapallo, it was clear that heroic measures were in order. Unity was involved.

Pershing did not go to Rapallo. Just back from an inspection of ports and services along his line of communications, he had breakfast with Lloyd George as the latter paused in Paris on his way to Italy and in the afternoon he called on Painlevé. With each he discussed the steering committee that was proposed to be erected to bring better order out of the Allied chaos.

There were three or four ways of securing team-work. Pershing thought rather well of honest conference and co-operation among generals of the several countries in the field; however, this called for a higher degree of self-denial than was usual among commanders with careers at stake. There were also possibilities of a council of war in the field (which commanders dislike); of a single commander (which France would have welcomed if assured that he should be French and which Pershing welcomed in principle); and of a steering committee in the rear, with some of the attributes of a consolidated general staff.

The last device was the best that it was practical politics to discuss, since English military opinion would not consider the subordination of the British Army to a French commander. Reason underlay this reluctance, for in Flanders lay the gateway to England, and none could be sure that in a moment of stress the road to Paris might not be regarded by a French commander as more important than the road to England. It might, in fact, be more important. German military skill had jolted British opinion into some compliance, but not enough for a complete surrender of control. The steering committee idea, a favorite of Lloyd George, was in weaker shape than Pershing liked, because the logical national representatives on such a committee would have been the chiefs of the several general staffs; whereas the British Prime Minister had a deep distrust of generals (even of his own) and insisted that the determination of policy should be, in the last analysis, political.

Lloyd George suggested to Pershing that he, too, ought to go to the Italian conference; but Pershing, having no specific instruction, suspecting the conference to be more political than military, and having no army ready for immediate use, preferred to stay away. He did not conceal, however, his desire for real co-operation between the English and the French, for 'when one was attacking the other was usually standing still.'

The Paris conversations were on Sunday, November 4. On Monday the Prime Ministers and their advisers met at Rapallo. On Wednesday they signed an agreement for 'the better co-ordination of military action on the Western Front,' in which they promised to set up in Versailles a Supreme War Council, with monthly meetings. The Council was to consist of the Prime Minister and a member of his Cabinet for each of the powers, with a permanent military representative of each to go to Versailles and act as technical adviser to the Council. The group of military advisers thus permanently installed was to receive reports and proposals, watch the day's battle, and consider the means at the disposal of the Allies. It was presumed that, upon their technical advice, the Supreme War Council would plan a common policy at its monthly meetings. The conduct of operations and the control of each army was left, specifically, in the hands of its Government. The crisis of the Austro-German drive had passed before the

Rapallo conference met, and the drive itself was shortly stopped with the Allied line in Italy mangled but not ruined. The business of the new Supreme War Council was with the future.

A month later the Supreme War Council met in the Trianon Palace Hotel for the first of its periodic sessions at Versailles. In the weeks since Rapallo the venture had been exposed to opinion in the constituent countries. Hindenburg joked about it: 'Such institutions are always a sign of helplessness. When they are at their wits' end, a war council is established.' The difficulty of popularizing even this much co-operation had become apparent. Cadorna, sent to Versailles as the Italian military representative, came with the handicap that he had been relieved of his command. France detailed Weygand (an assistant of Foch), who was the selection of a new Prime Minister, Painlevé being out. Clemenceau, now come to power, the bad boy of French politics, had at the age of seventy-six a single aim ahead of his driving power — France. Lloyd George sent Henry Wilson without trusting him; he nearly sent no one because his own outspoken remarks upon the ineptness of command and the need for oneness almost upset his Government. He might have been a less insistent co-operator if his distaste for the generals had not impelled him toward whatever course they disapproved. But a Paris speech, on his return from Rapallo, was so brutally frank as to necessitate a full explanation to Commons on November 14. His explanation was convincing to his majority, and it was reinforced shortly by a statement from Colonel House, who had arrived in England November 7. House put into words the substance of an instruction from the President: 'We not only approve a continuance of the plan for a war council but insist on it.'

Clemenceau desired to modify the Supreme Council, when it met on December 1, by bringing in the chiefs of staff, and he threatened if this could not be done to let the Council die in the hands of mediocrities. He acted, however, less destructively than he threatened and took part in the formal opening of the offices with their permanent military secretariat. House represented the President, having in his train Tasker H. Bliss who now wore the four stars indicating his rank as general. The rank had been revived in the autumn, so that Pershing, in command of the A.E.F., might hold his own with the leaders of the Allies, and so that the Chief of Staff might have at least a temporary rank as high as that of any of the officers to whom he might have to transmit the orders of the Secretary of War. Although on the verge of retirement, Bliss was being retained as Chief of Staff until a suitable younger successor could be found.

Bliss returned to the United States with reports for the War Department only to be sent back to Paris in time for the next meeting of the Council, to act as Permanent Military Representative. Pershing was not sure he wanted him, having preference for Hunter Liggett, and it took them some days to reach an understanding. But there is no note of criticism among the comments upon the service of Bliss once he was installed. He not only took an immovable position in support of Pershing, but also impressed his wisdom and fairness upon the military group regardless of nationality. Sometimes as a 'mountain,' sometimes as a 'benevolent pachyderm,' he earned the friendly judgment expressed by his biographer, Frederick Palmer, in *Bliss, Peacemaker: The Life and Letters of General Tasker H. Bliss* (1934).

Pershing was dubious about the Council when he joined the other commanders at its ceremonial opening; he thought it a 'kind of super-parliament.' He was more interested at the moment in getting troops to France than in the politics of their utilization. The Prime Ministers had no difficulty in completing the mechanics of the continuous services of the Council, but they were as yet unprepared with any plan for the military operations of the campaign of 1918. It was nearly two months before they were again in session, still without a program.

The third meeting of the Supreme War Council, at Versailles on January 30, 1918, found the Allied armies facing trouble, and the English Chief of Staff, Sir William Robertson, thinking that 'our only hope lies in American reserves.' Robertson was within a few days of resignation because of distrust of the principle upon which the Council was constructed. His office was out of it. He was offered either post: that which he held or that of Military Representative; but he wanted both, which Lloyd George would not let him have. Pershing and the generals anticipated so little from the Council that Clemenceau was asked to assemble the field commanders a week before it met, at the headquarters of Pétain at Compiègne. Here Pétain foresaw a necessity to stick to the defensive. Foch wanted a counter-offensive to be ready to start when the enemy opened in the spring. Haig and Robertson wanted independent offensives to be prepared. And Pershing discussed the obstacles interfering with his construction of his rear and with the shipment of his troops. Except that American troops could not be counted on for any early operations (the English thought that as an 'autonomous unit' they would be useless throughout the year), the generals had not come to an agreement when the Council met.

The Military Representatives made their report to the Council, which thereupon decided to establish an Allied military reserve, and created an Executive War Board to direct its operations. The reserve could not be more than a principle, since none of the commanders either admitted having enough troops for his own minimum needs, or released for duty in the reserve the divisions promised it. Adjournment came without a program. Nervous souls at home had to be reassured by Bonar Law in Commons that the Council had not created a *generalissimo*. The co-operation in counsel, inspired by nearness of defeat, went only thus far. It might never have gone farther had not the next German blow, falling in March, driven the Allies the rest of the way to unity and Foch.

Inadequate as the Supreme War Council was, it promised in military affairs a completer team-work than had been attained in diplomacy. The commentaries on the Fourteen Points had multiplied between the day of their announcement and the end of January. But there was no assurance that if the military picture should change, the terms of peace would not change with it. The spokesmen for the Central Powers were disposed to treat the Fourteen Points as destructive of their nations. The Allied Governments, and that of the United States, could not hear among the enemy voices anything that sounded like a note of acceptance. There was nothing for the war to do but to go on.

Yet the enemies of Germany were growing toward a unity. The Fourteen Points constituted a new outpost thrown in the general direction of the purpose of the war. The Supreme War Council, by the mere fact of its existence, recorded the making of some concession from the principle of national separateness. Moreover, a series of conferences held in Paris in December brought the Allies and the United States into a more businesslike relationship with reference to their joint support of the armies in the field.

The United States had assumed the position of banker to the Allies; but as such it lacked full knowledge of the resources, liabilities, and projects of its debtors. It had begun to earmark funds for their expenditure within a few hours after the signature of the loan act on April 24. However reluctant the Allies were to bind themselves to any joint purpose, beyond that of military victory, they were of one mind and conduct in the use of the resources between which and themselves stood only the necessity to procure the signature of McAdoo upon their paper. By November they had drawn 2717 millions against credits established to the amount of 3131 millions. McAdoo was guessing that they would need about 500 millions a month for the duration of the war. They would have welcomed an automatic allowance of this dimension, in place of the requirement to state the specific case every time a requisition was accepted. England was conscious of a status different from that of the Continental Allies, since it passed on to them, in loans of its own, substantially as much as it borrowed in the United States. Out of the responsibility resting upon the Treasury in authorizing these acceptances came much of the American pressure for co-operation in the rear of the Armies.

The Purchasing Commission for the Allies began to function in midsummer, lessening the losses due to indiscriminate competition among the several buyers in the American market. There was, at best, some doubt whether at the end of the year there would be anything left to buy, since war needs gobbled up the visible output and still clamored for more. The permanent British and French Missions (which were left behind in order to supplement the work of the Embassies) when the congratulatory Missions went home in the spring of 1917 had as detached a view of the possible volume of American material as the United States Government possessed. They were willing to make some sacrifice for the sake of output and economy; and for their own purposes they soon saw virtue in the idea that co-operative boards in Europe should do for their combined requirements something of what was being attempted in the United States by the War Boards.

In advancing this idea the Treasury took an enthusiastic part. It had reasons of strictly American character to make its support enthusiastic. Even had there not been American loans, the Allies must have continued to buy in the United States. International law had never even frowned upon the purchase of military supplies in neutral countries. Neutrality had never been construed to suggest that the neutral should prohibit profitable trade merely because the buyer was at war. What would have continued permissible had the United States refrained from war became obvious with the United States itself a belligerent. The War Missions persuaded themselves and confessed to the United States that the Allies had reached the bottom of their strong-boxes; but had the loans not been authorized they would have made additional effort to build up collateral in the United States against which to raise the credits for American purchases. The Allies would not have declared their bankruptcy and dropped the war.

In proportion as funds were lent by the United States to the Allies the strain upon the treasuries of the latter was eased. Moneys and resources that might have had to go for American food and munitions became available at home for whatever purposes seemed advisable. There were many fields of opportunity beyond the cash resources of the Allies which could be exploited when bought on credit. Not all of their purposes were revealed to the creditor. Their conception of the 'justice' to be done at the peace treaty involved in most cases some readjustment of the map to their

own advantage. In some cases they were rivals for the same territorial booty, and were ready to spend money, if they had it, to
entrench themselves or to head off the competitor. The American
Treasury could not avoid feeling, as the loans were poured out,
that the United States was in spite of itself assisting its associates to
fight each other. Such competitions were not part of the American
objective in the war.

When Jusserand or Spring Rice asked for loans it was both
embarrassing and non-productive to inquire too much. The
Secretary of the Treasury was in no position to be inquisitorial
about the purpose of the expenditure, or about the work to be
done at home by the funds which his loan released. A clearing
house in Europe, in which representatives of the several Allies
should check the requirements of each other and give them priority according to their deserts, promised to relieve the embarrassment. Charles H. Grasty, whose dispatches from Europe provided the United States with much of what it thought it knew,
was asking in August for an inter-Ally council. He was suggesting
that House, or Franklin K. Lane, be the American member.
The Trading-with-the-Enemy Act, and the War Trade Board
formed in pursuance of it, gave power to the American pressure.
They carried implications entirely clear to the practical borrowers,
who did not want to dam the flow of credit.

On the night of October 28 Colonel House boarded in New
York the special train carrying an American Mission to Halifax
on its way to London. He traveled at the head of an impressive
delegation that in a way returned the visit of the War Missions of
April. Each branch of the war effort was represented among his
associates. Benson, Chief of Naval Operations, and Bliss, Chief of
Staff, went with him. Oscar T. Crosby, who had been clearing
the loans, was detailed by the Treasury and took along the best of
legal advice in the person of Paul T. Cravath. Vance McCormick,
chairman of the War Trade Board, was his own delegate; the War
Industries Board sent Bainbridge Colby. Alonzo E. Taylor, a close
associate of Hoover, could speak for the Food Administration.
The American Mission arrived in London on the very day, Novem-

ber 7, when the Allied premiers sat at Rapallo in the Supreme
War Council set up as a last sacrifice for the sake of victory.
Northcliffe, who knew much, and whose papers dealt with him as
knowing all, was being quoted to the effect that half the effort of
the Allies was being lost through cross-purposes and waste.

The steps leading to the decision for the Inter-Ally Conference
for which the American Mission was heading had been taken in the
interval since August. Its germ was in the financial conference
asked by McAdoo. The Allies desired it, not only to secure
orderly continuance of supplies, but also to bind the United States
to themselves in the matter of policy. They were repeatedly inviting American representatives abroad to sit in with their councils, not so much because they craved American advice as because
the United States having taken part in the discussions might feel
bound by the decisions. The reply to the Pope indicated a tendency of the President to go his own way in stating policy; he might
go too far.

The negotiations between England and the United States at the
time the American Mission was determined upon had their center
in New York and Washington and ran through irregular channels.
Roosevelt had thought well of Page, admiring him as he had
admired 'no other Ambassador in London . . . with the exception
of Charles Francis Adams.' However, Page had little to do with
the negotiations. He had long since ceased to represent the President, and he was blocked out of the picture before ill health ended
his embassy and he came home to die. Lansing, technically the
correct channel for diplomacy, had little to do with this angle of it.
It was Colonel House who was the tool, and in House the affectionate confidence of the President was unqualified through the
autumn of 1917. Sometimes in the White House but oftener in
his apartment in New York, House was no farther from Wilson
than his arm could reach to their private telephone. Next him, in
an apartment not far away, Sir William Wiseman had been
planted by the British Government to receive and expedite decisions on matters of state. It was an unusual circuit, but one
that was highly effective. As with Page, it lessened the importance

of Spring Rice, who, crowded out of the business he ought to have conducted, died suddenly in 1918. The British War Mission in a large degree superseded the embassy. Northcliffe, and after him Reading, had the reality of authority if not the trappings; while Spring Rice was distressed by the tactics of the great newsman and chagrined by his own ousting. Unfitted for his post of ambassador because of his personal identification with American groups unfriendly to the Administration, Spring Rice occupied himself with an honorary degree from Harvard. He wrote intimate letters to the Roosevelts, and for Henry Adams he made graceful sonnets. He was carefully expressing no opinion 'unless I am asked for it.' But he admitted ruefully, 'No one has asked me.'

In the autumn of 1917, Northcliffe yielded his post as head of the British Mission to Lord Reading and took his penetrating knowledge of the United States back to London, while Reading pressed upon the American Government the idea of participating in the next inter-Ally conference on the conduct of the war. Wiseman briefed the arguments for such participation, and Wilson assented to them about the time he directed House to launch the Inquiry. The lack of an effective army made it inappropriate for the United States as yet to do much about strategy; the President was unwilling to be let into what might be described as diplomatic alliance, yet the logic of economic co-ordination was convincing, and Balfour was right in believing that 'tonnage conditions will be the deciding factor' in the spring operations of 1918. In mid-October Wilson agreed to participate in the conference. He asked House to lead the American Mission, and on October 24 he gave him his letter of credentials.

House had three weeks for deliberation and arrangement before the Inter-Ally Conference held its opening session in Paris, November 29, 1917. He had laid his foundations in London before he crossed the Channel, and in advance of his coming he had passed the word ahead: 'No public functions.' The days were spent in conference with those from the King down, who controlled the larger strategy. He had nearly a week before Lloyd George arrived back from Rapallo. In this week it was believed that Venice was sure to fall and that the whole war was at stake. House was more than ready to permit the Prime Minister to use him as reinforcement in the demand for a superior unity and to give to American pressure a somewhat greater credit than it deserved.

While House was occupied at the top, the lesser members of the Mission found their way into the subordinate British offices similar to their own, to talk the business of the war. They found this business in confusion, with each of the problems interlocked with all the rest. Military plans were in abeyance because of ignorance of the extent of the American reinforcement. Numbers could not be stated with any precision, because of ignorance of the tonnage that would be available for transportation. Shipping matters remained in doubt, because neither the freight requirements of the next year nor the amount of new tonnage that could be expected from the efforts of the Emergency Fleet Corporation could be foretold. But through the confusion ran a clear purpose that England and the United States should go to Paris arm in arm to advance the unity of all. The days in London were crowned by a sitting of the American Mission (without House, who stayed away) and the British War Cabinet in the very room at the Foreign Office in which, said Lloyd George, 'Lord North engineered some trouble for America, but a great deal more trouble for himself.' It was 'purely a business gathering,' from which Lloyd George sent the Americans to Paris with 'man-power and shipping as the two first demands.' Nothing had occurred to change his view, expressed in April, that ships would win the war.

The American Mission had a week in Paris before the first plenary session of the Inter-Ally Conference was held, clogged with the representatives of the little Allies. The clogging was unimportant, for the formal sessions were only decorative. Much of the real work had been accomplished in the week of waiting, so that what was left for the full gatherings was only the recording of decisions reached in private. Even the usual speeches were lacking. House engineered an agreement with Clemenceau and Lloyd George that the leaders should restrain themselves — which was less of an effort for him than for them. They adhered to the arrangement, and left time for the committees to do their work.

Out of the Inter-Ally Conference came projects for co-operation behind the lines. As to the lines themselves, House learned that a great controversy would shortly arise: whether the A.E.F. should be used as such or be broken up into companies and battalions to be directed by officers of the Allies. But with this left in abeyance, the plans for supporting the Allies in their efforts comprised a finance council, a shipping council, a naval council, a munitions council, a food council, and an understanding upon common policy in the maintenance of the so-called blockade. Blockade was still as inadequate a name for the investment of Germany as it had been before the United States entered the war; the maritime controls of trade continued to be based upon an inflation of the law of contraband rather than upon the rule of blockade.

The leaders of the Conference adjourned their sessions to assist in the inauguration of the Supreme War Council at Versailles on December 1. They completed their work two days later, and a month after landing in England the American Mission was afloat on the *Mount Vernon*, bound for home. Said Colby to House: 'We have been so used to potentates and kings that the first thing we should do . . . is to take a week's course at Child's Restaurant, sitting on a stool, and getting down again to our own level.' The stools at Child's, on Pennsylvania Avenue, could tell a long story had they tongues.

The seeds planted at the Conference budded and fruited as the weeks ran on. First of all, the Inter-Ally Council on War Purchases and Finance retained Crosby in London to complete its organization, open its offices, and preside over its deliberations. It proved to be less important than its prospectus, for the Allies in this tight winter could not find things to buy upon which to use up the funds easily available. There was no shortage of American funds. The Second Liberty Loan had been a success, and there were no fears for the Third when it should be expedient. But Crosby's Council was ready for business December 15, 'the first permanent Inter-Ally body in which the United States is represented.' From his

offices in St. James's Palace an American directed priorities in the
matter of finance, and his Council met alternately there and at
Paris in the Palace of the Legion of Honor.

Naval co-operation had been a fact since the arrival of Sims,
who did not gain rank of Admiral, equivalent to that of General,
until the war was over. The presence of Benson with the House
Mission made it possible to make the co-operation more specific
and fruitful than it had been, but the Inter-Allied Naval Council
did not add much to the unity of direction already in existence.
To the destroyers already operating in European waters it was
agreed to add a squadron of American battleships; and even before
Benson had left Washington he had placed on the desk of the
President, for immediate approval, a memorandum on a new
variety of American effort. The submarines while still a menace
were less of a menace than they had been because the system of
convoys had drawn some of their teeth, while the barrage and
patrol at the Strait of Dover had greatly lessened the availability
of that exit from North Sea waters into the ocean. The ordnance
men in the Navy had proposed that the northern end of the North
Sea be blocked as well, and had undertaken studies of the two
hundred and thirty miles of rough water lying between the Orkney
Islands and the coast of Norway which, after the closure at Dover,
the submarines must traverse. No surface patrol was able to close
this highway, and attention shifted to the possibility of a tight
barrage of anchored contact mines. After the war was over, the
British Navy believed the conception of the North Sea mine barrage to have been its own, but it could not weaken the conviction
of the American ordnance men that only their pressure had overridden British despair at the magnitude of the enterprise. At any
event, a mine was designed in the Navy, a mine-firing device was
improvised, arrangements were made for quantity manufacture in
a hundred different plants of which none was aware of the nature
of the job, and plans for laying the barrage were proposed to the
Admiralty in July. With the approval of the Admiralty and the
Navy a laying base was opened by the latter on the coast of Scot-
land in February, 1918; and on June 8 the first field was laid.

Lines of the mines made navigation of the exit from the North Sea hazardous at the surface, at periscope depth, at submergence depth, and at deep-sea depth; 70,263 mines in all, of which the American Navy anchored 56,611 in their position.

The Allied Maritime Transport Council was the response to the need for ocean tonnage. With four sections, one for each Government reporting directly to its Government, it did its first work in London on March 13. The basic decisions that were to provide for the needs of the United States were not yet made, but it was possible to set in motion the machinery for tabulating tonnage and estimating the requirements of the principal commodities of trade. The studies that Americans had begun in the planning and statistics section of the United States Shipping Board were expanded upon the larger scale of total tonnage. The business of war was at a stage at which politicians could not do their work without the aid of statisticians who knew their stuff. The adding machine had become a significant item in the list of war munitions.

The munitions Council and the Food Council were delayed in their inauguration, but became real when the summer of 1918 brought about a new series of inter-Ally conferences upon the campaign projected for 1919. Before the economic councils were far advanced in their work, the interest of the war shifted from planning to operations in the field. But when these operations began, with the German attack of March 21, the German high command found itself facing a coalition that had considerably changed its tricks since the close of the last campaign.

Organization of the effort abroad had caught up to and passed the organization of the effort at home. Before the United States could profit greatly from the improved unity toward which its argument had been directed, it was necessary to reach other decisions as vital to victory as those concerning war aims or inter-Ally war organizations. It had to be decided, by rough method of pull and push, who should command the American effort, the President or the Congress; and who should command the American field forces, Pershing or the Allied generals. It had to be discovered whether the American war machine could be made to work.

X. 'HE SHALL BE COMMANDER IN CHIEF
OF THE ARMY'

T HAT unity of purpose and that co-ordination of effort, to whose
promotion abroad the endeavors of the American Government
were directed, were brought near to breaking at home. The disruptive forces threatening the success of the domestic undertaking
were generated variously. They were derived from political interest that could not be overlooked even during war, from the structure of human character, and from the Constitution of the United
States.

The third of these disruptive forces was inherent in the American frame of government. The plain meaning of the words of the
Constitution, 'he shall be Commander in Chief of the Army and
Navy of the United States,' was hard to accept when things went
wrong or failed to go right. Congress cannot sit quiet and permit
the President to lose the day or save it. What interference its patriotic zeal does not inspire is inspired quite as easily by its self-
esteem as a co-ordinate branch of the Government. To the President belong the executive power and the responsibility, but upon
the Senators and Representatives falls the double burden of voting
resources and of explaining in detail to constituents why resources
have been voted or withheld. Congressional leaders, reassembled
in December, 1917, after a brief recess since October 6, could not
ease out of their minds the attractive picture of a committee on
the conduct of the war or its equivalent through which their hand
might be in every pot.

Human character has a hard time in war. The strain of responsibility upon ministers, as they exercise their powers, is matched
by the strain of hope or suspicion upon the lesser breed of states-

men. Into the ears of congressmen, during the recess of 1917, were poured fact, gossip, and insinuation concerning the status of the war. Lawmakers knew little of what was going on behind the screen of voluntary censorship. Their constituents had boys in camp; boys so fresh that they would not have known when things were going well and so unused to war that every inconvenience or shortage was soon reported from mouth to ear, growing as it went. Congressmen came back to Washington ready to believe that everyone was incompetent and doubting the capacity of the President, and Baker, and Daniels, and the group of emergency chiefs, to bring order out of chaos. They were sure it was chaos, but lacked agreement as to the order they desired. Jealousy grew out of the constitutional structure; suspicion out of human necessity. The United States had had only eight months in which either to flounder or to succeed. Congressmen might have been less uneasy (or perhaps more) if they could have known that the driving Prime Minister of England was convinced that his country had floundered hopelessly for twenty-eight months before he came to office in December, 1916. In the middle of November, when the admitted insight and power of Lloyd George had been in charge of England for eleven months, Lord Northcliffe declined the Air Ministry, warning the Prime Minister of the 'obstruction and delay' of London, in contrast with the 'virile atmosphere of the United States and Canada'; he stayed out of the Cabinet that he might not be 'gagged' by loyalty, and warned that 'unless there is swift improvement in our methods here, the United States will rightly take into its own hands the entire management of a great part of the war.'

If it was easy for Administration congressmen to doubt the capacity of the American leaders, it was much easier for members of the Republican minority to distrust the capacity, if not the devotion, of any Democrats. Accepting the position of a minority party was a trait only partially acquired by the Republicans of 1917. The tradition of Democratic incompetence had been restated so often that it was believed. Republicans were now, moreover, facing the preliminaries of a congressional election due in

1918, an election that might leave them still a minority or redound to their advantage. The political schism of 1912, healing in 1916, was still less than completely healed; the scars of party battle left the party stiff. But the Republican leaders had no notion of letting themselves be left after the World War in a discredited obscurity like that from which Democrats had suffered after 1865. Their Congressional Campaign Committee was due to be renewed in February, 1918, and the National Committee was ripe for a reorganization with 1920 in view. The party must close its ranks. Issues that would be both profitable and safe must be discovered. And thus it happened that political interest reinforced human instability and the mechanics of the Constitution to create entanglements from which the President must extricate himself before he might carry the War of 1917 into its third phase — that of operation. Six months, roughly, had gone into planning; and another six were going into setting up an organization which was now in many directions farther advanced than that of England had gone in twenty-eight months. Congress reassembled in December, 1917, prepared to challenge Wilson's constitutional position as Commander in Chief.

Only one American division had taken its place on the line of battle when Congress took up the business of the new session, with its mind crowded with doubt as to the effectiveness of what had been done. The First Division, whose initial units William L. Sibert had taken to France (and from whose command he was about to be relieved by Robert Lee Bullard), had moved into its sector on October 21, but its successors were not yet in sight. Lloyd George, with an interest in comparisons, could point out that in a similar six months in 1914 England had sent more than 350,000 men to the front. He could not understand why the United States had sent so few or had sent them so slowly. Nor could Pershing understand. The curtain whose folds of secrecy concealed the front from the rear concealed also the rear from the front. It seemed strange to the American general that troops did not come faster. He was aware that in Allied counsels the conviction was deepening that the next great aggressive must wait upon his army, and that the war would be won only with the Americans. He agreed with this, differing from the other commanders only in his idea as to who should command the Americans in battle; they or he. In conferences held in London in December it was agreed that he ought to have in France at least twenty-four divisions by the end of June, 1918, but there was no schedule of shipments that as yet promised any such total. The men were in camp. He knew that, the Allies knew it, and there was every reason to suppose the enemy knew it; but he distrusted their training. He had sent back Sibert, the earliest of his divisional commanders, and he would not have been of the old Army if he had not believed the War Department always to be lax.

It was certain that the performance after eight months was far less than had been hoped or enthusiastically promised. The Administration was bound to find out why and Congress could not fail to make its own inquiry and come to its own conclusion. Either more had been promised than could be delivered or the creakings of the mechanism of the war machine indicated fundamental errors of schemes or men.

The Adjutant-General knew that there were more than one million soldiers in various stages of preparation in the United States when Congress met. The initial notion that American participation would not include fighting in France had been forgotten. Statesmen, when they have turned to write their memoirs, have been disposed to forget they ever held it. Pessimists were now restating the notion in a different form: that progress was so slow that it would be better to send only goods and cash, and not waste ships on driblets of troops. A second American division was not expected to be ready for any front before March, and the training program in the United States was already under criticism from G.H.Q. at Chaumont on the ground of inadequacy.

It was a large program. The easiest of its parts was what had been feared as the hardest: the enrollment of men under the draft law. It was now open to debate whether the hardest part was the housing of the levies in their new camps, the equipment of them with uniforms and weapons, or their instruction in the duties of the soldier. Many things that had not heretofore been included among the essential processes of mobilization were absorbing time and attention, complicating the strictly military details.

The protection of the soldier, once he was drafted, had implications touching the effectiveness of the Army, the future of the Treasury, and the politics of the war. Every process in mobilization was somewhat retarded by the determination to make it adequate. The War Missions, full of advice, were full of warnings of mistakes to be avoided. Men who were taken by law from the normal channels of their lives, and who were to be exposed to death, were entitled to every safeguard that the Government could provide. This was both fair and prudent. Soldiers were entitled to be treated as willing components of a democratic army, and obvious treatment of them as such stilled many of the doubts and worries that would be inconsistent with their freest performance in the line.

Gompers, in his Labor Committee of the Council of National Defense, was one of the starting points for the consideration of soldiers' insurance. Early in July the insurance men were brought into conference since the action to be taken might involve an intrusion of the Government upon the field of private insurance. Judge Julian W. Mack of Cincinnati was commissioned to work out a scheme of compensation, and the insurance companies were found quite ready to let the Government undertake the special risks involved in war hazard. Baker accepted the idea; McAdoo gave it his approval because the Treasury was not only already involved in insurance matters through its duty to carry the war risks of shipping, but was certain to become more heavily involved if history should repeat itself after the war. The cost of the Civil War was only begun when the fighting stopped. Thereafter, until the last veteran died, the Pension Bureau was the protector of the old soldier and the target of raid after raid. Pension attorneys and 'professional' veterans, backed often by the Grand Army of the Republic, made a great demonstration of the power of pressure politics as they drove Congress into pension legislation. The Treasury had a keen interest in the adoption of a considered

policy respecting claims before the claims should be sentimental-
ized by blood and suffering, or exploited by pressure.

The importance of soldier protection in the larger politics of
war management was obvious. In a war for democracy — and
in the United States the World War had taken on this aspect —
it was necessary to avoid the appearance of loading the cost upon
a single class of citizens. The young men who went to war had
burden enough in the physical risk that they alone would carry.
The family solicitudes behind them were too real to be ignored.
The honest distaste for any draft procedure had been overcome;
there remained an equally honest reluctance to send an army to
fight abroad. The bodies and the souls of the fighting men must
be conserved while the war was on; their interest thereafter must
be protected by a national pledge.

Judge Mack's committee drafted its project so promptly that
it was ready for introduction in Congress early in August, and his
bill was so adequate that its progress was not retarded by debate.
It was delayed only by the crowded docket of the houses. The
Bureau of War Risk Insurance, created in 1914, was accepted
as the nucleus around which to assemble the machinery for ful-
filling the obligations now for the first time accepted in advance.
It would have been less easy to define them had not the long
agitation of the Progressive period for employers' liability, or
workmen's compensation, prepared the public and the congressional mind. As the bill became a law on October 6, at the end
of the session, its principal headings touched upon family allowances, soldier allotments, compensation, and insurance. To administer all of these the Treasury bureau in charge was expanded
to include some thirteen thousand employees, whose filing cases
soon held more than four million separate accounts that must
be kept accurate to the last cent, and in a condition to be explained
by correspondence to the soldiers themselves and to their ex-
pectant dependents.

The family allowance was an obligation assumed by the United
States in recognition of its responsibility to the dependent family
of the fighting man. It was less important in fact than in appear-

ance, for the draft boards were in the habit of giving deferred classification to married men, even when their greater average age would not have made them as a class less liable to duty than the younger bachelors. Up to fifty dollars a month, from enlistment to one month after death, was to be paid to dependents, according to a scale beginning with fifteen dollars to a wife.

The soldier's allotment was in recognition of the soldier's obligation to his own dependents. Where allowances were granted, allotments to supplement them were held back from soldier pay and passed directly to the dependents. At least fifteen dollars per month in every case, the allotments could not run to more than half the pay.

Compensation was a Government obligation. If the soldier died in the line of duty his widow, until remarriage, might draw a monthly income with a seventy-five-dollar maximum. Should he be disabled, the compensation during disability was based upon an elaborate table of rates; and behind it all was an assumption that the obligation of the Government to its mutilated defenders had no limit.

Insurance was another matter. The commercial companies had no basis upon which to compute the war hazard and shrank from entering upon a speculative venture that might result in disaster if the war should be long and the death rate high. The Government accordingly prepared to provide insurance at cost, carrying the overhead as a charge of war. It not only became permissible for every member of the armed forces to buy term insurance up to ten thousand dollars, with the premiums deducted from his pay, but earnest campaigns were engineered to persuade all of them to take advantage of the attractive speculation. In 1919 it was reported that 4,561,974 individual policies had been written aggregating insurance in excess of thirty-eight billion dollars.

The organization of the bureaus to carry the obligations incidental to the war taxed the Army and Navy, whose records of service and title must be complete and accurate, and the Treasury, whose duty to account for every cent could not be evaded, war or peace. The obligations other than financial assumed with reference to the armed forces touched upon the character and the morale of the soldier and induced trial-and-error approach to conditions of war that had never been portrayed by the romantic historian.

Raymond B. Fosdick was well known in the War Department before the draft law was passed, and even before war was declared. He had been sent by Baker to the camps along the Mexican Border in the summer of 1916, and upon his advice the Secretary had accepted as another of his duties that of lessening the scourge of venereal disease. The 'women of the army' had heretofore been regarded as the unavoidable accompaniments of war, and at times they had provided the themes for literature as though they were heroic. Commanding officers had never known what to do with them or how to get along without them. They had filled the armies with venereal disease, breeding long sick-lists to lessen effectiveness in action, and impregnating soldiers so that the curse of war descended to their children and their grandchildren after the war was over. The result was both indecent and expensive. It was now no longer necessary, for medical prophylaxsis had learned how to eliminate the disease, and needed only to be allowed to strip from it the hypocrisy behind which even the name of syphilis was rarely mentioned. Writing to Funston in August, 1916, after Fosdick had reported upon the open prostitution and the segregated districts of the Border towns, Baker had promised to 'support and sustain' every effort the commander should make to clean his camp. Fosdick carried by word of mouth the warning that a failure to eliminate venereal disease would bring about a change in command.

The Army had learned that Baker was in earnest before it undertook to prepare for war. The civil authorities near the camps learned it when in August, 1917, Baker warned the mayors that if they did not control alcohol and prostitution he would shift the camps from their vicinity to other sites. So far as the disease was concerned, the Surgeon-General was able to equip the forces with medical officers prepared to treat it. Fosdick continued at Baker's side, throwing his strength into an effort to prevent it. Prompt medical treatment was indeed to be provided, but the opportunity for infection was to be cut down, and a wide assortment of decent and wholesome occupations was offered to fill the soldier's mind and time when he went off duty.

A Commission on Training Camp Activities was at work before Congress met in December. Morale work around the camps was entrusted largely to the local fraternal organizations, Maccabees, Odd Fellows, and the rest. They were encouraged to organize activities in recreation. Athletic enterprises were promoted; so successfully in the United States and in France that a new heavy-weight champion was in due time manufactured out of a private in the Marine Corps, Gene Tunney. And the service agencies that were allowed to go abroad, whether in the uniform of the Y.M.C.A. or that of the Salvation Army, were given the mission to keep the mind of the Army clean.

It added complications to the already overcomplicated task of Army administration to have numerous civilian services working with the men, but it lessened the sick-list. It added difficulties, too, in France, where sexual irregularities and morals were less closely connected than in the United States, but it contributed a new chapter to the history of mass sanitation. The effort to support the morale services provided a basis for new drives to raise funds in the United States for their maintenance; and each of the drives had its results in solidifying still more completely the public opinion behind the American enterprise. But through the late autumn of 1917, when criticism of every aspect of war endeavor was getting ready to erupt in open attack, the determination to make war safe for the soldier added another to the long list of things that must be done. The Allied armies had escaped some of this confusion and experiment as they grew in size, for the emergency before them had been too pressing to admit of non-vital essentials, and their administrators had not before them for their guidance the experiences and mistakes of their associates.

The Congress resumed its work on Monday, December 3; the President addressed it on Tuesday; the declaration of war against

Austria-Hungary became a law on Friday; and on Wednesday of its second week the Senate Committee on Military Affairs began a searching investigation of the American effort in mobilization. Crozier, the Chief of Ordnance, was the first witness called to testify upon the capacity and intelligence of the Administration. In his cross-examination began the debate upon the fitness of the President to command the Army and to direct the war. There was politics in the investigation, but there was more concern. There was no obvious way by which the Congress could itself take the command from hands which it might believe to be incompetent; but the suspicion that the American effort had thus far miscarried drove members to a search for a way to speed the work.

The Committee on Military Affairs did not wait for a resolution of the Senate to direct it to its task. Senator George E. Chamberlain, its chairman, knew his own mind and had used his interest and driving power to advance the Army bills as they had come along during the first session. For fifteen weeks now, he and his associates listened to the testimony of men who were under fire and who often believed with him that there was something fundamentally wrong. They plowed through testimony bearing upon the activities of the War Department until it took twenty-five hundred pages to carry the record of the hearings. Chamberlain pursued the investigation until the winter changed to spring, until grave doubt had given way to hope, and until the War Department had by its own internal reforms increased its capacity to do its duty. But before the attack was abandoned, it had produced schemes for the reorganization of the war agencies and counter-schemes for strengthening the hand of the Commander in Chief.

The tales told by the witnesses carried more interest for contemporaries than value for the historian. They brought out details of what had or had not happened during eight months of effort. Many of the details were fresh to the public, however stale they were to workers in the Government. They related mostly to conditions prevalent earlier than December, and no longer in existence at the date of the hearings. They indicated both the enthusiasm of the effort and the inexperience of many of those who had to make it. And they were news. The press followed Chamberlain's string of witnesses, giving them much space in the dispatches out of Washington during the winter. The testimony had a tone different from that pervading the daily releases of the Committee on Public Information. It reflected long-restrained grievances of subordinates whose advice had been disregarded, and the tendential questions asked by the inquisitors indicated a willingness to believe that the grievances were well-founded. It was all the easier to believe the worst because when questioners approached what were to them the present conditions in the War Department there were good military reasons for withholding specific replies.

While the headlines carried the story of the unpreparedness with which the war started and related new details respecting attempts in organization that had failed, the current news of December and January fitted nicely into a picture of general incompetence. It was stated that production of war materials lagged, that clothing supplies for the troops were inadequate, that arms and equipment were insufficient. If Pershing's opinion of the War Department had been known to the public, and if the small total of troops in France had been revealed, the reaction adverse to the Government would have been even more bitter than it was. The curtain of secrecy concealed these things, but it could not hide a breakdown in the basic matters of railroad service and coal supply. 'Five months of crippled endeavor have passed,' wrote George Harvey as early as September. In December he asked: 'Are we losing the war?' In January he began the publication of his *War Weekly*, inquiring: 'How long can he [the President] carry the whole burden of war alone?' It is hard to reconcile his bitter criticism of the Administration and Baker in their conduct of the war with his avowed desire to assist them, but the very existence of his weekly vituperation testified to the earnestness of the doubt prevailing in many quarters during these, the darkest weeks of war.

The railroads were overburdened in spite of the desperate efforts of the Railroads War Board to operate them as a team. They had too much to do during the summer as camp materials were moved to camp sites and as men were moved into camp and out again. When in the late autumn the factories began to disgorge, long trains of coal, iron, and lumber, and of finished goods, started to the ports of shipment, and congestion swamped all facilities. Ships were too few, of course. Docks and warehouse space were inadequate. Freight yards could not hold the trains. And when snow and frost crippled the switches and impeded the operation of the terminals, the whole system of transportation in the United States began to creak and crack.

The Interstate Commerce Commission reported to Congress at the beginning of December that a strong arm was needed to direct the railroads and that unification was imperative. The lines east of Chicago, at least, needed to be operated as a national unit, regardless of ownership. The pooling of freight cars, an essential part of unification, was already authorized by law, but it was impossible for the roads under private management to pool the revenues and make fair compensations to the lines that were sure to suffer if competition was abandoned. The conditions prevailing in the Eastern freight yards, as Christmas approached, suggested a greater degree of confusion than really existed, and brought more blame than was reasonable, for neither private nor public management could have controlled the weather. But yardmasters could not receive the loaded trains as they pulled in or unload the freight. Warehouses could not hold it, even if unloaded. Ships could not hurry their 'turn-around' so as to move it. There were stories of consignments stored on the wheels, in trains that were routed back to the West still carrying the goods they bore from factories to ports.

On December 26 the rumors of impending seizure were confirmed by announcement that under the law of August 29, 1916, the President would in two days take over the management of all the railroads. The administration of the system was vested in a Director-General of Railroads, to which post McAdoo was named. The tireless energy of the son-in-law of the President seemed to have no limits as he now assigned a share of his strength to the railroad job. Before many weeks he took away from the officials of the roads the responsibility for their immediate management and vested the operation in his own appointees, who were sometimes the same persons, but who were now clothed with the authority of the United States. The railroad presidents became merely the executives of corporations owning property that the United States had leased. When Congress reassembled after its short Christmas recess it found an additional duty awaiting performance. Not until March was nearly over did it complete the law regulating the time and terms of Federal management of railroads.

The average earnings in the three fiscal years 1914–17 were made the basis for the rent to be paid by the Government during the period of control by the Railroad Administration. The private companies had found it hard to borrow for betterments. But betterments could not be avoided, and the law of March 21, 1918, put at the disposal of the Director-General a revolving fund of five hundred millions for capital investment. It was one of the consequences of war finance that the Government occupied the money market, making it next to impossible for private industry to borrow at reasonable rates; the Government accordingly assumed the task of financing the railways as a war cost. The Railroad Administration became the sixth of the great war agencies with which the normal mechanism of the Government was surrounded.

Railroad labor, as well as railroad finance, became a responsibility of the United States, for the unions felt the cost of rising prices, and their incessant demands for wage increases were among the burdens that made private management totter. And what had to be done by the Government in matters of railroad finance and labor became precedents for an extension of its authority into all the fields of finance and labor before the spring was gone. The railroad crisis, coming at a moment when doubts were strong as to the success of mobilization, made the doubts more serious. One of the specialized worries had to do with fuel, bringing Garfield and his Fuel Administration into the picture during January.

When the Fuel Administration was created, August 23, 1917, it was more clear that something must be done than just what it should be. Harry A. Garfield, blessed with a well-known name but cursed with academic connection, was not a coal man, and because of this he had to struggle against an expectation that he would be incompetent. The President, having rebuked the Council of National Defense for transgressing its powers in an attempt to fix the price of coal, had fixed it under his own powers just before Garfield was installed. To Garfield he left problems of production, labor relationship, and distribution. Price had a vital connection with the gross supply, because in addition to the great deposits of high-grade coal in the United States there is a wide distribution of inferior coal that can be mined and sold only when prices are above the average. There was a broad sector of the industry that could be occupied by producers who normally did not produce coal at all, but who could, under stress, mine the more easily worked veins of poor coal if the price were high enough. Since the highest price of the last ton mined would fix the national price of coal, it was certain that a price high enough to bring all the deposits into use would bring also unwarranted profits to the more fortunate producers. Some of these might be recaptured by the war excess-profits taxes, but not until after an inflated price of coal had done damage to the coal consumer. It was a nice task to set the price at the proper level.

The distribution of coal, one of the greatest charges upon the railroad system, was the crux of fuel control; and this became jammed in December with the rest of the program. McAdoo, hopeful that his Railroad Administration would work well, was optimistic about the fuel problem early in January. Garfield was pessimistic; and specially pessimistic because one of the causes of the congestion at the ports was the inability of the steamships to fill their bunkers. He was not ready as yet for the system of zone distribution that was later adopted to eliminate cross-haul by requiring each major division of the United States to get along on its own coal supply. He had appreciated the difference between the conditions governing coal as fuel and those of oil, and had on January 10 appointed Mark L. Requa of California, one of Hoover's associates, to be chief of an oil division of the Fuel Administration. But nothing had forewarned the country of the summary action taken a few days later in the announcement of the coal-less days.

On Friday, January 18, and for four days thereafter, and then on Mondays for nine more weeks, industry east of the Mississippi was directed to go slow on coal. Plants were required to close down to a Sunday basis. Exceptions were made for essential industries and for war manufacture; but the intent of the order of the Fuel Administration was to lighten traffic, clear the lines, and let coal get to the ships at the ports of embarkation. A wave of indignant protest was set off by the publication of the fuel holiday order. It brought home the war. Said the *Outlook*: it was a 'call of all hands to the pumps'; said the President, when efforts to induce him to overrule his subordinate reached the White House: 'We are on a war footing.' And the order stood.

But the necessity for the order, if it was necessary, or the outrage of it, if it was not needed, gave new acerbity to the discussions of the inadequacy of the Administration. Republicans, who might be expected to be critical, became more critical. Many Democrats were sunk in despair. And one of the latter, Chamberlain, the director of the investigations, went to New York on the second coal holiday, Saturday, January 19, to talk about the war before an audience assembled by the National Security League. Root was at the speaker's table, as was Roosevelt, who led the cheering at the end of the address, after the chairman of the Senate Committee on Military Affairs declared 'that the Military Establishment of America has fallen down. There is no use to be optimistic about a thing that does not exist. It has almost stopped functioning ... because of inefficiency in every bureau and in every department of the Government of the United States.' The issue was joined on Monday when the President, after securing from

Chamberlain a verification of his words, declared the charge to be 'an astonishing and absolutely unjustifiable distortion of the truth.'

The degree to which the military effort had broken down was and must remain largely a matter of subjective judgment. The whole program was too vast for any but the President to know or comprehend its whole, and his personal responsibility made his personal opinion of its success insufficient to establish it. But he, more completely than any of his critics, knew what it was about. For nine months the United States had been at war. The accomplishment, with all its defects, was distinguished when judged against the background of unreadiness as it existed in April, 1917. But the United States, after nine months, was still far from ready to meet the enemy on the battlefield. This seemed like failure to those who thought in terms of what there was, rather than in terms of distance gone.

At the moment when Wilson gave the lie to Chamberlain there came into clash two sets of forces out of whose combat was to emerge the solution of the problem of command. The President was himself steadily remodeling the war machine. He began this about the time when Scott retired from the War Industries Board and when Baker determined to let Bliss remain Chief of Staff until a younger general should establish himself as an adequate successor. The specific conditions displayed by the Chamberlain investigations no longer existed on the day they were brought to light. They had become historical. While Chamberlain was attacking set-ups that had been abandoned, the Administration kept its own counsel and continued to adapt set-up to changing conditions and experience. Chamberlain, as inquisitor, was forced into a greater prominence than he desired. It is possible that he had not yet forgiven Wilson for selecting Baker rather than himself to be Secretary of War upon the retirement of Garrison. He could not avoid being widely advertised by such political forces as were seeking grounds to attack the Administration. What he sought was not politics, but some new principle of command, consistent with the Constitution and better than that of sole presidential authority. Rumors of this search had floated through Washington in December when Congress reassembled, and had evoked from Charles Michelson, who was signing his dispatches as a Washington correspondent, the comment that a 'war council' idea 'jibes with the President's notions of carrying on the war like pickles in ice cream.' War council, coalition cabinet, munitions ministry, or something of the sort was in the air.

Theodore Roosevelt, whose friends were warranted in believing that behind the authority of his name the Republican Party would present a united front in 1920, reached Washington on Tuesday morning, January 22, with the slogan: 'Tell the truth and speed up the war.' At Longworth's home he was visited by those who agreed with him. He spoke the words of patriotism; meant them; but his conferences with Republicans in Congress gave a political color to his mission that could not be explained away. He could not forgive the military decision that kept him from the battlefield. He could not believe that good could come from Wilson. Even before he arrived, the news of his coming coupled with the President's rebuke of Chamberlain set tongues wagging in Congress. Stone of Missouri, who had been unwilling to fight Germans in April, was more than ready to fight Republican hecklers in January. He charged partisanship against them all; against Roosevelt, as 'the most seditious man of consequence in America'; against Wilcox, chairman of the Republican National Committee, who had called an unusual meeting for St. Louis on February 12, to name a new chairman and to prepare for both the congressional election of 1918 and the presidential campaign of 1920; and against Penrose, whom the course of the war had thrown into an unusual sympathy with the course of Roosevelt. Roosevelt countered the charges as a private citizen. Penrose countered them in the Senate, defending the duty of the minority 'to remedy inefficiency and abuses' by criticising them, and to maintain the integrity of their party in opposition. He and Roosevelt were alike in discarding one of the suggestions for improvement: that of a coalition Cabinet. Neither believed that bi-partisan administration had succeeded in England or desired to attempt it in the United States.

When the dust of combat subsided it revealed a concrete proposal for an improvement in administration to be obtained by the creation of a munitions minister or ministry. To this end Chamberlain presented to the Senate on January 21 a bill 'to create a war cabinet, to be composed of three distinguished citizens of demonstrated executive ability ... through which war cabinet the President may exercise such of the powers conferred on him by the Constitution and the laws ... as are hereinafter mentioned and described.' Chamberlain had discussed his project at the White House a fortnight earlier, and had been advised by the President as early as January 11 that the latter was fundamentally opposed to it. The British experiments with a munitions ministry and a small war cabinet were attractive precedents to those whose understanding of the British system of government was less complete than that of Woodrow Wilson. When Wilson now challenged the truth of the charge of breakdown, and indicated that it would be fought to the end, Chamberlain's bill was lost before it was printed. It was conceivable that the President was incompetent to wage the war, yet it was he and not Congress that was designated as Commander in Chief. His Cabinet was what he conceived to be a War Cabinet; and, lacking the power to take from him his constitutional right of appointment, Congress was impotent to elevate to control better men than he could be induced to name. It was not possible to dislodge him from the position of President as described in the Constitution.

While Chamberlain, losing confidence in the agents of the Government, was assembling testimony to indicate inept administration, and was advancing toward his explosion point, the President was shuffling the cards and arranging new combinations to advance the war. It is not possible to separate the part of this shuffling that may have been inspired by fear of trouble with Congress from the part induced by the experience of the eight months since the war began. The opposition declared that the changes were forced upon the Administration by criticism; it is not necessary to believe that the Administration told the whole truth in claiming them to have been entirely spontaneous. However they came about, they put the administration of the war upon a new plane between December and May.

The Chamberlain investigations were only a few days old when Baker announced the creation of a War Council, consisting of the Chief of Staff and the more important bureau chiefs, whose function was to 'oversee and co-ordinate all matters of supply of our field armies and the military relations between the armies in the field and the War Department.' He explained the new agency as not inspired by either the investigations or the situation reported from the Inter-Ally Conference. He told the Chamberlain Committee a few days later that it was a next step, now that 'initial supply and organization had been substantially disposed of.' When, eight months later, he dissolved the War Council and assigned its rooms to the statistical branch of the General Staff, George Harvey noted the disappearance in his *War Weekly*. Harvey was not sure whether the Council had been created because of the incompetency of Baker or as a device to get rid of inadequate bureau chiefs by promoting them upstairs. The fact that the chiefs were relieved of routine duties on account of their new responsibilities gave support to the latter interpretation. But whatever the reason, the War Council had outlived its usefulness by July, 1918. Two of its members had come to cast so long a shadow as to obscure their colleagues. March and Baruch had the American end of the war in hand. It had been more than suspected in the winter that one of the reasons for the creation of the Council was the impotence of the General Staff, with its brains picked for duty abroad. There may have been a chance that the Council, dominated by the bureaus that never liked the General Staff, would come to dominate it. But nothing could overshadow Peyton C. March, once Baker had chosen him and had installed him in the office of Chief of Staff.

At the desk of Sharpe, who moved upstairs into the Council, a place was at last found for Major-General George W. Goethals, as acting Quartermaster-General. The Emergency Fleet Corporation was not the place for the builder of the Panama Canal to function happily; in the War Department, however, and as chief of a section of the General Staff with oversight of the whole quartermaster business, Goethals found his rôle. He brought a young cavalry officer with him, Robert E. Wood, who had been his quartermaster at Panama, who speedily became a brigadier-general and who later turned his war experience into post-war advantage by rising to the head of Sears, Roebuck and Company. He borrowed another cavalryman, when Crowder was through with him — Hugh S. Johnson. Goethals drove the business of procurement with a maximum of courage and a minimum of red tape until his P.S. & T. — the Purchase, Storage, and Traffic Division of the General Staff — controlled the whole field. Even if he could not work with 'boards' he knew how to work under military superiors, the Chief of Staff and the Secretary of War. His admirers and the admirers of Bernard M. Baruch have not been able to agree which of the two, the military head or the civilian, was the great master of the material side of the American reinforcement. But between them, they were 'it.'

Goethals, who rounded out his career as a procurement officer, was as such only an experiment when in December he became acting Quartermaster-General. He was only one of Baker's guesses at good management. Stettinius was another guess, and one equally well grounded. Edward R. Stettinius had made himself head of the Diamond Match Company before the house of Morgan found him. The finding was consequence of a deliberate search for a new partner to take charge of the investment of Allied money in the materials of war. Stettinius had spent three billions of this money, to the satisfaction of the Allies and of the Morgans, before Baker annexed him to the War Department as Surveyor-General of Army Purchases. This was announced in the midst of the Chamberlain drive, and was hailed as the creation of the equivalent of a director of munitions. It preceded by a few days the announcement that March was to come back from France to be acting Chief of Staff. Stettinius was made an Assistant Secretary of War in April, and fulfilled with meticulous exactness the demand of Chamberlain for 'distinguished citizens of demon-strated executive ability.' A third of the good guesses as to per-sonnel had been made in November when Major Benedict Crowell had been induced to resign his commission in the Army to become an Assistant Secretary of War, with general oversight over muni-tions. Crowell was a Cleveland mining engineer, who had been with the General Munitions Board before entering the Army. He became Director of Munitions in 1918.

Unruffled by the investigations and keeping his temper under the barrage of criticism, Baker continued upon the job in hand. There was no sign of wavering on the part of Wilson, who stood behind him. The tactic of the Administration in meeting the storm when it broke was worked out promptly. Confidence in its success was so complete that, having called new aides to his side and having summoned March, the Secretary of War quietly disappeared from the news at the end of February. He arrived in France upon an inspection trip on March 10; and soon there-after his black civilian derby and his unimpressive stature made their appearance in the illustrated papers among resplendent generals, as he visited the front and the rear to see with his own eyes what the A.E.F. was doing. He had not only set the War Department upon a new and final course, but he had also drawn enough of the teeth of the Chamberlain investigation to lessen the hurt of its bite.

The hearings before the Senate Committee on Military Affairs increased in interest from December into January. They brought the inquiry to a crisis over the week-end of January 19–21, and they declined in consequence during the next few weeks. Public tension relaxed as it was discovered that heatless days did not mean disaster, as new news gave new subjects for thought, and as the rigors of winter were softened by the approach of spring. The relaxation was advanced by the appearances of the Secretary of War before the Chamberlain Committee to give direct testi-mony upon the state of preparation.

After extracting from his subordinates their impression of the difficulties under which they had worked and the lack of unison from which they had suffered through the summer, the Committee summoned Baker. He went on the stand on January 10; and thereafter he was in and out of the Committee until the end of the month. The first days of his testimony suggest to the reader that he underestimated the importance of congressional and public uneasiness and that he treated the hearings as routine and the inquisitors as contentious. He was well aware of personal and political hostility, such as that of Senator Sherman of Illinois, who described him as 'half pacifist and the other half Socialist.' But he was conscious, too, of White House backing, for on the day after his first session Wilson wrote emphatically to Chamberlain in disapproval of the war cabinet idea.

It was not easy for those who lived, worked, and slept with the war to realize how little the public knew of what was going on. But the flare-up set off by Chamberlain in New York reminded the Administration that the state of the public mind was as important as the condition of the Army, and that the distrusts, however ungrounded, were genuine. The Secretary, who had not done himself much good by his first appearance, asked for a second appointment with the Committee, returned to it on January 28, and at that time turned the drift of thought and feeling. He had a better text than on the earlier occasion, for Chamberlain had now not only launched his charges and introduced his law, but he had also elaborated both at great length before the Senate as he made a personal defense against the retort of the President.

There were few Americans more effective in exposition than Baker, when he took the occasion seriously; and now, as he reviewed nine months of war in the presence of the Committee on Military Affairs, he looked over the heads of his hearers to the great public that needed to be reassured. Even yet he spoke with caution; for in the background was an enemy watchful for every fragment of testimony that might reveal a military secret. He was, indeed, as Palmer has said, 'walking on eggs.' He could at least tell his hearers that instead of having, as Roosevelt had demanded, five hundred thousand men who could be sent to France in 1918, he would have that many actually there early in the year. He dared not say how bitterly the Allies were urging the American reinforcement, but he could tell of the million and a half who would be ready to be shipped if tonnage could be found. He could describe the welfare of the Army and ask, 'Has any army in history ever, since the beginning of time, been so raised and cared for as this army has been?' He could not tell precisely what he was soon going to inspect in France, but he could check the impatience of his audience by recollection, and remind it that 'France was a white sheet of paper, so far as we were concerned, and on that we had not only to write an army ... we had to go back to the planting of corn in France in order that we might make a harvest.'

The Secretary was not willing to reveal the uncertainty of the Supreme War Council, whose members were at the moment *en route* to a meeting at Versailles. If they had even yet no affirmative program of military affairs for 1918, he could not make one for them; but he could tell what Pershing had found in the preceding June, when France was demoralized and Pétain was at work restoring its morale. And his description of the day when first the advance guard of the A.E.F. appeared upon the streets of Paris still tingles the reader of the *Official Bulletin*, or of the *Congressional Record* in which the testimony was reprinted in spite of Republican objection, or of the daily press through which reassurance reached the citizen. Two days later Baker took lunch publicly with Chamberlain in the Senate restaurant; and on February 6 Overman of North Carolina introduced in the Senate a War Department draft that was the Administration alternative to the corrective legislation of the Military Affairs Committee.

It was the contention of the critics that the Administration was too lax to run the war; the reply of the Administration was that the war was well run, that it was out of the confusion of the first half-year of planning, that it was nearly out of the second half-year of organization, and that it was on the verge of operation. In place of new laws to tie the hands of the President and teach him his duty, the Administration asked a relief from red tape and statutory interference. Few statutes have in so few words surrendered so much; and none has vested more discretion in the President than was done by the Overman Act, which received his signature on May 20, 1918.

In the controversy over the command of the Army it was Wilson, backed by public opinion, who prevailed. Republican factionalists, so far as they were factionalist, sniped at him from party committees and from editorial sanctums. Democratic party leaders had difficulty in moving with him as rapidly or as thoroughly as he conceived that the public desired him to move. Leader of a party that had through three Congresses gained and retained the whole of the law-making machinery of the United States, Wilson was nevertheless, at one time or another, driven to lead without the support of his partisan lieutenants. Sometimes Clark was against him, though Speaker of the House; sometimes Claude Kitchin, chairman of the Committee on Ways and Means; sometimes Stone of Missouri, chairman of the Senate Committee on Foreign Relations. And now Martin of Virginia, party leader in the Senate, declined to stand sponsor for the measure vesting in the President full power of action. Burleson took the draft to Overman, who consented to manage it. Crowder had drawn it up for Baker, two weeks before.

The Overman Act remained in committee from February 6 until Overman called it up at the end of March. It passed the Senate April 19 by a vote of 63 to 13, amended only by a specific grant of authority to rearrange aircraft production. The House accepted it without amendment, with but two votes in opposition to a majority of 294. It cut through checks and balances. For the continuance of the war, and for six months thereafter (unless the President should designate an earlier date), the Overman Act authorized him to redistribute the functions of executive agencies as he saw fit; 'to utilize, co-ordinate, or consolidate any executive or administrative commissions, bureaus, agencies, offices, or officers now existing by law'; to create new agencies; to transfer, redistribute, or abolish the functions of others; and to utilize funds voted for any purpose for the accomplishment of that purpose by whatever means might to him seem good. The text of the act justified the jocose amendment hurled at it by Brandegee as it left the Senate: 'If any power, constitutional or not, has been inadvertently omitted from this bill, it is hereby granted in full.' It was possible to joke about it, and from the floor of either house to criticize its concentration of authority, but public opinion had made up its mind about the management of the war, and few members of Congress desired to be left in the uncomfortable isolation of opposition.

The American reinforcement was in full flow before the bill became a law; the First Division was in the line in front of Cantigny, ready for its earliest independent venture; and the war machine at home was functioning.

XI. THE 'SEPARATE COMPONENT'

FULL executive responsibility for the management of the war was left with the President after the discussions and the legislation of the winter of 1918. He demanded that he be left unhampered, and that he be granted sweeping new powers, and Congress acceded to both demands. Thereafter, he was in complete command. For whatever went well or badly, his became the accepted and unshiftable responsibility. The Federal Government, muscle-bound by American preference, had been freed from peace-time restrictions in the process that began with the President's fund of one hundred millions and ended with the passage of the Overman Act. The half-dozen huge war boards were as many evidences of American willingness to meet emergency with emergency methods.

The war boards were all functioning before the Overman Act was signed. Their directors were called in to meet with the President on March 20, at which time it was suggested that they were to constitute a War Cabinet, supplementary to the regular Cabinet, with its ten secretaries. The War Council, created by Baker in the War Department in December, was on its way out, since the new Chief of Staff had no use for it. Neither it nor the War Cabinet managed to become a creative entity, but each did its service as a symbol of improving team-work. Each had to do with the American reservoir of men and things out of which a military spearhead was being fabricated.

The direction of the military spearhead at the front in France was a matter in which the effectiveness of the American reinforcement was involved. Pershing did not become sure of his status as co-commander until July, 1918. In February, when the Overman

Act was introduced, his pretensions to be a co-commander were an
annoyance to the military authorities of the Allies. They had
given up hope of an American reinforcement large enough to
count before 1919, and he had presumed to sit in judgment upon
their needs. It is as well that the men who had to work together
through the morass of plan and execution were not fully informed
of what each of them thought about the others. This revelation had
to wait until their memoirs saw the light. The reader of the
memoirs and the correspondence can learn more about them than
they knew about themselves. Knowledge at the time might easily
have destroyed their capacity to work at all. 'The Allies are very
weak,' wrote Pershing, 'and we must come to their relief this year
[1918]. The year after may be too late.'

Pershing, like the President, had on his hands a fight for permission to do his work his own way. Though he did not know the
words in which his associates expressed their acid comments upon
his plan or his capacity, he was aware that through his period of
command he had against him most of the weight of professional
wisdom as the Allies possessed it. He differed from the President
in that the latter must rely chiefly on himself in conducting the
fight, whereas the commander of the A.E.F. had behind him,
persistently and loyally, the authority of the President of the
United States as well as that of the Secretary of War. Neither
Washington nor Grant could have believed in the possibility of an
American commander whose hand should be so well upheld by
the political agencies of the Government. Neither of them had
been so upheld.

The course of Pershing, in building an organization to carry a
great American army as a 'distinct and separate component,'
met with disapproval and sabotage from the Allies. The Administration backed him up, but he had to bear full responsibility for
his decisions. When he issued his basic orders from Paris in July,
1917, it was not suspected on either side of the Atlantic that the
United States would fight in force. When he demanded an
American sector on the Western Front, he raised a question that
the Allies would have preferred unraised, but one for which there

was no easy way to deny compliance. When he settled down in Chaumont, saw the importance of the reduction of the German salient at St. Mihiel and the road to Metz behind that salient, and directed his staff to begin the paper work for a first army enterprise at this spot, he had escaped for the moment from the menace of amalgamation. When he began the consolidation of his lines of communication, south of Paris, connecting his Atlantic ports with his Toul sector, his wisdom might be challenged, but not his certainty of purpose. He, like the military authorities of the Allies, had regrets over the thin stream of troops that landed in France even after the War Department had more than a million men in camp; but they, unlike himself, did not until after the close of their disastrous season of 1917 come to count on any heavy reinforcement. Thereafter, Lloyd George persuaded himself that they had all along been 'waiting for the Americans.' Eventually the British Premier convinced himself that the delay in providing what had not been contracted for constituted culpable delay.

Pershing never lost sight of his ultimate army. His requisitions for its first million poured into Washington and overwhelmed the bureaus and the committees. His specifications, of necessity, were amended repeatedly as his officers worked their way into the details of training and equipment. Equally of necessity, the procurement officers in the United States were driven crazy by changes in specifications after they had let contracts and arranged for the construction of new plants in which to make the munitions Pershing required. After his conference with House and Bliss, and the Supreme War Council, in December, 1917, Pershing set a specific goal for Baker: 'We should plan to have in France by the end of June [1918] . . . four army corps, or twenty-four divisions, in addition to the troops for the service of the rear.' This meant approximately a million men, for one man was needed at the rear for every two men at the front. The million men were, in fact, in France or on their way thither before July, but when Pershing demanded them he knew no way to get them.

As the deliberations of the Supreme War Council revealed the impossibility of a major Allied aggressive against the enemy until or if the Americans should arrive, the disapproval of Pershing's determination to command them when they came forced its way into counsels in Europe, and back to Washington. Few intimations of it reached the public, but on the very day that Pershing asked for his twenty-four division program, Lloyd George appealed behind his back to House for American troops — 'even half-trained' — to be mixed with seasoned veterans. He did not repudiate the desire for an army with a 'national identity,' but he wanted more than this. To this end he suggested that troops be shipped in excess of Pershing's program, to become replacements in the British ranks. Haig had a plan for using them this way.

By the time House and Bliss were back in Washington in mid-December the Administration was facing a choice between Pershing and Haig as its military adviser, or Pétain, for the French commander was pressing Pershing to let his regiments as they arrived be attached to French divisions. On Christmas Day Baker cabled Pershing, for the President, 'full authority to use the forces at your command as you deem wise.' This left the full responsibility for decision upon the table at Chaumont.

The British had powerful leverage in all matters connected with the decision, for they controlled the ships. So long as the extent of the reinforcement depended on American bottoms it was little more than academic because the bottoms were too few to carry the men and their supplies. It was too much to expect that Britain would sacrifice indispensable tonnage to carry troops to a destiny that Britain distrusted. When England, however, offered to find the ships for the carriage of troops in excess of Pershing's program, on the condition that Haig have a temporary right to use them, it provided a basis for a bargain. It did more; the admission that ships could be found made it increasingly harder for Sir Joseph Maclay, British Shipping Controller, to withhold on any ground of shortage the transport needed. Without the use of much British tonnage it was unlikely that even the minimum of twenty-four divisions would ever get to France.

The bargaining over troops and tonnage was never ended. Between December and March it provided many opportunities for the Administration to overrule Pershing, or even to displace him, had it been so disposed. Repeatedly the generals met, and the American general stood firm. Often the Permanent Military Representatives of the Supreme War Council, united in February as the Executive War Board in charge of the Allied (though non-existent) reserve, discussed amalgamation. Bliss sat on this Board, with Rawlinson, Weygand, and Cadorna as colleagues. Even the Prime Ministers tried their hand. Lloyd George and Clemenceau, convinced that Pershing's was not the way to win the war, attempted persuasion upon his chief. They might have been more persuasive had they been in agreement upon a better way. Lloyd George was an 'eastern,' thinking always of turning the German left wing in the Balkans or beyond; Clemenceau, a 'western,' saw victory to be reached somewhere along the direct route between Paris and Berlin. Jusserand and Reading (who replaced Spring Rice as ambassador in February) exerted pressure for their masters in Washington. The bargains reached in France sometimes received an unanticipated construction at the White House, and the conversations in Washington sometimes led hopeful ambassadors to believe that the President would overrule his commander in the field. Pershing found that in addition to the burden of preparing for his army he must take continuous part in a diplomatic fight to retain command of it.

He was saved, in part, by a determination in Washington to back him up. He was helped, from time to time, by jealousies between England and France, which led each of them in turn to assist him a little in evading the encroachments of the other. He was ready, in a pinch, to fight back. Early in January he cut across 'military channels' to rebuke Clemenceau for trying to settle with Washington by cable matters that could be settled only by conference among the generals in the field. Clemenceau, admonished, avowed himself ready to 'exercise all the patience' of which he was capable — which was not too much — but insisted that upon the settlement of the matter might depend the outcome of the war.

By the time the Supreme War Council held its third session, at the end of January, Pershing was certain that there would not be any general Allied offensive until his men were in France. He adhered to his position against amalgamation, noting that his colleagues, Haig and Pétain, made their own bargain and maintained it against the directives from the Supreme War Council. He had brought Bliss into full support of his position before the Council met. Since Bliss, still Chief of Staff, was technically his superior officer, this was vital; but it was not difficult, for Bliss had no delusion of greatness to make him think his four stars were superior to those of Pershing. The most that Pershing would promise was that if divisions should be brought over as a whole (rather than only the infantrymen and machine gunners whom the Allies craved), the regiments of infantry might receive preliminary training with the British while the artillery received training with the French; all of this conditioned upon the delivery to him of divisions as units after training. He was willing to let the troops take their chance with combat forced upon them while engaged in such training, but he refused to let them be counted as parts of the armies of either of the Allies.

In the face of Pershing's opposition to anything looking like amalgamation, the Supreme War Council had no option but to arrange matters as best it could with what it had. The American army was, after all, only a when-if-or-as reinforcement; not a certainty. Haig and Pétain, each in his own way, were as recalcitrant as the American commander. The recommendation of the Permanent Military Representatives was approved in principle, but was modified by the Allied commanders into a moderate extension by Haig of the lines he held, and a mutual agreement that each should come if needed to the aid of the other. The vision of an Executive War Board under a French chairman looked so much like a first step to a generalissimo that the 'black coats' of the Supreme War Council felt impelled to issue public denials that a generalissimo had been created.

In the British army, which had not been able to bring about effective amalgamation with its own colonial troops and yet desired to amalgamate the A.E.F., feeling ran high against any inter-Allied arrangement that might lessen the discretion of the field commander, or that of the Chief of the Imperial General Staff. In a fortnight Robertson was out of office over the issue of the Executive War Board and Sir Henry Wilson was in his place. In the middle of March the Supreme War Council met again, in London, to face the fact that neither of the existing armies would contribute its quota of divisions to the reserve. There was a real question whether the scheme of pooling the interests at Versailles had not broken down. So far as it depended upon the functioning of the Executive War Board, it had collapsed. The Board lasted, even in name, only until midsummer.

This fourth session for which Clemenceau came with bad grace to London, began as the Supreme War Council and ended as a political conference of the Allies. Foch, as French Chief of Staff, came with his Premier, and with Weygand, his *alter ego*, as Permanent Military Representative. The new British Chief of Staff, Wilson, was in harmony with Rawlinson who had taken his place as Permanent Military Representative. Bliss was there, an 'unswerving advocate of the army of maneuver under Foch,' as Lloyd George has described him; and hoping in vain that the Executive War Board might somehow come back to life and to the command of a real reserve.

The United States, absent from the political conference of the Premiers, had no political spokesman in Europe, and wanted none. Wilson, his own agent, had addressed Congress again on February 11, reiterating his aims in the war and summing up the comments that had reached him since his Fourteen Points address. The definitive peace between Germany and Russia, under dictation at Brest-Litovsk since December, was signed in March a few days before the Prime Ministers came together, and only awaited ratification by the Bolshevik revolutionists. Pressure was already upon the United States to provide troops for a venture at Vladivostok in an Allied effort to lessen the consequence of the withdrawal of Russia from the war. On March 11, as though he suspected the intention of the Allies, Wilson again stepped out alone, sending to the Russian congress which was about to meet a message of interest in the unimpaired sovereignty of Russia. Without his presence or approval the Allied statesmen in London proceeded to denounce the German deception of Russia and to prepare their intervention in eastern Siberia in support of a Russian minority against the Soviets.

Pershing had an opportunity to freshen his contacts with the War Department during the week in which the Premiers met in London. Secretary Baker was at hand. Wrestling with the congressional attempt to take the management of the war out of the hands of the President, Baker had kept on with his own revamping of the war machine. With Crowell, Goethals, and Stettinius attached to it and finding their level, and with the President on the verge of assigning to Baruch the management of the War Industries Board, and with March on his way home to take in hand the General Staff, some of the business on his desk began to thin out. He had found time, during the worst of the fight over a munitions ministry, to approve a new scheme of organization from the General Staff, which was published to the Army in General Order 14, February 9. In this the advisory functions of the General Staff were more clearly defined than before and the work was dissected topically in the interest of speed and accuracy. The war did not last long enough for the General Staff to be detached entirely from the jobs in administration that were foreign to its theory, or to be set free for the exercise of exclusively advisory functions. But the progressive reorganizations worked in that direction. As now redefined, the Chief of Staff, military adviser of the Secretary of War, was to work through five principal aides, each an Assistant Chief of Staff. These aides were charged respectively with administration, war plans, purchase and supply, storage and traffic, and operations. The assistants were to deal directly with the line units in the Army and with the various staff services, and out of what they thus learned they were to inform the Chief of Staff so that he might give sound advice to the Secretary. In practice the resulting orders commonly began: 'The Secretary of War directs ...'; but whether or not a given order was important enough for the Secretary to have seen it, he took the responsibility for what his military counsel made him say. The work was beginning to run through the new grooves when March reported for duty. He modified the procedure in detail during the next few months, but his military contribution was more in the field of dynamics than in that of mechanics.

With his reorganization started and with his dramatic appearances before the Senate Committee a matter of record, Baker slipped out of Washington to inspect the A.E.F. On March 10 he was reported in Paris; and here he began to take account of stock, with Bliss to write an attractive picture of their conference in a cellar under the hotel during a night air raid. When Bliss went off to London for the meeting of the fourteenth, Baker went on tour, leaving with the military authorities of France what comfort they could get out of his statement that his trip was that he might the better know how to support the commander of the A.E.F.

Pershing had much to show him; not much in the way of divisions ready for the field, but much already accomplished in preparing for the army when it should arrive. He had, in France, been doing work closely resembling that which Baker had left in Washington. His most recent job had been the erection at Tours of a new headquarters, bearing to his army something of the relation held in the United States by the War Department to the whole military establishment.

No more in France than in Washington did American officers, laboring for their first time over the vast problems of mobilization, supply, training, direction, and fighting, manage to settle to their satisfaction the relations between part and part that are most likely to help to win a war. Probably these are incapable of settlement and must depend in the last analysis upon the particular war and the personalities in charge of it. The first great question of the relationship between the political heads of a nation and its fighting force was settled basically in Washington. The second, that of the relationship between the commander and his subordinates, was worked out in the field. There can be little doubt that the commander should keep his desk free from detail in order to have time to survey the broad lines of his mission. There is as little doubt that each of his chief subordinates, being human, craves to hang directly on the word of the commander, without the intermediary —or the meddling— of the officials whose business is to free the commander from detail. The black braid on the cuff of the officer on the General Staff had not made that officer popular in the United States; it kept him unpopular in France. Many of the officers who were invaluable cogs in Pershing's machine were as much aggrieved by the inability of his personal staff to comprehend their needs as he was aggrieved by the inability of Washington to understand his requirements.

While the A.E.F. continued to be no more than a dream, for whose realization the headquarters group was busy drafting plans, it remained possible for the direction of the American venture to remain at Chaumont. The time had to come when the inevitable cleavage between those who directed the battle, those who fought it, and those who brought up to the line the men and their supplies would call for a decentralization of functions and control; all, however, remaining under the hand of the commander. When Pershing moved his G.H.Q. to Chaumont in September, he left behind him in Paris the subordinate headquarters of what was then called the Line of Communications. This needed every day to work in most intimate contact with the French authorities through whose towns and across whose country the lines would run. But Paris was no place for the Line of Communications after its plans were made and its blueprints drawn when it became concerned with construction first and operation next. And Chaumont was no place for it; for Chaumont must concern itself with combat, while the work of the Line of Communications was completed far in the rear when it delivered to the agents of the field commanders their men and tools.

During January, the American papers, naming no names according to their practice under the voluntary censorship, began to hint at the probability of a shift of the headquarters of the Line of Communications to a 'beautiful little city in central France,' Kernan, commanding the L.O.C., recommended this; a Chaumont board approved it; and in February the orders bringing it about were issued. Tours was the city. Situated on the Loire, with good railway connections to Paris, to St. Nazaire through which supplies were coming, and to the training areas behind the Toul sector, it was convenient. Being relatively empty of French administration, it gave room for growth. In a most attractive part of France, its environment gave to the officers detailed to work in Tours what compensation they could get to make up for absence from the front. Even Harbord, who later came to command it, felt that the physical separation from Chaumont deprived him of the direct contact with Pershing that he needed; but Harbord's argument against the possibility of keeping everything at Chaumont is conclusive against even his own dissatisfaction. The order directing the shift from Paris provided a new name for the Line of Communications, which now became the Services of the Rear. Before long this was amended to Services of Supply.

What could be decided at Tours was decided there. Pershing's general oversight was maintained by direct contact between the several divisions of the Tours staff and the similar divisions at Chaumont. The sections of the staff at Chaumont received a new nomenclature resembling that of the French Army, without greatly changing the functions distributed by Baker in the American reorganization of February 9. The five 'Gs' made their appearance; and military lingo used 'G-1' or 'G-5' with complete understanding of what was meant. The principal duties of the five Assistant Chiefs of Staff, thus designated, and their counterparts at Tours, and in armies, corps, and divisions as far down as the system extended, comprised all the great functions of the Army. G-1 was administration; G-2, military intelligence; G-3, operations; G-4, co-ordination and supply; G-5, training. The railroad men and those in charge of army utilities were never satisfied; and Atterbury, ever a railroad man in spite of being a general, believed that the Services of Supply ought to have been a civilian organization, dependent directly on the commander. There were some in Washington who thought that they might better have been directly dependent on the War Department. But, for better or worse, Pershing had organized the American effort his own way, and had his scheme of things to show when Baker undertook to see with his own eyes what had been done and what remained to be done. The army was taking shape before its men arrived. It had even its 'house organ.' The first number of the *Stars and Stripes,* edited in the army by its men for their morale, made its appearance February 8.

Baker saw it all: from the stacks of piles waiting to be driven at the ports to the staff offices at Chaumont and to the front-line trenches. Sometimes he had Pershing for a guide, but he hardly needed one, and with his lack of swank left many to wonder who the inquisitive little man could be. Always he had words with those in immediate command and with their men. Often he had to pause and speak to groups; and when he did this even Frederick Palmer, more or less his custodian and entirely case-hardened to official eloquence, was stirred to listen. The culmination of his tour brought him to the headquarters of Pétain, for luncheon at Chantilly, on Thursday, March 21. The program for that afternoon was to have been the Somme battlefield, which Palmer knew; but the program was modified, for the battlefield was again occupied by battle. That morning a desperate German blow, planned to end the war before the Americans arrived in force, broke upon the British Fifth Army which held the new extension of the line of Haig. Amiens was the objective of the drive, and the splitting of the Allies at their point of junction its immediate purpose. The Valley of the Somme provided the route of the advance. The first stroke drove Allied troops from their trenches along some fifty miles of front, with the spearhead advancing a little to the north of St. Quentin. During the next week Baker carried his tour to London, while the daily war maps showed the growth of the new German salient, with its base widening and its tip reaching almost to Amiens, through which ran the sole dependable line of communications between the French armies in front of Paris and the British forces in Flanders. On Sunday, the fourth day of the drive, Pétain let Haig know that he need not hope for immediate reinforcement if their line should break; that in such case it would be the duty of the French to cover Paris, leaving the British to shift for themselves between the German divisions and the Channel.

If the war had ended now, and for several days it had a fair chance of being ended, the historical *post mortem* would have attributed German victory to the inability of the Allies to subject themselves to disciplines other than their several own. The scheme for an Allied reserve, directed as a unit by the Executive War Board, had broken down. Perhaps there could not have been a reserve, since each of the principal Allies was a little beyond the crest of its man-power. Certainly there was none that could fill the breach at the left of the British Fifth Army. The agreement for mutual help, between Haig and Pétain, left each general the judge of the time and manner of the help, and in the crisis of the German drive neither felt warranted in endangering the national purpose represented by his army for the sake of the safety of the other. This could hardly have been otherwise so long as France and Britain were fighting separate wars. The American pressure for concentration of the command, so that there might be a single war, was interesting as evidence of American belief, but in the absence of an American army there was no military contribution of importance for Pershing to have made, even had there been a generalissimo. And the absence of an American army was due to the lack of ships in which to transport it, with Britain pardonably reluctant to invest ships in an unwise, or what it believed to be unwise, American adventure.

Six months later, had Germany won the war, with Pershing commanding his 'separate component,' the *post mortem* might have been justified in placing the onus all on him and his personal ambition to command an army. But in March, 1918, a collapse of the Allies, with their resources and man-power still far ahead of those of Germany, would have been fairly attributable to defective team-work.

The Allies did not lose. The British Fifth Army, weary when it received the blow, and perhaps not adequately supported during its engagement, fell back before the German thrust. It lost contact with the neighbor British army on its left, until there was a gap with nothing in front of the enemy but the road to Amiens. The French neighbor on its right was slow to appreciate the full urgency of the call for reinforcement. In the end, Haig healed his own breach, and the advance of the apex of the German salient slowed down. It slowed down as much because all salients tend to bring themselves to a standstill as because the barrier of resistance was too tough to be overcome. One of the German officers planning the drive had warned his superiors that

> in a successful offensive, the attacker will be forced to cross a difficult and shot-to-pieces battle area and will get gradually farther away from his railheads and depots, and that, having to bring forward his masses of artillery and ammunition columns, he will be compelled to make pauses which will give time to the defender to organize resistance.

The preparations for the drive, noted by the intelligence officers of the Allies, had produced suspicious warning movements along one hundred miles of German front, most of the way from Armentières to Reims. The German divisions themselves, making their adjustments, had not been allowed to know just where they would begin. The concentration had displaced the Allies, beginning with a thirty-mile front and widening to fifty; the penetration as the salient was advanced ran beyond thirty miles, far enough to have reached Amiens had not Haig managed to deflect the apex a little to the south, where it came to rest. Montdidier, in front of the French armies, and only some forty miles from Paris, was in German hands when the line of the new salient was stabilized.

At the week-end, the drive having begun on Thursday, the crumpling of the Allied line attracted attention in London even before Haig was stirred by great fear, and before Pétain warned him that he must close the gap or lose connection. If Lloyd George or Henry Wilson had trusted Haig more, they might have watched him less closely, or had less disappointment at his unwillingness to find divisions for the proposed reserve. On Saturday, after a meeting of the British War Cabinet, the Prime Minister asked Milner to go to France, and was ready to accept a French commander as less disastrous than defeat. On Sunday, Haig came to the same decision. Making desperate effort to back up the Fifth Army and restore the line, and warned by Pétain, Haig summoned Wilson and Milner, who was already on his way, to come to France to negotiate a better team-work which might mean a unified direction of the war. The historians will long debate the responsibility for the near-victory of Germany whether it was an undue extension of the British front, or the incapacity of Gough with his Fifth Army, or the default of Pétain upon his promise to send aid if needed, or the general unimaginativeness of Haig, or sabotage by Lloyd George because of his interest in 'eastern' adventures. But there is already agreement that the nearness of defeat broke down resistance to the theory of the war that President Wilson had endorsed when he said of the Supreme War Council: 'we ... insist on it.' On Monday, with the fate of Amiens still uncertain, the generals and the politicians scurried from conference to conference; on Tuesday, March 26, they came together for action at the town hall of Doullens-en-Picardie.

Pershing stayed on his job, for he was not involved in the battle except in so far as a handful of engineers, caught by the advance, exchanged picks and spades for weapons, turned themselves into scratch troops, and helped resist it. Poincaré, President of the Republic, presided at Doullens, back of the British front, and some eighteen miles north of Amiens. Clemenceau was there, bringing with him Ferdinand Foch, whom he had boosted to opportunity ten years before. In an earlier Cabinet, Clemenceau, free-thinker and radical, had elevated Foch, conservative and conscientious Catholic, to his brigadier-generalcy and the post of director of the École Supérieure de la Guerre. Already Foch's *Principes de la Guerre* (1903) and *De la Conduite de la Guerre* (1905) were the textbooks of the officers of France. Foch represented the theory of the war which had prevailed in France since the elevation of Pétain to the command of the Army in the spring of 1917 and his own resultant advancement to Pétain's post as Chief of Staff. Peter Wright, a member of the English staff at the Supreme War Council, thought he looked 'like a rustic French curé.' At Doullens, also, were Milner, and Haig, and Sir Henry Wilson. As the result of their out-of-conference discussions, Milner assented for England to the elevation of Foch to more than had been intended for him when the chairmanship of the Executive War Board was in hand. He was charged with 'co-ordinating the action of the Allied Armies on the Western Front.'

Foch left the conference still five months from his *baton* as marshal of France; he was still far less than commander in chief; his mission to co-ordinate the action of the commanders was less than sufficient to get the co-ordination carried out; and he had no reserve at his disposal. But resistance had been broken down at the very edge of defeat, and unity was in sight.

Insufficient as was the authority conferred on Foch on March 26, there was only one course indicated for the United States; this was approval and compliance. From Washington on the twenty-ninth Wilson cabled his congratulations to the new co-ordinator; and the press, when it received and carried the story, magnified co-ordinator into commander. It assumed, not knowing otherwise, that an extensive reserve was already in existence and would come at once within the jurisdiction of the new Allied chief.

Compliance came from Chaumont, too. The authority of Pershing to dispose of the troops under his command was such that even without the word of the President he was competent to act. On that Monday, when others were working out the agreement for the twenty-sixth, he drove to the field headquarters of Pétain at Compiègne, to offer the French commander the use of the divisions that could be sent into the line. These were the First and Twenty-Sixth, quite ready; the Second and Forty-Second, nearly enough ready. Behind these the Thirty-Second was due to be ready by the first of May. The plans of Pétain did not admit of their use in the active line at once.

On Thursday, the twenty-eighth, Pershing drove off again. The Doullens agreement was now in effect. This time he paid his respects to the co-ordinator at his headquarters at Clermont-sur-Oise. He took Foch out of conference with Clemenceau and Pétain, and in private repeated his gesture of temporary surrender: 'At this moment there are no other questions but of fighting.' The brief French sentences which he spoke, touched up for publication, stressed the honor of taking part 'in the greatest battle of history,' and placed his whole establishment — 'all that we have is yours' — at the disposal of Foch. It was promised that the First Division should go shortly to the front. The front could now be talked of. It was no longer a withdrawal to the rear, but had been frozen facing Montdidier. Before April was over the trains and camions brought the First Division into the line, opposite Cantigny.

There were many fingers in the pot in these days of acute crisis, including those of Secretary Baker and of the British War Cabinet, with whom Baker was in conference. Lord Reading had already been directed to advise President Wilson of the importance of the battle, to urge him 'to drop all questions of interpretations of past agreements,' and to appeal to him to send over infantry 'as fast as possible.' Pershing was already in agreement with Lloyd George that the battalions of the twenty-four-division program, if brought over by the British, should for the time be trained and used by them. Baker, on Monday, restated the matter to Pershing and followed his telegram in person. He relayed the British desire that divisions in France be given to the French, that engineers of the Line of Communications be lent to the British, and that infantry, to the exclusion of other types of troops, be forwarded from the United States. The American leaders were in personal conference in Paris on the twenty-sixth, they conferred with Pershing before the latter visited Foch on the twenty-eighth, and on the same day they considered the words and implication of a joint note to which the Permanent Military Representatives were driven in their desire to play a part. The promotion of Foch, who preferred to work with a French staff around him, was already raising some question of the future of the four secretariats assembled by the Supreme War Council in the Hôtel de Trianon at Versailles.

The joint note No. 18, destined to arouse considerable controversy as to its formulation and meaning, was agreed to on the twenty-eighth, after Pershing had withdrawn from its discussion. It had to be an expression of the unanimous agreement of the Permanent Military Representatives in order to become a 'joint note'; and Bliss assented to it. It recited the crisis, recommended the 'temporary service' of American units (other than the divisions) in the Allied armies, and urged that 'until otherwise directed by the Supreme War Council, only American infantry and machine-gun units ... be brought to France.' Bliss thought it embodied the idea of Pershing; Pershing thought it implied a retreat from his position that a separate army was the American objective. Jusserand and Reading, in Washington, thought the Allies had won out over Pershing, and in this conviction they explained the note at the White House, where they called on April 1. The President did not seem to have seen in the joint note any departure from Pershing's desire, agreed that 120,000 men should sail per month (roughly half on English ships), and sent Reading to March to work out details. He cabled to Baker, approving the joint note with the reservations Baker and Pershing had made in transmitting it, without taking specific note of the fact that in these reservations they had been willing to concede the change in plan of shipment 'only in view of the present critical situation.' They had emphasized the temporary character of the new plan, and had kept in mind 'the determination' as speedily as possible to have 'an independent American army.'

March, when Reading was sent to him for immediate action, had his own difference in interpretation, for he regarded 'men' as meaning troops of any kind, whereas Reading thought of 'men' as infantry. The differences in interpretation were never quite ironed out. But the essential of the matter was that, in the crisis, Britain found ships whose existence it had hitherto denied; the Embarkation Service used them, so far as troops were concerned; the Shipping Control Committee filled up the cargo ships and hurried their turn-around; the Allied Maritime Transport Council, set up after the November conference, dug tonnage out of its hiding-places; and all foreign trade of the United States was operated under licenses of the War Trade Board. The corner was turned, which must somehow have been turned before Pershing, or anyone else, could ever have had an American army. Before Baker was back at his desk in Washington on April 16 the accelerated flow was under way.

At each of the three corners of the negotiation, Washington,

London, and Paris, there was some confusion as to the meaning of joint note No. 18, and the President's assent to it. But Pershing had no confusion in his own mind, whatever misgiving or irritation he felt. He agreed that the situation might force some of his infantry units to serve temporarily with the British, but he insisted that they must not be treated as replacements; and no orders were issued depriving him of authority over his troops. He suggested to the President that England was trying to get American troops so as to avoid sending to France its own men who were held in England to defend the island against invasion from across the Channel. He clung to his divisions and his army corps, and to a policy of keeping his artillery ready to be assembled with the detached infantry in complete divisions 'when called for.' And on April 3 he went at call of Clemenceau to meet in Beauvais with much the same body that had reached the critical decision at Doullens on March 26.

Lloyd George came this time, as well as Clemenceau; and the meeting might easily have been listed as a session of the Supreme War Council, although it partook in fact more of the character of an inter-Ally conference. It was here that Pershing learned of what Reading thought Woodrow Wilson had agreed to on April 1, learning it when Lloyd George informed him that the President had assented to the shipment of 120,000 infantrymen and machine gunners monthly, beginning in April.

Here at Beauvais Clemenceau raised the question of a redefinition of the powers of Foch. Baker had advised the President that Pershing would accept under Foch any position that Haig and Pétain would accept. Foch pointed out that the Doullens agreement had defined his duties as 'co-ordination of action'; that the action was now over, since the drive had stopped, and that he was left with nothing to co-ordinate. Lloyd George agreed that the powers vested at Doullens did not 'go far enough.' Bliss and Pershing spoke out in favor of a supreme commander, believing that 'the success of the Allied cause depends upon it.' They agreed to a resolution vesting in Foch 'the strategic direction of military operations . . . of the Allied Armies on the Western Front';

but Lloyd George and Clemenceau would have left out of the resolution any reference to an American army had Pershing not insisted on its inclusion. He conceded that there was no army yet, but demanded that 'this resolution apply to it when it becomes a fact.'

The conferees left Beauvais with the position of Pershing emphasized to the point of irritation. His determination was unshaken and his backing unweakened, but his achievement of a 'distinct and separate component' was still in the lap of the gods. Yet the conferees did not leave until a unified command had been attained. The Beauvais agreement permitted the several army commanders to exercise 'the tactical direction of their armies' under Foch's strategic hand; it gave to each commander a right to appeal to his Government if by this strategic direction 'in his opinion his army is placed in danger.' By April 17 the President had confirmed Pershing's approval of a French request that with the strategic direction should go to Foch the title of Commander in Chief of the Allied Armies. The title did not as yet extend over the Italian Front, or over that of the Belgian army, of which the King of the Belgians remained in personal command.

XII. 'WORK OR FIGHT'

T HE Secretary of War returned to the War Department on April
16, the day before the night on which the First Division moved
into position opposite Cantigny on the Montdidier front. For it,
and for the A.E.F., as well as for the Secretary, the war at this
moment passed into its final phase. It became for the United
States a matter of combat.

The veil of secrecy which had thus far kept citizens at home
from knowing what was going on in France continued to obstruct
vision from either end of the effort, and it was still not discreet
to tell too much. The casualty lists, beginning now to come to
hand, revealed the fact of operations. They were small lists at
first, but they were more than lists of accidental casualty, and they
were of imperative interest to the folks at home. Yet the newspapers kept pretty well to their pledge of voluntary repression of
news that might aid the enemy, while the War Department sought
to find a way to give the prompt notice that a death demanded
without at the same time publishing data from which the intelligence officers of the enemy could compile lists ·of American units
in action and their places along the front. Much of what the
newshawks would have liked to print, they knew, but much of
what they would have liked to know was kept from them. The
new Chief of Staff, who was now very much at work, as well as
Baker who now joined him, believed that this secrecy could be
overdone. They were annoyed at the way in which officers,
returning to the United States from observation trips in France,
'leaked' indiscreetly, telling what they ought to have forgotten,
or, worse, what they did not know; but now that fighting was to
become the order of the day they knew that the news of fighting

had to be revealed. March had already begun to loosen up with congressmen, holding weekly meetings with the military committees at which the veil of secrecy became progressively thinner.

For the remaining months of the war the history of American democracy became the history of war. The supply and operation of the Army took precedence over all else, and all else was judged less on its own merits than on its relation to the military effort. Policies had been formulated during the first six months, by a people not yet aware how completely absorbing war would be. Agencies had been constructed during the second half-year, with a people as impatient for results as those had been who sent McDowell to Bull Run in 1861. Operations dominated now, with no McClellan to hold things back while he waited for absolute perfection.

Peyton C. March put the War Department on a twenty-four-hour day and a seven-day week. Bliss had described him as a 'man of positive and decided character,' and he lived up to the description. He had taken office saying: 'I know no gentle method of conducting a war of this magnitude'; and he was as rough with himself as congressmen and subordinates complained that he was rough with them. One of the congressmen, bitter because of the removal of a favorite major-general from command of his division, relieved himself by calling March the 'high priest of Prussianism' without realizing how much of praise his epithet contained. Even Baker, who did not often try to override, could not break down his Chief of Staff's determination that the management of the war should continue to be a military task rather than one distorted by politicians. As the last six months moved on, the regimentation of the American people behind their common purpose permitted the novel instruments of their purpose to function at increasing speed. The accepted slogan was 'work or fight.'

It was the Provost-Marshal-General who lifted these words to prominence by rulings made in connection with the second registration under the Selective Service Act. Under that act, on June 5, 1917, there had been a peaceful and willing enrollment of

9,586,508 young men. From this list the first draft had been taken by lot. Before those who had been drawn had all been sent to camp, there had come to light a good deal of waste motion because of preliminary work done on men who were finally left in 'deferred classification,' on such grounds as nature of employment or personal dependents. In November it was decided to classify by questionnaire the men who had not been drawn and probably would be left at home. Hugh S. Johnson, still working with Crowder, drafted the new rules, making as nearly automatic as possible the selection of the Class I men, those who were young and without dependents and who constituted the normal reservoir of man-power. After December 15 the new questionnaire classification was in operation; but immediately after June 5 the man-power reservoir had begun to be recruited from younger men, as each of these passed his twenty-first birthday. It was guessed that these would number three-quarters of a million, almost all Class I, before the first year after registration had elapsed. In May, 1918, Congress directed that the names of these be added to the list. The anniversary of the first registration was proclaimed by the President for the second. In July, when the new questionnaires had been counted, the *Official Bulletin* reported that 744,865 new names had been made available for selection.

The new names, arranged again by lottery, went to the bottom of the existing lists of which the several draft boards were custodian. In issuing rules to govern the draft boards as they certified numbers upon call of the Department, Crowder declared: 'We shall give the idlers and the men not effectively employed the choice between military service and effective employment. Every man in the draft age, at least, must work or fight.' He classed as idlers such as had no job, or made their living by gambling, clairvoyance, bucket shops, or race tracks. The 'non-useful' callings, carefully classified, were such as those of waiters, passenger elevator operators, footmen, ushers, domestic servants, and clerks. He opened, by indirection, a new range of occupations for women, and helped construct the new social classification that prevailed even after the men came back from war. Men not at work, or non-usefully at work, were to be listed immediately in Class I, instead of receiving the deferred classification to which their age or domestic responsibilities might otherwise have entitled them. And the Secretary of War, in July, pointed up the ruling by holding professional baseball players to be non-useful. Before any considerable number of Americans had seen the enemy, the War Department was carrying on in the expectation that the war might be prolonged through 1919 into 1920, that the A.E.F. might at the end be leading the fighting, and that all legal limits would be set aside as Congress brought the whole available manpower into the Army.

Between the critical days when the Allies gave Foch his commission and the day of the second registration, the war machine caught its stride. Crowell and Stettinius had fitted into the War Department. March, who was only acting Chief of Staff at the beginning, put on his four stars when Congress legalized the rank of General for the Permanent Military Representative at Versailles, thus enabling Bliss to be relieved as Chief of Staff and yet retain his stars in France. The Secretary's appeal for office aid through the authorization of two additional assistant secretaries was granted. Crowell was already first assistant and had presided over the Department while Baker was away. Stettinius became the second, in April. Keppel, the third, was specially entrusted with the relations of the Army to the civilian auxiliaries. On the day that Baker reappeared, Goethals was given his final position in the hierarchy.

Since December, 1917, Major-General George W. Goethals had been seeking a way out of the disorganization among the procurement bureaus of the War Department and the sections of the General Staff. The old battle between the heads of the permanent bureaus and the General Staff was not yet over, and at the time of Goethals' appointment as acting Quartermaster-General it was not yet certain which side would win. Knowing Goethals, it was easy to prophesy that the case of the side with which he was connected would be advanced, regardless of wounded feelings. He was now on both sides, being a bureau chief and at the same time his own principal superior in his capacity as head of a General Staff section on Storage and Traffic. The fight was adjusted for the time by merging bureau management with the General Staff, whose theoretical function was only to advise concerning management.

The decision to bring March back to Washington was a victory for the staff theory. Goethals annexed the Embarkation Service, at the immediate head of which Frank T. Hines functioned with distinction. He controlled the warehouses at the ports of embarkation and saw that smooth management called also for control of the Inland Traffic Service, for which in January he found a place on the organization chart under his direction. The coalless days in January at least made it possible to relieve some of the congestion at the ports. Thereafter Goethals' establishment fed cargoes into the ports while P. A. S. Franklin's Shipping Control Committee moved the ships in which they went to France. Storage and Traffic had chiefly to do with the supply side of the business of the Quartermaster-General. The procurement side, as indispensable as one blade of a pair of shears is to the other, was also normal business for the Quartermaster-General, except as munitions procurement had been specialized out to be the concern of the Chief of Ordnance. The functions, in orderly sequence, were those of purchase, inland traffic, storage, and embarkation. All of these, on April 16, were ordered into the hands of Goethals, now an assistant Chief of Staff and head of a Purchase, Storage, and Traffic Division of the General Staff. P. S. & T., as his division came to be called in the language of Washington, thereafter had control of what was needed, once quartermaster material came into the hands of the War Department. Its scope grew relentlessly under its driving head, swallowing up other separate agencies with each new revision of the organization chart, and functioning better every month. It took over much of the work to which the committees of the Council of National Defense had originally devoted themselves, while the organization of American industrial life so that it might the better produce goods for the War Department to use, also an original function of the C.N.D., was concentrated in hands as capable in their way as those of Goethals. Bernard M. Baruch was given custody of the War Industries Board on the day that March reported for duty at the head of the General Staff.

Lack of effective team-work between civilian production and Army use of American resources was never as complete as its critics made it out to be, although it was real enough to justify much of the worry when in December and January the war machine appeared to have frozen up and broken down. Frank A. Scott, destined for decades to continue to be an appreciated adviser of the War Department in procurement matters, cracked under his war labors. Retiring on October 17, his place as chairman of the War Industries Board was taken by Daniel Willard, who had on his hands also the railroad activities of his private life and heavy duties as chairman of the Advisory Commission, C.N.D. Just before the announcement in January of Stettinius as Surveyor-General of Purchases, Willard surrendered the War Industries Board so that he might give more of his time to the Baltimore and Ohio Railroad, now taken over by the Railroad Administration. He testified to the Senate Military Committee that the management of the civil end of procurement was a one-man job. The War Industries Board, however, did not receive a new chairman in his place until Woodrow Wilson decided that Willard's colleague on the Advisory Commission, Baruch, was likeliest of the men available. From January 16 to March 4 the Board had no head, and even then Baruch could not be given legal authority for action that Willard deemed necessary. Nevertheless he found it possible to wield power in fact by a shrewd reliance upon patriotic desire, indirection in the use of minor powers, and an element of bluff.

The Senate Committee on Military Affairs had been told by both Willard and Baruch, as it was told by the political critics of the Administration, that the handling of industry ought to be centered in a single office. From the Council of National Defense had come the statement that if the work was to be intelligently done 'somehow we should have a system for clearing the needs of the Army and Navy, and for having the needs brought before the people.' The word superman was sometimes used as suggesting the kind of man required. Clarkson, with wisdom after the event, is not far wrong in writing that the chief needed to be able to 'look any man in the face and tell him to go to hell.' Baruch could certainly do this, and he could keep his mind on a large objective without getting snagged in administrative detail or complexity of organization.

The President accepted the theory of concentration in a letter to Baruch which constituted the charter and commission of the War Industries Board after March 4, 1918. He wrote, 'the ultimate decision of all questions, except the determination of prices, should rest always with the chairman.' Upon this understanding, priority in its largest sense became the principal business of the Board. The Government was determined to procure the largest possible amount of material supplies for the support of the war program. The War Industries Board was to be kept informed as to the needs and hopes of the several 'purchasing agencies,' including those of the Allies. It was to encourage 'the studious conservation of resources and facilities'; to create new facilities and open up new sources of supply; to convert existing facilities 'to new uses'; and to advise the Government concerning the prices it should pay. The actual fixing of prices was the one matter kept out of the exclusive possession of the chairman. Power for this had by the Lever Act, August 10, 1917, been vested in the President, who now required the chairman of the War Industries Board 'in the determination of prices' to be governed 'by the advice of a committee.' This Price-Fixing Committee began to operate under Robert S. Brookings ten days after the appointment of Baruch. It received its instructions directly from the White House and made its reports to the President.

The Requirements Division, W.I.B., began to do business in April. A representative body, it included spokesmen for the several sections of the War Industries Board as well as agents of the buying departments of Army, Navy, Emergency Fleet, Railroad Administration, Food, Fuel, Red Cross, and the Purchasing

Commission for the Allies. Through these agents the war buyers were expected to keep the Requirements Division informed concerning not only their emergency needs and the requirements of their respective programs, but also their plans in formulation so far as these could be foreseen. It was the ideal that these needs should be balanced with the total capacity of American industry to produce. In practice the ideal was never reached; but out of the discussions in the Requirements Division came better knowledge of the bottle-necks, a clearer view of what might safely be let alone, and some modification of extreme and overlapping demands.

In the scheme of things, as the Requirements Division came into action, the contracts laid before it for approval were rejected, modified, or cleared. When cleared they were passed to a Clearance Committee where they were registered in order, after which they were permitted to be fulfilled. In the process of passing them to clearance, the various subsidiary agencies of the War Industries Board were drawn upon according to the necessities of the case.

The Commodity Sections, whose creation had been begun in some of the sub-committees of the Council of National Defense, were indispensable in nearly every negotiation. Where price was involved, the matter was referred to the Price-Fixing Committee, which drew upon the technical knowledge of the Commodity Sections and used the Federal Trade Commission in coming to its conclusion. The Commodity Sections, in their turn, did business with the War Service Committees, representing the various industries, and bringing to the attention of the Government the inside knowledge in the possession of the industries.

Where priority was as important as approval, the Commodity Sections were again drawn upon to advise the Priorities Board. Under Judge Edwin B. Parker there were drawn into this Board the powers and much of the personnel that had been used in the earlier phases of the war. As now reconstituted the Priorities Board determined not only what needs must be met first when the supply was inadequate for all, but also what demands were non-essential to the conduct of the war. In the light of these decisions the Priorities Board advised the War Industries Board upon the treatment of requirements as submitted to it. There was law behind priority. The right of the Government to seize and operate manufacturing plants was broad enough to cover lesser interferences with their operation. The Railroad Administration was in a position to back up the Priorities Board by withholding transportation. The Capital Issues Committee of the Federal Reserve Board might in its discretion withhold approval of demands for capital to finance private business. The law worked on priority somewhat by indirection, but it could be made to work. The Priority Board found great reluctance among the industries to be damned by the classification 'non-essential.' It managed to avoid that term yet reach the same result by adopting a different technique in which its lists gave prominence to industries that were indispensable. By September the Priorities Board had reached a point at which it could implement the work-or-fight order of the Army by publishing a Preference List, classifying industries, with munitions, food, fuel, ships, and railroads at the top. The service of these was not to be interrupted by demands contemplating a different use for labor, capital, fuel, or transportation. The Preference List provided, also, a basis for 'industrial exemption' from the draft, and locked the war effort into a vigorous unit.

In the course of determining how needs should be met, the War Industries Board did much to give comfort to both war industry and less essential industry. It steered the war industries into channels whereby they reached access to new capital for the construction of new plants or the reconditioning of old ones. It advised owners of non-essential plants how they might convert their property so that it might become useful. Its Conservation Division, taking over the task of the older Commercial Economy Board, brought continuous pressure upon industry to economize, to manufacture fewer styles, to cut the yardage in men's clothes and women's dresses, to standardize such things as paving-bricks and bedsprings. It sought economies by lessening stocks carried on hand; persuading jobbers and retailers to reduce their inventories, and urging manufacturers to speed delivery of goods from the factory, so that local stocks might be kept low. Some of its short cuts, tried for the sake of war, provided guidance for peace industry when, after the war, the Department of Commerce undertook to lessen the waste motion in business.

The Government met business across the council tables of the Commodity Sections, which varied in size and importance and in competence. The administrative skeleton of the War Industries Board remained flexible to the last, with never an official organization chart to freeze its processes to any pattern longer than Baruch believed the pattern to be productive. When the personnel of the Board, demobilized upon the return to peace, came together again at the parties where Baruch entertained his associates, the members could not always agree as to which of them had really won the war. They gossiped a little about the inefficiency shown in some corners. Yet they retained a high *esprit* as they looked back upon their share in the first real American experiment with a planned economy. Some of them remained flexible enough to help construct the next, when the 'lame-duck panic' made the United States, in 1933, willing to attempt the New Deal.

Always behind the sections and the organization was Baruch himself, shuttling between the White House and the business conferences. He was there to advise and to devise, to be called into any meeting to sweep away difficulties, or to be as rough with business in the interest of the Government as business was when it faced the Government. March approved him and his methods, commenting in his memoirs that 'the stage of the dictators had been reached.' The *Washington Post*, often chary of praise, gave its editorial blessing: 'The transformation of this country into a colossal war-making power, and the co-ordination of the manifold parts of this tremendous machine, have been accomplished with remarkable celerity and absence of friction.'

So far as the War Industries Board was anything more than the power of the President exercised through a structure of

Baruch's co-ordination, it was still a creation of the Council of National Defense and dependent upon its creator. As soon as the Overman Act gave the President the right to reorganize the administrative structure of the Government, he broke this connection and by Executive Order converted the War Industries Board into an independent agency under himself.

At many points in its work the War Industries Board was brought up against the problem of business which was expanding into war production at a time when the financial needs of the Government dominated the money market. Business had an imperative need for more capital if it was to undertake to execute war contracts. The Liberty Loans, and the short-term Treasury Certificates preceding them, absorbed more than the capital available for investment. To a considerable extent they were raised by credit inflation at the banks as purchasers of bonds borrowed from the banks the money with which to pay for the bonds. The needs of local governments and business for credit could not be met. There was good reason for discouraging capital flotations in so far as these were nonessential, with the war always the measure of necessity. There was equally good reason for permitting necessary activities of both local government and business to be carried on.

On the recommendation of McAdoo, the Federal Reserve Board, in January, created a Capital Issues Committee with branches in the reserve districts, to dissuade promoters of new loans from entering into competition with the Government for capital. They were also to approve necessary refunding operations and essential new issues. Working without power but with a strong public opinion behind them, these committees operated for three months before Congress took steps to back them up. A bill was drafted in the Treasury to make capital available to contractors who otherwise, unable to borrow, might have been unable to execute their contracts. The Senate and House debated simultaneous bills in March, worrying considerably over a new step in finance in which, through a Government-owned company, the War Finance Corporation, the Government was to borrow

from the people in order to lend to business. A precedent for
this was established, in the same month, when Congress made
half a billion dollars available to the Railroad Administration to
help finance the railroads. Another half-billion was now appropriated, in an act signed April 5, to be the working capital of the
War Finance Corporation, which body was authorized to borrow
three billions more in income-tax-free bonds. It was not to lend
directly to war contractors, but indirectly it was to aid them by
loans to banks which had taken the responsibility of making loans
to business. The Capital Issues Committee was given legal status
by the War Finance Corporation Act and received power to
scrutinize and pass upon new financing in amounts above one
hundred thousand dollars. It checked non-essential demands by
business on capital and restrained States and local government
from continuance upon local non-war building programs. The
school boards accepted it reluctantly, and wildcat promoters
properly disliked it. Yet it helped to make definite the economic
intent behind the slogan, work or fight.

There were no accepted tables to guide either those who advocated work or fight, or those who would have liked to oppose
the principle. Before 1914 there had been no war in which the
power of armies to destroy was as great as modern ordnance
made it in the World War. There had been no war in which,
through a prolonged struggle, it had been the desperate effort
of each contestant to keep in the field (with gaps promptly closed
by newly grown man-power) the largest number of soldiers the
productive effort of the whole people could maintain. It was impossible to say how many fighting men per million of population
any country could keep recruited and supplied without depriving
those who stayed at home of necessaries of life without which they
could not continue to produce.

It is still unknown how long a nation so organized can continue
to keep up its effort. Numbers of men do not provide the answer;
nor do things. The prevailing standard of life is involved. The
state of mind of the individual and the zeal with which he ap-
proves what he conceives to be the object of the war may take

the place of men and munitions and put off the day of final collapse. The relentlessness of the governing class may have something to do with it; and the determination of a few to continue to survive may enable them to coerce the many into extinction. The future of civilization may belong to fatalistic peoples with low regard for human life. Certainly the form of government and the understanding of its people must affect military outcome and endurance. Perhaps the rightness of a cause may be enough to carry a staggering nation through the one last day that results in victory. But in a democracy, staying democratic through the duration of a modern war, every menace directed at the enemy must be matched by explanation directed at the constituent so that the latter may continue approval and support.

Whatever number of men per million may be detached from the work of normal life and sent against the enemy, a larger number, even better skilled, must be diverted from their occupations of peace in order to provide those who fight with the supplies and weapons they must have. And what is left of the population, after these deductions, must, by a balance of production and conservation, support the nation while keeping alive themselves. There are no tables of proportion to which rulers may turn for guidance at the beginning of a war. Only experience, tempered from day to day by the nature of the war, can be their guide.

The Selective Service Act, designed in part to prevent the uneven wastage of productive strength through voluntary enlistment, made it the duty of the Army to select the men whom it could best use and to leave at home those who could best work there. The administration of the draft was intensely localized in the draft boards and the State boards of appeal. The definitions upon which these local bodies acted were handed down from the head of the Army. In these, as reordered in December, and amended before the second registration, the principle was laid down that young men should do the fighting.

Men of draft age were soon in the clutch of registration, tied to the fate of their numbers, to be used as needed. Those who received deferred classification and were left on the job at home, and those, younger than twenty-one or older than thirty who were not listed, were in no one's clutch. They could seek work as they pleased. Often the work sought them at fancy prices. Those of them who constituted the body of organized labor continued to support the organizations which they had created in order to bargain for wages and working conditions. The Government was ready to deal with organized labor to a degree to which business had not accustomed itself. Under the patronage of Government the unions grew in numbers. Never yet more than a small fraction of the men who worked, the organized unionists who claimed to speak for all workers reached a total of 2,371,434 dues-paying members. Their delegates met for their thirty-eighth annual convention in St. Paul on June 10, 1918. They had grown a quarter-million since their last meeting in Buffalo; they were to grow half a million more by the time they met in Atlantic City in June, 1919. At no time did their total reach that of the men and women in the military service, enrolled in the War Risk Bureau of the Treasury.

In general, although there were many individual exceptions where men went to war undriven by legal obligation, organized labor was not even asked to fight. The union workers, steady professionals in their crafts, with family obligations and definite places in the industrial machine, were commonly above draft age or in classes whose calling was deferred and never reached. The men who volunteered or who were drafted, again with many exceptions, were likely not to have acquired heavy domestic obligations or to hold key positions in their shops. Sixty per cent of those who had filed their blanks before the second registration for the draft declared that they had no dependents. War is a class business, in which those most likely to be maimed are the very ones whose influence in determining their service is least.

It results from these conditions that the organization of an army moves with military precision. Men march because they must. But the organization of the people who maintain the army is a matter of continuous negotiation. The men who work the shops and railroads, so long as their right to refrain from work is conceded, may do much to determine the conditions of their contribution. What they do not get by bargaining they may reach at when they vote. They bargained in 1917, inspired by the fear that war necessity would fall upon them more heavily than upon other classes, that hours of labor would be lengthened, that low wages would be forced upon them and made a matter of patriotic duty. The assurance of the Government, in the arrangements made through Gompers, that these disasters should not strike them, carried less than complete conviction. The mere confusion due to the shifting of labor to serve war needs and to the recruiting of labor from classes that had been accustomed to different work provided an abundance of occasions for controversy. Every war job, every war agency, found that before it could reach the stage of quantity production it must come to terms with individual citizens who, being free to work, were free to refrain from working.

The labor adjustment agencies of 1917, put together piecemeal as emergencies arose, had the common quality of a desire to maintain the continuous flow of production without the intermissions caused by strikes. If they had done no more than preserve a reasonable peace they would have served. One of them did much more. It brought into the picture Felix Frankfurter, who, as an assistant to Baker, was sent in September, 1917, to Bisbee and elsewhere in the West. The Secretary of Labor, William B. Wilson, was chairman of the President's Mediation Commission, but Frankfurter, its secretary, was the motive power. In the report, which he filed January 9, 1918, the Commission recommended to the President a 'unified direction of the labor administration of the United States for the period of the war.' The Council of National Defense came to a similar conclusion at the same time, advising that Wilson, one of its members and one whose Cabinet Department was of fact-finding rather than of administrative character, should reorganize his Department. This was to become a War Labor Administration, and approximated it before the year was over. It did not take on distended war functions comparable to those of the six great war boards, but it enlarged old activities and undertook new ones that proved to have more than a war importance.

As a part of the reorganization, Secretary Wilson called upon the American Federation of Labor and the National Industrial Conference Board to name five representatives each, as spokesmen for labor and its employers. Each of the groups so named chose a sixth from civil life. The selection of the labor group was one of its own kind: Frank P. Walsh, recently chairman of the Committee on Industrial Relations, who had had a turbulent career as labor lawyer. The employers' group chose William Howard Taft. Appointed in February, the National War Labor Conference Board, so constituted, debated in March and reported in April. At the heart of its recommendation was provision for something resembling a supreme court for labor controversy, to sit in a case only when all other machinery for settlement had been tried without success, and to give relief only in cases in which work was continued during the period of litigation.

On April 8 the appointment of the National War Labor Board to be such a court was made public. The conference members who had recommended it were named as members. Taft and Walsh were designated as joint chairmen, and in the procedure of the Board they presided alternately. Both Gompers and the National Manufacturers' Association approved the venture. In more than a year of service the Board listened to more than one thousand disputes, acting always as a buffer between the Government and the capital and labor that were serving the Government. The National War Labor Board was without legislative authority, being created without action of Congress, but the powers of the President were enough to give it teeth. When the Smith and Wesson plant at Springfield declined to accept a ruling it disliked, the War Department commandeered its plant. When the workmen at Bridgeport resisted a ruling they provoked from the President a sharp letter to the International Union of Machinists pointing out the fact that deferred classification or industrial exemption under the draft implied an obligation to work without interruption.

The Taft-Walsh Board was a court; but the great need of the Government was a procedure which might prevent cases from arising. In May the Board was supplemented by a War Labor Policies Board, with Frankfurter as chairman. In this body policy was discussed, that the Government might be advised. Each of the chief departments had its representative associated with Frankfurter as they worked out uniform standards of labor conditions and adjustment methods, since the United States itself had now become the greatest American employer of labor. By midsummer, as one of the activities of the reorganized Department of Labor, a United States Employment Service was in operation. In its regional offices the common labor of the United States was pooled and through its influence the competition of employers for labor was moderated. It claimed to have registered 5,300,000 laborers, and to have placed 3,700,000 of them in jobs.

The inability of boards to function sharply had become increasingly visible during the experimental period of the war, in 1917. They clashed with the unwritten law of administration that authority must be complete and that lines of command must not be clogged — a law not inconsistent with democratic control of policy. Above the whole machine the power of the President was completely established by the surrender of the opposition and the passage of the Overman Act. The delegation of great sections of this authority was administratively impossible until the task had shown its shape, and impossible politically until public opinion was ready to accept it. The magic of great names, or names that could be built up until they looked great, helped; but it did not make supermen out of the holders of the names. The notion that the day of supermen or dictators had arrived was bolstered by the concentration of power in the hands of such as March, Goethals, Baruch, and the chairmen of the various war boards. They were not supermen. They were dictators in only the loose sense that responsibility was concentrated upon their shoulders.

The program of the United States Shipping Board, to be brought into being by the Emergency Fleet Corporation, was audacious. On the inspiring idea of a 'bridge of ships' the Fleet Corporation had launched its schedule. With every existing yard fully at work, it became a matter of new facilities before there could be new bottoms beneath the freights of the A.E.F. No offer of assistance could be rejected if there were even a gambler's chance that there might be a contribution behind it. Yards were enlarged, which must be completed before the first new keels could be laid. New yards were authorized, which had to be worked up in blueprints before contracts could be let. Steel ships and wooden ships were authorized wherever builders thought they could construct them. Concrete ships, too, ultimately took the water and managed to keep afloat. And the great assembly plants, upon whose multiple ways ships would be put together out of parts fabricated in inland factories, were hurried toward completion while the naval architects sketched the ship patterns suitable for quantity production. But assembly plants had to be designed before they could be built. All the difficulties of site, labor, material, transportation, and capital had to be met for ships as for training camps. Moreover, the frigid winter, which froze coal in the open freight cars into solid blocks of ice, froze as well the river marshes through which piles had to be driven before any shipway could be built on firm foundation. Between 1914 and 1917 each of the Allies had had enough of confusion and waste motion in its own war plans, but each of the enemies had been similarly held back. The whole scheme of American preparation had to be telescoped into twelve months, as against the three times twelve months in which the Allies had advanced to the stage of fitness in which the United States found them upon joining the war in 1917.

Difficulties were inherent in the program of the Shipping Board because of the fact that the tonnage of the American merchant fleet, after a year of war, was only a bookkeeping tonnage reached by transfer to the Shipping Board of ships which would in any event have served some master. They were made more embarrassing by the American facility in exaggeration.

Those who issued grandiloquent press releases about the program often managed to believe themselves. Those who read them read only the totals without realizing what they meant. The

Allies, with a despairing readiness to believe the worst, found in the discrepancy between estimate and performance either deception or incompetence. The Shipping Board had given wide publicity to its intention to requisition some three million deadweight tons of ships already under construction and to build about fifteen million tons more on its own account. But no new ship of its own had been delivered to it before the Allied Maritime Transport Council began in March, 1918, to take account of stock.

By September 1, 1918, the Shipping Board claimed 8,693,579 deadweight tons of ships upon its roster. Most of these had been taken from their other owners by seizure, *angaria*, or requisition; 1,344,242 tons represented the requisitioned hulls that had been on the ways when war was declared; only 465,454 tons were in the form of new ships built for the Fleet Corporation. The war could not wait for quantity production of ships in United States yards to become a fact or a factor. Dissatisfaction with the visible results after great promises needed to be assuaged whether ships were built or not.

Charles M. Schwab was drafted the day Baker returned to Washington, April 16, 1918, with a new title of Director-General and full authority over the ships and shipyards of the Emergency Fleet. Hurley, chairman of the Shipping Board since July, continued as chairman, and he had at last found a head who was likely to make things move, or at least to make them look like movement. Schwab had had three predecessors since Goethals dropped the task. He was one of the wonder boys of steel, who had not ceased to be a boy when he became a magnate. Brought up among the mills, he began as a lad to drive stakes for the Carnegie companies. Before he was much more than a boy he was managing their plants; and when his master sold out to the great consolidation, Schwab was ripe to be president of the United States Steel Corporation. Always more interested in making steel than in managing corporations, Schwab left the Steel Corporation after a few years to devote himself to Bethlehem Steel. In 1918 he was as busy with contracts for munitions and steel shapes as it was possible to be, when the White House drafted him for the

duration of the war. His heavy contribution in 1916 to the
Hughes campaign fund made no impediment in Wilson's mind
or in that of the new Director-General.

Schwab found that his predecessors had started what it now
became his business to hurry along. Unfortunately, the program
had never a chance of fulfillment in a war that was over in nineteen months. Before he took the job he had an understanding
with Baruch that his yards should get their steel, and with the
Shipping Board that his hand should be free. The Board had
removed one of his predecessors for overstepping his authority
by ordering the Fleet Corporation out of Washington. Schwab
moved it immediately to Philadelphia where it might have room
to grow. He explained to a House committee that he did not
regard shipbuilding as a matter of engineering: 'I regarded as
the essential feature in producing ships the enthusing of the working people ... making them realize the importance of what they
were doing in conjunction with the men in the trenches.' If the
President had been able to command a similar personality to give
new tone to the other delinquent program, it would have been
well. Aircraft production was notoriously behind promise, and
was perhaps behind reasonable expectation.

On a single day in March, above a single training field in Texas,
as Mark Sullivan wrote in *Colliers*, one hundred and thirty-seven
airplanes flew more hours than had been flown by all the military
planes of the United States before April, 1917. An air service
was in the making, but the fleet of planes whose innumerable
wings were to darken the sun had not yet been built. The estimate
of 1917 that twenty-two thousand airplanes with their proper
spares would be required before July 1, 1918, was as far from
fulfillment as was the estimate of a bridge of ships. The *tour de
force* of the designers, in producing plans for the Liberty engine
in a few hours, was an encouragement to morale when announced.
But, in proportion as anyone had assumed that hopes would be
fulfilled, the disappointment was keen when the news broke in
January, 1918, that the planes had not arrived. A misleading
press release in February announcing the shipment of the first

American battle planes to France, five months ahead of schedule, made disappointment worse. Few were aware of the disproportion between the American promise and the reality on the Western Front, where, said Baker, neither side had ever had at once as many as twenty-five hundred planes. Rumor spread that a private investigator for the President, Gutzon Borglum, had claimed to have found dishonesty as well as incompetence in the execution of the program. In any event, the effort to expend the aircraft appropriation of 1917 did not produce until April 8, 1918, the completed model that was to be the 'main reliance of our service-plane program,' the De Haviland-4, with a Liberty twelve-cylinder engine. Benedict Crowell has described the welter of confusion and the pressure salesmanship from European manufacturers in the midst of which the War Department selected its types for quantity production.

During the midwinter period of reorganization the air program as a subject of gossip and suspicion would not down. When Stettinius went into the War Department it was hinted that perhaps he was to be placed in charge. Neither the public, nor congressmen who knew more than the public, could believe that American ingenuity was insufficient for the execution of the program. There had been change after change as the program expanded. When the Council of National Defense had launched its Aircraft Production Board in May, 1917, the responsibility for army aircraft had been only one of the many responsibilities of the Chief Signal Officer, Brigadier-General George O. Squier. Naval aviation belonged to the Chief of the Bureau of Construction. The two chiefs were legal sponsors for all contracts, but in neither Department had the work been specialized. When the aviation appropriation, $640,000,000, was made in July, the need for specialization and team-work became more clear. In October, an Aircraft Board representing both Departments was created by law and given the duty to advise both Army and Navy. But early in 1918 the law officers pointed out the strict limits within which the Board could give even advice. The old difficulty which had wrecked the sub-committees of the Council of National Defense helped to wreck aircraft. If the civilian advisers were not suspect among the manufacturers because of their connection with rival firms, they were suspect to Congress as having some interest in the execution of the contracts upon whose drafting they gave advice.

The uncertainty as to what to do retarded the program more than did the administrative organization of the Government. Whatever the type of plane and engine, there remained the problem of spruce. The wooden propellers and the wooden struts of the aircraft wings required the finest wood available, which was found only in small amounts in the logs as cut. Just as Pershing's men had to go into the forests of France to cut the piles for the docks at the American ports, the Army had to go into the Northwest forests to get its spruce. The American lumber industry was none too happy even before the war. Wood substitutes were beginning to change its balance with its market. Lumber fortunes, built up among the stands of pine and hardwood in the Northern States, had been swung into fir and spruce on the Pacific, and also into Southern pine. The industry was bothered by freight rates, by Sherman Act restrictions upon combination, by Government ventures in conservation, and by labor. The labor difficulty was harshest in just the region where stood the spruce needed to be logged for the airplanes. Here the migrant labor of the lumber camps, much of it American, had welcomed the organizing efforts of the I.W.W. It was mutinous and unpopular, threatening by its disposition to block the program.

As one of the preliminaries to building planes, the Army sent an officer, Brice P. Disque, into the Northwest to see what could be done. Upon his recommendation a Spruce Production Division was created in the Aircraft Board, and through his efforts an anti-I.W.W. labor organization was set up in the Northwest forests. His L.L.L.L. — Loyal Legion of Loggers and Lumbermen — reduced labor turnover and brought out the logs. Thirteen railroads had to be built before the logs reached the mills. Even then the lumber had to wait for plans before it could be fabricated into final shapes. A Spruce Production Corporation

(Government-owned) came eventually into existence to manage the business and to dispose of the greater fraction of the cut because only perfect lumber could be used.

The supply of cloth to cover the wings gave out. When England was unable to produce linen in quantity sufficient for this, the Bureau of Standards was invoked to draw specifications for a cotton substitute. This involved chemical search for a suitable 'dope' with which to dress the cloth. Factories had to be converted before they could turn out either 'dope' or cloth. Lubrication presented its problems, because the engineers believed that no other lubricant possessed all the advantages of castor oil. There were stories afloat concerning the vain efforts of an air officer to get from the wholesale druggists the castor oil, for it was in a medicinal way that the castor-oil bean had hitherto served society. It was not to be had in tank-car lots. Before the spring planting season arrived in 1918, an officer of the Signal Corps was placing contracts for acreage of castor-oil beans. The *San Francisco Call* believed (and the cautious *Christian Science Monitor* confirmed it) that as many as one hundred thousand acres were to be planted. The birds had been nesting in the trees that were to make the Shipping Board's wooden ships; the seeds that were to raise the beans that were in turn to make the oil for airplane engines had not themselves been harvested when the airplane program was first conceived.

In the intervals between his efforts to placate the politicians raging in committee, Baker was searching for a man big enough to direct the aircraft program yet in no way connected by business interest with automobiles or aircraft. He found him in the Red Cross organization. John D. Ryan, brought up in the Michigan copper country, had been picked young by Marcus Daly and made president of the Anaconda Copper Company in 1909. He left his business to work with the American Red Cross in 1917, was believed to be a Republican, and was scrutinized by Baker during the weeks in which the latter was deciding that Baruch was best choice for the War Industries Board. Ryan was placed in charge of the Aircraft Board in April, as another of the supermen. General Squier was left in charge of the Signal Corps, but was separated from his duties respecting aviation which were entrusted to a Bureau of Military Aeronautics with Major-General William L. Kenly in command. As soon as the Overman Act gave the President the power (in this matter the act was almost mandatory), President Wilson set up Aircraft Production as an independent bureau in the War Department. As head of this Bureau Ryan built on the labors of his predecessors and brought order, becoming in the summer Director of Air Service and an Assistant Secretary of War.

In large measure the defects of either head or heart that had occasioned criticism were on the way to a cure even before they became matters of gossip and suspicion. Borglum became a public figure as he maintained both the accuracy of his charges and his claim that a letter of introduction from the President had made him an official investigator. His allegations figured noisily during the last debates over the Overman Act; but five days before that act was signed the President permitted the Attorney-General to announce that Charles Evans Hughes had been retained, with full authority and a free hand, to investigate the execution of the aircraft program by the Signal Corps. The name of Hughes carried assurance that the investigation would be genuine, and the Senate Military Committee at his request called off a public investigation. When at last the Hughes report was given to the public in the autumn the power of initial ignorance and error to block the aircraft program had been nullified. Thus in the air and on the sea the American contribution to the war was one of promise rather than of performance.

Throughout the spring there was continuous discussion of a third appeal to the people for loans to carry on the war. The periodic emission of Treasury Certificates reached an accumulated total at which it was prudent to let the banks shift the load to the citizens as holders of bonds. How far the effect of criticism might blunt the popular willingness to carry on the drive for bonds and to subscribe to them was beyond prophecy.

On the first anniversary of entrance into the war McAdoo

opened the drive for the Third Liberty Loan, asking for three billions. Citizens marched the streets in local parades to give it publicity. Wilson had two days earlier signed the bill authorizing four and one-fourth per cent bonds, non-convertible, to run for ten years. The preparations, more intense with each successive drive, had been long in the making. Howard Chandler Christy and his co-artists had drawn their posters. Lapel buttons had been prepared by millions. The Four-Minute Men had been briefed for their appearances in movie theaters. Arrangements had been made to take care of private needs for finance, so that Government need might monopolize the field. The National Security League had put its private troupes of speakers on the road. And the President, speaking at Baltimore, had for the moment abandoned his 'wedge' that distinguished between the German people and their rulers, as he used the words 'force, force to the uttermost.' When the returns were in, in May, the loan was oversubscribed. In the four weeks' drive 18,376,815 subscribers had signed for $4,176,516,850 in Liberty Bonds. And when a few days later Crowder issued his work or fight ruling on the draft, it and the United States were in as nearly complete harmony as possible.

XIII. WAR MADNESS

SUBMERGED by the resounding roar of approval of the war doctrine were some discordant notes. When the war was over, and peace with victory appeared to be no peace at all, these notes were caught up with avidity, amplified by hate and hope, and used to the discredit of the doctrines that had overwhelmed them. In building up the case for a relentless prosecution of the war until victory should make it possible to organize a peace, there was hysteria that went beyond the need. It was unusual for democracy to find itself acting in agreement without a minority strong enough to impede it. As a consequence of this unusual agreement and of the intensity of its expression, democracy became a mob, ruled by mob psychology and injured by it.

The people of the United States, in their enthusiasm, lost sight of rights, whether of the individual or of the minority. Determination to defeat an enemy was stiffened by growing hatred of the enemy, by apprehension lest there be enemies at home, by contempt for the American who picked his words, maintained his balance, and by being less indiscriminate than the orator of the day appeared to be the opponent of the orator. At times volunteer speakers allowed themselves to denounce as traitorous audiences that did not applaud enough. Coercion supplemented persuasion as salesmen pushed the Liberty Bonds. The weeks during which the work-or-fight basis was established were also weeks in which American moderation was permanently threatened by the madness which goes with war.

The week in which the War of 1917 passed into its second year was a week of landmark events upon the several fronts. No one person in this week saw even all of the single front on which he fought. No one of the sequences of events was unrolled without involvement with all the rest. No individual could measure the degree to which they interlocked or know their course. No one yet knows.

In Flanders the German army let loose its second terrific wave of 1918, desperately determined to end the war before the American divisions should arrive. At Chaumont and Tours the A.E.F. plodded with its program, unable in the crisis to throw its weight. At Beauvais Pershing was shocked to hear the British opinion that his Administration had let him down. It had not let him down; but until he realized that his authority was still intact the shock was as great as though fully warranted. In Washington the Third Liberty Loan Drive was set for launching, and the War Finance Corporation began to function; both were to test the degree to which public spirit was behind the war. In sundry offices at the Capital, Goethals was preparing to step out in one-man charge of Purchase, Storage, and Traffic; the Emergency Fleet was getting ready to receive a new headpiece in the guise of Schwab, as near-dictator; and Taft was being drawn out of his prolonged campaign for the League to Enforce Peace to take over judicial functions in the field of labor. Under the dome of the Capitol and harried by their constituents, congressmen were deliberating laws to tighten the hold of the Government over war dissenters. In California the Hindoo plotters, admitting that German money had financed them, were being hurried to conviction. In Wisconsin, the election of a junior Senator to sit next Robert M. La Follette was measuring the intensity and the direction of war emotions. Philadelphia was preparing to receive, without blare of trumpets, a final convention to liquidate the affairs of the National German-American Alliance. And in a mining town in Illinois, one Robert Prager was done to death.

Robert Prager, as his Senator, Sherman of Illinois, explained on the Monday after he was lynched, had lived in the United States since 1905, and worked in a zinc smelter at Collinsville. He was by birth a German, by preference a union worker, and by conviction a Socialist. He was unpopular among his fellows before he was arrested, and on Thursday, April 4, he was in the local jail where he and others had been gathered on suspicion of disloyalty. Congress, while Prager lay in the lock-up, was debating amendments to the Espionage Act, in order that the crime of sedition might be so defined that juries could indict and courts convict. In case after case, when arrests on suspicion occurred, it was discovered that nothing that was actionable was capable of proof; and it was not practicable to bring suspects into court on mere suspicion. The dismissal of suspects, when the law provided no ground upon which to hold them, served the ends of justice but embittered the opinion of the mob. Fall of New Mexico was warning his colleagues in the Senate to describe crimes in clear language unless they wished direct action by the people or intervention by courts martial. Another Senator, Chamberlain, was preparing to support a bill entrusting to Army courts the suppression of sedition.

A dismissal of suspects had occurred in Collinsville at the end of March. Prager, unfortunate, was still in jail when a mob of miners succumbed to enthusiasm and alcohol and took him from his cell. No violence was needed. An officer at the jail testified at the inquest that he refrained from drawing a revolver on the mob because the telephone rang and he had to answer it. Other officers averred that they would have shot had the mob tried to hang its victim within city limits. Outside these, they disclaimed jurisdiction. The mob gave its victim time to write a pathetic letter to his parents in Dresden, then killed him.

The proponents of anti-lynching laws treated the Prager murder as another reason for a Federal statute. The temperance forces found in it another reason for the proscription of alcohol. The Cabinet, when it discussed the press reports of the disgrace on Friday morning, found in it further evidence of a rising tide of intolerance and pressed upon Congress for a law that should give explicit definition to crimes of sedition, enable courts to do their duty, and at the same time save the innocent from death. Myers of Montana, always extreme in demanding action against sabotage, syndicalism, and sedition, found reinforcement for his argument that Congress should take the laws of his own State as a model and put down dissent.

It was another matter to put it down without running foul of the Constitution and doing to free government more damage than any dissenter could inflict. The mobs, whose excess was feared, were less concerned with proof than with direct action. The American population of German or Austro-Hungarian origin, whether naturalized or not, had fallen victim to the unpopularity of its countries of origin. Enemy aliens were already under presidential regulation, but they had little more to bear than any Americans whose names testified to German parentage. Lutheran clergymen were delivering their sermons in English to avoid the curse upon the German tongue. School boards were eliminating the German language from their curricula, and university trustees, under compulsion, were investigating the loyalty of such of their professors as were of German birth. The foreign-language press was filing with the local postmaster translations of such of their columns as might have a bearing upon war issues. The volunteers who fed into the Department of Justice their comments upon the suspicious acts of alleged traitors were flooding the dockets with cases that must be investigated. German societies, however innocent they may have been in fact, were finding it difficult, if not impossible, to operate.

Greatest of all the incorporated objects of distrust, the *Deutsch-Amerikanische Nationalbund*, folded up its tents. When this society was formed in Philadelphia in 1901, there were already in existence in several States local German-American alliances for the preservation of the German traditions of their members. Delegates came to Philadelphia from twenty-two States to make an alliance national in scope. The avowed purpose was cultural and reminiscent, but around the written program there began to accumulate at once a suspicion that here was an agency of dangerous propaganda. 'The German Government cannot well prevent rattle-headed Germans from talking and writing' ran an immediate editorial, but there was some evidence that the German Government did in fact encourage it. William II, when the National

German-American Alliance was formed, was engaged in courting not only the Government of the United States but the Germans overseas. The visit of his brother, Prince Henry, in 1902, was used to strengthen the bond of sentiment. There was some doubt whether the Imperial Government regarded the duty of a German to the Fatherland as quashed by his acceptance of naturalization in the United States. And it was alleged that the Emperor had declared that no Government could stay in power in the United States in opposition to the German vote.

But the United States welcomed the Alliance. Congress had often provided for the incorporation of tradition. It had accepted the American Historical Association as a subsidiary of itself. It had given recognition to the Sons and Daughters of the American Revolution. It gave incorporation to the National German-American Alliance in 1907. The political parties, in the era before the United States became race-conscious, had found it expedient to set up sub-committees to carry their gospels to their foreign-language adherents.

The War of 1914 started the Alliance upon a course at variance with that of general American opinion, while the officers and chapters, fighting defamation of the Fatherland, brought the hyphen into disrepute. The German-language press, organized openly to block Wilson in 1916, had asked for the trouble that came to Germans when peace was replaced by war. The funds the Germans raised for the relief of suffering were easily believed to have been diverted to subversive ends in the United States. After 1917, no argument could convince American opinion that the incorporated Germans were not a menace.

Everything German was banned, in spite of the evidence that Germans were accepting the draft, buying Liberty Bonds, and serving on war committees wherever Americans of non-German names would let them. It was esteemed as patriotic to sign pledges never again to buy goods of German manufacture. Even the physical markers of the German past became objects of hostility. The statue of von Steuben, commemorating loyal service to the Revolution, could not escape disapproval as it stood across

Pennsylvania Avenue, opposite the White House. The statue of von Steuben's master Frederick the Great, presented to the United States when William II courted Theodore Roosevelt, became an embarrassment as a symbol of Prussian militarism. This statue, hardly welcomed when thrust upon the Capital, had been erected in an out-of-the-way corner in Washington on the terrace of the Army War College. When excited patriotism launched a resolution in the Senate to remove it, the Army did not wait to be driven. From Washington Barracks, where the Engineers held sway, a gang of men came quietly with a derrick to the terrace of the War College, lifted the statue from its base and stored it in the basement out of sight.

It was inevitable that among the minor actions of the war the Senate Committee on the Judiciary should investigate the charges of disloyalty clustering around the German-American Alliance, that the officers of the organization (when they had not already resigned) should testify to its innocence and loyalty, and that the repeal of the charter should become a law. The President signed the repeal on July 30, but the Alliance had already been dissolved. On April 11 it met in the city of its origin, voted to disband, emptied its treasury into the coffers of the American Red Cross, and became a victim of war intolerance.

The lesser victims of the mob had no redress. In more than one parade that celebrated the launching of the Liberty Loan they marched under compulsion, some of them forced to wear stultifying placards. The larger victims, with greater power to evade or to fight back, became subjects of intemperate debate. Greatest of these, La Follette, had recently suffered the humiliation of a rejection by his own State. It was not he who had been a candidate in the special election of Senator held on April 2, but his personality had with increasing prominence dominated the political discussions in and about Wisconsin since the unfortunate September meeting of the Nonpartisan League in St. Paul, where the Associated Press had mistakenly made him say 'we had *no* grievance.'

Within a few days of the St. Paul speech the demand was upon the Senate to expel him. The Minnesota Public Safety Committee formulated the demand. Senator Frank P. Kellogg read the speech to the Senate with grave disapproval and made the motion. The Senate Committee on Privileges and Elections was directed to investigate, and La Follette, on a matter of personal privilege, made a defense on October 6. More than his status in the Senate was involved; his control of his State was in danger. He brought suit at home against his detractors, while his friends prepared for him a militant mouthpiece in the Madison *Capital Times*, which made its appearance in December. It developed that the fight against him in the Senate was the lesser of his worries, since his colleagues, of whatever party, so valued their own personal right to be obstinate that they were reluctant to take extreme measures even against a Senator who blocked their action. And Republicans, however deeply they disapproved his war views or his Progressive principles, were not unwilling that someone should take the unpopular lead in baiting the Administration. The Senate Committee held meetings, received floods of telegraphic advice, heard testimony, took recesses, and managed to put off a report until, with the war a matter of history, it could safely recommend a dismissal of the charges. His case took a more painful slant when in October the junior Senator, Paul Husting, was accidentally shot while on a hunting trip and Wisconsin faced a showdown on its emotions in a campaign to elect a successor.

It was not usual for Wisconsin to have a Democratic Senator. Husting, a progressive Democrat, had won his seat in 1914 only because of Progressive votes given to him in the absence of a Republican candidate whom La Follette Progressives would approve. An American-born son of a Luxemburger father and a daughter of Solomon Juneau, who had a trading post on the site of Milwaukee long before there was a town, Paul Husting trained in politics with Woodrow Wilson. His speeches during the period of neutrality separated him from the La Follette wing of his supporters, since they made few concessions to the German-American point of view. His death let loose a struggle of Democrats to replace him with another Administration man, of La Follette to elect a Progressive, and of conservative Republicans to prevent the selection of a La Follette adherent. Every candidacy offered for party consideration at the primary, March 19, 1918, was tested by its bearing on the issues of the war and on those of local politics. It was the strategy of the opponents of La Follette to make use of his unpopularity, and to make the issue one of loyalty in order to belittle whatever effort the Senator might make in behalf of a candidate agreeable to him.

While the primary contest was under way the fight on La Follette reached its height. No public institution was closer to his heart than was his State University; yet most of its faculty turned against him in resolutions which just escaped denouncing him as traitor. The Madison Club expelled him. School boards and boards of supervisors resolved against him. The State legislature, in a joint resolution which it sent to Congress, affirmed the loyalty of the State, and condemned La Follette 'and all others who have failed to see the righteousness of our Nation's cause.'

In the primary vote in Wisconsin the 'loyalty' candidates received a clear majority over those cast for either La Follette's candidate or for Victor Berger, who took the Socialist nomination without opposition. La Follette failed to secure the nomination of a supporter. The election brought into three-cornered fight Berger, whose anti-war stand was open and avowed; Joseph E. Davies, a useful Wilson Democrat who resigned from the Federal Trade Commission to be a candidate; and Irvine L. Lenroot, once a La Follette lieutenant, who had abandoned his leader on the issue of the war. The President wrote a letter in support of Davies, who belittled Lenroot as a war supporter. J. Hamilton Lewis was sent into the State to speak for the Democratic candidate, and the Vice-President, Marshall, came for a great rally in the University stock pavilion, where his indiscriminate abuse of the opposition to Davies cost his candidate votes.

Since no La Follette candidate survived the primary, there was doubt as to the redistribution of the La Follette vote, but no one received it all. Lenroot was elected Senator, fully committed to the war. He and the other 'loyalty' candidate, Davies, received together 313,000 of the 423,000 votes cast, which came within a few thousand of the presidential vote cast in 1916. The 110,000 going to Berger (showing marked increase from his primary vote of 38,000) suggest perhaps the extreme dimensions of the anti-war spirit in the most German of the States. The *Chicago Tribune* thanked God for Marshall who had spilled the beans for the Democrats. The *San Francisco Chronicle* rejoiced that 'Wisconsin has voted herself loyal.' La Follette was more than ever a scapegoat, nursing wounds that rankled, which his followers kept open.

Victor Berger, whose vote on April 2 ran far ahead of the voting strength of Socialists in Wisconsin, was victim of a different sort. His *Milwaukee Leader* was excluded from the second-class mailing privilege. He was, even before the primary, under indictment by a Chicago jury for violation of the Espionage Act, but his offense was substantially that of being a Socialist in war time. There was hazard in this, for verdicts and sentences reached against a background of war emotion were taking on an aspect of persecution rather than punishment. Berger was not convicted until the war was over. His constituents had meanwhile re-elected him to Congress where he forced the House to decide what to do with Socialists and with members under indictment or conviction.

Jeremiah A. O'Leary, who had received uncomfortable publicity in 1916, was caught in the prosecutor's net. His Irishry had impelled him to join hands with any of the enemies of England and had made him an ally of the German intrigue before von Bernstorff was sent home. His *Bull* continued anti-English until Burleson ruled it out of the mails in August, 1917. When the State Department, in the autumn, released documents from its file of German dispatches his name was mentioned and a true bill was found against him. When his case was at last called in Judge Hand's court, on the day Wilson signed the Overman Act, May 20, it was discovered that he had jumped his bail. He became the objective of a little man-hunt, until he was picked up in the Northwest and brought back to New York to plead not guilty and to be tried.

In the period of stress in 1918 many of the critics of the war were not courageous enough to fight the currents of opinion. Not so Debs, whose convictions could be neither coaxed nor silenced. On June 16, 1918, he attended a Socialist convention at Canton, Ohio, and spoke out against the war in words that could be interpreted as obstructing enlistment. War justice moved promptly against him, for he was too well known ever to be inconspicuous. He was arrested in a fortnight, tried at Cleveland in the autumn, and there convicted and sentenced to a ten-year term. When the Supreme Court, in March, 1919, upheld his conviction he went to prison. President Harding released him from Atlanta on Christmas Day, 1921; but while in prison he had received in 1920 more than 900,000 votes for President.

The popular nervousness and the frenzy against spies and so-called traitors outlasted the period of work or fight. In the week in which Debs went on trial, Oswald G. Villard's *Nation*, carrying a leader under the caption 'Civil Liberty Dead,' was held up in the New York Post Office. The Government was pressing heavily upon critics and dissenters, and war extremists were, in turn, training their guns upon members of the Administration as lukewarm in the prosecution of the war.

There were three chief points in the indictment of the Administration as the nagging continued after the field-days before the Senate Committee in January. The first of these was incompetence; second, was softness with traitors and pro-Germans; third, was softness with the enemy. In varying degrees these provided themes for those who desired to criticize without risking the odium of disloyalty. No other public character attained the prominence of Theodore Roosevelt as he prodded the Administration by editorials in the *Kansas City Star*, or let himself be sent on speaking tours. Root, Taft, and Hughes had found tasks in connection with the work of the war Government, but Roosevelt had been unacceptable and remained equally devoted to the war and implacable in his criticism of the Administration.

None of the minor characters took up with more verve than George Harvey the rôle of volunteer gadfly, to teach the President the responsibilities of his office. Harvey used the editorial section of the *North American Review* until his earnestness outran its flexi-

bility. In the month of contest for a different kind of war government, January, he turned these pages into a personal journal, the
War Weekly, and used his skilled pen without restraint. Had any of
the proposed laws, forbidding words used in 'disrespect' been in
force, Harvey would have become a weekly culprit. He professed
that he brought support to the President to win the war. Occasionally he spoke well of Wilson or of others in the Government, but
the tenor of his comments, apart from his hostility to the enemy and
to the league that was to enforce peace, was to undermine their
repute and their authority. He used the word 'mannikins'; with
the result that Lodge urged him to use it oftener and to stress the
idea that Woodrow Wilson feared to have around him any but
little men. He was going at high speed when Baker came back
from the inspection tour in France, derided the Secretary as 'cooty'
Baker, denounced him as 'shockingly and dangerously unfit for
his job,' and expected from him 'nothing but piffle, piddling,
pacifist piffle.'

The fate of Leonard Wood provided material for many of the
critics who believed that the Government was afraid of big men.
The other of the two major-generals who might have been sent to
France, Wood had become a sort of martyr for even those who
had no fault to find with Pershing. Work had been found for
him to do at Camp Funston, where under his command the
Eighty-Ninth Division was prepared for embarkation. He was included among the officers sent abroad to see war as it was fought,
but he was no sooner abroad than word dribbled back that he was
too important to be a subordinate. He had been Chief of Staff.
On the rebound from Pershing's stubborn insistence, his European
hosts played Wood as a favorite. He talked too much — until
finally Pershing hurried him home. At home he still talked to
committees, to Republicans, and to the young men who found his
magnetism irresistible. His division was moved to Hoboken in
May. Baker had decided to keep him at Camp Funston, but Wood,
moving without specific orders, preceded the Eighty-Ninth to
New York. Detached from his command at the very port of
embarkation, the blow appeared to be more cruel than it was

intended to be; but neither the Secretary nor the President would yield to Wood's personal appeal to be allowed to fight. His rejection could be interpreted as a rejection of ability, and it was so treated. It could also be interpreted as politics intruding upon war policy, for talk had begun to deal with him as a Republican candidate in 1920. The footnote to the episode, revealed only when the President was dead, was written in a personal letter to the editor of the *Springfield Republican*, in which Wilson gave praise to Wood's great ability, but recorded the belief that he was troublesome and insubordinate. Even if the Administration had wished to use him, it would have refrained, for it was aware that Pershing did not want him. It may even have known of Pershing's intention, should Wood appear, to order him home.

The attack upon Baker was a one-sided battle as he refrained from answering back. Others in the Administration, when picked out to be whipped, sometimes indulged themselves in retorts that made the matter worse. George Creel, at a post of danger since he stood between the press and its prey, was as often as any in trouble and at times could not restrain himself.

Baker had inadvertently invited trouble when he suggested that the American preparation should be interpreted in the light of the fact that the battle line was three thousand miles away. Wilson had invited it as early as the *Lusitania* sinking, in the words, 'too proud to fight.' Creel, with the same ideology in his mind, gave an opening at the beginning of the Liberty Loan drive. Speaking to an audience of lecturers, he declared himself 'proud to my dying day that my country was inadequately prepared.' His congressional critics took it up, the press repeated it with zest; and Creel forgot himself and yielded to indiscretion at the Church of the Ascension in New York, early in May, before a radical forum whose members heckled him after an address. If relentless Senators thought he was soft and socialistic, the left wing thought he was an oppressor who delighted in the suppression of free speech. One of his hecklers demanded his opinion about 'the heart of Congress.' He flashed back with a wise-crack, 'I have not been slumming for years.' The newsmen picked it up. His critics roared in denunciation when the words reached the *Congressional Record* and were not appeased by his abject apology. The papers of the Committee on Public Information found their way eventually into the National Archives, but Congress had taken its revenge by bad-tempered scrutiny of Creel's accounts and by refusing funds to let the affairs of the Committee receive orderly liquidation when its work was done. The official propaganda under Creel's direction was never violent enough to please the extremists; the National Security League at times diverted part of its strength from fighting the enemy to fighting Creel, the mouthpiece of the Government.

The battle on the domestic front would have been easier to fight if it had been possible to see under the Constitution a sharp margin at which the right of the United States to repress sedition came into contact with the right of the citizen to freedom of speech, of the press, and of petition. The First Amendment to the Constitution is explicit and peremptory; yet there was no serious doubt of the duty of the Government to maintain the United States against subversive attack. The complete right of the citizen to argue for his policy and to vote for his candidate was never denied. It was no more complete than his obligation not to interfere with the operation of a law, once passed. The dangers to the common purpose arising from overt acts in interference must be avoided without alienating too roughly those who saw in the measure of avoidance an attack upon the American theory more dangerous than the attack by any enemy. No one could have satisfied the extremists on either side.

The result was that the two ends were led into grotesque union to play against the middle. On the left, the minority — more important in their individual quality than in power of influence — kept up a continuous attack under the banner of free speech. They had addressed the President in a round robin while the Espionage Act was still in Congress. And the President, just before his powers were enlarged in the Trading-with-the-Enemy Act, had written convincingly to Max Eastman on the theory of free speech in war time. On the right, the advocates of relentless war fought under the same banner, with such as Theodore Roosevelt and George Harvey urging that Congress refrain from putting into the hands of the President more power to curb opinion. When the left took to the rostrum it attacked the Administration as fighting a war to save dollars at the cost of liberty. From the right came charges that the Government was brave with small enemies and cautious with large ones. Tom Watson's little *Jeffersonian* had been excluded from the mails, as had other journals of small reach like the *Masses* and the *Milwaukee Leader*. Why, the right wing inquired, was Hearst let alone? Roosevelt collected anthologies of utterances, some over the pen of Hearst, some from the editorial columns of his chain of papers, and declared that from the press of a little publisher they would have led to jail. On May 2, Hearst absorbed the *Chicago Herald*, thus bringing its Associated Press franchise into the hands of the resulting *Herald-Examiner*. When it was discovered that out of the White House Tumulty had promptly written in congratulation, anticipating from the *Herald-Examiner* the 'same good Democratic fight,' it became impossible to convince right-wing critics that politics was not being played. The right wing and the left had nothing in common but their determination to resist the demand of the Administration for a better definition of existing crimes and an extension of the law.

With the passage of the Trading-with-the-Enemy Act, October 6, 1917, the power of the Government to cope with interfering dissent was considerable though insufficient. In the Espionage Act, in June, 'willful' attempts had been struck at, whether their intent through false statement or argument was to interfere with the prosecution of the war, to cause insubordination in the ranks, or to slow down the recruiting of the armed forces. The law gave no power over those opinions expressed in public which were not aimed at individuals or things, but whose presumed consequence might be conviction in the mind of another leading to an overt act. Conspiracy requires a coming together of minds. Obstruction requires that the obstructer be shown to have been in some kind of contact with the thing obstructed; and a denouncing of a law as bad, or an administrative act as evil, may not be treated as obstruction if government is to be free. Altgeld of Illinois, pardoning the anarchists of 1886, brought reproach upon himself as an enemy of government; but the conviction, spread by his passionate argument against a doctrine of 'constructive conspiracy,' was accepted even by those who were human enough to feel that he had, somehow, let society down.

The *Revised Statutes* contained provisions helpful in the prosecution of such interference with the laws as might be tangible; but what was resented and feared in 1918 was opinion out of harmony with mass conviction, and the expression thereof. The Selective Service Act had put additional weapons in the arsenal of prosecution, but did not touch opinion and its mere expression.

The new powers of the Postmaster-General, conferred by the Espionage and Trading-with-the-Enemy Acts, reached out to control what the courts could not yet touch. Using the admitted right of the Government to refrain from carrying in the mails what it regarded as unmailable, these laws permitted Burleson to make administrative rulings based on his personal opinion. He could exclude, and exclusion from the mails was a near-equivalent for silencing. It was no concern of his whether or not the courts followed up his rulings by attempts to convict those against whom he ruled. His victims, if they sought to compel him to display and prove his reasons for action in the courts, were impeded by the cost and delay accompanying litigation, and while they sued for redress, the exclusion orders continued to operate. The alleged subversive activities against which the Post Office ruled were precisely those which the law forbade; Burleson had no power to define new crimes and no right to act on mere suspicion of guilt. But to his opinion was given the force of law, unchecked by the safeguards that inhere in courts. Not only the second-class mailing privilege, which is the very life of newspapers and periodicals, was under control of his judgment, but the law directed him to refuse to carry subversive matter of any kind. It gave him large powers in the examination of private correspondence.

In the opinion of the Department of Justice, these powers, sweeping and unchecked as they were, were insufficient. Gregory, the Attorney-General, complained in April, 1918, of 'the lack of laws relating to disloyal utterances,' attributing to this lack the 'danger of disorder' and the growth 'of disrespect for legally constituted authority.'

The excesses of the I.W.W., and the general willingness to believe in the power of mischief possessed by this labor union, contributed much to the further protection of loyalty by law. Frank Little, one of the inner circle of the I.W.W., was on August 1, 1917, taken from his boarding-house in Butte, Montana, and hung from a railroad trestle. Little had recently arrived in the Northern copper country after an active career as agitator ranging from the San Joaquin Valley in California to Bisbee. He preached labor war against the Anaconda Company. That company attributed to labor strife a twenty-three per cent decrease in its output of copper during 1917. There was the disorder usual when labor conflict broke out in company towns. Facing this disorder, Montana, like the other States, was less than usually able to preserve the peace because its organized militia was outside the State. The complete drafting of the National Guard for service in the United States Army occurred on August 5. Mob violence ran unchecked. Someone fastened to the garments of Little a legend in code which, being translated, was the symbol of those vigilantes who had done rough justice when Montana was a mining camp.

Deep distrust of the purpose of the I.W.W. was not dispelled by the avowals of the union leaders that they fought capitalism, not the United States. The files of *Solidarity*, their journal, were indiscriminate in attack, so that Burleson issued an exclusion order without arousing loud protest. The liberals of the left defended the right of Socialists to exist; but having to draw a line somewhere they left *Solidarity* outside. What purported to be actions of the executive board of the I.W.W. ordered the expulsion of those members who joined the armed forces of the United States.

On the day preceding the departure of the drafted men to camp in September, 1917, Charles E. Hughes assured the members of the American Bar Association at Saratoga that Congress had ample power under the Constitution to protect the country. 'The power to wage war,' he said, 'is the power to wage it successfully.'

On that same day the Department of Justice was putting the final touches upon its preparation to strike a blow. At 2 P.M. (C.S.T.) on September 5 the local offices of the I.W.W. were raided throughout the West. Officers were arrested, papers were impounded. William D. Haywood, the president, was picked up in Chicago. For seven months the evidence was studied as the Attorney-General prepared against more than one hundred members, large and small, the case of the United States. The case came to trial in the court of Judge Kenesaw Mountain Landis on April 1, 1918. As a result, during the weeks when assertive loyalty was most intense, each day brought to the press new excerpts from the testimony upon which the charges of disloyalty were based. The trial dragged out through four months, but it ended as abruptly as the raids had been sprung, for the jury came back quickly to the courtroom with a verdict of guilty as charged. A fortnight later Landis distributed sentences among the hundred, according to the degree of their guilt, beginning with twenty years at Leavenworth for Haywood.

Myers of Montana, inspired by the lynching of Little, offered the Senate a sedition bill two weeks after the hanging. He proposed to eliminate the requirement that the words complained of have a provable connection with an overt act, or a provable intent. Words that were 'calculated' to 'incite or inflame' were for him enough to constitute a crime, leaving it to the jury to determine whether such was their tendency. He was well ahead of Congress, but he renewed his proposal in various forms until at last, in the tense spring months of 1918, the Congress was ready to revise the law. Meanwhile his own State, with patriotic emotion and industrial pressure forcing it on, amended its own criminal statutes.

The Montana legislature met in February to bring its law down to date. In a brief session it gave definition to 'criminal syndicalism' in an act signed by the governor on the twenty-first. On the next day Governor Samuel V. Stewart, later to be elevated to the supreme court of Montana, signed a sedition law which opened a new chapter in American criminal jurisprudence. The Montana statute protected the form of government in the United States, the Constitution, the flag, the soldiers and sailors and their uniform against 'disloyal, profane, violent, scurrilous, contemptuous, slurring, or abusive language . . . or any language calculated to bring [them] . . . into contempt, contumely, or disrepute.' It did all that law could do to take the place of conscience and good manners, and it provided a text for debate when Congress, pressed by the emergency, prepared to amend the law of the United States.

Driven by the rising spirit of intolerant loyalty, guided by an Administration anxious both to save the innocent and to convict the guilty, held back by a coalition whose recruits were drawn equally from the extreme left and the extreme right, Congress provided the Department of Justice with two new laws. The first was passed easily and signed on April 20. It concerned sabotage, the weapon of the syndicalists. American labor had not taken kindly to this newest importation from the ideology of European class warfare. Among the avowed intentions of syndicalism was the expulsion of the capitalist from his plant. Among the methods were those of slowing down production and mutilating the product until the ownership of the plant would have no value and the workers might come into possession of it. This was sabotage, an industrial weapon which the I.W.W. endorsed as soon as the word reached its organization, and with which neither State nor Federal law was phrased to cope. When the war raised the possibility that it might be practiced as a seditious crime, the Attorney-General without avail recommended a law to Congress in 1917. A year later he reminded Congress that the Government had no law under which it could 'prosecute men who attempt to destroy factories, munitions, and other stores necessary for our armies.' So distinguished an historian as Albert Bushnell Hart wrote in the *New York Times* to allay the fear of the nervous that pro-German workmen in the bakeries were putting ground glass in the bread. The Sabotage Act fixed pains and penalties for the willful injury or destruction of war material, or of utilities or tranportation, whether public or private. It was a useful law, but it caught small fish. The first reported arrest was that of a worker in a factory making waterproof cloth for gas masks, a German lad of seventeen, who slashed two bolts of cloth. He confessed, asking to be believed that his intention was loyal, and avowing that he slashed the cloth to symbolize the appearance of Germany when the wearers of the masks had done their job.

If Army opinion had had its way the laws against sedition would have been entrusted for enforcement to the hands of military authorities and summary processes would have reached ends not attainable by jury trials. The section of the General Staff devoted to Military Intelligence had a large field over which it operated. Counter-espionage was one of its natural duties. The names of candidates for commissions in the Army, by tens of thousands, were passed through Military Intelligence for investigation of the background and loyalty of the applicants. The correspondents and agents, necessary for these inquiries, covered the United States with a close net, so close that it would not have had to be made much closer if the whole matter of sedition had been in hand. The files of Military Intelligence — never perhaps to be made public — were filled with names and reckless suspicions. One of the assistants of the Attorney-General went so far as to prepare a law giving jurisdiction over disloyalty to courts martial, but his chief disavowed him and the President wrote explicitly against it.

Except on the field of actual combat American tradition ran contrary to toleration of any courts other than the ordinary civil courts of justice. More important than tradition, the Fifth Amendment guaranteed: 'No person shall be held to answer for a capital, or other infamous crime, unless on a presentment or indictment of a Grand Jury,' except within the armed forces. And the Sixth Amendment added to this guaranty the promise that 'in all criminal prosecutions' there should be 'the right to a speedy and public trial.' The militant minority which wanted courts martial for the citizen faced a hostile majority in Congress, backed up by the prospect of a veto should such an act reach the White House.

The Attorney-General felt that his was the obligation to enforce the law, if only Congress would enact it. He believed in the effectiveness of his machinery for investigation and discovery.

In April, 1918, he was receiving and checking 'upward of 1500 complaints per day' caught in the dragnet operated by the 200,000 or more voluntary coadjutors whom he had begun to attach to the Department of Justice even before war was declared. Most of the complaints were based on mere suspicion and most of the suspicion was unfounded — sometimes hysterical, sometimes malicious. Enough probable cases were left on his docket to lead him to urge Congress to give him more power. A week after the lynching of Prager he begged for authority to deal with 'disloyal utterances,' and thereby he reinforced the pressure from the Government that the Liberty Loan be protected from the lukewarm and the malevolent.

The Sedition Act, not to be signed until May 16, 1918, was called up in the Senate on April 4, two days before the Loan Drive began. Overman, who had it in charge, urged haste, not only to aid the loan, but because 'The people of this country are taking the law in their own hand.' That night, some of them lynched Prager. The bill was brief, containing matter that Congress had been unwilling to incorporate in the Espionage Act a year before. The House had passed it in March without a roll-call or a dissenting voice. To support it in the Senate, Myers presented from the legislature of Montana a memorial praying for a more rigorous punishment of sabotage and sedition with copies of the Montana laws of February as models. His colleague Walsh explained the route by which Montana came to its enactment. In the District Court, in the case of the United States *vs*. Hall, the Federal judge had spoiled a prosecution, in which disloyal and bitter language was admitted, by charging the jury that the act committed must have some reasonable connection with ensuing event. The defendant had scolded against the war, speaking to rural neighbors sixty miles away from a railway. Such behavior, however improper in war time, could not be treated as a willful attempt to interfere with the operation of any law. The judge conceded that such language ought to be criminal, but found nothing in the Espionage Act to warrant a conviction.

It was impossible to hurry the Senate, and the course of the drive

showed that the Liberty Loan needed no protection. Not until
April 10 did the Senate accept an amended bill. Not until April
24 did the bill come back from the conference committee. It was
May 9 before the House sent it to the White House, and another
week before it received the approval of the President.

The debate was harsh, uncovering in the Senate an opposition
to further increase in the powers of the President, a solicitude for
free speech, and a disapproval of the Postmaster-General as a
censor of opinion. Senator William J. Stone, ten days before he
died, feared that even Joe Cannon might be caught within its
sweeping prohibition of language disrespectful to the Government,
for Cannon had told the world why 'volunteer swivel-chair war-
riors wore spurs.' It was 'in order that their heels might not slip
off the desks so easily.' Roosevelt joined the fray. The Associated
Press had carried, mistakenly, a story that the President was by
title to be protected against contemptuous language, whereupon
the ex-President hurried into the *Kansas City Star* a vigorous editorial
protesting against anything that might make that office sacred.
The measure was generally supported by the Northwest Senators
— Jones of Washington, Chamberlain of Oregon, King of Utah,
and both Myers and Walsh of Montana — among whose constituents the I.W.W. was a menace. The Senators of Progressive mind
were generally against it: Johnson of California, Borah of Idaho,
Norris of Nebraska. In the Senate 46 yeas overrode 26 nays to
pass the conference report. In the House only Meyer London,
Socialist, stuck to his nay.

The final text of the Sedition Act extended the power of the
United States over speech and opinion, regardless of provable
resulting consequence. It retained the word 'willfully' in the interest of the culprit who might be brought to trial. But once his
willful intent to speak or utter was established, it became unnecessary to prove any intent to injure or impede or any ability to
do either. The list of adjectives describing the proscribed language
was impressive: 'disloyal, profane, scurrilous, or abusive.' 'Contemptuous' was stricken out in conference.

The law forbade the abuse of 'the form of government of the

United States, or the Constitution of the United States, or the flag of the United States, or the uniform of the Army or Navy of the United States.' And since the lexicographers of the Senate could not agree how sweeping was the meaning of the word 'calculated' (which the Montana law used), they substituted a more definite word 'intended'; forbidding language 'intended to bring' the protected ideas and institutions into 'contempt, scorn, contumely, or disrepute.' They gave point to their legislative determination by rejecting a safeguard clause advocated by France of Maryland:

> That nothing in this act shall be construed as limiting the liberty or impairing the right of any individual to publish or speak what is true, with good motives, and for justifiable ends.

The Department of Justice joined hands with Military Intelligence in protesting that the specific guaranty of a right to prove the truth of utterances would so impede prosecutions as to destroy the usefulness of the statute.

Sweeping as it was, the new clause on dangerous utterance aroused less spirited opposition than the new clause enlarging the power of the Postmaster-General. This officer was empowered, 'upon evidence satisfactory to him,' to close the mails to persons using them in violation of any provisions of the act. The phrase 'upon evidence satisfactory to him' was old; as old as the lottery and fraud laws, under which the control of the mails was used to retard the circulation of material injurious to public welfare. The Postmaster-General was directed, with no more right of protest than he might himself permit, upon such evidence to return to the sender as 'undeliverable under espionage act' all mail directed to the culprit against whom the evidence might point. He was not given the right to examine this mail, or to open it without a search warrant, but by returning it unopened he cut off the individual, in non-guilty matters as well as in guilty, from postal contacts. Hiram Johnson, who had supported in vain the France amendment, opposed also this extreme administrative privilege. He was willing to punish those proved guilty, but he could not reconcile with freedom of speech and of the press an administrative ban upon free action. The minorities, whether on the left or on the right, whether inspired by conviction or prodded by politics, were voted down until finally the Sedition Act became a law. In the interest of the war, and driven by an excited opinion out-of-doors, the majority in Congress pushed aside the sound comment of the California Senator: 'There is a difference between refusing a man a privilege and holding him responsible if he abuses it.' Moderation and reason had a hard time with democracy at war. Work or fight, established among the agencies of government, reached out to control the actions of the mind.

XIV. THE ATLANTIC FERRY

T HE Allied Maritime Transport Council, conceived in November, 1917, at the conference of the Allies, was formed in February, 1918, and met at Lancaster House in London to begin business on March 11. Its task was to balance the bottoms afloat with the tonnage requirements of the enemies of Germany, to fix priorities among different kinds of freight, and to uncover and bring into use 'concealed' tonnage. The only important increments in sight were the Dutch ships whose seizure was in train and the output of the Emergency Fleet Corporation, on which no prudent planner dared to build. The British yards were clogged with ships which had been damaged by submarines and required emergency repairs.

The maritime burden had fallen heaviest upon England. England not only possessed the lion's share of ships, but also had lost more than half the total war losses, whether to the submarine or to other war risks. In the month of American entry, April, 1917 — the 'darkest hour,' as C. Ernest Fayle has described it in *Seaborne Trade* (1924) — the losses through enemy action reached for the British a ceiling at 545,282 gross tons out of a total of 881,027. Prior to this month the accumulated losses had mounted to 5,450,363 tons, of which 3,155,186 had carried the flag of the British merchant fleet. It had never been safe to tell the truth about the sinkings. The German submarine had nearly fulfilled the guaranty of its proponents — almost winning the war before the Allies managed to set up a defense against it. The monthly losses steadily declined after April, 1917, although still in excess of monthly replacements. They averaged for Britain alone 265,000 tons a month during the next year, but April, 1918, was the last month in which the British losses ran above 200,000 tons. Thereafter, they continued to decline.

The Council could do little more at its first meeting than gasp at the magnitude of its assignment and order the paper work upon which it might try to take action when next it could meet. When it assembled for a second session, in Paris on April 23, the tide was turning. The basic decisions on which depended the dimensions of the A.E.F. had been reached. The submarine showed signs of being brought within control. There was still ahead a race between the sadly depleted maritime equipment of the Allies and their increasing requirements which was made harder by the certainty that every American soldier who came to France would occupy the space of two deadweight tons of freight, and would keep perhaps one ton of well-managed shipping busy thereafter until the war should end. One of the possibilities was that the war would be lost through inability to carry sufficient ocean freights, but the future threats against maritime success were less those of enemy inteference than those of internal inadequacy.

The decision to fetch an army from the United States, impelled by fear that one of the German drives might end the war and recorded in the complicated four-cornered negotiations of London, Paris, Washington, and Chaumont, was clearly reached by the time of the joint note No. 18 which was signed by the Permanent Military Representatives on March 28. There was painful lack of unanimity as to the way in which the American troops were to be used, but the Allies had come round to Pershing's view that the war could not be won without them. With the crisis as it was, no future need of the Allies could be as great as the need for help at once. There were too few ships for what the Allies were sure they needed for themselves in order to feed their people or to outfit their forces. In the decision to risk future maintenance for the sake of immediate reinforcement, England upset all shipping schedules in the month between the first and second meetings of the Allied Maritime Transport Council. The hope that American ships or the commandeered Dutch ships might aid in provisioning the Allies was laid aside, since now all shipping from the United States must concentrate upon the requirements of the A.E.F. and, more than this, out of European tonnage troop and cargo tonnage must be diverted to the Atlantic Ferry. When the decision was made there was no way of foreseeing that after April, 1918, the submarine would be tamed.

The submarine brought Germany near to victory and filled the filing cases of the Allies with gratuitous suggestions of how to cope with it. There were no tested naval tactics that could be depended on to foil it, and no ready-made precedents in international law to cover and to regiment its use. From the beginning of the submarine 'blockade' in 1915 until the earliest flotilla of American destroyers reached Queenstown in May, 1917, the war against the new weapon was one of trial and error — mostly error. Thence, up to the Armistice, more trial and error brought success, without uncovering any certain panacea. In *The Victory at Sea* (1920), Rear-Admiral William S. Sims stressed the secrecy that went with the experiments. Tactics on land and the new weapons of the war became common property as soon as used. Those of the ocean, on it or beneath it, were sometimes so effective that neither of the combatants knew the full extent of success or loss. And neither told the public what it knew. Even eternal vigilance was no guaranty of safety against an enemy who was often invisible until after he had struck.

Most concrete of the American contributions to the defense against the submarine, and most impressive as a structure, was the North Sea Mine Barrage which had been approved before the November conferences. The Navy Bureau of Ordnance was secretly at work upon its component parts before Senators began to ask embarrassing questions in January. To the lay mind the attempt to 'bottle up' the submarines was continuously attractive, but the navies knew that whatever could be planted could be swept away. The barrages fixed by the British at the Dover Straits were repeatedly cleared by the German destroyers while escorting submarines to sea. Yet the British kept on replacing the Dover mine fields and accepted the American lead in building across

the northern outlet of the North Sea. Here the first mines were
not planted until June, 1918, and the task, so far as it was capable
of being completed, was nearly done by November. What help
the North Sea Barrage might have rendered after 1918 is beyond
determination. Its undertaking is evidence of the thoroughness
of the anti-submarine effort rather than a contribution to victory.
The barrages and the mine fields were of less importance than the
endless cruising of destroyers, the depth charges, and the organization of ocean traffic in protected convoys.

At the Admiralty offices in London, where was concentrated
the completest information about the submarines, it was known
from day to day where most of them were at work. Corrected
each morning, the ocean map told the story. The observations
made by ships at sea and wirelessed in provided some of the data
for the map, but since these ships reported in good faith many
times as many submarines as were ever built their information
was of greatest use in checking what was already known. The
best data for plotting the position of the submarines were submitted
by the submarines themselves. They persisted in conversing
with each other by wireless. They made reports to Germany
almost daily — or nightly, when it was safest to rise to the surface
and lift the antennae masts. And whether British naval intelligence could decode their messages or not, the direction finders
made possible a system of triangulation by which the submarine
gave itself away. Knowing the speed, and hence the possible
cruising radius of the submarines, it was possible for the Admiralty
to draw a circle on the map showing the limits within which the
next day's operations must take place. The circles showed as well
the hunting grounds for chasers.

The arming of troop and cargo ships with guns with which
to repel submarine attack was a measure whose effectiveness
remains in doubt. A matter of political and diplomatic controversy
during the period of American neutrality, it became a naval controversy after entry. It gave to Germany ground for contending
that the submarine must attack without warning or else run the
risk of destruction. On many of the merchant ships it was difficult

to find deck space clear of rigging where naval gun crews could have free room to operate. If guns were placed amidships their use swung the vessel broadside to the enemy, improving the target. If fore and aft, their range was somewhat limited, and their presence anywhere aboard was too often a temptation to fight the submarine instead of running away. British regulations were explicit, directing ships to run when attacked and in no case to come to the rescue of another ship in danger from the submarine. The American instructions were less explicit; but sound tactics were the same. After 1917 the use of convoys placed the burden of defense upon agile little fighting ships built for the work. During 1917, before the convoy system was standardized, four American sinkings out of five came from torpedoes that could not have been stopped. Yet no possible system of defense could be ignored and the Navy armed the ships.

A dozen merchant ships with gun crews and guns for use against illegal submarine attack went to sea between March 13, when arming was ordered, and the declaration of war. With six-inch guns as the chief reliance, some three hundred and sixty-seven merchant ships were similarly equipped during the war. The troop transports, which were never seriously attacked, were more heavily armed than the cargo ships, but all owed their increasing safety to defenses other than their guns.

The destroyers and chasers were the best means of protection. England was working to the limit to guard the approaches to Europe when the first six United States destroyers reported for duty. By July, 1917, there were thirty-five of them, and the Navy was planning for a fleet of chasers that could be fast enough to outrace the submarines, quickly built, and constructed out of light, stamped plates. Henry Ford took a contract, set up an assembling plant at River Rouge, launched *Eagle I* in July, 1918, and promised a fleet of two hundred by February, 1919, with unlimited more to follow. But only seven of the Eagle boats had received their guns when the Armistice was signed; and so this effort joined the long list of enterprises for whose impact against the enemy the war was too short. More than four hundred smaller ships of other type, chasers of the 110-foot class, were put to work.

Much of the loss of merchant shipping could be charged to the necessity of England to concentrate the British destroyers as a curtain around the Grand Fleet and at the Channel ferries. Even England was desperately short of the small craft made unexpectedly necessary by the submarine campaign. Neither the Grand Fleet nor the Channel transports were got at by the enemy. It was sound strategy to let the need of the fleet come first and that of the ferry next, but it left merchant shipping as a bad third. Until American aid arrived, the approaches to British waters from the Atlantic were the scene of a vast guessing game with a few submarines on one hand and too few destroyers on the other. By the end of 1918 Daniels could report to Congress that Navy patrolling ships under the commander in Europe were cruising 516,000 miles a month; and the tonnage sunk declined steadily after April.

Promiscuous cruising by destroyers and chasers brought an element of chance into the guessing game, but left the advantage still with the submarines. It was the use of the small craft as guards for convoys that made shipping safe. The relative safety of the Grand Fleet and the Channel transports, both always guarded by destroyers, had pointed to the convoy as the best defense even before American entry. Sims pressed the point, but its adoption was blocked by the belief of the British merchant captains that their ships could not steam in formation suitable for convoy. It could be insisted that the speed of the slowest vessel must determine the speed of the convoy, with the result of slowing down the voyage. Daniels believed that about twenty per cent of theoretical efficiency was lost in convoy; but against this, the ships were saved.

Over the disapproval of the merchant captains, England experimented with a convoy from Gibraltar in May, 1917, which escorting destroyers brought safely into port. A Hampton Roads convoy was tried with equal success. The first dozen transports carrying the A.E.F. sailed as convoy on June 14 and reached St. Nazaire in safety, and, except for the great fast passenger liners carrying troops, which trusted to their own speed until they reached an escort off British shores, the United States sent its men to France on transports and in convoy groups. Eighty-eight fleets, averaging a dozen transports, sailed from the United States to the war zone, losing no transport on its way to Europe. Escorted out of American waters and to the edge of the zone by a cruiser, the convoys were picked up at prearranged spots by the destroyers and zigzagged their way to Brest or St. Nazaire or Liverpool.

The work of the camouflage artists, widely advertised as a device to fool the submarine by lessening visibility and blurring the edge of the target, gave a circus aspect to every harbor where shipping congregated. Yet it deceived the submarine less than did the habit of zigzag cruising. The problem of the submarine captain, having sighted his victim, was to identify its course. His torpedo moved slowly through the water, often slowly and visibly enough to permit maneuvering to escape it. To get the course, the simplest method was to cruise ahead of the intended victim until its masts came into line and then to lie hidden a little to sunward off the course until off its beam. By frequent and irregular changes of direction the convoy upset many of the calculations, while its enveloping little fleet of destroyers, racing around it, made it dangerous for a periscope to break the surface.

By the spring of 1918 the defenses against the submarine produced results. It helped, when in April the exits from the German submarine base at Bruges were directly attacked. Zeebrugge was closed on April 23, Ostend on May 9. Quite as significant was the regularization of the convoys. To avoid some of the loss due to the uneven speed of ships, the vessels came to be grouped according to their ratings. A fast convoy (thirteen to fourteen knots) left New York for Liverpool on its first regular run on April 9, 1918, with the convoy committees determined to deliver 140,000 troops a month and to increase the capacity of the sixty ships assigned them by cutting down the round trip to an average of forty days. There were slower convoys, also running on regular schedules, out of Halifax, New York, and Hampton Roads. Their schedules were so timed that their destroyer escorts could deliver a fleet at Dover or Liverpool and instantly pick up a fleet of empties going back for more troops and cargoes. Shuttling more rapidly as troop ships, the *Aquitania*, *Mauretania*, and *Olympic*, assigned by England to the carriage of the A.E.F., and the *Leviathan*, which the Navy had repaired, overtook and passed the convoys. Among them they carried more than a division on every turn-around.

The Navy took much pride in the speed with which it had converted into effective carriers the interned German ships — 'completely disabled,' as the German Embassy had overhopefully reported to Berlin before Bernstorff left. The sabotage upon them had been badly done by wrecking crews who failed to take into account the skill of Navy artificers at electric welding. Cylinders that had been burst, boilers burned out, connection lines askew, set new problems and called for the devising of new techniques. Yet twenty of the ships were back on runs before November, 1917, and the renamed *Vaterland* on December 15 sailed with its first installment of the nearly 100,000 men it was to take to France. Because it could get into Liverpool only at high tide, it was shifted in April to the run to Brest. By bunking its men in relays it once transported nearly 11,500 on a single trip.

It is difficult to disentangle the share of credit and responsibility for the ocean services due to the British Admiralty, the Navy at home, Sims and the Navy overseas, and, in a lesser degree, to France. Each had its independent organizations. All were linked in co-operation. The Allied Naval Council, reinforced after the conference in November, pooled their wisdom. The Allied Maritime Transport Council acquired a specialized job and served it after March. The officers and men at sea worked more as individuals than Army men could work. But they made a team.

The assembling, classification, identification, and loading of men and stores was a problem in itself, and sometimes it had to happen that fodder for Army animals went to Brest with the men, and rations for men went to St. Nazaire with the mules. But when ships were waiting for cargoes the cargoes that were waiting for ships had to go aboard. It was another matter to recruit the able-bodied — highly able-bodied — longshoremen to load and unload without delay. Released from Army duty though they were, it was not easy to keep them happy. At the British docks there was petty trouble when the laborers on night shift clamored for access to their beer at midnight and asked why they should be inconvenienced by the early-closing law, whereby the 'pubs' were locked when they came off duty. They got their beer.

The actual navigation of convoys and escorts called for high seamanship. Sims pointed with pride to the emergency Navy training that converted landlocked college boys into capable watch officers and navigators within a few weeks. He was equally pleased with the work of their professors of physics who took up the challenge of underwater listening devices. The latter made it possible for the navigator to make a fair guess at the distance and direction of an approaching submarine.

With official title as 'Commander of the U.S. Naval Forces Operating in European Waters,' William S. Sims had a position analogous to that of Pershing, yet different in that his degree of independence was less and his necessity for co-operation more. Daniels declined to agree that Sims, directly under the Secretary, was as free from Navy 'channels' as Pershing was from those of the War Department and the General Staff. Sims went to England as rear-admiral, was at once given temporary rank as vice-admiral, and was made temporary admiral only in December, 1918, when all was over. Upon his return he reverted to his pre-war rank of rear-admiral. A Republican Administration made him Admiral of the Navy in 1930, eight years after he had retired. He had a restive mouth which even before the war had let escape senti-ments inappropriate to be spoken by an important naval officer; it continued to be restive after the war, when he engaged in a too-free discussion of the Irish and entered into controversy with Daniels over war policy. But his skill and his congeniality with his British colleagues made him an effective servant of the Ameri-can determination to defeat the submarine.

Sims could not have fought such a fight for a separate command as Pershing fought. By naval necessity, the investment of European shores was indivisible. He worked under the British or himself commanded British forces as occasion required. His American units on all the ocean fronts, but most numerous in British waters, filled his headquarters with business. He was forced to be an admiral whose flagship was a block of 'remodeled dwelling houses in Grosvenor Gardens.' Yet he had forty-five naval bases under his control at the Armistice, all of which he kept in harmony with the British Admiralty offices in Whitehall.

The British Grand Fleet, held together in the North Sea with a mission to prevent the German fleet from reaching the high seas, was at the heart of the naval strategy of the Allies. Stationed there, waiting, in an inaction that irked its men and irritated lay critics, it did its work by continuing intact. Its existence was a guaranty that the smaller craft could do their share. Sims contributed to its strength. A squadron of five American battleships, under Hugh Rodman, was as much a part of the Grand Fleet as any of Pershing's divisions while fighting with the British or the French was part of the army with which it was associated. But there could be no intention of withdrawing them, since they would be helpless if alone and their effectiveness lay in their reinforcement of the British strength. In addition to this squadron, three American dreadnaughts were kept on emergency station off the southwest coast of Ireland, at Berehaven, to be ready in case a naval disaster in the North Sea permitted the escape of the German dreadnaughts or the emergence of any powerful raiding vessel.

The naval mission of the Allies was to prevent the enemy from provisioning himself, to keep his High Sea Fleet from doing damage, and to keep the sea lanes open for the supplies of the Allies and of the American reinforcement. Had this reinforcement continued to be only what was envisaged in April, 1917 — a reinforcement in money and supplies — both the merchant tonnage and the power of naval defense of the Allies might still have been insufficient. The submarine at that time appeared to have established a control. As this control was progressively broken by an improving organization of Allied strength and by

American assistance, the Allies postponed defeat without much improving the guaranty of victory. Replacements could not repair the damage done or even make good the continuing new losses. Without the foodstuffs and military supplies that must be brought across the seas, the Allies could not maintain either their home populations or their armies in the field. Without an American military reinforcement it seems probable that the Allies must have lost their war.

Yet this reinforcement of their strength on the line of battle made every aspect of Allied supply more difficult to manage. There was no increase in effective merchant tonnage; what the United States Shipping Board promised was not delivered before the Armistice. Upon what was left of merchant tonnage, as of April, 1917, fell the additional burden of moving American troops and keeping them fed and armed. It was possible by strong-arm work upon the neutrals to get access to some of their shipping, but neutrals were squeezed in such a way that, yielding to pressure from one side, they were likely to experience retaliation from the other. Before American entry England began to coerce the Continental neutrals by cutting off their supply of bunker coal at British coaling stations unless they carried freights and served ports agreeable to England. The danger of destruction by submarines or at the mine fields impelled the neutrals to keep their ships at home. Their vital need for coal and food forced them to make some sort of terms with the Allies, although there was always danger of armed intervention from Germany. Sweden, Denmark, and the Netherlands, most threatened by this intervention, were slowest in yielding to Allied pressure. After the organization of the War Trade Board the United States joined in exerting the pressure, as whole-heartedly as though the United States as neutral had not resented it. But the neutral ships, chartered, coerced, or commandeered, met only a fraction of the Allied need.

Every American soldier put on the line put as well a permanent burden on the ocean trade. It took only simple arithmetic to compute the tonnage, sorely needed for Allied use, that must be kept busy on A.E.F. supply when there should be a million Americans in France, or two millions, or even more. If each American required fifty pounds of overseas freight per day (and the requirement was not far from this), the first million would pre-empt twenty-five thousand deadweight tons per day for American use alone. The curves of requirement, when the statisticians superimposed them upon the curves of Allied necessity and the sagging curves of tonnage in hand, pointed to a moment when ocean supply would collapse, inadequate. If Germany should not have broken down before the war reached this moment, the war was lost. So many different factors 'won the war' that it is invidious to single out any one for emphasis; yet it is certain that on the Atlantic Ferry was fought as critical a battle as any fought on land.

It was late in the autumn of 1917 before the War Department quite realized that it had been committed by Pershing to the delivery of twenty-four divisions, which with supporting troops would make a round million, by the end of June, 1918. Three months later, when the great drive opened March 21, there were in Europe only five divisions that could by any stretch of the imagination be regarded as ready for the front. The Allied distrust of an American army that should be a 'separate component' was so great that the British Government had not ventured to endanger the endurance of England by diverting tonnage to the carriage of the A.E.F.

Pershing was clearer in his mind about what he wanted than was the War Department about what it could accomplish or what could be shipped. Immediately upon laying down his scheme for a headquarters organization in France, Pershing had in July, 1917, demanded his million. To this, the War Department replied with an estimate of maximum possibility, which comprised twenty-one divisions (small divisions of 20,000 rather than the larger divisions of 28,000 which Pershing specified and finally obtained) and a grand total of 634,975 men by the middle of June. In addition to the First Division, its schedule of shipment provided for some 288,000 men to be floated before March 1.

THE DIVISIONS AFLOAT OR IN FRANCE*

	1917							1918									
	Je	Jy	Au	Se	Oc	No	De	Ja	Fe	Ma	Ap	My	Je	Jy	Au	Se	Oc
	1	1	1	1	1	1	1	1	1	1	1	1	1	1	1	1	1
			2	2	2	2	2	2	2	2	2	2	2	2	2	2	2
				26	26	26	26	26	26	26	26	26	26	26	26	26	26
						42	42	42	42	42	42	42	42	42	42	42	42
								32	32	32	32	32	32	32	32	32	32
'Combat divisions,' of which twenty-nine saw active service								3	3	3	3	3	3	3	3	3	3
									5	5	5	5	5	5	5	5	5
										77	77	77	77	77	77	77	77
											82	82	82	82	82	82	82
											35	35	35	35	35	35	35
											28	28	28	28	28	28	28
												4	4	4	4	4	4
												27	27	27	27	27	27
												6	6	6	6	6	6
												33	33	33	33	33	33
												30	30	30	30	30	30
												80	80	80	80	80	80
													78	78	78	78	78
													89	89	89	89	89
													92	92	92	92	92
													90	90	90	90	90
													37	37	37	37	37
													29	29	29	29	29
														79	79	79	79
														91	91	91	91
														36	36	36	36
															7	7	7
															81	81	81
															88	88	88
Six depot, training, or replacement divisions							41	41	41	41	41	41	41	41	41	41	41
													83	83	83	83	83
														76	76	76	76
															85	85	85
															39	39	39
															40	40	40
Seven late divisions; broken up and reassigned																87	87
																84	84
																86	86
																34	34
																	31
																	38
																	8

* Table based on War College handbook, *Order of Battle of the United States Land Forces in the World War, American Expeditionary Forces* (1931); Leonard P. Ayres, *The War with Germany* (1919).

There was no certainty that tonnage for so many as this could be assembled by the United States or borrowed from Great Britain. But the War Department substantially fulfilled this portion of its estimate when before March 1 it had shipped 291,000 men.

Despite the reluctance of the War Department to promise more than it could hope to fulfill, Pershing continued to hope. In October his 'shipping schedule No. 1' contained the order of shipment of the components for a force of thirty divisions, grossing 1,328,448 men, whom he asked to have in hand before the next July. He asked for more than he expected to receive, and each month when his receipts came up only to his expectations he allowed himself to be a little disappointed in the War Department. After he had attended the November conference and had conversed with the chiefs of staff, Bliss, Robertson, and Foch, he wired Washington of the 'utmost importance' of having at his disposal by the end of June 'twenty-four divisions, in addition to the troops for the service of the rear.' He was immediately involved in bargaining with the British for ships, and in fighting off their attempt to get mere man-power in exchange for tons. And when whispers of the bargains reached the French, they showed grievance and demanded man-power for themselves. His army in sight continued to be depressingly small, while his conviction grew that without a great American army the war must be lost.

The flow of troops was accelerated in March. No more than twenty-seven transports had carried troops from the United States in any month before March, but in that month there were forty-five, with more than 85,000 troops aboard. The tables of Vice-Admiral Albert Gleaves, who commanded the convoy operations and recorded them in *A History of the Transport Service* (1921), account for 2,079,880 in the American personnel taken overseas before the Armistice. Eighty-two per cent of these were convoyed by the Navy; forty-three per cent were carried in ships of the United States. The record of March, 1918, seventy per cent better than that of any preceding month, was broken by the April total of 120,000 men; and April was left behind by each of the next six months, with top figures of 311,359 in July, and a monthly average of 263,000. The Allies, driven to find the ships by their fear of defeat, did not give up their hope that they could drive or bargain Pershing from his contention that he would command the men. But once the ships were found, the army came.

The Atlantic Ferry had fetched most of the components of the First Army Corps before the German drive began in March. Major-General Hunter Liggett, who had organized on the West Coast the 41st Division which was arriving in France between November and February, was given command of the First Army Corps in January. He proceeded with the organization work necessary in anticipation of the time when the corps should complete its training and take the field. It was July before this time arrived and his command became tactical as well as administrative; meanwhile it remained administrative over such of its troops as were not specifically under French command. Six divisions were in theory allotted to an army corps, and sometimes a corps had that many; but it took more than divisions to make a corps. There were also 'corps troops,' not a part of any division, but attached to corps headquarters to be used directly under the corps commander. Most prominent among these were air service, artillery, engineers, medical, and signal troops, and a little cavalry.

The tables of organization, printed in *Order of Battle of the United States Land Forces in the World War* (1931, 1937), make it possible to determine with considerable accuracy where divisions and smaller units were at work from day to day, but the commanders of division or of corps rarely knew of what their commands consisted until they saw the day's table of strength. Detachments, transfers, and replacements were such as progressively broke down the entity of units, and approached an ideal of interchangeability of parts for the whole A.E.F.

Basic for the First Army Corps was the 41st Division, which never fought as such. Its fighting units were used as needed, but the headquarters organization was kept near the Loire, a little east of Tours. Troops poured into it from the docks of St. Nazaire and Brest. It did depot duty, maintained a reservoir from which men and units were dispatched toward the front and kept its fluid personnel busy with drill and instruction through the interval between arrival in France and allocation to duty. If divisions had come as divisions, ready to be sent immediately to the training areas around Chaumont and Neufchâteau, its duties would have been lessened. But men came in large numbers, ascribed to non-divisional tasks, or simply as 'casuals.' They must be trained and sorted out before they could go forward. After fighting began, there were continual calls for replacements.

Grouped around the St. Aignan area, where the 41st was stationed, were numerous service establishments, halfway between the ports and the front. Tours, itself, was made headquarters of the whole Services of Supply in March, 1918. Northeast was Blois, where officers were sorted out. If they came as casuals, here they remained until work was found them. If they proved inadequate at the front, hither they were sent to wait until some different task was found, or until, not needed, they were returned to the United States. A little east was Gièvres, rapidly becoming a huge warehouse center. Southeast was Issoudun, where the aircraft schools were concentrated.

The combat divisions, sufficient for the initial set-up of the First Army Corps, were all on hand by March. Beginning with the 1st and 2d Divisions, whose units were not assembled as divisions until after their arrival in France, the First Army Corps received also the 26th (New England National Guard), the 32d (Michigan and Wisconsin National Guard), and the 42d (Rainbow) Divisions. Describing the divisions as Regular Army or National Guard, which was somewhat misleading from the first, became deceptive within a few weeks after the opening of head-quarters.

The Army scheme, contemplating the use of troops derived in three ways, included sixteen divisions in which were to be grouped the partly trained militiamen of the National Guard. It was sought to bring the National Guard regiments to full strength by voluntary enlistment before the Selective Service men were sent to camp. After the National Guard had been distributed among its sixteen divisions and these, on August 5, 1917, had been drafted *en masse* into the Army of the United States, it was determined to form a seventeenth division, known as the 42d, to go to France earlier than any of the rest and to join the Regular Army 1st and 2d. This was announced August 14, the 42d Division being comprised of selected units from twenty-six States, all presumably more advanced in their training than the rest of the Guardsmen.

There were recently enlisted raw recruits, in all of the units, whether in name from the Guard or the Regulars. There were so many, indeed, that certain of the units looked like awkward squads when they reached France and none of them were instantly ready for the front. Even their officers included quotas of second lieutenants fresh from the Officers' Training Camps. They were not professional soldiers, whatever they were called.

There was even more dilution of the pre-war trained soldiers than that involved in new recruits and training-camp officers. As the divisions were headed toward Hoboken and the Embarkation Service they were rarely of full strength. Their ranks were filled to something resembling strength by drafts drawn upon other divisional camps, not yet ready to sail. It was a heartbreaking experience for divisional commanders to have their ranks repeatedly depleted in order to meet such levies and to have to start anew upon the training of men inducted under the Selective Service. At least a quarter of the men who sailed in National Guard divisions came to them through the draft. Whatever character the divisions started with was weakened by the scrambling process.

The 1st Division, whose people were both flattered and embarrassed by its designation as the 'nursery of the High Command,' set up its headquarters in the Gondrecourt training area, within striking distance of both Chaumont and Neufchâteau, in mid-July. This was a month after sailing. The division suffered endless losses as officers and men were set to other tasks than that of training, but it managed, alone among the twenty-nine combat divisions, substantially to complete its period of training according to schedule.

It was hoped that divisions might be seasoned by at least three months of experience in France before they were sent to the front. The schedule provided for a month of drill as division, after arrival, while officers and men were getting used to France. There was a second month planned to be spent in training with the French, for which purpose the division was broken into small groups. A third month was assigned to training as a reassembled division. And after this the division was expected to be ready for introduction to actual war on a quiet front under its own officers.

Participation in combat began for the A.E.F. when on October 21, 1917, the earliest battalions of the 1st Division moved into the line of the French army, on the Sommerviller sector, northeast of Lunéville. Pershing has described them as short of winter clothing, rolling kitchens, horses, and officers. Out of the line at the end of November, they resumed divisional training at Gondrecourt, changed commanding officers, and found themselves operating a sector on the south face of the St. Mihiel salient on February 5, under the command of Major-General Robert L. Bullard. Here they were kept until, after Pershing had placed his force at the disposal of Foch on March 28, they were shifted to the Montdidier front.

The 2d Division, only less than the 1st, was a training school. Its organization was directed in September, 1917, after the draft men had begun to report to camp and while its component units were variously in the United States or in France. Some of the Marine Corps men (the 5th and 6th regiments of which were to constitute its 4th infantry brigade) had gone to France with the first convoy. Its divisional headquarters were assembled in France in October, and in January its divisional training was well under way. The German drive in March found the 2d Division brigaded with the French on the west face of the St. Mihiel front. There was reason in training the divisions on the quiet sectors east of Verdun, and special reason in permitting them to serve on the faces of St. Mihiel; for the elimination of this German salient had already been ticketed as the first independent assignment of the A.E.F., when there should be an army.

Third in seniority of the divisions of the First Army Corps, which Pershing could offer to Foch in March, was the 26th, which Major-General Clarence R. Edwards commanded. Edwards had had thirty-four years of service in the Army, had been long in Washington at the head of the Bureau of Insular Affairs, and was in command of the Northeastern Department (headquarters in Boston) when assigned to the division. The division was never together in the United States but was shipped in fragments from Montreal, New York, Hoboken, and Newport News. Its roster was unusually free from men acquired by transfer, and it was at sea before draft men were available at the National Army camps. It began to arrive in September, was trained in the Neufchâteau area, and on February 5, when the 1st Division received its own sector, the 26th moved in with the French along the Chemin des Dames, northward from Soissons. Its historian — for most of the divisions and many smaller units have historians of considerable, though uneven, merit — admits that its men still had many of the tricks of war to be learned, 'from calculating fire data to burying garbage.' But he speaks with enthusiasm of the French troops of liaison under whose experienced eyes every activity was conducted at the start. The division was historical-minded enough to save and send back for preservation in Massachusetts the case from which its artillery fired its first shell on the afternoon of February 5. On April 3 it replaced the 1st Division at St. Mihiel, when the 1st was sent to Montdidier.

Much as all the divisions tended through interchange to become alike, there was a difference between those derived from the National Guard and those assembled in the Regular Army. Some of this was in the matter of junior officers. In the Regular divisions the lieutenants and many of the captains were Training Camp men, who did not pretend to know the art of war, and who took counsel avidly from the Regular officers who commanded them. The Regular officers whom they saw most had commonly, up to April, 1917, at least, been in the grades they occupied them-

selves, because war expansion resulted in the speedy elevation of
the Regulars one, two, or three grades above their peace-time
rank. It is to be borne in mind that throughout the months of
American participation every officer, from Pershing down, was
trying to function in a rank for which peace had not fully prepared him and that only the rigorous activity of the Inspector-
General's force kept inexperience from doing damage.

The junior officers in such a division as the 26th were earnest
amateur soldiers, many of them with years of service in the
National Guard. Their units, some with a military past extending
to the Revolutionary War, had an *esprit* based upon tradition,
local residence, and sometimes social standing. Among them there
was an undercurrent of resentment at a military policy which
broke down local connection and which appeared to be based on
a belief that National Guardsmen could never be more than
amateurs. The long legislative struggle to fit the organized militia
into a scheme of national defense had left scars on both sides.
The draft of the National Guard, effective August 5, had destroyed
the Guard. Its personnel retained a recollection of long service,
but in the Army of the United States they had no history prior
to induction.

Before the 26th was ready for the front its officers had come to
feel that Regular officers were prejudiced against them, and that
the cards were stacked. When, in the midst of the Argonne
fighting, Edwards was relieved of his command and a brigadier-
general from the 1st Division replaced him, a long post-war controversy was started in which the grievances of the National
Guard had a field day. It was Army policy, when vacancies occurred among the officers, whether from death or transfer, to fill
only a few of them by promotions from below. In a great army,
with uneven incidence of vacancies, it would have produced great
unevenness of rewards had the officer below invariably gone up.
But the 26th felt that too many of the vacancies were filled by
new officers transferred to the division and inferior to the juniors
over whom they took command. Too many of the Guard officers,
for their happiness, were allowed to end the war in the rank in

which they entered it. Too many others, because of proficiency in some civil craft, were sent away to work behind the lines at what were essentially civilian duties, even though performed by men in uniform. They ran the railroads, and the camp utilities, the laundries and the warehouses. Better men than they, indeed — Regular officers unfortunate enough to be skillful — were taken from jobs at the front to serve the rear or to return to the United States to train recruits. The Chief of Artillery, A.E.F., March, was sent home to be Chief of Staff; the Chief of Staff of the A.E.F., Harbord, whom Pershing seems to have regarded as his best, was sent back to Tours to run the Services of Supply. But the Guardsmen, prepared to be unhappy with the Regulars, based their complaints upon the rapid promotions accruing to Regular officers, particularly from the 1st Division.

In the American scheme, the direction of a fighting army must be in the hands of the professional officers found in the army at the beginning of the war. This sets up an unavoidable conflict between the officer caste and the mature and accomplished civilians who have taken commissions of their own volition. The belief in deliberate discrimination sharpened the grievance.

The Rainbow Division, fourth to arrive, followed the 26th to France. Its personnel included Charles P. Summerall and Douglas MacArthur, both destined after the war to become Chief of Staff. Its first commander, Major-General William A. Mann, although on the verge of retirement, assembled it at Camp Mills and brought it overseas. Major-General Charles T. Menoher, who succeeded him, had risen from colonel to major-general in a few months, and was to rise farther, for in November he was shifted to command of the Sixth Army Corps, in the Second Army. The 42d was brigaded with the French near Lunéville, until at the end of March it relieved a French division in the line, taking over the Baccarat sector as its own.

It was not allowed to be known while the divisions were training in the camps in the United States what use would be made of them overseas. But it was known at Chaumont. Here it was early decided that the first four divisions to arrive should be groomed for combat; that the fifth, which proved to be the 41st, should be assigned to odd jobs around the depots, and that the sixth should be kept in the immediate rear of the front to hold replacements for the First Army Corps. When, in February, 1918, the units of the 32d Division came in by way of Liverpool and Le Havre, they came prepared to fight, only to learn that their destiny was different. They were the sixth to arrive.

Some of the regiments of the Michigan and Wisconsin National Guard were still near the Mexican Border when the forces of these States were merged in the 32d Division and assembled at Camp MacArthur, near Waco, Texas. The first commander, Parker, was soon shifted to Battle Creek, Michigan, to train the Michigan and Wisconsin draft men in the 85th Division at Camp Custer. His successor, Major-General William G. Haan, rescued the 32d from its fate as non-combat division only by convincing Chaumont that it was fit to fight. It had been equipped to sail only by stripping the less happy 33d (Illinois National Guard, at Camp Logan, near Houston) of its 'ordnance, and all its overseas supplies,' and of its reserves of clothing. It served for a few weeks as replacement, losing meanwhile a Wisconsin regiment that was filtered into the 1st Division; but after the crisis of March 21 it was redesignated for combat. By the middle of June, Haan was in tactical command of a sector of his own, facing Mulhouse, at the extreme right of the front in Alsace. First of the divisions to get on German soil, its men had an advantage over most, in that German was for many of them a second tongue. Its divisional performance was a rebuttal of the German belief that Americans of German parentage were still a reliance for the Fatherland.

When Pershing went to Foch on March 28 offering his divisions, the Atlantic Ferry was still working only as though there was no real intention to bring a fighting army to France. The 1st Division, alone, had been tested on a sector of its own. The 2d, 26th, and 42d were still learning how to behave on quiet sectors, under their French tutors. The 32d had not escaped its destiny as a replacement division; three of its infantry regiments had been detached from it before it took station at Prauthoy, in Haute-

Marne; and it lost seven thousand men as replacements during March, including its fourth infantry regiment, which it lost forever. When Pershing believed he had four divisions ready to fight, and a fifth nearly ready, he was more sanguine than were the French officers who had watched them train. These had admired the spirit of the men and the energy of the new officers, while marveling at their initial ignorance. The new men coming were progressively less well trained, for the confusion in American camps, caused by repeated transfers back and forth and repeated drafts of divisional men for special services, was breaking up programs of instruction as fast as they were planned. No one of the divisions in France had undertaken an independent action, worked out by its own staff and directed by its own commander. Service on quiet sectors — good service, which the French intelligence officers praised in their reports — was different from independent action. Six days after offering the divisions as they were, Pershing went to Beauvais.

He left Beauvais not quite sure that Bliss had not let him down by agreeing to joint note No. 18, and that President Wilson had not deserted him by accepting the British interpretation of its recommendation. To Allies, who could see how slowly the divisions were arriving, it seemed ridiculous to wait for American man-power until Pershing's craving for divisions, army corps, and army should be gratified. They had information from every level of the American effort. Their officers in the American camps described the confusion prevailing in many of them. Other officers with A.E.F. troops after arrival reported on their rawness and the unevenness of their equipment. The liaison officers knew nearly as much about Pershing's force as Pershing knew. There was more than mere delay involved, for there was no certainty that the staff work at Chaumont would be good enough for the safe direction of an army once in action. But whatever rumors came through to Pershing from Washington, no orders came directing him either to surrender his men or to give up his idea of a separate component. Baker left him on April 7 to sail for home, leaving him still in complete command, and stating explicitly that neither the British nor the French were to get 'an exaggerated idea' that the transport arrangements were to provide means 'by which their losses will be made up in the future.' Pershing went to London for a conference with Lord Milner on April 24.

If the Allies thought the American commander was too stubborn, Pershing was convinced that they were 'at last thoroughly alive' and that 'America was their reliance.' Just as the 1st Division moved to its station near Montdidier, he pressed Foch to name the day when the six divisions might operate as a corps and found the Generalissimo ready to accept in principle but unable to fix a time or place. When, during the next few weeks, it became possible that the accelerated divisions (nine reached France in May) might end by reinforcing the British, it became easier to persuade the French that Pershing ought to have his way. A separate army would fight on the French front, whereas a brigaded army would stiffen only the British lines. At the London conference Pershing concluded with Lord Milner the details respecting the shipment of the May divisions and the degree upon which the British, behind whom they were to train, might rely upon them as a reinforcement. He was met, in conference, by the British interpretation of joint note No. 18, but he clung to his power of command despite the 'heavy "verbal artillery"' that was turned upon him.

At Abbeville, where the Supreme War Council held its fifth meeting on the first of May, it was apparent that the Council, as a technical co-ordinating agency, was breaking up. Its diplomatic aspect, given it by the ministers, was clearer than ever before. The Permanent Military Representatives were falling into the background, since the personal staff of Foch was doing their work. The Executive War Board, upon which they had had an institutional existence, was abolished. By common consent the principal tasks of this session were to weigh the relative disadvantage of a loss of the Channel ports as against the breaking of the Western Front by German penetration, to expedite American arrivals, to reconcile the rivalry of France and England for the use of

American troops while training them, and to work on Pershing. Despite pressure from Clemenceau and David Lloyd George that the May agreement giving preference to infantry and machine gunners be extended through June, Pershing declined to commit himself. Washington, he thought, had already yielded too much. He refused to let the Council dictate his course.

The bitterness of the struggle for his power of command, not publicly sensed while the war was on, was first clearly displayed after the close of the Washington conference in 1922, when George Pattullo published his papers on 'The Inside Story of the A.E.F.' in the *Saturday Evening Post*. When Pershing retold the tale in the chapters of *My Experiences* serialized by the *New York Times* in the spring of 1931, he quoted freely from the record of the Abbeville session and said something about striking the table to emphasize the point he made. Upon assembling the articles in book form, he edited the table-thumping out of the text; but its spirit is as of the record. To Foch's point-blank question whether, holding to his independence, he was willing to let the line be backed down to the Loire, he answered, 'Yes, I am willing to take the risk.' In one of the most intelligent critiques of the A.E.F., *It Might Have Been Lost* (1929), Thomas C. Lonergan measured the significance of Pershing's decision, and the burden there would have been upon him had the venture failed. That it succeeded in the way it succeeded was largely due to Pershing's insistence.

They ended at Abbeville in an agreement that through June the May shipments, at least, should be continued, and that the matter of shipments in July should be considered later in the light of conditions as they might then exist. They agreed, as well, that 'an American army should be formed as early as possible under its own commander and under its own flag.'

The events of May shook the Allies again. After holding off defeat in March, at Amiens, and in April, in Flanders, they faced its possibility once more when Germany poured down in May and broke the line along the Chemin des Dames. When the Supreme War Council met on June 1 to take its inventory and make its plans, the German advance was at Château-Thierry on the

Marne. It was 'the very crisis of the war,' wrote Bliss, who had time to put himself on paper since most of his business as Permanent Military Representative had been drawn from beneath him. The British and French found themselves in too warm a controversy over the cause of the French collapse along the Chemin des Dames to give undivided attention to Pershing. They even agreed with him that the character of the American troops was not a proper concern of the Supreme War Council, but was suitable for consideration 'outside the Council' by the persons most involved. They listened to his statement of the embarrassment caused to President Wilson by hearing through the British and French ambassadors in Washington 'representations' on matters that were proper to be settled directly between himself and Foch. Upon this, Foch urged him to ask of Washington an army of one hundred divisions, combat troops, to be forwarded at the rate of 300,000 men per month. The June agreement was, in substance, extended over July, but since it committed only 140,000 troops, and 311,359 were actually floated, it was no longer a serious interference with the plans of the A.E.F.

The ministers of the Allies, and Foch himself, were discouraged; but Pershing left the Council on June 3 not dissatisfied — the Atlantic Ferry had come to life. This was the last important meeting of the Supreme War Council until the very end, when armistice terms came into sight. The July meeting, which Pershing attended only because of a personal urging by Lloyd George, was concerned with marginal matters. Troop shipment agreements were now settled elsewhere. Pershing had in hand work more important than any the Council could put on its agenda. On the third of June his divisions were on the line at the very tip of the German salient, at Château-Thierry. And on the twenty-eighth of May his 1st Division had been tested at Cantigny and had proved itself.

XV. THE TEST OF QUALITY

CANTIGNY was not featured in the *Guide to the American Battle Fields in Europe* (1927). That convenient handbook for the patriotic tourist — prepared by the American Battle Monuments Commission, to which General Pershing gave many years of service after withdrawing from more active duties — allowed it only one page out of the many which were devoted to the field activities of the fighting troops. As the war went, it was a trifling encounter. Cantigny was just another town. But as a test of quality its capture was undertaken by the staff of the 1st Division, and was watched by solicitous officers from Chaumont and by the various Allied officers of liaison. On May 29, when it was of the past and the division was consolidating the fragment of new line it had established, there was no longer any question whether American troops could fight or whether civilians in uniform could be taught something of the technique of command. Major-General Hunter Liggett, in administrative charge of the division, since he commanded the First Army Corps, wrote about it in *Commanding an American Army: Recollections of the World War* (1925). Cantigny was, he said, 'the first cold foreboding to the German that this was not, as he had hoped, a rabble of amateurs approaching.'

Within a week the Allied argument against a separate American army began to shift. Beneath it thus far had been the assumption, not always masked, of American incapacity except under Allied lead. Now entered the note that the fine fresh soldiers were so great an inspiration to the wearied Allied troops as to make them invaluable to boost the effort. It suited Pershing to magnify the usefulness of his force, although he had no delusion as to the military significance of one village. It suited the Allies as well to advertise the fact that Americans were on hand and could be used. It has been rumored that German orders directed immediate recapture of whatever Americans should gain, lest news of prowess should penetrate the censorship. A prompt *communiqué* let the United States know in the morning papers of the twenty-ninth that on the Picardy front, a little west of Montdidier, a village had been taken, and was held.

The region around Montdidier, at the tip of the Somme salient, became a quiet front when the German drive slowed down at the end of March. The 1st Division was shifted hither in April to relieve French troops, and to build up a nucleus in reserve for an Allied counter-stroke which Foch was never able to advance beyond the stage of contemplation. Near the end of April, he slipped the infantry into the line opposite Cantigny, where Bullard received command of a sector on the twenty-seventh. Facing the division, the German holders of the village — not much more than a crossroads — sat on a low plateau, with an uncomfortably clear vision of the American line and with their own artillery and services well masked behind them. In the middle of May the 2d infantry brigade did a week of service on the line, after which its 28th regiment (the regiments in the Regular Army divisions retained their old Army numeration) passed to the rear to rehearse on selected ground, in full scale, the task assigned it. It was back in line in time for 'H-hour' at 5.45 A.M., on the morning of May 28. With French artillery covering the assault, the occupation of Cantigny was complete and successful in time for early breakfast. There were seven different and unsuccessful German attempts, within the next day or two, to reoccupy the village. The victors held their position, widened their sector, built up its systematic defenses, and remained in place until they passed back to the rear on July 8. Pétain cited the regiment. Hanson E. Ely, its colonel, rose to command his own division, the 5th. Beaumont B. Buck, the brigade commander, rose to the 3d. Bullard, divisional commander, received the Second Army. It is possible to minimize the significance of the enterprise, though without destroying its value as a symbol, by stressing the preoccupation of the German forces in the larger venture to which they devoted themselves the day before Cantigny became a station on the line of the Allies.

Battle was expected somewhere, sometime, in May. The first German attempt, in the Somme, the second in Flanders, made certain a third, because the German determination to break the Allied line was not doubted. The investigations from the German side, since 1918, have confirmed this. Where the next thrust would come, and when, were kept from the knowledge of Foch. Few maneuvers of the war were more perfectly concealed than those connected with the German concentration of forces north of a line that might be drawn from Compiègne, through Soissons, and east to Reims. The intelligence officers of the A.E.F. diagnosed German intentions and were right enough, but their contribution was disregarded at French headquarters. The valley of the Aisne, which runs westwardly through Soissons to Compiègne, was in French hands. North of that valley, parallel to it, the rough heights of the Chemin des Dames were too rough to be taken easily from the Allies. They commanded too good a view of their own northern slopes, of the Ailette at their foot and of the German center across the Ailette at Laon, to be easily surprised. Tired divisions had been parked there to recuperate, including five of British troops wearied and torn by the battles of the early spring. Newspaper strategists in the American press discussed the impending attack, studied their maps of France to pick the spot, and forecast it for any other place than where it struck.

But on the early morning of May 27 the heights of the Chemin des Dames and the slopes behind it, down to the Aisne, were drenched with gas and enveloped in German artillery fire that cleared the way for infantry. The batteries came from nowhere, unknown until they spoke. The infantry came from nowhere, brought up at night and kept deceitfully under cover by day. The aircraft photographs had not discovered the concentration. Rushing across the Chemin des Dames, meeting little resistance because little that could resist was left, the Germans reached the Aisne itself before noon; and before sundown the advance was heading for the Vesle, which runs through Reims to enter the

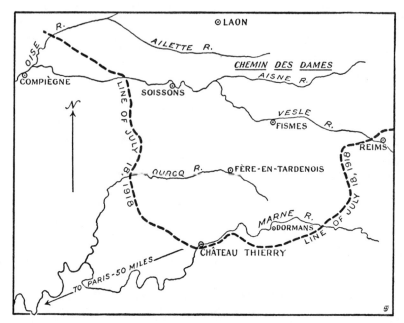

THE MARNE SALIENT

Aisne, above Soissons, from the south. On a front of about forty miles the Allied line was penetrated some twelve miles on the first day; penetrated so easily that the Germans fell over themselves, missing chances to penetrate more deeply and more widely. Yet they were ready on the second day, along the Vesle, midway between Reims and Soissons, to continue the advance. The second day was as dreary for the Allies as the first had been. On the third, with the German left washing around the fortifications of Reims — these held — the German right enveloped and occupied Soissons, while the center pushed the tip of the salient past Fère-en-Tardenois, where the French railroads met and where were great dumps of supplies. On the fourth day of the drive, May 30, the center crossed the ridge north of the Marne and could look down upon Château-Thierry and Dormans, and the rail and highway systems which follow the Marne and constitute the great east road to Metz.

It was again no time for Pershing to stand upon his dignity. The German gain was greater than the High Command had anticipated. As the troops at the tip of the salient raced ahead, the plan of battle was developed in accordance with the gains. Since Reims resisted, the armies pushed beyond it, risking their left for the sake of greater penetration. Soissons, yielding, let the salient widen on the right among the woods and hills between the Aisne and the Ourcq. Across the line of advance, all the river valleys sloped to the right in the general direction of Paris. By the fourth day, the Marne was within reach, and once across the Marne a swing to the west made Paris a possibility. South of the Marne lay the battlefield on which the war had, in 1914, changed from one of maneuver in the field to one of attrition in the trenches. Between Dormans and Château-Thierry was the place to cross. Southward and westward was the thrust, and ahead of the German line the roads were clogged with farmers hurrying from trouble and with French units in various stages of retreat. It was mostly one-way traffic; Allied divisions were not pressing against it to the front. Bliss had trucks in readiness to move his files, in case Paris should have to be abandoned.

The 1st Division, busy at Cantigny, was too busy to be of use elsewhere. The 26th was still in charge of a sector at St. Mihiel. The 42d was on its Baccarat sector in Lorraine. The 32d, now reconsidered and made a combat division, was on the line in front of Mulhouse. Only the 2d was ready for heavy duty. It had completed an assignment on the west side of St. Mihiel and had been moved, ten days before the drive, to the vicinity of Beauvais. Here, Major-General Omar Bundy was continuing its training with the French. It was near enough the 1st Division for it to be suspected that it was part of a concentration that Foch was preparing for use east of Montdidier. When Pétain on the fourth day of the drive asked for troops, the 2d Division was put on trucks, spending the last day of May *en route* to Meaux, on the road to Metz.

There were no other divisions ready for use. The 5th Division, arriving in installments like the rest, through April and May, had not yet had the experience of a quiet sector and was training near Chaumont. Major-General Joseph T. Dickman, with the 3d, which had arrived a month earlier in France, was also near Chaumont, where Pershing had watched his maneuvers within the week. The commander had been to the British area to see something of the still fresher arrivals, the 4th, 28th, 35th, 77th, and 82d, when he wrote in his diary on the last day of the month: 'The French situation is very serious.' But such as he had, he handed his men to Foch. Even before the 2d Division was started east to Meaux, the 3d, as man-power and without artillery, was started west. It began to move on the 30th of May. One of its units, the 7th machine-gun battalion on its own motor transport, arrived at the Marne on the afternoon of the thirty-first, and as the German advance pushed down the right bank of the river toward Château-Thierry the machine-gunners crossed the bridge, took station on the north edge of the town, and set to work. While they awaited the rest of the division, which was temporarily attached to a French division, they covered the retreat through Château-Thierry, retarded the German advance, held their stations on June 1, and on June 2 retired slowly through the town. They crossed to the south bank just before the bridge was destroyed by General Jean-Baptiste Marchand, of Fashoda fame, commanding the 10th French Colonial Division. Along the south bank of the Marne the 3d Division filtered into place. By June 6, Dickman had a sector to the left of the 10th Colonial with his own left touching the 2d Division, which had followed the 3d into action.

The 2d Division, in its trucks on May 31 when the units of the 3d went into action, came up to Meaux in the afternoon and was sent ahead astraddle of the Paris–Metz road. Bundy, by protest, kept it from fighting piecemeal among the French. His men marched all night, coming into line on the morning of June 1, without knowing where the line was, or whether it had even an existence. The German divisions in the salient were swinging westward, and between them and the retreating French there was no fixed force. As, after the event, eloquence grew more impassioned and less careful, Daniels was one of many to rejoice that the Marines had saved Paris. The regiments of Marines attached to the 2d Division had an advantage in publicity over all other varieties of troops. When the censors passed the word 'division' in the stories of the correspondents no reader could tell who was meant thereby — since censors' rules forbade the naming of specific units. But when they passed the word 'Marines' (which no one had thought to forbid) everyone recognized at once the regiments that had been taken over with the earliest troops. A Marine legend was built up at the expense of troops just as useful and many times as numerous. The recruiting officers of the Marines made much use of the words 'first to fight'; and the Secretary of the Navy, their commanding officer, played them a close second. The gallant units on the road to Metz were headed toward an overstuffed legend as misleading as that of the Rough Riders in the war with Spain. But neither the Marine Corps, nor the 2d Division as a whole, seems to have saved Paris.

The saving of Paris may have been accomplished south of the Marne, where the German armies, once through between Château-Thierry and Dormans might have swung west around Hill 204, had not the French, with American assistance, checked the advance. It may have been accomplished north of the Paris–Metz road, where the French constructed a new line which left the 2d Division in command of the sector to the right by June 4. But it was more probably done by the decision of the German High Command. As the salient advanced, it was hampered by its own success and endangered by its long and exposed flanks. Château-Thierry and a line running nearly north from the Marne at that point were as far west as it was safe to press, or intended to press, until the salient should be sufficiently enlarged to allow room for maneuver for the crowded attacking divisions and for the operation of the services of the Germans.

Yet the 2d Division, weary as it was with all day in the trucks and all night on the march, managed to establish a line where there had been no semblance of a line. It held its stations while refugees poured through it, escaping the invaders; it listened to the talk of dire calamity on the heels of the refugees; and it watched a new French front being pushed up alongside it. It waited for the Germans, but the latter did not strike it in force on the first, the second, or the third of June. In front of the sector of the 2d the new German line enclosed Hill 204, just west of Château-Thierry in the angle between the Marne and the road to Metz, and Vaux, upon that road, and the villages of Bouresches and Belleau together with the wooded hill in front of the latter. To the left of the 2d the new line ran north, crossing the Ourcq, passing well in front of Villers-Cotterêts and the forest behind which it was hidden, and on to a crossing of the Aisne about seven miles west of Soissons. From the Marne to the Aisne is about twenty-seven miles, of which the 2d held some five. Not until June 9 did the Germans undertake seriously to widen their salient on this western side, and from this effort they were beaten back by the Tenth French Army under General Mangin.

On June 6 the 2d Division began a corrective operation of its own to bring within its lines Vaux, Bouresches, and the woods in front of Belleau. Here for the first time an American division undertook a protracted enterprise. The terrain was difficult, the resistance stout, and the regiments were so green that they blundered into each other, lost contact, and got lost in the woods. Beginning at Bouresches, which was taken without great difficulty on June 6, the fight dragged out, with troops learning their business as they fought. Hill 204 to the right of Vaux, and the Belleau Woods to the left of Bouresches, tested the endurance of the division and the skill of its officers. The hill was taken by June 10, in co-operation with French forces and the left of the 3d Division. The Belleau Woods were cleared out, clump by clump, and gun-pit by gun-pit, but were not fully in American possession until June 25, when the Marine Brigade finished what was its particular task. The enterprise had sentimental values which the French recognized by renaming the woods as Bois de la Brigade de Marine. The division had suffered some 9500 casualties. Congress in due time incorporated the Belleau Wood Memorial Association which bought the ground on which they fought. Vaux was at last taken on July 1, and in a few days more the responsibility for the sector passed to the 26th Division. The command of the 2d was changed on July 15, giving to Major-General James G. Harbord his brief moment in the field. He had been Pershing's chief of staff from the organization of the A.E.F. until May, had then commanded the Marine Brigade until July, and was reluctantly to accept non-fighting duty before the month was out. Bundy went up, to command in turn the Sixth and Seventh Army Corps.

The position of Foch, Commander in Chief on the Western Front, became stronger every day. The mythical reserve, which was to have been contributed by the Allies and managed by the Executive War Board of the Supreme War Council, had remained without reality except in the minds of news writers outside of France. While the heavy pressure was upon the line in March and April the Generalissimo could do little but watch and hope, and contemplate the action he might some day take if he should have the strength. The three months after the line was stabilized around Montdidier brought him the strength, such as it was. The Atlantic Ferry, in these months, carried 648,000 American troops.

It is an impressive list of divisions, seventeen in all, that made appearance in France in these same months. If they had been divisions trained as in the schedule, and floated as complete units, they would have been more impressive. But they came as the convoys could receive them, with the first and last units of many of them two months apart. They came faster than the War Department had provided, until camps in the United States were drained and divisional strength was made up at the last minute by transferring men, wherever they could be found. The case of the 33d Division, arriving mostly in May, is to the point.

Not all the war units were as happy in their historians as was the division put together at Camp Logan, in Texas, out of the Illinois National Guard. Frederic L. Huidekoper, adjutant of the Division and a lawyer by trade, had written a textbook of controversy, *The Military Unpreparedness of the United States* (1915), before he took a commission. He served with the Illinois troops through the war and was commissioned by the State to write *The History of the 33d Division A.E.F.* (1921). His four volumes have none of the college-annual spirit that lessens the usefulness of many divisional histories. They contain weighed text and reprint a large share of the official orders on which the text is based; and they reveal the tribulations of Major-General George Bell, Jr., as he sought to prepare his troops for service.

The 33d was in motion overseas from April 23 until June 15, 1918. Its first units had begun to arrive at Camp Logan on September 10, 1917. Here they had found an incomplete camp and General Bell with his divisional staff waiting to receive them. Before Bell had more than a fraction of his men in hand, he was sent abroad on the inspection tour with other divisional commanders, and was away from September 19 until December 7. While he was in France his understudy rearranged the units as they came in accordance with the divisional structure and size preferred by Pershing. Some were enlarged, some reduced, some broken up. All were short of men, and the complement of officers, of whom nearly one thousand were required, suffered all the time from the loss of selected groups sent away for special instruction or ordered away to other military units. Short of personnel as the division was, it was overwhelmed by the way in which its shortage was relieved. Drafted men, 6600 of them, were sent it from the 86th and 88th Divisions; and with these men instruction had to begin again from scratch. Among these, moreover, were so many 'unable to speak English' and so many physically unfit (2189 were discharged for physical disability) that they could not be assimilated. The weather went back on them and their canvas tents were no protection against heavy snow and a temperature of 11°, which is low for Texas.

When intimation of early shipment came at the end of November, it was necessary to report to Washington on the unreadiness of the division, and the shipment was cancelled. But its supplies were sent, being transferred to the 32d Division. When Bell returned in December, organization and training began again, with numbers still inadequate and with many alien enemies among the drafted men, whose disposition the War Department was slow to settle. In March, Bell was protesting to the Chief of Staff, urging that his letter get to General March himself and not to some assistant (Bell 'having been a Staff officer' and knowing the procedure), and reminding him that Pershing had 'personally declared to me that no divisions should be sent overseas unless they were thoroughly disciplined and equipped.' It was no wonder that members of Congress, who had visited their home camps, went to the December session in Washington full of grievance and dismay.

The 33d Division moved at last in April. Its gaps were hurriedly filled by robbing the 84th, 86th, and 88th Divisions. Arriving variously at Brest, Bordeaux, and Liverpool, they settled with the English near Abbeville, and a few companies fought with the Australians at Hamel on July 4. Not until mid-August did the division, still without its artillery, go into action with the British.

A division on the roster was not always a division for the field — the more rapidly the men were shipped, the less was there to be expected of their readiness when they arrived. But the acceptable performance of the earlier divisions at their first test made good

news at home. Cantigny, Château-Thierry, and Belleau Wood
heartened the citizen. If the achievements were as dangerously
magnified as the complaints of maladministration had been six
months earlier, it was no more than was to be expected under war
stresses. The half-knowledge with which men wrote and the gaps
in fact due to the military censors at the European ends of the
cables distorted the story for a public mind that was too greatly
disturbed to have drawn correct conclusions from the whole truth.
No one, in office or out, was in a position to know the whole truth.
The 'supermen' installed during the spring were by June appearing to get results; and results were being got, whether because of,
or in spite of, the supermen. Schwab's launching party of July
4, with its nearly one hundred ships, conveyed a promise that the
tonnage need would be met at last. The American camps had
a soldier population of nearly a million and a half, while Baker
timed for the Fourth of July a letter to the President informing him
that on July 1 '1,019,000 men had been embarked for France.'
His figures were interpreted in the light of the performance of
those who had led the way. Foch had his man-power in sight.

A young Virginia officer, Jennings C. Wise, watched the
operations near the Marne and wrote of them while memory was
fresh. His *Turn of the Tide* (1920), one of the earliest measured
narratives of American participation, is still of value. His title fits.
The tide of the World War, flooding against the Allies since 1914,
slackened when the Marne salient was stabilized in June. It turned
to ebb in July, as the enemy attempt to enlarge the salient and
to put it to use broke down, and as Foch brought into action what
was now his superior man-power. The testing of the quality of
the new American divisions was continued and extended as the
dynamics of the war reversed direction.

There are few advantages inherent in the military possession of
a salient. Its external lines are of necessity longer than the base
from which it has been thrust, and more costly to defend. They
run where the enemy has held them, rather than from point to
point determined by sound strategy and the convenience of the
attacker. The terrain within the salient, likely to be cut up by

shell fire, must, at the least, be reorganized to carry the services behind the new fronts. It may easily happen that by advancing into the salient the successful troops have walked within range of defenders' guns.

All of these disadvantages came to Germany with the less than success of the May attempt to gain territory and to break the Allied line. Unless one of these objectives could be attained, the drive to the Marne was a liability rather than an asset. The German documents have made it clear that this was the last huge liability which Germany was able to assume. The only specific advantage gained was the interruption of communication on such highways as ran eastwardly from Paris toward Reims or Verdun and on the roads along the south bank of the Marne. This gain to Germany was less than fatal to the Allies. The German armies could not advance south of the Marne without broadening the base north of the Aisne from which they operated; could not withdraw without confessing defeat; must broaden the base or charge off a loss.

In the Valley of the Oise, above the junction with the Aisne, the result of May was to leave French forces in a blunt angle between the south face of the Somme salient and the west face of the Marne salient. A German advance here would straighten the German line, shorten it a little, and perhaps make practicable a renewal of the thrust at Paris. The advance was attempted on June 9, in what is sometimes described as the fourth drive of 1918. It was so promptly stopped by Mangin that the effort makes an unimportant showing beside those which preceded it. There was a slight gain on either side of the Oise, but none along the Aisne; and the German situation was not materially improved.

It was so certain that life was inconvenient for the German divisions crowded in the Marne pocket and that the thrust must be renewed that the faces of the salient were kept under closest scrutiny. Concentrations were found on the east side, toward Reims, where a companion effort to that in the Oise was in preparation. Pershing, dining with Pétain on Saturday, July 13, recorded the opinion of his host that the advance was near at hand.

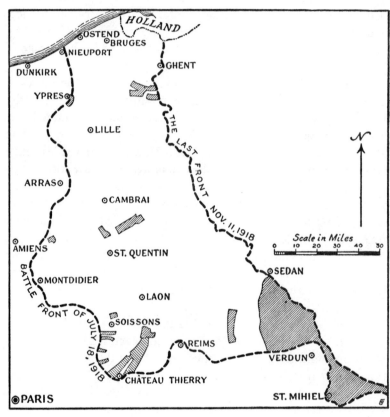

AREAS OF DIVISIONAL OPERATION, A.E.F.,
JULY 18–NOVEMBER 11, 1918

The intelligence officers had assembled evidence of activity on either side of Reims, where success on either side would bring about the fall of that city even though it were not itself attacked. A convenient prisoner, taken on the evening of Bastille Day, July 13, carried the time schedule for the artillery fire and the infantry advance. It is possible that the German High Command had counted upon overcelebration of Bastille Day as likely to produce a Monday morning slackness. But when the advance began on Monday morning, July 15, the Allied forces were so disposed as to receive it where and as it came.

The American divisions along the Marne had a share in the reception of the drive. They had been readjusted since the original salient took shape. Liggett had taken command of the front west of Château-Thierry on July 4, in tactical control of his First Army Corps. The 26th Division, having relieved the 2d, was in the line, with the 2d in second position, and Liggett had also a French division. There were French troops on his right, with elements of the 28th among them. This 28th (Pennsylvania National Guard) had arrived in May, trained a few weeks with the British, and been stationed with the French since July 1. The 3d Division, still brigaded with the French, was farther to the right, south of the Marne, where it had prepared trenches in the open for the German artillery to fire upon and positions under cover to be used. East of Reims the 42d Division was slightly behind the line in a position to be reached by the Germans on the second day.

For the first time Foch fought a battle on his own terms. His front lines, lightly held, were made to be abandoned. Behind them, in prearranged positions, his artillery was fixed to range over the river crossings and, more important, the next positions where German divisions, tense to take trenches, would be relaxed when they found the trenches empty. To the east of Reims, Gouraud yielded on July 15, but held the Germans on the second day. West of Reims, the heavy fighting was at the Marne crossings, well below Dormans. The country directly between Reims and the Marne was too rough for advance and compelled the German armies to detour west around it, before they could push east, up the valley. They made their gains in the Dormans region, against the French. Where the 3d Division held the line on the Marne bank, east of Château-Thierry, the line held. Both fact and legend built up the fame of its 38th infantry regiment, which found itself alone, fought simultaneously on its front and both flanks, and held its ground. Jusserand was wont to tell American audiences of one of the American generals, insubordinate when ordered to withdraw, basing his disobedience on a point of honor: that he had still three thousand shells in his possession belonging to the enemy and that he was bound to return them to the owner. The German drive made its little gains on July 15, was on the sixteenth stopped on ground determined for it in advance, was uncertain on the seventeenth in face of a new kind of reception, and on the eighteenth was abandoned because Foch had made it futile.

The Germans were embarrassed in the occupation of a salient that they dare not deepen without widening and that they could not widen. Their embarrassment was visible to amateur strategists as well as to those, Pershing among them, who advised that an attack upon the flank would be appropriate. The east flank, where Reims sat among the hills which had compelled the German armies to make a detour, was strategically impossible. But the west flank, from which further drives toward Paris might be anticipated, was inviting. Not far within the German lines the roads, once carrying French supplies between Soissons and Château-Thierry, were now congested with German supplies essential to the troops at the tip of the salient. They were already within range of the French guns, while the advance west of Soissons had brought the German troops nearer to the dumps where Foch had been concentrating supplies against the abandoned project of a drive east of Montdidier. Knowing where the blow of the fifteenth would strike, Foch arranged to let it take its course, confident that it could lead to nothing. He planned to break it, not only by tactics at its tip where it was best prepared to win, but on the side, robbed to serve the tip.

Two days before the blow he caught the 1st Division, *en route* from its Cantigny sector to a rest region which it badly needed, and shunted it back to his line west and south of Soissons where it slipped in behind the 1st Moroccan Division on Monday night. On Wednesday night it sidled alongside that division, on its left, upon the line of battle. Major-General Charles P. Summerall became its commander while it was in motion, relieving Bullard who had been lifted to the command of the Third Army Corps, to administer American troops in this new adventure. He had been assigned the promotion a week earlier, while Pershing had in mind a grouping of divisions and corps near Château-Thierry in an American First Army. He was given the 2d Division as well as the 1st, and also the French 1st Moroccan; but since the rearrangement was too recent for the staff to be ready, the tactical direction of the corps remained with the French.

The 2d Division, relieved by the 26th in its Château-Thierry sector on July 10, had its rest broken by orders on Sunday, July 14, to join the Third Corps in the French Tenth Army southwest of Soissons. Harbord relieved Bundy in its command on Monday, organizing his staff as he moved into a position of which he was not fully informed. The forest of Villers-Cotterêts, facing the German lines, had held them back a little, so that it constituted a small salient for the French. It provided cover in which the concentration of troops could be concealed by day and a near-jungle through which it was almost impossible for troops to find their way as they moved to station by night. Mangin, of the Tenth Army, commanded the projected operation. Gouraud, east of Reims, was reinforced and directed to prevent German gains in his direction. This he did on Monday and Tuesday of the drive, with considerable assistance from the 42d Division.

Wise speaks of Foch's determination upon a counter-offensive as 'superb audacity.' It was bold enough, but it was less than this; sound strategy pointed to it when the time should come and when there should be troops at hand. Troops were at hand when the early testing of the American divisions revealed their enthusiasm, if not their experience. The time had come as soon as it was clear to Foch that the German drive of July 15 was proceeding upon his schedule rather than upon its own. He borrowed British divisions as well as Bullard's army corps, concentrated fifteen divisions between the Aisne and the Ourcq, and selected the American units for the spearhead. When his attack began at 4.45 A.M. on Thursday, July 18, of the nine divisions to advance only three had been close to the front the day before. They started fagged by a night march. They were unheralded and unsuspected.

The whole line pressed on the morning of July 18. On each of the three sides of the Marne salient it was demonstrated that the tide had turned. The Germans knew it before Foch sensed it; von Hertling writing later: 'even the most optimistic among us understood that all was lost.' So far as the American component was concerned, there were three active divisions in addition to the Third Army Corps. The 4th Division, south of the Ourcq, advanced with the French. The 26th, a bit farther south, from its Belleau Wood sector pushed into the heart of the salient. East of Château-Thierry the 3d moved in a parallel direction across the tip. The 28th Division, also on the line, to the right of the 3d, kept close to the Marne. With the enemy busy on all of his Marne fronts, the chief business of the effort was to penetrate the German flank at Soissons, to endanger the highways around that city, to advance the Allied guns until they could reach the transportation lines at Fère-en-Tardenois. Not Pétain who urged, or Foch who approved, or Mangin who executed, foresaw the penetrating power of the troops at the spearhead, tired though they were; or that what was now begun was to continue, with ever-broadening front, until the German armies were stalemate and the Imperial Government was broken.

The withdrawal of the German armies from the Marne 'pocket' is likely long to provide material for case study of tactics. It was professional in the highest sense. During the first two days of Foch's counter-thrust the whole west face of the salient was pushed back from six to eight miles, endangering the rest of the salient through interference with the transportation lines. The artists who translated the Allied advance into maps and cartoons for readers of war news in the United States pictured the pocket as a bag, with a drawstring along the Aisne and Vesle, from Soissons to Reims. They had Foch pulling the drawstrings, with von Boehn's Seventh German Army as the catch. But the catch escaped, losing to the Allies what stores they could not burn or move, yet saving the force. As soon as the meaning of the first two days was appreciated, resistance stiffened around Soissons, for here was the hinge at the German right on which the front must swing back. Not until August 2, the sixteenth day of pressure, did the French lines reach the outskirts of Soissons, and by this date the town had been evacuated because the German line had swung in brilliant and orderly retreat from the Marne to the hills south of the Vesle. On August 4 the 32d Division came to Fismes and on the next day Bullard took tactical command of the Third Army Corps along the Vesle. The salient was off the map.

The behavior of the American troops in the Marne pocket was more significant than the performance of the same number of men could be in any later phase of combat. The maneuver here was first fruit of the Supreme Command under Foch, the first consequence of a superiority in man-power given to the Allies as the result of the shipping decisions of March, the first testing on a considerable scale of the raw divisions for whose command Pershing was waging so persistent a battle. While the engagement was on, the Supreme War Council held its meetings on the first of June, and of July, with Pershing gaining in his power to insist through the behavior of his men. It no longer required persuasion to get ships to move more men as fast as they could be brought to Hoboken. The enemy made discovery that the A.E.F. was real and noted in the intelligence reports that some of the units behaved 'almost like shock troops.' The discouragement in Allied headquarters turned to hope until it was almost forgotten that in January the wisest of the military men had agreed that American troops could not be relied upon as important in action until at least 1919.

American opinion, quickened by the realities it knew about — for the censors were generous — and by the exaggerated forms in which realities were magnified, caught a glimpse of victory and of a grateful Europe. The investigations of mistake and incapacity in war preparation were no longer worth pushing; their reports fell flat. The political opponents of Woodrow Wilson lost hope, until even the kindly persuasiveness of Will H. Hays could hardly divert their attention from the war maps and the casualty lists. With the war a-winning they could not hope to turn the Democratic majority out of office. Against war Democrats it seemed almost impossible to run a serious competitor without inviting a charge of disloyalty. Against Democrats of the South, whether they were for the war or lukewarm, no Republican could hope to have much chance. And there were Republicans coming up for re-election in November who could not even be supported, if they survived the primaries, without suggesting that the party preferred politics to victory. Wilson, speaking for the Liberty Loan on the day the Germans crossed the Chemin des Dames, had uttered the phrase 'politics is adjourned.' It was more than possible that the adjournment was 'without day.' The American mind, geared to its war acceptance of work or fight and impatient with either indifference or dissent, lost its inhibitions as to scale or cost and was prepared to see things through.

While the early divisions were undergoing their test, more troops were floated in July than in any other month of the war. It was not, chiefly, as divisions that they went. Indeed, after the end of June, only six of what were to figure as combat divisions arrived in France; three in July and three in August. The high figures were high because of the great number of casuals packed into the ships and specialized troops badly needed behind the lines or in the equipment of corps or armies. As the operation in the Marne pocket came to an end in early August, with the pocket gone, and with the 4th and 32d Divisions abreast on the Vesle at Fismes, the American force in France was intricately engaged. In every process, save that of army fighting, from elementary instruction to heavy combat, it was spread along the front from Ypres to Mulhouse. The conveyance of the force to Foch, in March, had not been recalled.

As of August 4, when Bullard took tactical command of the Third Army Corps, three of the combat divisions were mostly at sea, fifteen were behind the lines resting or preparing, eleven were at the front. It was as well that Pershing had insisted on his large division, twice as large at least as those of the Allies or of the enemy, for he had trouble enough in providing twenty-nine with adequate command and staff. Had he, with smaller divisions, possessed twice as many, he would have had to outfit them with officers unready for the burden of responsibility. Only in the early divisions had officers revealed enough of quality to warrant promotion. Most of the divisional assignments were based on pre-war records and hunch, not always happy. Half of the pre-war officers had been left at home for indispensable duty there.

The eleven divisions on the front on August 4 began at the extreme left with the 30th (Tennessee, North Carolina, South Carolina, National Guard) and the 27th (New York, National Guard), brigaded with the English at Ypres. Next, on the north face of the Somme salient, the 80th (Virginia, West Virginia, Pennsylvania, National Army) and the 33d (Illinois, National Guard), who were training with the British on the line. On the Vesle, the drive through the center of the Marne salient, begun by the 26th (New England, National Guard) and the 3d (Regular), continued by the 42d (Rainbow) and the 32d (Michigan, Wisconsin, National Guard) with the assistance of the 28th (Pennsylvania, National Guard), had been completed by the 4th (Regular) and the 32d, both now ready for relief.

One division, not figuring in the tables because it was struck from the list in May, was represented on the line of August 4 by three regiments fighting with the French. This was the 93d, a Negro division, built around Negro units from the National Guard, but never filled to strength. It had been a matter of delicacy and difficulty to deal with the Negro citizen, whether he was called to duty by the draft or already enrolled as a Guardsman. An officers' training camp for Negroes was organized at Camp Dodge, whence came junior officers to command troops of their own race, it being the intention of the War Department that all of their higher officers should be white. By December the Department had decided to concentrate in Negro units the Negroes as they came to camp and to group these units in two Negro divisions.

The idea for the 93d was abandoned, its regiments being permitted to remain with the French. The other Negro division, the 92d, was assembled while on the way to France, sent overseas in June, and stationed in a Lorraine sector at the end of August. Most of the Negro troops to reach France were sent in labor units, without divisional organization, and served behind the lines.

Of the eleven divisions on the line of August 4, five were in quiet sectors, east of Verdun. Of these, the 82d (Georgia, Alabama, Tennessee, National Army) stood on the south face of St. Mihiel. The 37th (Ohio, National Guard) was directly east of Nancy; the 5th (Regular) had the St. Dié sector in Lorraine; the 35th (Missouri, Kansas, National Guard) and the 29th (New Jersey, Virginia, Maryland, District of Columbia, National Guard) were in Alsace, in front of Mulhouse.

It was not an Army of the United States that Pershing as yet commanded in France; it was in truth only a great armed force. But as fighting in the Marne salient ceased, events were in train to make Army a fact. In Washington, March had announced an impending change at the end of July, following on August 7 with an order whereby the several designations as Regular, National Guard, and National Army were stricken from the record. The whole force became the Army of the United States. The scrambling process had already made the special designations misleading in the case of most of the units. The collar insignia were changed, dropping the qualifying initials 'N.G.' and 'N.A.' which all but Regulars had hitherto been forced to wear. There was less than one chance in twenty that an officer or private, in uniform, had known its feel before April 6, 1917. All, hereafter, looked alike; and so far as they were able behaved alike.

And there was recognition in France, that could not be delayed indefinitely after the 1st and 2d Divisions had moved toward Soissons on July 18. On August 10, at La Ferté-sous-Jouarre, where Liggett on July 4 took tactical command of the First Army Corps, Pershing was permitted to assume a new duty. Remaining Commander in Chief of the A.E.F., and with the consent of Foch, he became also commander of the First Army.

XVI. THE PROGRAM OF ONE HUNDRED DIVISIONS

'To win the victory in 1919' ran the first sentence of a cable to the War Department, sent on June 23 from Chaumont. Here Pershing had been in conference with Clemenceau and Foch, and with André Tardieu whose knowledge of Washington affairs was perhaps more intimate than that of the Commander in Chief. It is not always remembered that after fighting has begun there is little the commander can do about any particular battle. It has passed out of his hands and into those of the field commanders on the line. The Commander in Chief may watch and worry, or interfere (if interference be his habit), but his chief business is to be ready to deal with its result. While the troops fight, he must prepare for the next battle, and the next.

The insistence of Pershing for the separate army was partly based upon knowledge that as the war should be protracted it would become increasingly a burden upon his component among the Allies. The insistence of the Allies for American troops was as reasonably based upon their recognition of the need for manpower. They knew their limits. They had fear, too, that the collapse of Russia would make possible the transfer to the line in France of German divisions from the Eastern Front, whose presence might make the German rifles more numerous than their own. This was a reason for the Vladivostok adventure, and that at Archangel, to which the United States contributed unwilling aid. Both fruitless efforts were based on a hope to lessen the consequences of Russian defection. When the British and French ministers came together in the Supreme War Council to make their plans — in what the American officers sometimes described as the 'town meeting' — they spent time in bickering upon their relative performance in calling to the colors all the men they had. Each felt certain that the other was somehow holding back. Yet they agreed, and rightly, that neither possessed any considerable source of recruits except as growing boys reached military age. The personal literature of the war is full of bitter pictures of schoolboys forced too early into uniform. That of the European belligerents, Allies or enemy, is equally full, with equal bitterness, of tales of older men kept long in the line after they had lost their resilience. The only untapped reservoir of man-power was in the United States.

Neither British nor French, nor Pershing, now expected to win the war before 1920. Within two years without setback, they foresaw an advance across the Rhine that should bring the enemy to terms. The American factories were preparing heavy munitions for this advance, which would first have to crush the German forts. For 1919 the commanders craved a preponderance in the field with which they might drive the Germans back from France and Belgium. To this end, Clemenceau, Lloyd George, and Orlando, at the Versailles meeting of June 1, had addressed themselves to President Wilson, urging 'the raising of fresh American levies' and their shipment at 'not less than 300,000 a month' until there should be in France 'a total American force of 100 divisions at as early a date as this can possibly be done.' At the Chaumont conference of June 23 the demand was reduced to schedule. Pershing and Tardieu doubted that the demand could be met. But Pershing was ready to join in asking it, to set a goal. His goal, attested by his signature and that of Foch, called on the United States for troops at the rate of six divisions a month, which, with troops for army, corps, and rear, would mean 250,000; and for replacements which, accepting the French experience, would call each year for twenty per cent of the total strength. Eighty divisions were demanded for April, 1919; one hundred by the end of June.

Before the turn of the tide was visible in 1918, the battle of 1919 was in preparation. Its first skirmishes were in France, where the estimates were made and where Pershing had in hand a comprehensive reorganization of his services of the rear. He had reached a point at which upon this would depend the effectiveness of everything in the zone of advance. The second of the skirmishes was in Washington, where the new demands confused every schedule in preparation in the War Department and frightened by their scale. The third was again in Europe, whither hurried in the early summer the representatives of every branch of the procurement services to work out with the Allies an international co-ordination of effort. The American war machine was working on both sides of the Atlantic. Each crew believed its own to be the better effort and thought critically of the deficiencies of the other, but both could join in a certainty that victory would strain the powers of each.

Just as the American mind had accepted from the start the principle of a supreme commander for the armies in the field, it now accepted the comparable principle of a complete team-work in the supply of the armies. The United States differed from the Allies in that it had a single goal: victory. Freed from desire to save something, or to attain some end directly useful to itself, it was freer than the Associated Powers to press for solidarity. Before the line of August 4 could even be guessed at, the basis of a solidarity had been laid down.

It was in March that the Lines of Communication behind the A.E.F. were redesignated as Services of Supply and shifted to Tours, where Kernan set up headquarters. Here was done the planning, and hence came the directions, described in sympathetic detail in Johnson Hagood, *The Services of Supply: A Memoir of the Great War* (1927). Hagood was on the board to recommend the organization and became a fluent (and insuppressible) advocate of the principle emphasized with new solemnity in the World War. With the whole nation in arms, devoted to the maintenance on the front of the whole fighting power, and with the civilian population in the rear devoted to war effort, the connecting links between front and rear, procurement and supply, had become more important than military direction in combat. The Services of

Supply would have preferred an organization scheme in which they might have depended immediately upon the Commander in Chief instead of being physically apart and restricted in communication to channels running through G–4, the assistant chief of staff in charge of co-ordination. They always felt hampered because of this, even after Harbord, personal intimate of Pershing, became their chief. But segregation, with consolidation at Tours where the supply agencies were within reach, was a master step, and Harbord knew ways to cut red tape and get through to the commander in matters of emergency. The S.O.S. was a little hampered, too, by another control, which cut across military channels and was saved from doing damage only because of the remarkable skill of its chief, Charles G. Dawes.

Not many generals went to war with a terrier and a piano, or did distinguished service from a residence in the Ritz Hotel in Paris. Dawes was the exception. A prominent banker and old enough to have shown his skill in organization by preparing the capture of Illinois for the nomination of William McKinley, Dawes took a commission in an engineer regiment, coming to France as major. He and Pershing were youths together when Dawes was struggling for a law practice in Lincoln while Pershing was studying law and commanding the cadet corps at the University of Nebraska. An incorrigible civilian (he tells of Harbord, by the direct order of the Commander in Chief, buttoning him up to military propriety in public), Dawes never permitted his modest rank to handicap him in dealing with the great. Pershing took him from his regiment in the summer of 1917, made him General Purchasing Agent for the A.E.F. and chairman of a General Purchasing Board. In due time the Commander pinned his eagles on him, and the War Department permitted his promotion to the rank of brigadier-general. But Dawes remained the business man in uniform and retained a diaristic habit that produced an enlightening document in his *Journal of the Great War* (1921).

The jurisdiction of the General Purchasing Board spread over all of the buying agencies of the Army in France as well as over those of the Red Cross and the Y.M.C.A. The same reasons which induced in the United States the creation of the War Industries Board and the consolidation of buying in the Purchasing Commission for the Allies made it reasonable to consolidate the buying abroad. The principal supply branches of the Army (Quartermaster, Engineer Corps, Ordnance, Signal Corps, Air Service, Chemical Warfare, Medical Corps, and Navy) did their procurement under the critical eye of Dawes. They contributed representatives to his General Purchasing Board, whither the representatives came not to discuss but to be told. They debated only such trifles as the allocation of office space. Dawes made the policies — ever with the idea: 'to save shipping space from America.' He reported at the end of 1918 that, as against 7,675,410 ship-tons of trans-Atlantic freight unloaded in France, there had been bought in Europe, under his eye, 10,192,921 ship-tons.

The unification of buying, which the War Department had not before the war worked out in the United States, added another layer to the controls upon the S.O.S. Kernan had a complete organization at Tours, with a staff to direct the service departments behind the line. He was under the oversight of the General Staff at Chaumont and for a long time the S.O.S. was not permitted to deal directly with Washington, whence came its men and much of its material. Its buying in Europe was under a third control: that of Dawes, who as General Purchasing Agent was subordinate to S.O.S., but whose General Purchasing Board was of the whole Army in France. Behind the complex scheme was the determination of Pershing to keep in his own hands the control of his rear as far as the ports. When the time should come that the A.E.F. was carrying the heaviest of the burdens, this would be unavoidable. If the time should come, and come it might, when the Allies should crack, the surest safeguard of the A.E.F. would be an unbroken line of communications. The S.O.S. protested, and even Dawes had his complaints, but Pershing stood his ground. He could not let it lose its identity any more than he could let it be commanded from Washington or give to it his undivided attention. As the priority tables were studied with reference to the one hundred-division program and estimates were figured for tonnage requirements of the second million, and the following millions, it became ever more certain that the war might have to be won from the rear. With all the buying that could be done in France the fraction of supplies that must still be carried overseas was larger than any tonnage in sight for 1919, even if the Shipping Board should reach its schedule of production.

To the dual relationship of Dawes to Chaumont and to Tours there was added a third. He became in a sense an ambassador of the A.E.F. in Paris. His purchasing duties required him to maintain close and continuous liaison with all of the French supply departments as well as with Allied and neutral business. Paris was the place for him. His presence in Paris and his close connection with the Commander in Chief made it possible for the latter to use him for various contacts that he would otherwise have had to make himself. There was a basic difference between the Allies and the United States in relations with their armies. The Allied ministers handled directly their inter-Allied business, while President Wilson left to Pershing such a complete control over the A.E.F. that the latter spent much time in diplomatic duty. Dawes could help with his skill in organization and his facility with men. He took pains not to make the task of his official superior at Tours impossible by going over his head, but with his varied functions he was outside the ordinary scheme of Army organization. The Army does not produce in either peace or war generals who can be expected to be as competent in business as they are in military matters.

The co-ordination of purchases was perhaps the simplest of the tasks. The several bureaus did their own buying, with Dawes pressing on their chiefs for common action. It was his special task to uncover resources in Europe, whether in Allied countries or among the neutrals, and to tempt them out with dollars. In buying in these markets it was essential to have understanding with the Allies, lest they and the United States should bid against each other. It was useful to persuade the supply departments to use as many 'standard categories' as possible and to buy them in common. It was helpful to France to provide work for French women and *mutilés* in the factories and repair shops working on A.E.F. account. Dawes was called upon to run a labor office, recruiting civilian labor from neutral countries, and to make arrangements with the Allies for the interchange of supplies and the incidental bookkeeping. He acquired valuable experience in procuring mules from Spain, for it took diplomatic ability to manage both the mules and the Spanish. He found in Tardieu, who had been High Commissioner in Washington, a sympathetic coadjutor. When the War Trade Board had reached its stride, he negotiated through Sharpe, the American Ambassador in Paris, for pressure to be exerted through the War Trade Board to make neutrals more accommodating. The General Purchasing Board and the General Purchasing Agent, Pershing's own ideas, were created by the Commander in Chief on August 20, 1917, over the adverse recommendation of a staff committee to which the idea had been submitted.

As the dimensions of the job grew and as useful results followed the closer co-ordination of purchase, the mind of Dawes expanded with reference to the conduct of the war and of the critical campaign of 1919. He found each of the three great armies in France living out of its own warehouses and upon its own independent supply system. Here again was reason for an independent American army, for when the exigency of March to May compelled the dispersion of the A.E.F. units along the whole line it became almost impossible for the S.O.S. to serve the force. There were fleets of motor trucks belonging to one army lying idle while the neighbor army was immobilized from lack of trucks. There were dumps and storehouses belonging to one while another needed the supplies they held in dead storage. In the middle of April, as the 1st Division was preparing to operate on the Montdidier front, Dawes addressed the Commander in Chief with an argumentative memorandum in favor of a military control of Allied supply systems; a control that would place a single service behind all the armies, under the direction of a general, in the rear, who would have an authority comparable to that which was at the moment being fully vested in Foch. Pershing responded favorably. He may, indeed, have asked for the memorandum. On May 22 he joined with Clemenceau in signing an approval of the principle of unification of policy. He offered as his contribution, as he had done with respect to the Generalissimo, to join the Allies in placing the whole rear under a single commander other than himself. He did not see in this a complete amalgamation of the rears, but rather a military co-ordination of their policies. Dawes took the agreement to London. The mission was delicate and diplomatic. England was as solicitous of the British rear in France as Pershing could be about his own. Dawes secured an accord. It was less than a single commander, yet was far in advance of current practice. The British Quartermaster could not surrender his initiative. France, whose military rear was inextricably involved with the whole economic life of the country, could not merge civilian business in the Army or go as far toward this as the United States had gone in the development of the War Industries Board. But as the result of the effort a Military Board of Allied Supply came into existence and held a first meeting in Paris on June 28. Dawes thought that in it he had found the 'beginning of an inter-Allied Staff.'

Hereafter Dawes' duties included service with this Board in addition to his other responsibilites. As its American member he reported directly to the Commander in Chief, communicating to Chaumont for execution the decisions of the Board. When the representatives of the three armies were in agreement, their decisions, through military channels, had the force of orders.

Communication and transport, whether by train, truck, or wire, were among the earliest 'must' tasks of the Military Board of Allied Supply. Ammunition was pooled, forage for animals was regulated, gasoline was conserved, labor was studied. As proud parent of the scheme, Dawes believed that even the chiefs of the independent armies and their General Staff officers learned from their occasional sittings with the Board 'how their activities ... could be conducted in better co-ordination' and were better for learning it. The Executive War Board of the Supreme War

Council fell apart as Foch, once Generalissimo, drew controls into his own hand. Having no commander, the Military Board of Allied Supply functioned until the end.

Before the end of June, 1918, the organization of supply was approaching system, while the one-hundred division program of June 23 promised to test it to the limit. Dawes' new Board was no sooner a fact than a threat to the new system was heard from Washington. Here, General March, well set in his saddle, was no better satisfied with Pershing than Pershing was with the War Department. He believed that Pershing was no diplomat and had no right to be entrusted with the inter-Allied negotiations. He fitted himself to the War Department idea that the Department should serve all of the rears, while the Commander in Chief should concentrate his attention upon the fighting. If Baker and the President had acceded to this idea there might have come about a sweeping change in the structure of Pershing's machine; but Baker, though he wavered, did not yield. There came, however, a letter from Baker, dated July 6, 'desiring in every possible way to relieve you of unnecessary burdens' and wondering whether General Goethals might not, if sent to France, 'take charge of the services of supply' and thereby leave Pershing free to be a 'fighting general.' The Secretary wondered, too, whether Bliss (now with lessened duties as Permanent Military Representative) could not become a clearing-house for diplomatic matters.

Gossip had named Goethals to Pershing even before Baker suggested him. There are bits of testimony indicating that Goethals was directed to get ready, and that he was even packed and on his way to Hoboken, when the Secretary withheld his hand and ordered Goethals back to his duties as director of Purchase, Storage, and Traffic for the General Staff in Washington. Pershing replied to Baker's letter (the exchange was made by the carriers who shuttled with important pouches between Washington and Chaumont) telling how he had worked to 'get our troops out of leading-strings,' and how Foch had at last consented to the organization of the First Army. He regarded as unimportant the burden of his diplomatic work, since it was chiefly concerned with troop shipments in which under any arrangement he must have a hand; but he had no objection to the use of Bliss for other diplomatic matters. As to Goethals, he was emphatic: 'Mr. Secretary, our organization here is working well.' He emphasized the importance of full power on the spot and that if his rear were controlled from Washington 'it would be impossible to make it function.'

The Commander in Chief was 'puzzled' about Goethals; had believed that he was necessary in Washington to handle P., S. & T; and was in any event certain that General Harbord could administer S.O.S. and 'pull in the team.' Whether he feared that Goethals, probably as lone-handed as he was himself, could not pull in *his* team, he did not say. He had already acted as Commander in Chief before the messenger carried his letter back to Washington on July 28. Having cabled to Baker objecting to the Goethals mission and asking that action be deferred until the arrival of his letter, he terminated Harbord's service with troops in the field. Brigadier-General John A. Lejeune, with rank in the Marine Corps, took over the command of the 2d Division *ad interim* on July 26, and permanently on July 28. Harbord was ordered to Tours to meet Pershing on July 29, and to assume at once command of the Services of Supply. On the same day they, with Dawes, started upon a week of thoroughgoing inspection of ports, railroads, service establishments, and storehouses. On August 7 Pershing cabled to the Secretary that with Harbord in command 'I am as confident of the organization... as I am of ultimate military victory.' He had acted so promptly that it was impossible for Washington to send him Goethals unless it was prepared to humiliate him in public. It held its hand. Three days after this, Pershing took command of the First Army, having conferred with Foch about the future of its use and having secured agreement that it should be concentrated in the region of St. Mihiel.

The formal appeal for one hundred divisions, forwarded on June 23, was earmarked for the attention of the President. It received attention in every office having to do with the preparations for 1919. It was 'studied' — the Army word for deliberation upon a proposal and the framing of the reply. March replied in a few days, warning the Commander in Chief not to hold out expectations that the United States could meet the requisition. Conferences brought into the study the War Industries Board, the War Trade Board, and the Shipping Board, as well as the General Staff of the Army. The problem proved to be 'full of burrs,' as Baker soon wrote Bliss; for the shipping men reported that all the ships' berths in France would be insufficient for the vessels that would be required to meet it. Before the study was completed, the delegates of the War Boards had been sent to France for sessions with the inter-Ally boards created by the November conference, for heart-to-heart discussion with Pershing and for planning schedules in connection with the next campaign.

As the war passed into its last half-year there remained for the political agencies in the United States few things to do, and many to watch. So, too, with the people. There was no more voting to be done until November. The missteps in preparation were crowded out of the news by reports of success in action. A large fraction of those whose normal capacity and tendency was to help build public opinion were attached to the several networks whose sole excuse was winning the war. Hays cut short his visit to the Indiana Republican convention on May 29 so as to be free to go on the stump for the Third Liberty Loan. Roosevelt and Taft, meeting by chance in a Chicago hotel while both were on war tours, made of the meeting a public reconciliation in the interest of the war. If there had been more serious issues to divide the public mind in the third half-year, it is unlikely that the small amount of uncovered sedition could have produced the noisy uneasiness about 'loyalty' in the spring. If Congress had not completed its basic work, it would have been too busy with more pressing legislation to give its time and its passion to the Sedition Act. It was in April and May that the structure of work or fight was substantially completed and that emotion took its fling at dissent. Public opinion thereafter, as it watched the war, dealt more and more with terms of peace: Wilson's terms.

And Congress, with little on its docket except a revenue act which could not be completed because no one could say how much money would need to be raised, took partial recesses through the summer. It was not until autumn, September 6, that Claude Kitchin brought from the Committee on Ways and Means what was to grow into the Revenue Act of 1919 and found there was no quorum on hand to receive it.

Between July 13 and August 19 the two houses obeyed the constitutional injunction not to adjourn for more than three days at a time, protecting itself by a gentlemen's agreement that no business should be brought into the semi-weekly meetings without full notice. A handful of members would meet twice a week, discover that no quorum was present, and adjourn for three days. Most of the members went on vacation, some of them going as far as the battle-front, where their parties visited trenches, were received at headquarters, and picked up what they could. When the hundred-division program reached the United States there was little that Congress need be asked to do about it.

The minor events of the summer, which were putting only finishing touches upon the war structure, were designed to improve the working of the machine. The Emergency Fleet Corporation, crowded for space in Washington, had slipped away to Philadelphia, leaving Washington still overcrowded. Every War Board and every bureau that grew with its load brought to the Capital its clerks by the thousand; to the profit of house-owners, but to the despair of those who sought lodgings. Wherever there was a new munitions plant, or one enlarged, there was the same trouble and performance was slowed down. To remedy the housing shortage Congress in May allocated to the Department of Labor fifty millions; and ten millions more for expenditure in the District of Columbia. Another of the red-tape cutting devices of the emergency made its appearance in July as the result. This was the United States Housing Corporation, chartered in New York, with all of its stock owned by the Government. By November the Housing Corporation had ninety-four projects under way, and nearly as many more under contract or ready for bids. In the

District, the plaza before the Union Depot blossomed with more-or-less Georgian apartments, of wood and plaster, to provide residence for the girls who did the paper work in the Departments.

In July, too, the United States Sugar Equalization Board was incorporated under the laws of Delaware, to deal in sugar for the Food Administration, to control its price, and to capture the whole of the Cuban sugar crop for the use of the United States and the Allies. Two months later, wheat was dealt with again. Congress and the President, between them, had already taken care of the guaranteed minimum price for the crops of 1917 and 1918. Now, to be certain that the planting for 1919 might be ample to the need, a board advised and the President fixed a guaranty at $2.26, based on No. 1 Northern at Chicago. On August 1 the telegraph and telephone services passed into the hands of the Postmaster-General to be administered as a unit by the United States, while radio and cables remained within the power of the President to take over at his discretion. The action was empowered by a law of July 16, which Wilson demanded. He was hurried to this by a strike already ordered for July 8. With the help of Gompers the strike order was recalled and senatorial fears that taking over the wires would mean a censorship of opinion were assuaged. Burleson was more than willing to assume the responsibility, since he regarded the wire services as natural adjunct of the Post Office. He permitted the actual operation of the lines to remain in charge of the existing officers of the companies.

The need to provide more man-power brought the Senate back from its intermittent recess and was the most important matter upon which action by Congress was asked and taken during the summer of 1918. Some action in this direction would have been necessary even if the demands for 1919 had not loomed up so sharply, for the list of Class I eligibles under the Selective Service Act was approaching exhaustion.

The initial registration, June 5, 1917, as corrected by the addition of late-comers to the list, ran to 9,925,751. A supplementary registration brought in 735,834 more, who reached the age of twenty-one before June 5, 1918. A second supplementary enrollment found an additional 159,161 who had come to military age by August 24. The grand total of 10,820,746 represented the discoverable man-power in the age range twenty-one to thirty, but there was neither possibility nor expectation that the whole of the group could be called to the colors. When the process of selection was revised, in December, 1917, and the registrants were classified by their questionnaires in five groups according to their availability, Class I became the reservoir from which troops were to be drawn. In the other four classes were those whose family or industrial status entitled them to deferred classification. About thirty-five per cent of the registrants, 3,706,544 in all, proved to be in Class I. Most of these were ready to serve; conscientious objectors were few and deserters and evaders were believed by the Provost-Marshal-General to be under two per cent.

With no greater difficulty than was involved in finding beds in camp and uniforms, the first levy of 687,000 men was raised from Class I (or from its equivalent, since most of them had gone to camp before the five classes were differentiated). The number in Class I was more than sufficient even after nearly one in three had been disqualified on physical grounds before induction or sent home from camp after passing the local medical examinations. Not all of the first levy could be received in camp until the end of February. In subsequent levies, drawing from the same Class I, the basis of State responsibility was shifted from total population, which proved to be unfair because of uneven distribution of exempt aliens and physical defectives. The new basis was the better one of total Class I registrants, with credit allowed for voluntary enlistments. By the end of March more than 750,000 men had been drafted; by the end of June 850,000 more. The bottom of the reservoir of Class I men was in sight.

There were only two ways to get more men: to summon those of the twenty-one to thirty age group whose call had been deferred, or to enlarge the age group. It was apparent before June that more troops would be needed than the original Class I could provide, even when recruited by the supplementary registrations. No one could tell how rapidly it might become necessary to summon them. General Crowder's work or fight rule of May 17, 1918, carried a warning that non-essential work was not a sufficient excuse for deferred classification, but this could not greatly enlarge Class I. Baker took the problem to the military committees in May, vague in mind as to the correct age limits for a larger group, and hopeful for a grant of authority to the President to call men as needed without legislative limit.

Except for moral advantage in the minds of men already registered or called, there was little to be gained by age extension at the top. Men above thirty were likely to fall within the deferred classes or to be less than effective if within Class I. The ages below twenty-one had positive military advantage, offset in part by sentimental disadvantage in calling out boys who could not vote. Boys of nineteen and twenty were mentally and physically fit for service and most of them would have Class I status.

The Class I man-power, so far as the administration of the draft was concerned, was less than it appeared to be. Volunteering, as a substitute for which the Selective Service Act had been accepted, had been permitted in part to break down the principle of selection. Before the numbers of Class I men were called, they, as well as others in the deferred classes, and others not of draft age, had been able to enter the armed forces on their own initiative and choose their service. It was part of the theory that Regular Army, National Guard, Navy, and Marine Corps should be filled by recruiting, which could be hurried along before the draft machinery could be put in motion. Some of their recruits came in under the same stimuli that have always built up volunteering; others sought to escape odium by avoiding the draft. Permission to enter in this fashion meant some loss of men who were too useful to be spared from industry. In a large proportion of cases it meant also a diminution of Class I, in which these volunteers would have found themselves had they waited for their numbers. By December the Army had closed most of its doors to volunteers; but the Navy and Marine Corps continued to accept them until on August 9,

1918, all volunteering was stopped. By this time nearly 1,360,000 had already entered the services by enlistment, while 2,288,000 had by the end of August been inducted under the draft. Class I, as originally conceived, was empty.

Early in August the man-power bill went to Congress. It was socially unwise to recruit Class I by throwing into it men with heavy family burdens. It was doubly difficult to enlarge it by lessening the number receiving deferred classification on industrial grounds. The industrial need of the war was greater than ever, with 1919 in sight, and labor was disposed to resent a revision of burdens aimed at its exemptions. The bill, signed on August 31, carried the extended age limits, eighteen to forty-five, both inclusive. It promised to add more than two and a quarter million Class I effectives, and it probably fulfilled the promise. The registration on September 12 added 13,395,706 names, making in all 24,234,-021. Never in the history of the United States had so much information been accumulated about so many citizens as was contained in their questionnaires. Their education, their health, their intelligence according to the new Army tests, their aptitudes, their financial and domestic status, all became matters of record, from which Crowder drew conclusions of far more than military significance in his *Second Annual Report of the Provost-Marshal-General* (1919), and his *Final Report* (1920). But he never knew how completely Class I was reinforced by the spread of age limits, because the classification of the new registrants, done in the several States, was no more than in process at the Armistice, and was never completed. On November 11, however, whether by draft or by enlistment, there were 4,791,172 in the various military and naval services; thirteen times as many (378,619) as were in all of them when the war Congress met on April 2, 1917.

It was possible when the call for one hundred divisions arrived to forecast the willingness of Congress to assent to the enrollment of total man-power and to the military employment of so much of it as might be necessary. It was equally possible to deliver to the Embarkation Service as many men as Pershing desired. They could not be completely trained on sailing, as he demanded, for too few weeks elapsed between the calling of their numbers and their departure for Europe, and hardly enough competent divisional staffs could have been found to do the training had they had time for it. But possibility was thrown into doubt, if not destroyed, when it came to estimating the burden on the Atlantic Ferry. No estimate of overseas freight required by the force in France ran below thirty pounds per man per day. The guesses ranged between thirty and fifty pounds — between full supply with ample reserve and minimum supply with shortages to be filled up by Dawes. But at the lowest figure the requirements of four million men would indicate sixty thousand tons that must every day arrive in France. There was no month before the Armistice in which as many as half this number of tons reached Pershing daily; and there were only five months in which a daily average of twenty thousand tons was attained.

Facing these facts, and they were facts even though precision was impossible in the forecast, the War Department could not promise one hundred divisions by the end of June, 1919. A much smaller number might prove to be too many to be supplied. In the event of military reverses, even fewer might yet be completely at the mercy of the enemy and without friends among the Allies because of the certain Allied conviction that Pershing's demand for an army of his own had caused *débâcle*. There was some gambling to be done which could not be too reckless in July, 1918, since with all the turn of the tide there was as yet no promise of early victory. But the good news coming in daily from the Soissons sector after July 18 warranted a risk. A week later the President approved a War Department program of eighty divisions to be in France in June, 1919. Allowing 27,000 to the division, and 13,000 more to serve behind it, this made a total of 3,200,000 men. The ships were not in sight to move the freight for these, but the United States took the chance. Pertinent to the decision, and so preserved by Dawes, was Dwight Morrow's description of a father telling his little boy a story: ' "The alligator had his mouth open and was about to close it on the turtle, when the turtle suddenly climbed a tree and hid himself in the foliage."

"But, papa," said the little boy, "a turtle can't climb a tree." To which Papa replied, "But *this* turtle *had* to." '

The Government in Washington had trouble in adjusting itself to the fact that the scene of war was far away and that its own task was to follow the leader, not to call the tune. The President left Pershing in command of the military effort. The military censors relaxed much of their rigor after American troops began to appear in action, and before the summer was over the War Department permitted publication of complete lists of divisions in France and of their higher officers. The publication was, however, historical. The news was not released until the enemy was as fully aware of the facts as the Department. Plans for the future were kept in the realm of military secrets; at times because the Army censors would not pass them to the cables, at times because Washington was not even aware of them. Pershing's quick shift in the management of the Services of Supply put an end to whatever move there was to relieve him of the control of his rear; and Washington continued to be forced to confine its work to the home end of the line that had become closely articulated from the trenches back to every citizen in the United States.

But Washington could not do its end of the work without a clearer view of the underlying purpose than could be gained through correspondence or through the distorted picture of events brought to the Department of State by the honest efforts of Lord Reading or Jusserand. It could not plan for the battle of 1919 without face to face contacts with both Pershing's assistants and the Allied agents who were at work on the French and British programs. With inspection and conference as objectives (and perhaps with curiosity), the procession of war work representatives on the road to Europe grew to impressive dimensions, until Rudyard Kipling could speak jocularly of an American invasion of England.

The health and morale of the troops were not lost sight of as their number grew. Behind the lines the American plant devoted to rest, recuperation, and recreation increased in size with every increment of troops.

No more in Europe than in the United States did the Army concede that venereal disease must remain a necessary accompaniment of war. The taboos which had hitherto defeated the effort to control it, by preventing the public mention of its name, were broken down. The people wanted their sons to come home well. It was wasteful for the Army to carry men to France in order to keep them there on sick-list from preventable causes. Education and prophylaxis did what could be done to keep the army clean; recreation and rest helped to keep young minds in wholesome habits. The *Stars and Stripes* had a sound editorial policy when it dealt with its readers in the tone of the sporting page and as though they were college boys. Forty or more camp papers in the United States did much the same thing on a smaller scale. Singing masters were taken over to encourage release of emotion through the lungs. Dawes, a skilled musical amateur as well as banker, engineered the assembly of a gigantic Army band, for which Pershing summoned Walter Damrosch as adviser. Baseball, boxing, and field sports established their therapeutic values in the camps behind the lines, while no body of troops could move far without bringing in its train the Red Cross worker and the huts of the Young Men's Christian Association.

It was customary to swear at the Y.M.C.A., but it was in most cases kindly profanity. Katherine Mayo, asked to come to France and to report, produced in '*That Dam Y*' (1920) a homely picture of its work. There were snarls and harsh judgments, arising largely from the accident that the army canteens were handed over to the Y.M.C.A. for administration and that the supplies there were sold instead of given out as rations. But the shelves of the 'Y' carried the stock of sweetmeats and cigarettes dear to American youth, and the men and women in charge, in uniform but not with military rank, kept their stocks wherever there might be men off duty.

The Red Cross, close to the army, had gone far since the drive for a hundred million which it undertook under Henry P. Davison in 1917. It went out for another hundred in May, 1918, when the President marched down Fifth Avenue at the head of its procession. Davison was among those in France in the early autumn to work out with Pershing a closer relationship between the medical personnel of the Red Cross and the Army Medical Corps.

The other volunteer agencies ran second to Red Cross and Y.M.C.A. tending to become something of a nuisance because of their earnestness and their insistence that weeks must be allotted in the United States to their drives for funds. The Salvation Army, the Knights of Columbus, and the United Hebrew Charities were all in the picture, while within the Army the chaplains' service was expanded under Charles Henry Brent, an Episcopal bishop whose flexibility Pershing had known in connection with the Philippine Opium Commission.

The morale services, borne with gladly for the help they gave and doubly useful because of their effect upon the mind at home, were essential in a democratic war; but they and the men who went out to inspect them were but a small link among the many between the American effort and the armies in the field.

Late in July it was announced that the Assistant Secretary of the Navy was abroad and that on the twenty-second he had begun his tour of inspection of the Navy establishment by lunching in London with Balfour, Milner, and Sir Eric Geddes, First Lord of the Admiralty. For the next two months Franklin D. Roosevelt was up and down the front. His travels took him in public to Italy, in semi-public to the destroyer base and to the fleet, in private to the offices where contracts were to be inspected and to the ports where the facilities for handling ships were nearly adequate to the load then on them, but in need of expansion for the eighty divisions when these should come. Before he was reported home again, September 19 — sick with what was beginning to be called the 'Spanish flu' — he had in his mind the picture of the Navy need.

Most important of the visitations of the summer were those having to do with food and munitions; the former accompanied with wide publicity because the success of the food program depended on publicity; the latter almost kept from the news because its business was secret until the time should come to make it public with projectiles.

Herbert C. Hoover (the middle letter still in his name) was reported in England the day after the arrival of Roosevelt was noted. The Food Administration had a more sweeping commitment than that of most of the American War Boards. Its reason for existence was less the American need than the need of the armies in the field and of the civilian populations of the Allies. The American machinery of the Food Administration was functioning in all the States, where its branches were carrying out its rules in close co-operation with the State Councils of Defense. Hoover went abroad to arrange the quotas for the next crop year, to discover minimum requirements, to search for tonnage, and to discuss the balance in which it would be safe to gamble civil sustenance against military maintenance. There were no fears about sufficiency of food for the United States. War gardens had been added to the patriotic efforts of co-operators. The consumption of sauerkraut had picked up. Banned for its German name in the first surge of patriotism, it had been saved as 'liberty cabbage.' The acreage under contract with the farmers north of Chicago made it already clear that in 1919 the cabbage plant was enlisted for the war.

The Food Administrator was already a notable figure in Allied circles where to the courtesy extended to him because of his past performance there was added more consideration because in his hands were future benefits. He was lunched at the Mansion House, dined by the Government, and received as key member of the conference of Allied food controllers which opened on July 23. He took with him a considerable staff. Alonzo E. Taylor, who had been one of his agents abroad since the war began, joined him in England. Hoover opened the conferences with the comforting assurance that the food crisis was past. During the next few weeks he repented somewhat of this assurance and reminded the public through his press releases that it was past only if economy continued to be practiced. However, his tables and graphs showed wheat, meat, sugar, and fat in sight in quantities sufficient for the minimum needs of the Allied populations and the armies in the field. With the submarine danger subsiding, it had become chiefly a matter of getting the cargoes overseas; but that was a matter of maritime transportation, not of food production and conservation. 'It might be said,' said David Lloyd George, who introduced him at the Government dinner, 'he represented Providence.'

Out of the conference of food controllers an Inter-Allied Food Council was set up as a permanent agent in London, with offices in Trafalgar House, Waterloo Place. It was promised that war bread in the future would be better bread, but those who ate it were admonished still to regard it not as bread but merely as consumable food. American hotels were released from their no-wheat pledge. Consumers were told they might eat as freely as they chose of 'light' beef. From both sides of the line the food information was such as to give hope to the enemies of Germany. As against the Hoover assurance of sufficiency, the figures from Germany told enough of the true story to warrant a belief that the German Army ration was kept up only by the starvation of the population at home. Dieticians began to figure and guess about the point at which food and the lack of it would win the war. Back in New York before the end of August, Hoover told the reporters little of his detailed plans, but he let it be known that Germany was not yet hungry enough to surrender, that food was clearly in sight, and that the remaining problems were those of building up a reserve for 1919 and of getting ships. By 'conservation measures,' he said, reverting to the slogan of April, 1917, 'the Allied cause has been saved.' But victory was more than ever a matter of ships.

The arrival of Edward R. Stettinius, Second Assistant Secretary of War, was made public simultaneously with that of Hoover and Roosevelt. Coming into the War Department in January as Surveyor-General of Purchases, Stettinius had with Goethals reorganized the procurement work. He came now to France to stay, soon vacating his Washington position, when Crowell and Ryan absorbed his job and divided the work. He had with him Samuel M. Felton, a railroad expert, specializing in military railways; Walter S. Gifford of the Council of National Defense, specially skilled in telephones and telegraphs; and Charles Day, a mechanical engineer from the Emergency Fleet Corporation. The munitions conference, for which he was headed, became a permanent body under the name of the Inter-Allied Munitions Council. Giving no publicity to its deliberations, it worked for the future, worried by the difficulty of getting to France the material needed by the eighty divisions without at the same time reducing the food supplies below a safe reserve. The munitions problem, like that of the War Industries Board in the United States, had advanced far beyond the implements of war as such. It was concerned with basic raw stuffs without which munitions could not be made and whose uneven distribution made bargain and balance prerequisite to any program.

The War Industries Board had on hand to take part in the commodity discussions a delegation of its own headed by a consulting engineer, Leland L. Summers. The complicated nature of the arrangements they had to make resembled poker quite as much as war. They were illustrated by the case of the Spanish mules which Dawes so urgently required. Spain had the mules, needed them, and was indisposed to sell for cash. But Spain was short of fertilizers, whereas the Inter-Allied Nitrate Executive had control over the whole available supply. By withholding nitrates it was possible to persuade Spain to see reason in the matter of mules. But before the transaction was finished and the Army drivers had the mules, the War Trade Board, with its power to control the issuance of export and import licenses, had been brought into the arrangement.

The complications were not limited to those due to the reluctance of neutral dealers. There was the matter of jute for bags, particularly for sand bags to be used in the trenches, of which the United States had ordered 100,000,000 for delivery in France. Most of the world supply of jute was raised in India, whither the war demand had brought great profit and where the native peoples had rallied loyally to the British Empire. England was reluctant to impose on India either an allocation of the crop or less than a competitive price, while the jute farmers and the merchants who controlled the trade were slow to accept a regimentation. It happened, however, that India had been short of silver for use as currency and had turned to the United States to remedy the shortage. When the United States now found difficulty in releasing more silver, India found a way to co-operate. An Inter-Allied Jute Executive was about to be set up when time was called at the Armistice.

Inter-Ally 'executives' and agreements to pool and ration the common stock of basic commodities became nearly as numerous as the commodities themselves. Tin, rubber, manganese, and platinum — none of which Nature has distributed conveniently to the great industrial nations — were key commodities, and insufficient at best. The task of the Munitions Council, supplemented by the 'executives,' was to compare needs, to maintain control of supply, and to keep down the costs. Some of the intricacies of the business are revealed in *American Industry in the War: A Report of the War Industries Board* (1921), which Bernard M. Baruch filed with Wilson on his last day in office; and *Report of the War Trade Board* (1919), which its chairman, Vance C. McCormick, transmitted when his organization had been reduced to a dimension small enough to be absorbed in the State Department. In the last analysis, in matters of munitions as well as food, ships were the neck of the bottle.

The Allied Maritime Transport Council met again at the end of August, after its preliminary sessions in March and April, to consider shipping in the light of the enlarged needs of the American program. In spite of the checking of the submarine the tonnage deficit was still alarming. The building of new ships was slowing down because of the diversion of labor to the repair of injured shipping. British labor was overshadowed by the threat of strikes, which evoked from the Prime Minister the counter-threat that exemptions from military service must be cancelled if men refrained from work. American bottoms, on which reliance had been placed after the glowing initial prospectus of the Shipping Board, were not to be supplemented by much new United States tonnage during 1918; and what new tonnage there was, instead of relieving the pressure upon Allied tonnage for Allied necessity, was insufficient for the enlarged American need.

There were, at the end of August, 1842, ocean-going steamers under some form of control by the United States. They aggregated 6,405,388 gross, or 8,693,579 deadweight tons; but only five per cent of these represented new ships built to the order of the Emergency Fleet. The Council could do little in August with the commitment for 1919. When it next met, at the end of September, Secretary Baker was on hand as advocate of an even larger allocation of tonnage to the American service. Hines was there, too, from the Embarkation Service, stating troop and cargo need. The war had passed into a phase in which quick returns ousted the long run from consideration. Baker was ready (if not quite safe in doing it) to promise that after April, 1919, the new American tons would become a reality.

The procession from Washington to the front and back to Washington to take up again the conduct of the American end of the contract was ended by Baker. He had once more made his rearrangements at home. On August 27 he named Benedict Crowell Director of Munitions and elevated John D. Ryan to be Second Assistant Secretary of War and Director of the Air Service. He slipped away to France, with his departure a secret until his arrival was noted on September 8. With him were Ryan, Hines, and Gorgas from the Medical Corps. He came to put the capstone on the agreements for the battle of 1919, and arrived in time to join Clemenceau and Pétain on September 13, in entering the town of St. Mihiel, from which on the preceding day the First Army, A.E.F., had driven the enemy. The last sharp German salient had been eliminated from the Western Front.

XVII. THE FIRST ARMY, A.E.F.

AMONG the most intriguing of the battles that have never been fought is the one that might have been just beginning when the Secretary of War entered St. Mihiel on the heels of the departing Germans. The first engagement of the First Army was completed, with the army held on leash by Foch. But in the mind of the army, from the commander down, a belief lingered that the second day, September 13, 1918, might as well have been the first day of a definitive movement leading to a peace coming earlier than it came in fact. Liddell Hart has had the same idea. Author of an admirable first-aid to the uninformed, *The War in Outline* (1936), Captain Hart developed his critical skill upon a long series of special writings on personalities and strategy. In one of these, he considered the consequences after St. Mihiel 'if Foch had listened to Pershing instead of Haig'; and since the attack on Metz did not take place it remains possible to conjecture concerning its possible success. A seasoned correspondent of the New York *Sun*, Thomas M. Johnson, weighed the matter in *Without Censor: New Light on Our Greatest World War Battles* (1928), and inclined to believe that events would have proved Pershing to be right.

St. Mihiel, on the right bank of the Meuse, was at the tip of a salient projecting into France after the field armies of 1914 settled down to a war of attrition in the trenches. South of the southern face of the salient the country rises to the Vosges Mountains and to the Plateau of Langres, progressively rougher as it rises and un-manageable for large modern armies. Only at one spot near the Swiss border, where Belfort guarded against Mulhouse and Épinal against Colmar, and where Mulhouse and Colmar guarded

THE ROADS TO GERMANY

Germany against French invasion, was a major operation even conceivable; and none took place. Flowing from the hill country, northward and roughly parallel for sixty miles or more, the Moselle and the Meuse start on their journey to the Rhine. They separate only when the Belgian Highland — the Forest of Ardennes — interposes its bulk to force them apart and its rough terrain to forbid large-scale maneuvers across its hills. The roads from Germany to France were only three; or from France to Germany if the time should come to cross the Rhine. The approach at Mulhouse–Belfort remained a quiet zone of war; that which ran north of the Ardennes through Belgium brought upon Germany, for its use, the reproaches of the world; the third was in the region where the Moselle and the Meuse begin to separate in order to circle the borders of the Ardennes.

Through this middle highway the German armies came in 1870. Confronted on the Upper Moselle by the French fortifications around Metz, they laid siege to the fortress, circled around it, and accepted its capitulation in the end. They passed across the narrows between the rivers to Verdun, marched down the valley, and at Sedan captured the town, the French army, and the Emperor Napoleon III. Metz was the guardian at the gates of France; but failed to guard. Verdun had slight military importance in 1870. But when the armies moved again in 1914, Metz had been rebuilt into an impregnable German fortress, while France had selected at Verdun the point around which to construct every manner of defense that military science could command. Built to hold back a German invader, it held him back. The whole power of the enemy could not reduce it when its reduction was made the major German effort of 1916.

Between Verdun and Metz, a distance of about thirty-five miles from river to river, the invasion of 1914 was checked by the outer fortifications of Verdun. To the north the German armies swept around them, across the Meuse, to the region of the Aisne. To the south they pushed a salient reaching the Meuse twenty miles above Verdun, and they could get no farther. Metz became a German center of supply, key to access to the armies in northern France.

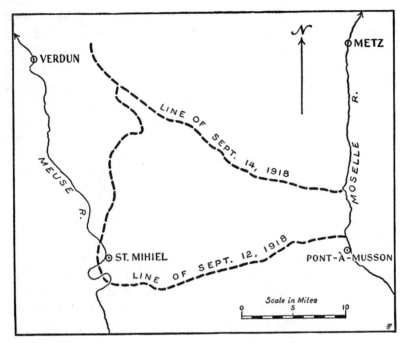

ST. MIHIEL, SEPTEMBER 12, 1918

The mineral fields, Briey and Longwy, northwest of Metz, were worked by the invader. Germany was short of iron and determined to retain these fields. The salient at St. Mihiel was treated as a correction of the borders of the German Empire, fortified to be held, and filled with military cemeteries that were designed to last forever. Along the south face of this salient, from the Meuse to the Moselle, the American divisions took their tours of service in the trenches. The American officers let their minds range over the nearness to Metz — whose fixed guns could reach the country at the base of the salient — and over the military significance of the reduction of Metz. They had a hope that this might be the mission of the A.E.F.

Upon the erection of headquarters at Chaumont the reduction of the salient became the objective of the war plans unit of Pershing's staff. Before Christmas, 1917, Pétain was apologizing to Pershing for having revealed this to Colonel House as to be the first American venture in the field. And when at last the First Army took shape the strategists at Chaumont conceived St. Mihiel to be but the first paragraph in a chapter which might end with Metz and peace. The doubts as to American ability which pervaded the atmosphere of the French and British headquarters were not entertained at Pershing's headquarters.

When the salient was at last cleared away in two days' fighting, the army in motion could not forgive the leash that held it back. It was natural to forget the defenses encircling Metz, which might have made it as impregnable as Verdun had showed itself to be, and to think instead of the short mileage and the value of a victory. But Foch listened to Haig instead of Pershing; as the result, when Baker visited the captured town of St. Mihiel, the battle was at its end instead of at its beginning. Haig had put forward arguments for continuous pressure in the west, in which Verdun should be the pivot, so as to compel German withdrawal. He feared that failure by the A.E.F. might lessen what was now a chance to win; also that initial success might set up a new position whose maintenance by the Allies would interfere with more profitable progress elsewhere. He argued against the American desire, rejected it coming and going, and won his point. The battle of Metz remains only a theme for speculation.

Second, much second, among the battles never fought, was one whose paper work Bundy directed. When he was removed from the command of the 2d Division on July 15 he did more than make a place for Harbord. He was given the Sixth Army Corps in the Neufchâteau area, and in August he was sent with the headquarters of his corps to Belfort. Here, planning on the use of seven divisions, he prepared for a drive on Mulhouse to begin in September. His divisions moved toward the new center; or at least their headquarters radio outfits moved, ever talking, and triangulated daily by German military intelligence. Each day brought them closer to Belfort. The evidence of their movement was mystifying at German headquarters, for military opinion could not believe in a major venture near Belfort. Yet it had not believed that a million could be transported to France, and had been forced to accept reality. It could not completely disregard the evidence. There was more evidence. A colonel in Pershing's confidence carelessly lost the corps orders in his hotel. A military attaché in a neutral country (Kahn of California told the story in the House) lost his papers in a café, and was publicly distressed by his carelessness. Each relied successfully upon the vigilance of the German secret services. The troops of the Sixth Corps, who reconnoitered the front line, let themselves be seen. It was Pershing's conviction that the ruse succeeded to the point of confusing the enemy. When St. Mihiel had been taken he called the Sixth Corps off its task, set its staff to the creation of a Second Army, and found a place for Bundy in command of the Seventh Corps.

The Genesis of the American First Army (a monograph published by the Army War College, 1928) relates the sequence of events in which the Abbeville decision of May 1 is an early step. Here the Supreme War Council agreed to the principle of an American army under its own commander and its own flag; though naming no day and hoping none would come. At Beauvais, early in April, Pershing had been obliged to insist that the American army should be named among those over which Foch was to act as co-

ordinator. The interferences with Pershing's plan, apart from
those based on Allied distrust, were not yet ended. He had surrendered his divisions to Foch on March 28, in the face of emergency. He must surrender them again at the end of May when
the Germans neared the Marne. The renewal of the drive on July
15, and the counter-stroke of Foch three days later, delayed him
again: but since he could not bring his divisions to his corps, he
had sent his corps to his divisions, with Liggett taking command
behind them on July 4. As the German retreat from the Marne
pocket became visible, and as the American divisions showed their
mettle, his bargaining power grew with the Allied hope of victory.
On July 24 he sat in a conference at the headquarters of Foch,
and emerged with authority to proceed.

Haig and Pétain were at the conference. Pershing attended with
a draft of an order creating an army ready for signature, but with
an acquiescence with which to sweeten the Allies. He bore to Foch
the news that the President would take a part in the occupation of
the Murmansk Coast. Neither March nor Pershing regarded this
as anything but an improvident waste of troops, but the Allies
were set upon it. With the other commanders Pershing listened to
Foch in exposition of a program for the rest of 1918; and for 1919,
when it was beginning to be hoped the war could be won. With
man-power now at his disposal, Foch was disposed to keep the
enemy at work along his whole line, to wear out his front-line divisions, to keep the German Staff guessing, and to keep immobile
what reserve divisions the Germans yet possessed because of the
impossibility of determining where they might best be used. The
thrust at Soissons had been started only as a minor operation to
retard the drive across the Marne. Its success had started a general
withdrawal which must be followed up. From the British view-
point the most profitable field for military investment was at the
extreme left of the line, along the Channel. Here Haig needed
room for maneuver, wanted reinforcements, was conscious that
Lloyd George distrusted him, and was sensitive at every suggestion
of the withdrawal of the American divisions with him and at his
rear. The assent of the French to the creation of the First Army,

A.E.F., was unpopular with the English and irritating to the British Prime Minister who allowed himself to threaten to cut down American tonnage if the American armies were to operate east of Verdun. But the conference reached its decision; Haig and Pétain went back to their armies to prepare for advance in concert, and Pershing returned to Chaumont to sign that night his order, effective August 10, for the assembly of the First Army.

The components of the First Army were still in the Marne pocket, where on July 24 the German line still sagged down to the Marne although it had everywhere been withdrawn from its advanced positions of July 18; or they were in quiet fronts, Lorraine and elsewhere, learning how to be soldiers, or in training camps behind the armies. Those on the Marne were functioning in and out of the line as the French Sixth Army pushed across the salient to the Ourcq and to the Vesle in the seventeen days before the order became effective. The new staff of the First Army had been hand-picked at Chaumont, where the General Staff itself had never before organized an army or directed its use.

The personnel of the army staff faced a new task in organizing it; and Hugh A. Drum, its chief, had been at work near Liggett's First Corps since the day, July 4, when Liggett took tactical command. It was proposed that the First Army, when assembled and organized, should relieve the Sixth French Army wherever that army should find itself. Since the latter was advancing every day, the staffs pursued the component troops from Marne to Vesle, never knowing the line on which the First Army might take over. And when at last, after the elimination of the Marne pocket, the line was smoothed about August 4, Foch and Pershing were on the verge of a decision to defer still longer the tactical functioning of the First Army. They were considering its shift to a different mission on another front.

On August 10 Pershing took command, to retain it until there should be a Second Army. But he deferred tactical control, informing his staff that the outfit was at once to be removed to the sector north of Toul, facing St. Mihiel. The French Eighth Army became the one to be relieved. Army headquarters were moved to Neufchâteau, whose location made it possible for watching Germans to suspect that its effort might be at either St. Mihiel or Belfort, without being certain of either until the blow should fall.

The opening of the frontier railroads to unimpeded Allied use was the immediate objective. Haig took the responsibility for the line north from Paris, through Amiens to the Channel ports. Pershing was at least to free the east line, Paris–Nancy, with its connection along the left bank of the Meuse through St. Mihiel to Verdun. During the last week of August the units of the First Army came into control of the line on both sides of the salient, from the vicinity of Verdun, around the apex on the Meuse, and across the narrows between the rivers to Pont-à-Musson on the Moselle. Pershing commanded the whole enterprise, his army constituting one among the armies of the French group 'of Armies of the North and Northeast' commanded by Pétain. Pétain issued a directive making Pershing's plan his own. The French agreed to lend artillery, airplanes, and tanks, and to place French divisions as needed in the First Army under the American commander.

The army and the army corps were operating mechanisms rather than military entities, and neither was certain to retain its components for more than a military moment. The fighting entities were the divisions, whose number in the A.E.F. was now sufficient for Pershing to include fourteen (plus two French divisions) and a French army corps in the First Army as it was put together in the three weeks after August 10. Grouped in army corps, and subject to transfer as need suggested, the resources of the divisions were supplemented by those of 'corps troops'; artillery, engineers, aircraft, and what not, which were administered through corps headquarters. The number of divisions to the corps, normally six, was often proved to be five or seven.

Administering the corps, and through the corps the divisions, the army organization at the top directed operations. There were army troops under the direct command of army headquarters. These, like the corps troops, were mostly air and artillery units, with detachments from all of the service corps such as tank, signal, medical, chemical warfare, and occasionally even a little cavalry; but this was not a war in which the cavalry commander had a chance to ride around the enemy and earn distinction. John Buchan, however, in his well-informed and contemporary *History of the Great War* (1922), has a footnote on the 'surprising adventures' of a cavalry substitute, a whippet tank, surnamed 'Musical Box,' which pushed through the German front and cruised on its own behind the lines.

Above all line organizations and army services, the General Staff from Chaumont represented the Commander in Chief and scrutinized everything. Staff officers were everywhere, always resented by men of the line, and were like the men of the line in being not too well grounded in their business. On their recommendation commands were changed and orders interfered with on slightest suspicion. The whole process of A.E.F. fighting was so telescoped in time that while there was much occasion for interference there was rarely time to correct injustice. The Commander in Chief was a relentless disciplinarian. There was no chance that war popularity with his men would lay a foundation for post-war politics.

That action was in the air was certain. The enemy knew it; perhaps somewhat confused by the demonstration staged around Belfort. The correspondents in France knew it; but the censors would not pass the news. The press in the United States suspected it, if for no other reason than that the flow of detail which had accompanied the reduction of the Marne salient shrunk suddenly at the end of August. Only half a dozen of the American divisions had had much combat experience, as such experience went in the A.E.F. On the capacity of these, and the untested capacity of the others, the success of the enterprise must depend. Getting them to the new front was a matter of complex paper work, and much explicit profanity on the part of the military police, as they moved on crowded roads with truck transport never adequate. Dawes was working with his Military Board of Allied Supply upon an Allied pool of trucks; but he could not improvise them.

While the preparation for the St. Mihiel offensive was under way, the whole front of the Allies came into action, in general accord with the directive which Foch discussed with the commanders on July 24. There was plenty of news for the American press even though the American divisions were for the moment out of it.

Haig put the British armies in motion on August 8. Ever since the line was stabilized in the Somme after the drive of March, the railway running north from Paris through Amiens had been in danger. Direct communication between the French and British armies had been impeded. The German front, crossing the Oise above Compiègne, had swung around Montdidier and run nearly north across the Somme and its branches to Albert. A third battle of the Somme now began here, to relieve the railway line and recover the ground lost in March. It was successful from the start, confirming for Germany what had been foreseen since July 18 — the end of the hope of a German victory. Montdidier was retaken early in the drive, with the French helping on the British right. The 33d Division, brigaded with the British, had days of fighting on the left before it was withdrawn and entrained to join the First Army. By the end of August the Somme salient was blunted, the Hindenburg Line was crossed in front of Arras, and the German withdrawal was accelerated by continuous pressure, not ending until the war was over. This was what Haig regarded as the major operation, and was the basis for his reluctance to approve what he regarded as wasting of the American divisions in American adventures.

Ten days after Haig put on the pressure, up the Somme, preparations were completed to supplement his pressure at either side. The movements on Soissons (July 18) and on Montdidier (August 8) had shifted the stresses in the valley of the Oise, where the line crossed the river a little above Compiègne. There, back of the German front, Noyon was important to the whole region as a railway and supply center. Mangin, with the Tenth French Army, was started up the Oise on August 18. Eleven days later Noyon fell, but the pressure did not stop. The fighting in this advance confirmed the growing impression of the temper of the A.E.F.

The 32d Division took Juvigny on August 30; 'fighting for three days,' as Pétain cited its 64th infantry brigade, 'without stopping, without rest and almost without food.' Juvigny was not much of a village, but was important as an approach to the western end of the Chemin des Dames. Well to the right of Juvigny as it fell, the 28th and the 77th Divisions were advancing across the hills from the Vesle to the Aisne, making the eastern end of the Chemin des Dames equally precarious. The 28th and 77th had continued on the course set across the Marne salient, in the revival of pressure here following the lull of August 4.

On the day after Mangin started up the Oise, August 19, the British left moved in the Ypres salient in the direction of Armentières. They had feinted here, to mislead the enemy, when Haig delivered his main blow above Amiens. The 27th and 30th Divisions were with the British and were soon on the line. Lille and the industrial region of northern France were the Allied objectives, while every mile the British could gain would relieve the severe compression under which they had labored in Flanders from the first. But upon the retention of Lille the orderly evacuation of the German right depended. Less than twenty miles from Ypres, it was not occupied by the British until the middle of October, when the Belgian coast had been freed as far as Ostend; but the activity on Lille was both continuous and ominous. Meanwhile, from Amiens north, the British armies had been advancing toward St. Quentin, and were near Péronne before the end of August. The Foch directive of July 24 had called for experimental pressure in many places to be kept up until resistance in any one spot should make it useful to deflect it to another point. As things worked out, with 286,000 Americans floated in August, and 259,000 in September, pressure once started was not obliged to cease. German strategic withdrawals became a general retreat, with confusion and collapse certain unless the retreat should be prompt.

By the end of August the Allied line was active all the way from Reims to Ypres, and the hope was born that the Germans might be out of France before winter stopped fighting in the field. The line

of the Western Front was smoothed, except for the salient at St.
Mihiel. More than this, a renewal of the drive behind Saloniki
was impending, and the Bulgarian front was believed nearly ready
to collapse. Allenby, in Palestine, was preparing to attack Damascus. Diaz was considering a resumption of the Italian effort on the
Piave. But not until the German documents emerged after the
war was it known that on August 14, following a conference at
Spa, Ludendorff offered to resign his command and urged the
Imperial Government to make what peace it could.

Before the end of August the evidence of success compelled a re-
examination of the decision taken July 24, whereby the First Army
was to assemble north of Toul, and to fulfill its mission at the St.
Mihiel salient. Pershing was again compelled to fight to retain the
army for whose creation he had so long and so obstinately struggled. The existence of the salient at St. Mihiel indeed marred the
symmetry of the Western Front as now reshaped; but the salient
had lost much of its significance with the German armies yielding
ground. If the pressure from Reims to the Channel should be continued and if reinforcements in quantity should enable it to be increased, the German withdrawal might be turned to rout. As a
matter of professional strategic skill the retreat was winning the
commendation of all military experts. But every mile from which
the German line drew back, no matter how deadly the rear-guard
actions, shortened the distance between the battle front and the
railway lines from which the German force was served. And behind these railway lines, the Belgian Highlands forbade direct
retreat. The Germans must go out of France as they came in:
north of the Highlands or to the south. If Allied artillery should
be advanced until the lines, and freight yards, and warehouses
came within range, these last would become untenable. The vital
flow of men and supplies would cease. German unity would be
superseded by confusion as the forces crowded on the detours that
would take them home.

The need for heavy mobile guns was among the problems of the
ordnance departments of both Army and Navy. Several months
before the German long-range guns, from fixed emplacements in

the vicinity of Laon, threw their shells sixty-eight miles into Paris, both branches of the American services were constructing mounts, designing guns, and converting heavy calibers built for coast defense or Navy use so that they might follow the armies in the field. Pershing had requisitioned many to be available in 1919. The Navy had five such, fourteen-inch guns, sixty feet long, ready to take their place behind American line in September, 1918. Heaviest of all the field guns available to the Allies, they had shorter range than the 'Big Berthas' which shelled Paris on March 24, 1918, but unlike the German guns which required built-up emplacements they were mobile, each on its own special train. Manned by Navy gun crews they could fire within ten minutes of bringing the train into position. Foreknowledge of these affected Pershing's view of strategy. The Navy guns had a range of twenty-five miles; the distance from the base of the St. Mihiel salient to Metz was considerably less.

From Metz to Lille, vulnerable wherever they could be reached, ran the French railways whose seizure in 1914 had enabled Germany to convert them to the service of its own armies. Whereas the French front was commonly served by lines at right angles to it, which could be simply shortened when retreat was unavoidable, the continuance of the German armies in France was based upon the continuous operation of a railroad system parallel to the German front. The system made a first-class base for victorious action, but its very nature made retreat doubly hazardous.

On August 30, Pershing as commander of the First Army took over his sector, and on the same day he was visited by Foch who bore proposals that the St. Mihiel enterprise should be modified because of the change in the military situation. It was of consequence that the French railways along the Upper Meuse should be regained, and that communication should flow unimpeded from Paris to Nancy. But the French had managed for four years to get along with this line blocked. It could endure it a little longer. St. Mihiel was no longer feared as a base from which Germany could throw confusion among the Allies. The salient was reputed to be impregnable. If effort upon it should fail, it would entail useless loss. If it should succeed, it could do little more than make a beginning of an attack upon Metz, where Allied investments might yield less valuable returns than could be got by reinforced pressure west of Verdun. It was in the Valley of the Aisne, Foch believed, that the 'fate of the 1918 campaign will be decided.' He wanted Pershing to get through with what he had to do at St. Mihiel as cheaply and as quickly as he could, so that most of the American divisions might be shifted to participate in operations on the front between Verdun and Noyon. Noyon had fallen to the Tenth French Army the day before Foch's visit, and the line ran almost straight thence to the Meuse at Verdun. Forty miles ahead of it lay the German railway junctions, Hirson and Mézières, upon whose smooth operation depended the security of the German front.

There was merit in the contention of Foch, even though it involved one more postponement of action by the 'separate component.' But it involved, also, the near certainty that if independent action should now be stopped, the time to undertake it would not recur.

Between the Aisne-Vesle front, a new line every day, and the railways of German supply, lay the French *Département* of Ardennes, up whose grades the French battle was to be fought. It had been fought over in 1914, occupied by the invader ever since, dug into fortifications, and was to be shot to pieces as the autumn of 1918 advanced. When the French reconstruction services took over the task of reimbursement of citizens who had suffered loss, it was found that of 741,993 houses destroyed or damaged in the ten invaded *Départements*, 78,000 were in Ardennes. From the owners of these, and of other property damaged in Ardennes, came 247,567 claims for restoration, to be passed through cantonal commissions, to be heard on appeal, and to be awarded more than four billion francs by the Republic. L. Lucien Hubert, in *La Renaissance d'un département dévasté* (1924), has told the story, typical of all of northern France. To get the Germans out of France, and to bring back into production in farm and factory the sixteen per cent of the population who had paid eighteen per cent of all French taxes before 1914, was vital to French interest; more vital than the feelings of the American commander who had appeared to the Republic to come too late and to want too much.

The reaction of Pershing to the new proposal was immediate and determined. Foch wanted to limit the attack to an advance upon the south face of St. Mihiel, in place of simultaneous advance upon both faces and at the tip. When the operation was over, the A.E.F. was to have to hold only another quiet sector. Metz and the mines of Briey and Longwy were out of the picture as Foch saw it. It may be true that he desired to get the enemy out of the mines by maneuver rather than by combat which would destroy them. He clung to his demand for a limited attack even on the south face, while Pershing clung to his point of the independent army and complete maneuver. The latter was ready to fight where needed, but only 'as an American army, and in no other way.' When Foch reproached him for his shortage of artillery and service troops, he reminded the Generalissimo that France had begged to supply the artillery, having more than it could use, and that the shipment of service troops had been cut down to meet what the Allies described as temporary emergency. There was a show-down on the thirtieth. Pershing believed that when Foch left his headquarters 'very pale and apparently exhausted' the latter had allowed himself to be persuaded by someone to take the stand he did, and he thought Pétain agreed with him as to the importance of complete action at the salient, but believed that it would be unwise to proceed toward Metz.

Three days later, September 2, Pershing and Pétain went into conference with Foch, at the Bombon headquarters of Pétain, and there the atmosphere was cleared. The Metz project was cancelled, in order to permit the First Army under Pershing to take part in a general movement west of the Meuse after St. Mihiel. The whole of the St. Mihiel salient was left under American command for the completion of the First Army operation which Pershing had been preparing since August 10. The Commander in Chief went back to American headquarters with double weight of responsibility upon him: he must not only win his battle, but he must also win

it so completely as to justify his determination not to let it be interfered with by the different strategic desire of Foch. He carried on
two operations for the next two weeks; in one capacity he made
the arrangements for a shift of his whole fighting strength to the
new field west of Verdun; in the other he safeguarded the St.
Mihiel operation upon whose success his status as a commander
probably depended. No one has brought to light the alleged
memorandum in which Foch asked that Pershing be relieved by
an American more pliable; but it may exist. What the British
really felt about the enterprise Pershing learned when Lord Reading talked with him on September 6, stressing the advantage to
be derived by having the American force in operation near the
British; and when General Diaz, asking for twenty American
divisions for the Italian front, interrupted himself to ask for
twenty-five. But Diaz himself did not expect to be able to attack
on his own front until the spring of 1919. There was satisfaction,
though melancholy, to be derived by Pershing from the information of his Chief Surgeon, Merritte W. Ireland, that 100,000
hospital beds were ready.

While Foch and the American Commander in Chief were
debating whether the battle of St. Mihiel should not be number
three among the American battles never to be fought, the staff of
the First Army was bringing additional divisions from the French
and British rears, to supplement the efforts of the divisions already
north of Toul. Once the decision was reached on September 2,
Foch did his part. Artillery and aircraft sufficient for the attack
were made available; the latter to be commanded by Colonel
William Mitchell, Chief of Air Service; the former to be under
Major-General Edward F. McGlachlin, Jr., Chief of Artillery.
The First Army was short of tanks; and those which it had were
French.

As the salient lay within the wings of the First Army, its western
face along the Meuse below St. Mihiel was on high hills east of the
river, from which German artillery could cover both the Valley of
the Meuse and the Woëvre Plain sloping behind the hills toward
Metz. The south face cut across between the rivers to the Moselle,

just below Pont-à-Musson. Behind the German front lines were fortifications, wire entanglements, defensive positions in the rear; and behind all these the defenses of Metz. There were enough defenses to throw doubt upon the ability of the drive, once started, to have been continued to victory at Metz. It was later learned that Germany was prepared to evacuate the salient if it should be attacked. Sharp German writers have blurred the success of the First Army by insisting that withdrawal was under way when the blow fell. American critics of the engagement have found captured German orders contradicting the claim, while the troops participating had no reason to believe they were taking part in a rearguard action.

The four corps of the First Army, as they faced the salient, had various functions assigned them in the orders which were drafted, examined, redrafted, and handed to their commanders. On the extreme left, and nearest to Verdun, the Fifth Corps, with the 4th, French Colonial 15th, and 26th Divisions (from left to right), held the angle where the salient jutted south from the main front. They were to cross the heights, and the 26th was to press into the salient. On their right the Second French Colonial Corps held the tip at St. Mihiel and ten miles on either side, with mission to keep occupied the German divisions which they faced. The main advance was entrusted to the Fourth Corps, at the right of the French, and to the First Corps extending from its right to the Moselle, and designed to act as pivot. On the line for the Fourth Corps were the 1st, 42d, and 89th. Of these the 89th, well trained by Leonard Wood, had completed no more than its tour of quiet duty on a sector in Lorraine. The First Corps had on the line the 2d, 5th, 90th, and the 82d. The 5th, 90th, and 82d, like the 89th, had not seen duty on an active front. Of the nine divisions upon which Pershing staked his untried reputation as a field commander, four were untried in action. In all of the divisions there were troops newly assigned, and of these some had not even received the full training of private soldiers.

The main attack, launched early on the morning of September 12, fell upon the center of the south face, midway between the rivers. There was enough preliminary artillery fire to disturb the enemy without giving him time to bring up reserve divisions before the infantry advanced. The most experienced of the divisions, 1st, 2d, and 42d, were at the spearhead. The Secretary of War, 'from his observation point near the battlefield,' was given the chance to watch more of a battle than was usually possible. Before night on the twelfth the divisions on the south face had reached the lines drawn on the staff maps for the second day's objectives. Before daybreak on the thirteenth the German divisions in the pocket were in confusion and the roads out of the salient were blocked to north and west. Pershing reported the capture of some 450 guns and 16,000 prisoners, at a cost of 7000 casualties. By afternoon on the 13th all that was left to be done was to correct the new line across the base of the reduced salient, so that it could be held after the First Army shifted its position across the Meuse to get into place for the next engagement.

There remains some reasonable doubt as to the military necessity of the risk taken at St. Mihiel, considering the situation along the Allied front in the first week of September; doubt not entirely dispelled by complete success. But there is no doubt that the existence of the 'separate component' depended upon the risk being taken. The success gave inspiration to men and leaders, and to the Americans at home, who, after the event, heard enough about it to compensate for the mystifying silence that had preceded the first independent operation of the First Army.

XVIII. THE MEUSE–ARGONNE

The character of John J. Pershing, rather than his military ability as a commander, stands out in clear visibility. It was his persistence that gave to the American effort in France the shape it took. No one can prove that the effort might not have been more effective if of a different shape. No one can know enough about Pershing to know where to place his professional talents in comparison with those of his colleagues in command, Haig and Pétain, or with those of his superior, Foch. There is material enough to provide foundation for a first-class military reputation in his administrative achievement whereby two million men were brought to the support of the Allied line of battle, and in his direction of a battle lasting for seven weeks. But he had no chance to uncover talents in the larger strategy, or to reveal lasting qualities through the ups and downs of successive campaigns in the field.

It is as impossible to prove Pershing's rating as a general as it is to prove the degree to which the American reinforcement made it possible to defeat the enemy. Thrown by the strategy of his chief into a holding position not of his own choosing in the last engagement of the war, Pershing did more than hold. The human weight of the forces under his command was at least a vital factor in victory; the economic weight contributed by the American Government was another; the unity of direction, to which the United States had contributed greatly, was still a third. But the victory in the field which broke the Central Powers was the victory of a team in which the abstraction of co-operation was perhaps more significant than the weight of any single concrete factor.

Upon the elimination of the salient at St. Mihiel, Foch acquired

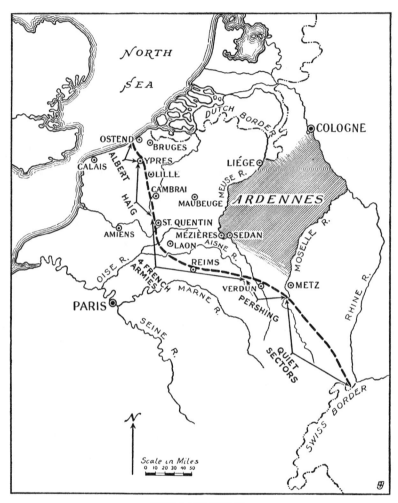

THE LAST PHASE
September 26–November 11, 1918

control of the final chapter of the war. The picture of the American share in the events of the last seven weeks gives, of necessity, some distortion of its significance; for great and successful as the American effort was, it was only one among many efforts, and owed as much to the timing of the others as they owed to it.

On the Allied left, as the American divisions were pulled out of the St. Mihiel line and redistributed, the King of the Belgians was preparing for a major effort. The one monarch to take the field in person, Albert had a group of armies, Belgian, British, and French. He had also, eventually, the 37th and 91st American divisions which contributed something to his success. The Allied gains of August, pushing the Germans back from Amiens, Montdidier, and Château-Thierry, had so endangered the German right that its withdrawal was begun early in September as the German High Command sought some defensible line in France upon which to come to rest for the winter months. As Foch came progressively into control of the initiative, the hope grew that the enemy might be out of France before winter; and one by one the lines prepared in the rear of the German armies were reached and passed. Aggressive pursuit made it impossible for the retreating armies to stop. While Pershing did his job with the First Army at St. Mihiel, the armies of Albert were making ready to leave the trenches for a follow-up in the open. The decision reached at Bombon on September 2 called for similar and simultaneous action along the whole Western Front. On the early morning of September 28 the armies on the left began to move; and to move so successfully that after three days they were forced to pause to organize a new rear, to marshal into prison camps their thousands of captives, to dispose of *matériel* of war abandoned by the German armies as they yielded ground, and to build service roads across country so fought-over that it was desolate. In October Albert's armies advanced again, reaching by the eighteenth Ostend and Bruges, with the whole Belgian Channel coast in Allied hands. On November 11 the 37th and 91st Divisions were in the line when it came to rest across the Scheldt River, east of Audenarde.

The right wing of Albert's group was the British Second Army, which advanced from the vicinity of Ypres. Lille, in its front, was evacuted by October 18.

Next to the right, in the general advance at the end of September, the British armies under Haig resumed activity in the recovery movement which they had begun on August 8. The British Fourth Army (Rawlinson) had started it, east and southeast from Amiens, heading toward St. Quentin. In the ensuing weeks the fan-shaped movement had broadened, right and left. French armies on the right had extended it toward Reims. Left of Rawlinson's army the British Third Army (Byng), First Army (Horne), and Fifth Army (Birdwood) spread the engagement to Armentières on the River Lys. Here Birdwood's left joined the right of Plumer's Second British Army which was under King Albert. As all prepared in mid-September for the British part in the general advance, they had immediately in their front, behind the German lines, Lille on the left, Cambrai on the River Scheldt, and to the right of Cambrai the St. Quentin tunnel through which passes the canal connecting the headwaters of the Scheldt with those of the Somme.

If there was any one 'key' to the Hindenburg Line, back to which the German armies had made a strategic withdrawal early in 1917 and from which had started the opening drive of March 21, 1918, it was here. The ancient tunnel — built by Napoleon — and its canal were worked into the defensive system. The deep cut through which the canal runs was a fortification in itself. The tunnel provided coverage for troops and storage for supplies, and ingenious death-traps for enemy troops that might try to penetrate it. The adjacent country was netted with wire, ranged by machine-gun nests, and covered by artillery on the heights. It lay in the zone of Rawlinson's Fourth Army; and two days before the British action became general Rawlinson sent against the outposts two American divisions borrowed from the A.E.F.

The 27th and 30th Divisions, both organized around National Guard units, and the former unusual in being still commanded by a general officer from the National Guard, Major-General John F. O'Ryan, saw their combat service as the Second Army Corps under Major-General George W. Read. Not always trusted by the High Command of the A.E.F., the National Guard divisions were used profitably by the British and the French, when they could get them. The British had learned how to deal with Australian and other Dominion levies under their own commanders. Continuously with the British, these two divisions were attached to the Second British Army in front of Ypres at the end of August. Transferred to Rawlinson's Fourth Army in September, they were selected by him for a preliminary testing of the German defenses on September 27, and for the advance upon the canal and tunnel when the British armies moved in force on September 29. There were thirty British divisions fighting with them. John Charteris, biographer of *Field Marshal Earl Haig* (1929), counts 35,500 prisoners taken on September 29–30, when the Hindenburg Line was crushed. The Guardsmen had an admirer in their gallery, who came to see the front and found a battle. Sir Arthur Conan Doyle, there on a visit, opened his letter to the London *Times* about it with 'Mine eyes have seen the glory of the coming of the Lord.' Doyle returned to London to complete six volumes of a popular *History of the Great War* (1920), in which he mingled his pride in the Americans with that in the Australians, who fought beside them; but he left it to 'some Antipodean historian' to tell the story in detail. For more than three weeks the American divisions stayed in the line and out as the British armies kept up their pressure until on November 9 they entered Maubeuge, and on the eleventh, Mons. Maubeuge was significant as a railway junction on the main retreating line, north of the Ardennes, upon which Germany relied for its service through Liége to Cologne. Mons had a more sentimental value. Here the legendary angels had appeared in August, 1914, when the Germans pressed Haig back in the first British battle of the war.

To the right of the British armies, the armies of France in the last week of September held the line from St. Quentin to the edge of the Argonne Forest, east of the Aisne. In a long, smooth, concave curve they faced St. Quentin and Laon at their left; but east of Laon was no near town of importance. The great curve of the westward-flowing Aisne ran across most of their front, cutting a southern segment off the *Département* of the Ardennes. A northern segment of the same *département*, cut off by the Meuse, contained the railway junction of Mézières, where the main military railway of the German front was reached by a branch running down the Meuse to Namur, and thence through Liége to Cologne. Here, too, was Sedan; and no Frenchman could fail to pray that before the war should end, the humiliating surrender of 1870 might be avenged by the recapture of Sedan. It was one of the minor ironies of the war that when it did end, Sedan had not been entered by the Allies. American troops had been near enough to take it, but had been ordered back. The French, after warning their 'brave neighbors' to stand aside with the grim sentence, 'I am obliged to use my artillery in that region,' had failed to do more than look down upon Sedan, on November 11, from the hills across the Meuse. Mézières, however, had been taken, giving France the reality of victory if not the sentiment.

Of the four French armies in the group to the right of Haig, those of Debeney, Mangin, Berthelot, and Gouraud, it was the last that headed toward Mézières and Sedan, with the additional mission of keeping in touch with the First American Army at its right. Pétain had made free use of American divisions during the reduction of the Marne salient, surrendering them as they were drawn away in August to be used against St. Mihiel. Moving across Champagne toward the Meuse and the French border, the French reborrowed two divisions. Gouraud was timed to resume his advance as Pershing opened his own battle on September 26. The French right was retarded by resistance unexpectedly desperate along the Upper Aisne. Pershing sent Gouraud the 2d and the 36th; the former staying on the line for a week to take Blanc Mont and St. Étienne-à-Arnes, the latter relieving the 2d and continuing to the Aisne at Attigny on October 27. For the 2d Division this was but one of many assignments. For the Texas and Oklahoma Guardsmen of the 36th, their three weeks with Gouraud constituted their first engagement and their last. By mid-October Gouraud's right and Pershing's left were out of the

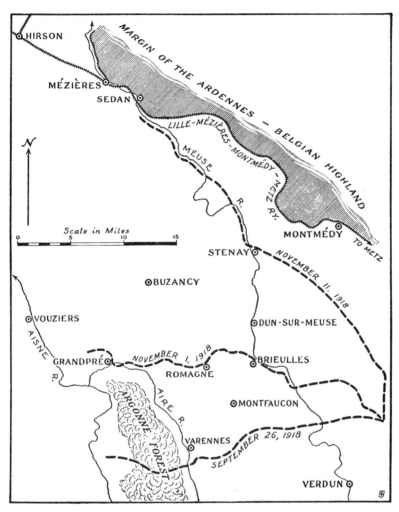

THE ADVANCE OF THE FIRST ARMY, MEUSE–ARGONNE
September 26–November 11, 1918

Argonne Forest and in co-operation between Grandpré on the Aire and Vouziers on the Aisne, above Attigny.

The American part in the general engagement at the end of September was on the pivotal position at the extreme right of the advancing line, which was to play 'crack the whip'; with the armies of Albert on the free end at the left. The quiet sectors east of the Moselle were expected to remain quiet, although after the American bluff at Belfort the Germans anticipated a drive upon Metz. Where the front line crossed the heights east of the Meuse, below the fortifications of Verdun, the pivoting was to begin. West of the Meuse, and thence to a junction with the army of Gouraud on the farther edge of the Argonne Forest, was the front across which the American First Army was designed to swing north and northeast, keeping its left in step with the wider swing of the French, British, and Belgian armies. Of the two hundred miles of active front between Verdun and the Channel, twenty-four were in Pershing's hands.

The terrain facing the First Army, when the whole line was set in motion, was the most refractory section of the front. Most difficult to take, with its hills, ravines, rivers, and forests, it was easiest to hold. Easiest to hold, it was for the German armies the most important sector to be held, since here the Allied front lay nearest to the railway arteries upon which depended the free circulation of German army life. Heavy guns at Verdun could almost reach the freight yards of railway lines connecting Metz with Sedan–Mézières. Only a few miles of Allied advance here were needed to make the railways untenable and to break the German front. The country in front of the Americans was fortified to be held until the end. Beyond it were concentrated German troops perhaps twice as heavily as elsewhere on the line; not because of fear of American prowess, but in recognition of the vital nature of the spot.

The A.E.F. had been pulled back from the attack on Metz because Metz was deemed impregnable. The region of the Meuse–Argonne was equally impregnable so far as military foreknowledge could anticipate. If the American forces had merely held their line, enabling the extension of the Allied front to swing without fear of being flanked from the right, they might have fulfilled a reasonable mission. That they should do more than this, and make an essential stroke for victory, was assumed at Chaumont, whether or not it was expected at Senlis and Bombon. When they did much in the forty-seven days, having been counted on for little, they were censured for not doing more. The concentration of American divisions in the First Army was begrudged by Allied commanders, who had taken samples of the divisions and would have been glad to use them all. Pershing had, after all, a limited experience as a commander; but it was of the hardest.

After the Bombon decision of September 2, the commander of the First Army had two operations on his agenda. The first was vital to him, the second to the war. So much depended upon the reduction of St. Mihiel that the operation must not be allowed to fail. But while he prepared to make the operation a success it was necessary to arrange a new First Army crew to open the new engagement, drawing heavily upon divisions which had not seen even as much of combat as those used at St. Mihiel. Foch watched with both understanding and apprehension the shifts necessary to 'all improvised armies,' recognizing the degree to which the American commander lacked not only experienced commanders of corps and division, but also trained staff officers to direct their work.

With the St. Mihiel salient eliminated, it was not possible to withdraw divisions for several days, lest a serious German counterstroke should undo the victory. The nine divisions engaged in the reduction — nine out of the twenty-nine that were used in combat — required reorganization hardly to be completed in a fortnight. It was impracticable to refill their ranks, reshuffle their officers (no one of them received a new commander), and shift them to positions on the front line west of the Meuse, in time for action again on September 26.

Back of the twenty-four-mile front whence the new line was to be set in motion, divisions were to be brought up for the line, for the corps reserves, and for the army reserve. They came from

DAILY BATTLE FRONT OF AMERICAN DIVISIONS IN THE MEUSE–ARGONNE

French Corps and Divisions serving under Pershing, in italics

FIRST ARMY, A.E.F., PERSHING Commanding

[West] ⟵ → [East]

Date	I Corps (Liggett)	V Corps (Cameron)	III Corps (Bullard)	*XVII (French)*	*XXXIII (French)*	*II (French)*	IV Corps (Dickman)
Sep 26 Thu	77–28–35	91–37–79	4–80–33	*18–10–15*		*26–2–39*	42–89–78–90–69
Sep 27 Fri	77–28–35	91–37–79	4–80–33	*18–10–15*		*26–2–39*	42–89–78–90–69
Sep 28 Sat	77–28–35	91–37–79	4–80–33	*18–10–15*		*26–2–39*	42–89–78–90–69
Sep 29 Sun	77–28–35	91–37–79	4–33	*18–10–15*		*26–2–39*	42–89–78–90–69
Sep 30 Mon	77–28–35	91–37–79	4–33	*18–10–15*		*26–2–39*	42–89–78–90–69
Oct 1 Tue	77–28–1	91–32–3	4–33	*18–10–15*		*26–2–39*	89–78–90–69
Oct 2 Wed	77–28–1	91–32–3	4–33	*18–10–15*		*26–2–39*	89–78–90–69
Oct 3 Thu	77–28–1	91–32–3	4–33	*18–10–15*		*26–2–39*	89–78–90–69
Oct 4 Fri	77–28–1	91–32–3	80–4–33	*18–10–15*	*15*	*26–2–39*	89–90–69
Oct 5 Sat	77–28–1	32–3	80–4–33	*18–26–10–15*	*15*	*26–2–39*	89–90–69
Oct 6 Sun	77–28–1	32–3	80–4–33	*18–26–10*	*15*	*26–2–39*	89–90–69
Oct 7 Mon	77–28–82	32–3	80–4	*18–26–10*	*15*	*26–2–39*	37–90–69
Oct 8 Tue	77–28–82	1–32–3	80–4	*33–29–18–26–10*	*15*	*79–2–39*	37–90–69
Oct 9 Wed	77–82	1–32–3	80–4	*33–29–18–26–10*	*15*	*79–2–39*	37–90–92
Oct 10 Thu	77–82	1–32–3	80–4	*33–29–18–26–10*	*15*	*79–2–39*	37–7–92
Oct 11 Fri	77–82	1–32–3	80–4	*33–29–18–26–10*	*15*	*79–2–39*	37–7–92

FIRST ARMY, LIGGETT · SECOND ARMY, BULLARD

Date	I Corps (Dickman)	V Corps (Summerall)	III Corps (Hines)	*XVII (French)*	*XXXIII (French)*	*II (French)*	IV Corps (Muir)
Oct 12 Sat	77–82	42–32	3–5–4	*33–29–18–26–10*	*15*	*79–2–39*	37–7–92
Oct 13 Sun	77–82	42–32	5–3–4	*33–29–18–26–10*	*15*	*79–2–39*	37–7–92
Oct 14 Mon	77–82	42–32	5–3–4	*33–29–18–26–10*	*15*	*79–2–39*	37–7–92
Oct 15 Tue	77–82	42–32	5–3–4	*33–29–18–26–10*	*35*	*79–2–39*	37–7–92
Oct 16 Wed	78–82	42–32	5–3–4	*33–29–18–26*	*10–35*	*79–2–39*	28–7–92
Oct 17 Thu	78–82	42–32	5–3–4	*33–29–18–26*	*10–35*	*79–2–39*	28–7–92
Oct 18 Fri	78–82	42–32	5–3–4	*33–29–26–26*	*10–35*	*79–39*	28–7–92

DAILY BATTLE FRONT OF AMERICAN DIVISIONS IN THE MEUSE-ARGONNE

French Corps and Divisions serving under Pershing, in italics

	[West] FIRST ARMY, LIGGETT					[East] SECOND ARMY, BULLARD		
	I Corps (Dickman)	V Corps (Summerall)	III Corps (Hines)	*XVII (French)*	*XXXIII (French)*	*II (French)*	IV Corps (Muir)	VI (Ballou)
Oct 19 Sat	78–82	42–32	5–3	*33–29–26–26*	*10–35*	*79–39*	28–7–92	
Oct 20 Sun	78–82	42–89	5–3	*33–29–26–26*	*10–35*	*79–39*	28–7–92	
Oct 21 Mon	78–82	42–89	5–3	*15–29–26–26*	*10–35*	*79–39*	28–7–92	
Oct 22 Tue	78–82	42–89	90–3	*15–29–26–26*	*10–35*	*79–39*	28–7–92	
Oct 23 Wed	78–82	42–89	90–3	*15–29–26–26*	*10–35*	*79–39*	28–7	92
Oct 24 Thu	78–82	42–89	90–3	*15–29–26–26*	*10–35*	*79–39*	28–7	92
Oct 25 Fri	78–82	42–89	90–3	*15–29–26–26*	*10–35*	*79–39*	28–7	92
Oct 26 Sat	78–82	42–89	90–3	*15–29–26–26*	*10–35*	*33–39*	28–7	92
Oct 27 Sun	78–82	42–89	90–5	*15–29–26–26*	*10–35*	*33–39*	28–7	92
Oct 28 Mon	78–82	42–89	90–5	*15–29–26–26*	*10–35*	*33–39*	28–7	92
Oct 29 Tue	78–82	42–89	90–5	*15–29–26–26*	*10–35*	*33*	28–7	92
Oct 30 Wed	78–82	42–89	90–5	*15–29–26–26*	*10–35*	*33*	28–7	92
Oct 31 Thu	78–77–80	42–89	90–5	*15–79–26–26*	*10–35*	*33*	28–7	92
Nov 1 Fri	78–77–80	2–89	90–5	*15–79–26–26–10–35*		*33*	28–7	92
Nov 2 Sat	78–77–80	2–89	90–5	*15–79–26–26–10–35*		*33*	28–7	92
Nov 3 Sun	78–77–80	2–89	90–5	*15–79–26–10–35*		*33*	28–7	92
Nov 4 Mon	78–77–80	2–89	90–5	*15–79–26–10–35*		*33*	28–7	92
Nov 5 Tue	42–77–80	2–89	90–5	*15–79–26–10–35*		*33*	28–7	92
				II (French)		*XVII (French)*		
Nov 6 Wed	42–77	2–89	90–5	*15–79–26–10–35*		*33*	28–7	92
Nov 7 Thu	[1]42–77	2–89	90–5	*15–79–26–10–81*		*33*	28–7	92
Nov 8 Fri	42–77	2–89	90–5	*15–79–26–10–81*		*33*	28–7	92
Nov 9 Sat	42–77	2–89	90–5	*15–79–26–10–81*		*33*	28–7	92
Nov 10 Sun	77–2–89		90–5–32	*15–79–26–10–81*		*33*	28–7	92
Nov 11 Mon	77–2–89		90–5–32	*15–79–26–10–81*		*33*	28–7	92

other positions on the fighting fronts, from quiet sectors in Lorraine, from training areas where they had not yet learned how to function as divisions. They came with borrowed artillery, borrowed aircraft, borrowed tanks. Army trucks carried 428,000 of their men, with an average haul of forty-eight miles. In all, 600,000 troops were moved into the line to replace 220,000 who had held it until now.

The railways and the roads that carried them had to have each its time-table and its military police to handle traffic at every intersection. The movements had to be in as profound secrecy and silence as are possible in a war where the enemy has eyes in the air and tapped telephone wires on the ground. At St. Mihiel military necessity had compelled the use of four out of nine divisions that had not seen battle. Four out of nine, again, as the line was arranged for the morning of September 26, had had no more experience than could be got from trench occupation on an inactive sector.

The arrangements for the general advance, in which the A.E.F. was to co-operate, assigned to the First Army a zone extending from the western edge of the Argonne Forest eastwardly to the Moselle, where some of the American divisions were still on guard along the new line established after St. Mihiel. Over some ninety-four miles of front, Pershing was in command; but the ninety-four miles broke down into three sections of variant character. The moving front, twenty-four miles, ran from the junction with Gouraud to the Meuse River, nine miles as the crow flies below Verdun. East of the Meuse, the fortified area around Verdun was occupied by the Seventeenth French Army Corps, for which no immediate advance was contemplated. Farther east, the Second French and the Fourth American Army Corps (each embracing troops of both nationalities) held a generally quiet line, with the Fourth Corps (Dickman) having its right on the Moselle.

It was behind the moving front, ready to slip into position as few hours as possible before the guns began, that the nine American divisions were prepared for the 'jump-off.' They were lined up:

77th–28th–35th	91st–37th–79th	4th–80th–33d
First Corps	Fifth Corps	Third Corps
Liggett	Cameron	Bullard

Each of the divisions had its mission, described in orders and illustrated with maps which, unhappily, would not always check with the terrain. Each had before it a 'no-man's-land,' almost without roads, beyond which lay the enemy. Each had an objective, to be reached over unfamiliar country. There had been little reconnoitering, since reconnaissance on any large scale would have advertised intention to the enemy. And each corps was held to the rule that any advance beyond the objective named in the orders was forbidden.

The line of the A.E.F. began on the left with the 77th, 28th, and 35th Divisions, constituting the First Army Corps (Liggett). Of these, the 77th, whose affectionate commander, Major-General Robert Alexander, characterized his men as 'hardy backwoodsmen from the Bowery, Fifth Avenue, and Hester Street,' was to hold the forest while the other divisions of the corps should 'reduce the *Forêt d'Argonne* by flanking it from the east.' The 77th took off in the middle of twenty-two miles of a forest six miles wide, covering the hogback between the Aisne and its tributary, the Aire. Until the common front should have been pushed north of the forest and the junction of the rivers just beyond it, the hogback would constitute a bastion impeding operations. Alexander had four and a half miles of divisional front, and discovered, once started on his way, that the flanking process was a failure. Neither the French division on his left nor the 28th Division on his right could do on schedule the work assigned it. Gouraud had troubles of his own; and the portion of the 92d Division charged with maintaining connection between his right and the left of Alexander failed to connect. The New York troops (New York, by courtesy only, since at the last minute the 77th had absorbed nearly 4000 replacements, mostly California men) found themselves bound to flounder through the forest, picking out by hand and in detail the enemy that should have been flanked from his ravines and machine-gun nests. It continued at the task through fifteen days of uninterrupted work, in a little war of its own, without contact on either flank. It had its high spot when a New York lawyer, Whittlesey by name, found himself with a lone battalion ahead of the divisional line, and isolated. Whittlesey dug in, and defied the world (in the form of German guns on all four sides) until after six days the line caught up to him. Famed as the 'lost battalion,' his battalion was never lost. It knew only too well just where it was, and its division knew. It put up white signs for aircraft beacons; and when the enemy construed these as overtures for surrender, it pulled them down, and preferred to starve until relieved.

Next to the 77th, the 28th Division (Pennsylvania, National Guard) undertook to advance down the right edge of the Argonne Forest, on the left bank of the Aire. The 35th (Missouri, Kansas, National Guard), new to fighting, was across the Aire to its right. Working as a team, the two were commissioned to flank the enemy out of the hogback; it being assumed that Gouraud, on the other side of the Argonne Forest, would carry out his half of the flanking operation, until the German troops occupying the bastion should be withdrawn from their untenable position. The 35th, at the right of the First Corps, was also to maintain contact with the left of the Fifth Corps (Cameron). From Vauquois, immediately in front of the 35th at the 'jump-off,' to Varennes, two miles north, where the main road crosses the Aire and descends the river on its right bank, the team advanced. But the Germans in the forest, far from being flanked out, discovered that the enemy had advanced into easy range. Deadly gunfire from the left cut across the 28th and the 35th. What was intended to be carried with a rush had to be taken in detail. The left of the 28th could not get far enough into the forest to establish liaison with the right of the 77th. The advance of the First Army, on its left, bogged down.

Cameron's Corps (Fifth) was expected to make the major advance. The hill, Montfaucon, four miles in front of it was the immediate objective. Before great reinforcements could be thrown into the German line, it was hoped to reach the road beyond Montfaucon which cut across between the Aire and the Meuse,

from Varennes to Dun-sur-Meuse, and to take Romagne —
heights, forest, and village. On the line of the Fifth Corps were
the 91st (Pacific Coast, National Army), 37th ('Buckeye,' the
Ohio National Guard), and 79th (Middle States, National Guard)
Divisions, none of which had been in action. Pershing thought it
reasonable 'to count on the vigor and the aggressive spirit of our
troops,' and let these take the place of 'technical skill.' The initial
orders of the corps assigned it more than could be accomplished
in the time allowed. The ruins of the town of Montfaucon, after
the greatest of American battles had swept across them, were to
provide a site for the most impressive of the American war memori-
als in France. On the outskirts of Romagne-sous-Montfaucon,
the geometric ranks of fourteen thousand marble crosses were to
tell something of the story of the men who fought in the battle and
remained forever in France. The height of Montfaucon, at the
least a dangerous enemy observation post, proved to be a center of
resistance, holding back the Fifth Corps long enough for the
whole German front to be stiffened. Stiffened here, and held persistently in the Argonne, the German line prevented the First
Army from completing in a rush the first operation which was to
have set up a new line north of the Argonne, from Grandpré to
Romagne, ten miles from the 'jump-off.'

The Third Corps (Bullard) came into position at the right of
Cameron, with a mission to pivot on the Meuse. At its left, the
4th Division (which had taken part at St. Mihiel) made the longest
advance, with Montfaucon well on its left. The 80th Division at
the corps center, with drafted men mostly from Virginia, swung to
the right as it advanced, until it faced the Meuse. The 33d (Bell,
Illinois, National Guard) pivoted on its own right, through ninety
degrees, until it was lined along the Meuse and facing east. Only
the Third Corps reached its objective on time. Its order directed
it to 'assist in neutralizing hostile observation and hostile fire
from the heights east of the Meuse.' But just as the German guns
on the east slope of the Argonne ridge held to their stations to en-
filade the 28th and 35th, the other German guns, on the heights
east of the Meuse and not even attacked, enfiladed the Third

Corps from its right as its divisions changed the direction of the
First Army front.

The memoirs of the commanders and their official reports,
naturally enough, emphasize the dimensions of the accomplishment of the First Army when it went into action on the morning
of Thursday, September 26, 1918. Just as naturally they fail to
stress the difference between the hope of Chaumont while the
orders were being drafted and the reality in the field at the end of
the first, second, third, and fourth days of combat. The divisional
historians, and they are legion, dwell upon the difficulties due to
inexperience, poor liaison, slack team-work with the artillery, and
refractory terrain. Every mile gained made it harder to bring up
supplies and to evacuate the wounded. The artillery at the beginning had selected positions and acknowledged range. As divisions
advanced into the forests, not knowing themselves quite where
they were, the guns could not know how to cover them. As the
guns were advanced over roadless devastation, to catch-as-catch-
can new stations, the artillerymen were late in readiness to resume
their fire, and when ready were uncertain where to shoot. Signal
corps crews trailed wires to batteries and outposts with personal
heroism greater than their accuracy. Runners started with messages through the woods without getting to their destinations.
Officers lost their units. Units mislaid their posts of command.
The writers, loyal to their units, pass the buck, each to the flanking
divisions, for failure to keep step. From one side is stressed the inexperience of training-camp officers and the stubborn ineptness of
National Guard officers; from the other, the unfitness of many of
the Regulars who were ordered to relieve Guardsmen alleged to
have broken down. Pershing has described 'the vast network of
uncut barbwire, the deep ravines, dense woods, myriads of shell
craters, and a heavy fog' that impeded advance. The difficulties
of the first hours were chiefly due to these factors and to the factor
of inexperience, for Pershing testifies that 'the strength of the
attack came as a complete surprise to the enemy and his forward
positions were quickly overrun by our troops.'

At the end of four days the gains were great, though less than had been hoped; and to the west of the First Army the whole Allied front was busy at its task. The outcome of the initial push was a new line where German resistance had held it, fatigued divisions of which some had to be replaced, and a restive Foch who still believed that Pershing was less competent than another to command the American effort. A letter was sent, with Weygand to reinforce it, suggesting a change in mission and scope for the First Army. Let it surrender the divisions of its left to a French army that should command both sides of the Argonne, and let it concentrate what divisions remained upon its right, on both sides of the Meuse. The letter was written on Monday, September 30, the day after Clemenceau had followed up victory by visitation. He had started for Montfaucon, taken later than expected, yet taken on Friday. Prime Ministers were not welcome anywhere in the midst of battle or close behind a dangerous front, but the old man had insisted on going. He was turned back by traffic. In addition to the heavy congestion due to ordinary supply from rear to front, the First Division was making a difficult march across the lines serving the Fifth Corps to a new station at the right of the First Corps. A less experienced observer than Clemenceau, and a less stubborn one (for he liked to do what he liked to do), might have been forgiven for carrying home the notion that American supply had broken down. Between Sunday, when Clemenceau saw the jam, and the next Friday, the service of the front was obscured by the cloud of traffic as tired divisions were pulled back and relief divisions were sent ahead. Pershing was clear in his vision of what was happening and what he proposed to do. There was no compliance with the suggestion Weygand discussed with Pershing on October 1. There was no pressure from Washington for compliance. Baker, in Europe on the business of the 1919 campaign and fresh from exposure to all the British arguments for amalgamation, wrote to Pershing on October 2 the comforting words: 'that the American Army as such was the thing we were trying to create.' He had been blunt with Lloyd George, telling him that 'we had no intention of feeding our soldiers into the French or British Army.'

The Argonne and the Meuse remained for the American commander essential parts of an indivisible whole and his army remained his own. The line between the 77th and the 33d constituted the base of a triangle, whose right side was the River Meuse, and at whose apex forty-five miles ahead was Mézières. Instead of breaking the unity of the operation by assenting to the detachment of his left, Pershing drew upon his reserves to reconstitute his line. The 77th was allowed to work out its mission in the Argonne. The 28th was left in place, patched with dependable Regular officers. The 35th, which had gone to pieces as, with both flanks exposed, it had pushed for four days down the Aire, was withdrawn, to be sent after rebuilding to a quiet sector. In its place the 1st Division, which had been held in army reserve, was pushed in between the 28th and the 91st. The 37th was replaced by the more experienced 32d, and before the end of October it was dispatched with the 91st to the assistance of the King of the Belgians. The 79th was replaced by the 3d Division, of Château-Thierry fame. The 80th was temporarily withdrawn.

Delayed, but not at all dismayed, Pershing prepared to resume advance in force. The enemy had imposed upon him a line and had reinforced it. On his left the 77th was still to be brought out of the forest to Grandpré. In his center the heights of Romagne blocked the advance of the Fifth Corps, as it faced the Kriemhilde *Stellung*. On his right, the Third Corps, with some eight miles of front along the Meuse, was under continuous gunfire from German batteries. The line of Grandpré–Romagne had to be established and the German guns had to be dislodged east of the Meuse, before the next grand phase of his battle could be undertaken. He held stubbornly to Mézières–Sedan as his destination, but until he could construct a smoothed front, until Gouraud should project it to the west, and until the heights of the Meuse should be in Allied hands, he could not advance upon it. He depleted his reserves by lending Gouraud the 2d and 36th Divisions, and he counted on the line before him twenty-seven depleted German divisions, all of which were smaller than his when they were full. He had in the A.E.F. on September 30, 71,172 officers, 1,634,220 enlisted men.

On October 4 he struck again with his line repaired and with all participants educated by the experiences of the first week to the supreme necessity for liaison. There were eight divisions on his revised front, still in the same three army corps:

77th–28th–1st	32d–3d	80th–4th–33d
First Corps	Fifth Corps	Third Corps
Liggett	Cameron	Bullard

He was approaching now the complicated positions of the Hindenburg Line. The four great defense positions of the German armies, converging upon Metz, were far enough apart at the western end of the Allied front to permit regions of relatively open country between them. There was some room for maneuver. But at Pershing's end, where the positions were packed together east of the Aisne, the rear of one was interlocked with the front of the one behind it. The most advanced was the line attacked on September 26. The second ran through Montfaucon. The third, the Kriemhilde *Stellung*, cutting across on the line Grandpré–Romagne–Brieulles, had been picked by the First Army as the limit of its first operation. Beyond it, the fourth and last, in front of Buzancy and Dun-sur-Meuse, became increasingly important to Germany as the others fell. What had been hoped to be carried in a rush was not yet gained when after refurbishing the First Army advanced on October 4. It took a second period of rush, pause, reorganization, and attack on October 14, before Grandpré and Romagne were in American hands. And after this, yet another period of rebuilding the line and reorganizing the rear before at the end of October the drive on Buzancy could be prelude to breaking through.

During the ten days after October 4 the active American line was lengthened, and by freeing each of its ends it gave its center greater freedom. The 77th at the left, plugging along down the hogback of the Argonne, was given help. On October 7 the 82d Division (All-American), which had been held in army reserve, was inserted in the line of the First Corps between the 28th and 1st Divisions, that the three by increasing pressure down the Aire Valley toward St. Juvin might pinch the Germans out of the northern extremity of the Argonne Forest. Coming in with the 82d was Sergeant Alvin C. York, Tennessee mountaineer and conscientious objector, who proved to be almost a division in himself. On his second day in the woods, bothered by German machine-gun nests, he set off in a party of seventeen to smoke them out. Casualties whittled his squad to eight and lifted him to its command. Almost single-handed he reported back to his unit, having impressed a German officer as his interpreter. His captive, who understood English because he had worked in Chicago, understood better the language of York's gun in the small of his back. Through his willing interpreter York had ordered out of their trenches and nests one hundred and thirty-two prisoners, and compelled them to carry into the American lines thirty-five German machine guns, and the wounded Americans. He was back on duty the next day, to have his story extracted from him by cross-examination, and in due time to have Foch commend his feat as the 'greatest thing accomplished by any private soldier of all of the armies.' On October 10 the 77th came out of the woods so that it could look down upon the Aire and Grandpré after what its historian designates as the 'Wilderness Campaign.'

On the same day that the 82d joined the line the 33d Division was transferred from the Third Corps to the French Seventeenth, on its right. On October 8 the 29th Division ('Blue and Gray,' with Guardsmen from Middle States and Virginia) was put in between the 33d and its French neighbor; and the Seventeenth Corps moved over the Verdun battlefield of 1916, to clear the heights of the Meuse. In the next week the heights were cleared, relieving the divisions west of the Meuse from the murderous enfilading fire of German guns. The operation east of the Meuse lengthened Pershing's active front, costing him troops. But it cost the enemy more, since it tied more German divisions into active defense of the 'vital pivot' of the German line.

With the battle spreading out before the A.E.F. and with an extension of activity east of the Moselle under consideration, the Second Army was created on October 12. Liggett of the First

Corps, promoted to succeed Pershing in command of the First Army, was nominated to Washington to be lieutenant-general, and made way for Major-General Joseph T. Dickman to command the left. Bullard, from the Third Corps, was given the Second Army and similar promotion, making room for Major-General John L. Hines. Cameron of the Fifth Corps was allowed to go back to the command of his old 4th Division, making room for Major-General Charles P. Summerall. The new commanders were finding their way to their new stations, while the front was undergoing revision for the new wave of advance of October 14. When Liggett took actual command of the First Army on October 16, Pershing reverted to his single status as commander of the A.E.F.; now for the first time he became in fact a General of the Armies.

As the commands changed, Pershing was satisfied that the First Army carried out a splendid achievement in a battle 'suddenly conceived' and 'hurried in plan,' fought in harsh weather, against a desperate enemy, with inexperienced troops. Every division in the line needed to recuperate. Everywhere there were local operations designed to 'secure a suitable line of departure' for the next advance. Even the raw divisions had been carried well along the route to veteran status in the eighteen days preceding the fresh advance. Liggett found his divisions under corps commanders promoted, as he had been, upon confidence in their proved capacity:

77th–82d	42d–32d	5th–3d–4th	33d–29th, plus French
First Corps	Fifth Corps	Third Corps	XVII French Corps
Dickman	Summerall	Hines	(east of Meuse)

The end was in sight by mid-October, when the line advanced again. Army headquarters could sense its nearness, and Haig, who had hoped hard enough for it in early summer, thought he had foretold it. London, Paris, and Washington were conscious of its approach. In Washington Republican leaders, searching for an issue, were pointing up their demands for 'unconditional surrender,' while in Berlin the obvious end was determining policy.

An Austrian feeler for informal discussion of terms of peace was brushed aside in September; 'declined in sixty-eight words,' as the *Christian Science Monitor* reported Lansing's brusque statement that the United States had already stated the terms. An altered German Government had approached Washington, asking for a conference. The Fourteen Points, nonsense to Germany in January, 1918, had by September become the one anchor to windward. It could not be known until the German archives disgorged their papers that on the fourth day of the Meuse–Argonne, while Clemenceau was grumbling about the crowded road to Montfaucon, von Hindenburg had notified the Imperial Chancellor that peace must be sought at once; or that on the seventh day he had conceded that there was 'no longer any possible hope of forcing' it. Between hunger and dissension at home and relentless pressure along the line of battle, the German front was crumbling. There was general German retreat, retarded with desperate military skill only where such retardation was essential lest retreat should turn into rout and compel surrender in the field. The one great hope was to get the armies home. That the absence of a surrender could in twenty years be distorted into a voluntary cessation of attack was more than any responsible German could have conceived. The officers of the Imperial General Staff knew the facts, admitted them to each other and to the Imperial Government, and hoped without believing that they might by bluff of resistance deceive the Allies into a peace negotiated as though with free agents.

Germany suffered military defeat, with events along the Allied Western front determining the time and place. The naval front was real enough; so real that the high seas were a liability to Germany rather than an asset. It did not take a victorious naval engagement to spell victory here. In no other war had the possibilities of an economic front been conceived or explored. This new front made life nearly as impossible for the neutral as for the lesser of the belligerents. No longer a status in which a powerful nation could remain at peace, neutrality became but a position to be held until the weight of events should indicate to the neutral which enemy it must resist. And beyond the economic front, where a victory was won, lay the even less tangible front of the human mind. Here, too, campaigns were planned and carried out, and according to the degree of their success helped by October to undermine the foundations of the German military power.

There is no way of proving cause and consequence in matters of the mind. Subsequent action may be established and may plausibly be connected with an alleged cause, but the line of connection remains only circumstantial, however plausible it may appear. It is fact that Caporetto was preceded by a flood of German propaganda within the ranks of the armies of Italy; and it is fact as well that subsequently many of the Italian units folded up. The connection may be causal, but the historian cannot prove it. It is fact that the Allied mind was imbued with the idea that the Imperial German Government had precipitated a war of conquest for its own advantage, naming the very day. To this was added the fact that the President of the United States, urging a 'peace without victory,' had drawn repeatedly a distinction between the German *people*, against whom he professed no war, and their *Government* which he alleged to have brought them to disaster. Propaganda, a weapon of the war, as definitely designed to break down the will to war as any other weapon, was continuously used by every Government at war. Its primary purpose was the amalgamation of a national will to win the war. Its secondary purpose was to break down the will to win of the people of the enemy.

There was little in the Allied propaganda, built around the charge of attempt at conquest and a situation of alleged atrocities, that had value for the secondary purpose of breaking German unity. But there was much in that of Wilson. His series of public statements, before 1917 and after, gilded the picture of a fair world, without war. His emphasis upon the handful of persons constituting the German Government as the devils of the machine produced documents likely to appeal to common folk, hungry and bereft, and to bring about results weakening their loyalty to that Government as the German front fell back. Wilson had two motives as he laid down American doctrine: one, to make it harder for the Allies to ask for a peace unable to win American support; the other, to divert the attention of enemy peoples and troops from the channels of their own national propaganda. It may be believed, though it may not be proved, that he succeeded in the latter purpose.

George Creel was his agent for this purpose. From the Committee on Public Information there went to Europe a flood of press releases comparable to that which had drenched the United States from Europe in pre-war years. He planted his agents in the Allied and neutral capitals to disseminate the American version of the truth. He reached the Allied mind with print, picture shows, and oratory. *Pershing's Crusaders* and *America's Answer* (official films) raised some of the hopes in France and Britain that Pershing found it so difficult to fulfill. It was Creel's belief that the best propaganda, if he could get it past the German censor, was the fact of American reinforcement and the doctrine of Woodrow Wilson. In July, 1918, while the various war boards were holding their 'round tables' with colleagues in Europe, Creel had one held in Paris, upon ways and means of getting propaganda into Germany. Advertisement in neutral papers helped. Translations of dodgers into the languages of enemy belligerents was undertaken; smuggling them into Germany and Austria was harder, but was accomplished. Dropped in loose bundles by aircraft, they settled down upon soldiers in the trenches. He once sent 400,000 greetings floated by paper balloons, east across the Belgian border; but he had to lament that he could not always trust the winds, and occasionally propaganda intended for Alsace came down in Kent. When the German people set up a cry for peace, based upon the Fourteen Points, it was partly Creel who had explained the Fourteen Points and by explaining them had diverted some of the German mind from conquest. The prisoners who streamed over the Allied lines during the autumn drive produced propaganda leaflets when their pockets were searched. Army Intelligence picked up German orders imposing drastic penalties upon soldiers even picking up papers from the ground. It is impossible to repudiate a connection like that between cause and effect. That the weakening of the German will to win was one of the victories, on one of the fronts of war, is plausible at least. But it was on the army front that Germany lost the war.

Liggett took over from Pershing the command of the First Army two days after it had resumed the drive on October 14, with its line not yet as far advanced as Pershing had hoped to get it in the first operation of the battle. From the heights of the Meuse to the Channel the position changed each day. That line in France, where von Hindenburg and Ludendorff had once expected to come to rest for one more winter, had vanished repeatedly before the German armies reached it. Even better than the Allied strategists, who could look at the map, read on it the line of the moving front, the immobile line of the railroads, and the barrier of the Belgian Highlands at the German rear, the German strategists knew that once the railroad was broken their armies could not be withdrawn and would lie at the mercy of the enemy. They placed no confidence in that mercy and surrendered at home before they yielded at the front. They advised the political leaders to seek shelter in the phrases of Woodrow Wilson. He had spoken eloquently about 'peace without victory.' What they needed now was 'peace without defeat'; and that on any terms.

The Allied line, just lengthened by Pershing's operations east of the Meuse, was correspondingly shortened by German withdrawal on the left, in the first days of Liggett's command. Moving too rapidly to make a stand, to evacuate *matériel*, or even to destroy all of it, the enemy pulled back toward the French frontier and the road home through Liége. Albert entered Ostend on October 17; Lille was evacuated by the eighteenth; and the streams of German prisoners testified to the willingness of German soldiers to end their individual war on any pretext. Across the front from Haig's armies resistant evacuation was the order of the day. The way out through Belgium started at Maubeuge. In front of the French armies, and along the Aisne, the withdrawal was slower and called for more hurrying by the Allies, because the Upper Aisne is near the Meuse. But here, too, there was withdrawal. The divisions of

Gouraud were turning the eastern end of the Chemin des Dames and opening for France the road to Mézières–Sedan. At the west end Mangin 'hustled' the enemy out of Laon on October 14, with time only to loot the city, not to destroy it. Liaison with the American left was established near Grandpré just as the 77th worked its way out of the forest. Hence to Sedan was a matter of twenty-four miles. Pétain had been unimaginative when he advised Pershing that Montfaucon was quite as far as the A.E.F. might hope to advance before winter.

Liggett took over the conduct of the drive which he found under way on a front where the enemy made few voluntary withdrawals. Before the next general advance could be arranged there were local corrections to be made, or completed, in the face of each division. The whole line was held back by the hilly country west of Romagne, which must be occupied before any concerted push could be directed against the last of the great fortified positions in the vicinity of Buzancy.

Romagne itself was taken on the fourteenth. And on the same day the Côte Dame Marie, which Pershing described as 'perhaps the most important strong point of the Hindenburg Line on the Western Front,' the 'dominating feature' of the Romagne heights, was stormed by the 32d Division, in Summerall's Fifth Corps. Around the Côte Dame Marie and across the highways converging on Romagne, and around Romagne, ran the works of the Kriemhilde *Stellung*. The hills were a natural fortress even before they were covered with trenches and enmeshed in wire. To the 32d, which had been working continuously on its problem of ejection since October 8, the starting of the new drive made no difference: the old drive had not stopped. The change of corps commanders was unimportant, since Summerall, until his elevation, had commanded the 1st Division, working with the 32d, at its left. Worn out for the moment, the 1st Division was replaced by the 42d Division for the final assault on the position. When a regiment of the 32d dashed across the top of Dame Marie, after nightfall of the fourteenth of October, it found 'the wicked machine-gun nests deserted by all but the dead.' With Romagne hill within American lines, Liggett's center could mop up and get ready to move again.

The left was corrected on and after the fourteenth, when the Aire between Grandpré and St. Juvin along with both of these towns, was brought within the front. The 77th, replaced by the 78th, took a needed rest, only to be brought back to relieve the 82d when the advance began again. East of the Meuse, on Liggett's extreme right, there were only local changes to be made on the extension of the front established by the 33d and 29th Divisions. The next mission of the First Army was to clear the country north of the Aire, whose 'wooded bluffs and mutually supporting spurs' made it as easy as it was supremely important to hold it; and to drive the enemy east across the Meuse.

There was no more room on the American front for additional divisions to be brought into action, although the Atlantic Ferry had in October contributed a net increase to the A.E.F. of 162,000 men, so that Pershing could note 76,800 officers and 1,790,823 in the ranks. The divisions that were concentrated on the line, with corps and army troops behind them, covered the country. Concentrated as heavily as space would allow, the troops were concentrated more heavily than would have been prudent had the war been expected to last indefinitely. Harbord, at Tours, complained that the Services of Supply were undermanned below the point of safety. Officer shortage compelled Chaumont to rob non-combatant units of their officers, as line officers fell in battle. Ocean tonnage was failing to deliver to France the material requirements now that the battle had taken on its grand dimensions. The Commander in Chief, with the immediate existence of his army on his soul, had to save corners of his mind for the extension of battle activity in the near future and for its continuance in 1919 should the enemy show power of resistance. To the War Department he had cabled on October 3: 'Unless supplies are furnished when and as called for, our armies will cease to operate.' Clemenceau had again tried to get rid of him, citing to Foch *'son invincible obstination'*; and Foch had blocked an appeal to Wilson for a new commander.

It is customary among military historians to write of that phase of the advance which began on November 1, 1918, as the final phase. It proved to be final; but it should be remembered that to those who took part in it the end of the war was still uncertain in both time and space. No one could avoid knowing that events were in train whose results might be the end of the war, but that knowledge of necessity for instant peace, which inspired German action, could not be more than suspected by the enemies of Germany. When at last it came, the completeness of the German collapse went far beyond expectation. At the end of October, with no confidence in the sincerity of the enemy in proposing a truce, it was necessary for the Allies to consider terms upon which a cessation of the drive might be profitable; but it was hard even to hope that Germany would assent to the only terms which the Allies, with victory in sight, must certainly demand.

Strategically, it was natural to suppose that when service on the field railroads should be interrupted the German armies would be endangered, and that they would be unable to make another serious stand until they should reach new posts along the Rhine. But it was supposed that the enemy commanders would somehow get their armies out of France. The Allied counter, growing in spread and intensity every week, warranted a hope that France and Belgium might be cleared before winter. There would come a time when that law of the salient, which bears down upon the victor as his rear gets clogged with patchwork roads and half-repaired railways, would operate against the Allies to slow them down. But victory was inspiring the Allies, as lack of it was demoralizing the enemy. The request sent through Switzerland to the United States, October 5, begging truce pending the negotiation of a peace on Wilson's terms was distrusted as a trick. With Allied armies gaining ground each day and with Germany retreating in increasing disorder, it was essential to continue to make gains while they came easily. Intermission or truce would at least permit the enemy to regain breath; at worst, it might enable him to make a new stand and prolong the war.

The Allied commanders proceeded to advise Foch on terms that would spell victory, whatever they should be called, while pressing the war as though Germany was to be beaten back to the Rhine and defeated on German soil. Liggett had for his immediate mission the reoccupation of the line of the railroad and the forcing of the enemy army back of the Meuse. The A.E.F. was ready and anxious to proceed upon the road to Metz. East of the Moselle, encircling Metz, Foch had in contemplation an extension of the active front. For this, Bullard, with half a dozen American divisions, was selected to co-operate with twenty French divisions under Mangin. The name of Second Army was to be taken with its commander into this adventure. The American troops on the inactive line between the heights of the Meuse and the Moselle, which had constituted the Second Army since October 12, were redesignated as the Third Army. Dickman of the First Corps was assigned to lead them. Orders shifting him to his new command were issued November 7; Bullard's engagement was dated for November 14.

It was not until October 23 that President Wilson notified the German Government that he had transmitted to the Allies its overture for an armistice. He did not promise that the Allies would give assent, but made it clear that there would not be any cessation of hostilities on terms that would permit Germany to resume the war, and that the military terms of any armistice would be drafted by the Allied command, which meant Foch. House, as Wilson's agent, was already at sea, hurrying to take the place of the President at such meetings of the Supreme War Council as might be necessary. He reached Paris on October 26, a day after Foch had assembled his commanders at Senlis, now his headquarters, to discuss the military language in which they should write their determination that Germany should not resume the war. Pershing attended with the others, convinced that 'surrender of the German armies' should be demanded, and willing to consider less only if the political leaders should so decide. He found Haig believing that Germany was capable of considerable resistance on a reduced front. He found Foch wary, with Germany at bay, yet convinced that the German army was, 'physically and morally, thoroughly beaten.' To Foch and House he pressed the point that any arrangement should provide 'guaranties against a resumption of hostilities.'

Pershing used the word armistice, as all did; and unfortunately. The only reasonable meaning of the word contains the implication of an unchanged ability on the part of both parties to resume a contest, after an interruption of hostilities. What Pershing and Foch and their associates had in mind, and what Germany was being driven relentlessly to accept, was something other than armistice. It contained all the substance of an unconditional surrender, lacking only the actual transfer to the victor of custody of the troops of the vanquished. No other word in modern times has, by its misapplication, caused the world so much trouble as this word armistice.

The commanders drafted the memorandum on military terms, while the Supreme War Council held its first formal session on October 31. 'We can continue it if the enemy desires it to his complete defeat,' said Foch, presenting the draft, to which the political leaders added political and diplomatic annexes. Not until November 4 was the last comma in place, so that the Supreme War Council could formally endorse the terms. The next day Woodrow Wilson notified the enemy, not of the terms, but of the readiness of the Generalissimo to deliver terms to the agents of the defeated enemy, should he be asked directly for them.

Pershing, meanwhile, went back to his two armies, with the project for the third ready for announcement, and in agreement with Foch that if the negotiations should fail or be a fraud no advantage should be allowed the enemy because of them. His latest reinforcement was on hand. Rear-Admiral C. P. Plunkett, with his fourteen-inch naval guns, had come ashore. Two of the guns, with the French, had ranged the yards at Laon before that city was abandoned. Others were in the rear of the American armies ready to be used. With the operation on Metz in view, two were assigned stations east of Nancy, to get the range of the eastern projection of the railroad beyond Metz. Two were brought down the Meuse below Verdun, and threw their shells into the yards at Longuyon and Montmédy, interrupting communication between Sedan and

Metz. On November 1, as scheduled, the advance began upon what could not until a later date be described as the last operation of the war. Italy had on October 24 resumed activity on the Caporetto front, a year to the day after the *débâcle* of 1917. Bulgaria and Turkey were down and out, in unconditional surrender; and it was only a matter of hours until Austria-Hungary should follow them.

John Buchan — Lord Tweedsmuir — has recorded his opinion that now began the hardest part of Pershing's task. Between the front of November 1 and the line of the Meuse the country continued rough and nearly roadless, even though less infested with fortified positions than the region south of Buzancy. The American troops were better skilled than when they began on September 26, but had lost their freshness. They were so closely crowded on the field that only superior liaison kept them from mutual interference; and as they crossed each other's lines in the rear they created hopeless confusion. To take advantage of the opportunity they must press ahead, each as far as possible, without waiting to rebuild — or build — the roads behind them; and the farther they got ahead, the greater the hazard if things went wrong. Much was to be risked if the war was to be won now.

When Liggett moved once more, he had again rearranged the units of the First Army:

78th–77th–80th	2d–89th	90th–5th	79th–26th–35th
First Corps	Fifth Corps	Third Corps	(plus Fr. *15, 26, 10*)
Dickman	Summerall	Hines	XVII French Corps
			east of Meuse

The First Army and Gouraud's French army to its left were in a close co-operation now that Gouraud had successfully reached the Aisne. From Attigny (where the 36th Division had on October 27 completed the assignment which it had shared with the 2d) to the extreme right, where the French 15th and the American 79th were to widen the front east of the Meuse, was a single operation. Its intent was to drive the enemy across the Meuse, away from his railroad, and up against the barrier of the hills in

Belgium and Luxemburg. Orders as to objectives had been changed. The program of limited objectives that had dominated thus far had been replaced by one of unlimited advance in the direction of the attack. Foch had published the new doctrine as a tactical suggestion; Pershing had antedated him in instructions issued to the First Army.

Across the American front, from the Meuse near Dun-sur-Meuse and through Buzancy, ran a ridge whose occupation would bring the Lower Meuse in sight and flank the German armies. The Fifth Corps faced Buzancy, in the center. The First Corps, with the Bois de Bourgogne on its left, maintained such connection as it could with the French army, with the line of the army limit running east of north from the Bois de Bourgogne to the Meuse opposite Sedan. The Third Corps, next the Meuse, had still the duty to pivot on its right until it faced the river between Brieulles and Stenay, to cross the river, and to push on with Montmédy and Longuyon as possible objectives. Pershing was human enough to wish the war might last until he had justified his program by gaining both Sedan and Metz.

The last fortified German front was broken on November 1 and four days later it had disappeared. There was no German strength left for serious counter-attacks. The divisions abandoned or were driven from their positions in quick succession, while the High Command published for home consumption the cryptic *communiqué*: 'We have readjusted our position to a depth of ten miles.'

On the extreme left, Dickman's First Corps found no enemy on its front after the first day of the new advance, and hurried in trucks and with motor-cycle units to pursue the retreating German rear over country whose roads did not invite such methods of pursuit. Liggett bewailed the absent arm for which the war had had no room, the cavalry. Advance was here, and now, a matter for the 'traffic cops' and was hastened when, on November 5, there came to Dickman a memorandum from Drum, chief of staff for Liggett: 'General Pershing desires that the honor of entering Sedan should fall to the First Army.' Sedan was beyond the zone of the First Army, on the right margin of the French; but Pershing's hopes were less orderly than his assignment. 'Boundaries,' Drum wrote, 'will not be considered as binding.'

The work of the First Corps was nearly done, since action was to pause along the new line stabilized on the Meuse while Mangin and Bullard took it up to the east of the Moselle. Dickman's 78th Division was withdrawn from his line November 5, and his 80th left for new duties on November 6. The 42d replaced the 78th for five days and was gone on November 8, when even the First Corps organization disappeared. Dickman was on his way to his Third Army, while the Fifth Corps absorbed what were left of his First Corps troops. The French had claimed and taken the Meuse sector opposite Sedan.

Working in front of Buzancy, the Fifth Corps carried its ridge with the 2d and 89th Divisions, Harbord noting the fact that there were now no National Guard Divisions on the aggressive line. The Third Corps had the Meuse to cross. On its left was the 90th Division; on its right the 5th, which had corrected the line by occupying Brieulles on October 30, was at the river. The railroad here, the local line from Verdun to Sedan, ran down the left bank of the Meuse. Across the river, on the east, was the Meuse canal, and each of the waterways called for pontoon bridges to be constructed under fire. By November 3 the 5th Division was across the river at Brieulles and two days later it had made another crossing at Dun-sur-Meuse. The 90th swung with it, lagging a little, carrying the corps front down the river to the outskirts of Stenay. By November 7 both were plunging east of the Meuse, 'against the enemy' as Foch had suggested, 'in the direction of attack.' They were within six miles of Montmédy when the Armistice checked their course on November 11.

After November 5 the American advance was a free pursuit of an enemy who could do no more than worry overeager pursuers from his rear, as he sought safety. The west of the Meuse had been cleared well below Stenay, while the First and Fifth Corps were also pivoting toward the east and the hills along the river, and while the French had become nervous lest others than themselves should take Sedan. The pursuit was so one-sided that by November 7 Pershing could safely give directions to 'use lights on all motor transport'; and the advantage was so great as to justify orders to unit commanders to 'push troops forward wherever resistance is broken, without regard for fixed objectives and without fear for their flanks.'

The spirit of the A.E.F. and the words of the commander account for one of the most remarkable maneuvers of the war, and one for which success has perhaps quashed the indictment. The 1st Division, out of the line since October 12, came back. From a position in reserve behind the central corps, the Fifth, it pushed out of the corps sector on the afternoon of November 6, occupying the right of the First Corps, whence the 80th had just been withdrawn. Someone misconceived his orders; whether at the issuing or the receiving end, remaining still in the dark. But through the night of November 6 the 1st Division made a forced march across the rear of its next neighbor to the left, the 77th; and the next left neighbor, the 42d; blocking the roads and delaying the advance of both. On November 7 it raced with the 42d 'for the possession of the heights south and west of Sedan.' Nothing quite like it had occurred in an American army since on the night of June 23, 1898, the First Volunteer Cavalry had marched through the Cuban jungle to a battle-front of its own choosing, the next morning, at Las Guasimas.

On the heights west of Sedan, with guns completely commanding the city and the German railroad, in a sector reserved by the French but not yet reached by them, the First Army came to its goal. That day, the field receiving sets picked up a radio from Foch, *via* the Eiffel Tower station, directing the enemy how emissaries 'requesting from him an armistice' could safely cross the lines to reach him. The naughty division, peremptorily ordered back, disappeared from the active front. That afternoon, unfounded news that the Armistice had been signed was cabled from Brest by the United Press. Roy W. Howard, who signed the message, has managed to escape moral responsibility for the error; but the United States broke out at once in riotous celebration of the 'false armistice,' only to learn that rejoicing was premature.

The German envoys, delayed in crossing the lines, came to Foch in his *wagon-lit* on the morning of November 8, stood embarrassed until Foch had compelled them to say they had come asking for peace, and received from him the ultimatum prepared by the Allied command. Seventy-two hours later, in the last minutes of the expiring time limit, they signed as the Armistice what in any proper military sense was the equivalent of unconditional surrender. At 11 A.M., Monday, November 11, 1918, the American reinforcement passed into history. The German Emperor was a political refugee seeking hospitality from the Dutch, and the German people, by revolution, had taken over the conduct of their own affairs.

XIX. PEACE AND POLITICS

THERE is reason to believe that the military share of the United States in the defeating of the Central Powers was great. Without the weight of the American armies to reinforce the line of the Allies, and without the pressure which they exerted upon the sector most vital to the continued operation of German armies in France, it is not easy to see how Germany could have been brought to terms acceptable to those who fought. Without this weight it is quite possible to conceive of a German military victory and a peace imposed by the Imperial German Government. Any estimate of the human significance of the Armistice must take into account the conjectural relative values to the world of a victorious Germany or a Germany not victorious.

But the military contribution that helped make possible a defeat of Germany months — or years — ahead of prophecy was a less significant factor in victory than was the American contribution to ideas. Washington alone was not bound by the Pact of Paris. The United States alone was not paralyzed by a fear of conquest or a requirement for security. The President of the United States, alone among the rulers, was able to think and speak of a world that ought to be, and by his position of disinterest to give voice to a vision of double purpose. The concept of a 'world safe for democracy,' illusory, perhaps, was vital enough at once to give purpose to fagged majorities among the Allies and to lessen among enemy peoples the willingness to prolong the war.

From his study in the White House, Woodrow Wilson conducted the campaign whose result made him the greatest general of the war. The last chapter of his effective leadership must deal with a tragic paradox. Most lasting of the war executives in his term of unbroken power, he was first to fall after victory had been attained. While the Allied world acclaimed him as a savior, and enemy peoples looked to him as their buckler, his own people turned against his leadership. The greatest demobilization in history had begun before Foch accepted the German signatures to the Armistice. Before the battle was quieted on November 11, Wilson, by parliamentary defeat, had been discredited. Discredited, too, he was by a people whose mass mind at the moment marched with his, and who, like him, beheld beyond victory the dawning of a better world.

For ten months after his suggestion of the Fourteen Points to a world unready for them, Woodrow Wilson faced three audiences, with as many preferences. Never for a day was he able to forget the requirements of each. All must be carried with him if his goal was to be attained. He was, in three rôles, prophet, President, and politician.

Before the world, he was prophet. Already he had the ear of liberal and weary groups as he gave to the war an objective worth fighting for. British labor had adopted him, American labor stood behind him, a world league seemed so reasonable an imitation of the American Federal Government that his fellow citizens could follow him, and the common folk among the enemies began to sense his meaning. Before a world audience whose willing consent was essential to the functioning of a new world order he was bound to elaborate the logic of the order. As the war neared its end he had much to overcome.

Within enemy countries the Governments struggled not only for victory but for existence. Ruling classes were against Wilson. Hence the wedge, repeatedly slipped between the German people and their rulers.

Among the Allies, each with an end not wholly covered by the plea for safety, and some quite willing to be party to agreements to divide the spoils, the American President had to win followers to outvote their rulers. So long as peace was remote, the latter bore with him; with victory approaching, general principles were certain to be threatened by demands for quick returns. The hard-boiled statesmen who persisted in the belief that life is a succession of temporary equilibria, backed by force, may have been nearer right than Wilson; but right or wrong they feared the enemy, distrusted their allies, disliked his program, and evaded when they dared. They had taken their profits, as his disruptive program softened enemy resistance, but no Government had pledged itself to support his terms.

In his own land, American tradition ran against him, for isolation was a habit. To break this down, Wilson had described 'peace without victory' as a 'disentangling' alliance — as a Monroe Doctrine for the world. But at best the American willingness to think in terms of a league to enforce peace was beset by the American habit of approving the avoidance of entangling alliances. First among statesmen to appeal to the world constituency created by growing nearness and instant information, Woodrow Wilson had yet to learn how easy it is for men to commend world doctrines and yet, at home, to vote with national groups for more immediate objectives.

Prophet to the world, he was President at home. As President his was the task to hold the United States to an undiverted prosecution of the war, every part of which was strange in scene, scale, and method. Accepting the war, Americans stepped above their parties, leaving no organized opposition to impede it. The rosters of the armed forces, of the War Boards, of the emergency activities, show how completely Wilson was President of all the United States. There was no room for Theodore Roosevelt, or Leonard Wood, each of whom fell into the pit of his own digging; but Root was used, and Taft, and Hughes. The organic support from both parties becomes more striking when the politics of the Civil War, the War of 1812, or even the Revolution are brought forward for comparison. The handful of war dissenters, scattered through all parties, were too few to give their tone to any major group and remained in painful isolation from start to finish. From the ranks of the Republican Party came indeed those who had done the most useful spadework for a league. Even Roosevelt had given it countenance; Lodge had spoken for it. And William

Howard Taft, busy with war work, was busy also with public advocacy of permanent peace based upon a league of nations. Before the American audience, Woodrow Wilson must act the President, playing no favorites, and directing the good-will of a nation in arms.

Prophet and President, he was politician, too. The constitutional structure of the United States, which gives its administration a continuity unknown to governments of parliamentary type, creates hazards likewise unknown to them. Parliamentary governments could, and did, set up coalitions and postpone elections for the period of the war. But no power in the United States could defer the mechanical incidence of election days, coming with the calendar and without reference to the status of pending public business. With the world on his hands and his people behind him, Wilson was yet forced to conserve his party structure. None knew better than Democrats the partisan mendacity of a Congress at variance with the Chief Executive. They had exhibited it while Taft was President; and many who had hazed Taft then were in office now. A congressional election was approaching, and they had to expect that if they lost it their own political guns would be turned against them, and that a Republican Congress under a Democratic President would be racked by the opposing pulls of patriotism and party gain. A statesman, to be useful as a statesman, must stay in office. Much more, a politician, to stay politician, must get re-elected.

The American peculiarity with its automatic days of political reckoning and its lame-duck sessions, could not be ignored by a party leader, even though he was also President and prophet. The Democratic interlude in which Woodrow Wilson did his work had been prolonged six years. It owed much of its doctrine to independent men, outside their parties; and much of its power to a group of legislators sitting in seats captured from normally Republican constituencies in 1912. The six-year terms of Senators elected with Wilson were coming to an end. On the ability of the President, as politician, to hold these seats against the normal habit of their voters, hung the political fate of the United States

for the last two years of his office. Neither before 1918 nor since
has the American Government, on dead center, failed to lag.
Prophet and President depended on the politician.

'Politics is adjourned,' and the election 'will go to those who
think least of it,' said the President, speaking to Congress on May
27, a few hours after the Germans drove the French from the
Chemin des Dames and headed for the Marne. He hoped he
spoke the truth, for it was his duty as politician that was least
consistent with his success as President or prophet. He asked for
quick passage of a second revenue bill, and returned to the White
House to read that night the disturbing dispatches telling of the
French retreat. The next morning came the more encouraging
bulletins on the neatness of the First Division effort at Cantigny.
The Overman Act (May 20) had just given him authority to
adjust the Government to the requirements of the war. The re-
staffed war machine was functioning under the names of supermen. Roosevelt, the night before, had brought diners to their
feet at the Blackstone in Chicago, as he shook hands with Taft.
Will H. Hays was on his way to Indianapolis to sound the keynote
of a country's war before a State Republican convention. There
he was welcomed as chairman of the Republican National Committee, yet he spoke not as Republican but as chairman of the
Indiana State Council of Defense. The applause that welcomed
Hays drowned the complaint of Senator Harry S. New, from the
same platform. New, who was not up for re-election in 1918 and
hence was free, called the President 'the most uncompromising
in his partisanship of any man who has occupied the White House
since the days of Andrew Jackson.' Hays may have agreed with
New, but he held his words, for it was his business to carry his party
through the war and leave it solvent. Neither he, nor the State
chairmen whom he called into quiet conference in Chicago on
Labor Day, could see a way to contest the November elections
without risking the loyal status of their party.

As spring gave way to summer, and the American divisions
behaved in action creditably to themselves and satisfactorily
to all concerned with them, it became almost possible to believe

that politics had in fact been adjourned. The President having stated his doctrine in the Fourteen Points, had concentrated on the war. The enemy had aspirations at variance with his doctrine, and the Allies were not ready to commit themselves. Wilson opened the Third Liberty Loan drive at Baltimore in April with 'force, and force alone.' Germany had compelled it. Only force could determine 'whether Right, as America conceives it, or Dominion, as she [Germany] conceives it, shall determine the destinies of mankind.' As against this program no important political group could make headway. Politics lay groggy for the moment, knocked out by patriotic determination to defeat the enemy.

The party gatherings of the summer were tame affairs, dealing with win-the-war oratory, and enlivened only by Wilson's own effort to purge his party of lukewarm representatives. He called their numbers, one by one. Jeff: [sic] McLemore was repudiated in Texas, losing every county in his Seventh District. Slayden, of the Fourteenth Texas, although he had been eleven times elected as a Democrat, withdrew from contest when the President described him as against the war administration. Hardwick of Georgia and Vardaman of Mississippi fought it out in their senatorial primaries, weighted down by presidential letters favoring their opponents, and both were dropped. Republican leaders were cautious with their words, seeing few openings through which it would be safe to attack sitting Democrats who had voted for war measures.

The New York Republican conference, held July 18, met just as the First Division, with a Roosevelt in it, struck the right flank of the German salient on the Marne. At the conference Theodore Roosevelt, saddened but not broken by the loss of his aviator son Quentin, spoke to the leaders on a 'lofty idealism here at home.' He permitted himself only a side remark in abhorrence of 'mock idealism.' Hays spoke from the same platform, and Root, and Taft (describing himself as a 'ghost emerging from the past'). With patriotism dominant, their political depression was measurable by the memorial, carrying on one paper the names of Root and of William Barnes of Albany, inviting Roosevelt to become a candidate for governor again. Said Barnes, explaining his support of a despised critic, 'The people will vote for him because he is Theodore Roosevelt.... Had this nation been led by vision the war would have been already won.' In the ensuing primary Whitman was nominated as candidate to succeed himself; the Democrats brought out a new name, Alfred Emanuel Smith, after a trial balloon carrying the name of William Randolph Hearst had been hauled down.

The political staffs in charge of the approaching canvass were unevenly matched. Woodrow Wilson was his own chief of staff, and Homer S. Cummings, vice-chairman of the Democratic National Committee, played no part comparable to that assumed by Hays in the Republican reorganization of February, 1918. Vance McCormick, Democratic chairman, was too busy with the War Trade Board to do much in politics. The chairman of the Democratic Congressional Committee, Scott Ferris of Oklahoma, who had sat in the House since the admission of his State, made little impression on events. There was small hope of winning new seats from Republican incumbents. It was as much as could be done to try to retain the normal Republican seats already held by Democrats; and since most of these were north and east there was little that Ferris could do about them. When Republicans in Congress made sharp remarks about those individual Southern Democrats who had been lukewarm, there was no net loss in sight, since those, if eliminated in primary, would be succeeded by other Democrats.

The Republican Party, defeated in three elections, in 1912, 1914, and 1916, was determined upon reunion and aimed at 1920. As nearly as any could foretell, Roosevelt was to run again. His reconciliation with Root and Taft suggested that the wounds of 1912 were healing or disregarded. It was the business of Hays to hasten the healing, and until the record of his quiet party talks is published it will be impossible to do more than guess at how he went about it. From the moment of his election as chairman of the Republican National Committee in February, 1918, he moved about the country, scratching none and comforting many. The picture he might have painted was that of a disintegrated party, indefinitely out of office should the war be won, the peace be won, and Woodrow Wilson be allowed to stand on the pinnacle of a new world order. For the moment it was completely inexpedient to bare the wounds of party or to do other than support the war to the uttermost.

The existing set-up of the Republican Congressional Committee was no help to Hays, because its chairman, Frank P. Woods of Iowa, re-elected to the post in January, 1918, lost his renomination to the House in the early summer on his war record. Woods had, before American entry, written letters early in the war that were being used to discredit him as though he were pro-German. Likely to be deposed after his defeat, he resigned as chairman at the end of August, making way for Simeon D. Fess of Ohio who was immediately elected to his post. Three days after Fess accepted the chairmanship, Hays went into conference with Republican State chairmen, thirty-two of them, in Chicago on September 2. What he said there and what they planned are not of the record, since the meeting was given scant publicity. Enough of it leaked out, however, to inspire Tumulty from the White House to inquire of Hays whether he really told his associates that the Democratic Administration 'would even end the war with any kind of compromise if that would ensure continuance of the Democratic Party in power.' Hays met the inquiry with indignant denial, quoting words that said less than those ascribed to him. But before the Austrian peace proposal of September 15 was received and rejected, it was clear that the adjournment of politics was an over-statement. There was, however, even yet no safe aggressive for Republicans to undertake.

What the party could not do, as such, could be done with less danger by outside volunteers. The National Security League was still at work. Having launched itself for preparedness in 1914, it held successive conventions for 'constructive patriotism' and 'national service' thereafter. It announced in midsummer a campaign to eliminate disloyal members from Congress. With Elihu

Root and Alton B. Parker as honorary officers on its letterhead and with an aggressive secretariat in New York, it compiled an 'acid test' for candidates. Eight roll-calls in Congress comprised the test, ranging from the vote to table the McLemore resolution in 1916, to the vote to eliminate volunteers in 1917. Six of the votes were taken before American entry, and only forty-seven of the 435 members of the House came clean. Of these only four were Democrats, and only four came from districts south and west of Pennsylvania. The League sent its questionnaires to every candidate as he raised his head, and flooded with literature the districts of Northern Republicans of whom it disapproved. It did little in the South, where Democrats would succeed Democrats, but concentrated its efforts upon districts in the Middle West. Attacking Democrats more numerously than Republicans, its campaign was suspected as being partisan. It concentrated, too, upon George Creel and his official publicity which it regarded as too soft with Germans.

Quite as important as the installation of party chairmen whose war records were unimpeachable was the installation in August of a new leader of the Republican minority in the Senate, Henry Cabot Lodge. Jacob H. Gallinger of New Hampshire, 'stalwart and standpatter,' in his fifth term as Senator, died on August 17. Next him among Republicans in seniority was Lodge, most bitter perhaps of the congressional critics of Woodrow Wilson. Already Lodge was drafting a personal speech on the 'irreducible minimum' in terms of peace; a speech which the death of Gallinger turned into an utterance from the leader of the opposition. With the Marne pocket cut off and the initiative shifted to the hands of Foch, it was possible to hope for victory and to suggest that only Republicans would know what to do with it. The maps in the papers were showing the daily gains of Haig in the battle of the Somme, renewed on August 8. The letters from the newsmen in France, now passed with details of the fighting of the early summer, set up a picture of victorious Yanks. The world read of the German conference at Spa on August 14, although it did not know that the German High Command knew the war was lost. 'We intend,' said Lodge, with irony directed at the President, as he made his speech on August 23, 'to make the world safe for democracy. But what exactly do we mean by democracy?' He made it clear that he, at least, was not fighting for democracy in the meaning of the President. 'We are fighting ... for security.' And he traversed the Fourteen Points, endorsing only those that pointed to a Germany 'in a position where she can never again attempt to conquer and ruin the world.' 'In a word,' he said, 'we must go to Berlin and there dictate peace.' He warned his colleagues, from his position as senior Republican on the Senate Committee on Foreign Relations, against a negotiated peace and the treachery of the Hohenzollerns. When the next day his party conference formally elected him floor leader, the lines had begun to form for the political campaign. A week later he told the correspondent of the *New York Times* why he hoped his party might win in Maine on September 9, and carry both houses in November: 'it will best promote the one great object ... speedy and complete victory'; and he went on to describe his party as the one best adapted to the intricate task of reconstruction. Fess followed him with a formal manifesto: 'Republican success will not only insure the most vigorous prosecution of the war, but it will be a guaranty against a compromise, and, therefore, an inconclusive peace, a "peace without victory." ' He declared that after peace the United States would need in Congress 'the nation's best talent.'

It was impossible for Republican leaders to oppose the war, even had they desired it, because their constituents had gone fully to war and would have rejected them. It would have been suicidal in the party sense, since such a course would have invited the Administration to turn the election into a test of loyalty, would have guaranteed a Democratic victory, and would have left the Republican Party tainted as disloyal. The Lodge manifesto, suggesting a war loyalty greater than the President's, offered a way to fight; but it was difficult to determine when and how. The two houses of Congress, only in intermittent session during midsummer, had little business on their hands, and many of their members were on vacation. The Democratic Senate whip, Lewis of Illinois, was abroad, 'whiskers, spats, rainbow vest, and all,' as a caustic Representative described him. He was making victory speeches to Allied audiences instead of working on easy renomination at home. The faithful remnant on the Capitol front had bills involving more detail than principle while they waited for the revenue law to run the gantlet of committees. There was a huge deficiency appropriation bill; and the eighteen-to-forty-five enrollment bill, which became a law on August 31; and a matter of war-time prohibition which made Northern constituencies restive and upset the budget by cutting off the revenue from alcohol; and the proposed Constitutional Amendment for woman suffrage which was hung up in the Senate. This last continued hung up, even after the President visited the Senate on September 30 to urge approval as a war measure — 'a vitally necessary war measure.' He needed the passage as a politician if for no other reason, because militant suffragists were holding him personally responsible for the delay in Congress, and Democratic members up for re-election were facing organized opposition because of the failure of the party to endorse the vote.

The events of the autumn kept the canvass slow, deferring an opening for a party fight. Irrepressible voices from either side attacked the other on its record on the war, making small headway. But leaders watched their step. By tacit agreement the adjournment of major politics was prolonged into October, for the Fourth Liberty Loan was under way and McAdoo had announced the necessity to raise six billions, by four and one-fourth per cent bonds, to run for twenty years. The curt rebuff to Austria, released September 16, was curt enough for Lodge; 'The Government of the United States . . . will entertain no proposal for a conference upon a matter concerning which it has made its position and purpose so plain.' As politician the President could not have afforded to speak otherwise. As President he was expected to speak this way; and Lodge characterized the answer as one to meet 'with universal approval.'

The fourth drive for funds, organized in the Federal Reserve Districts with even greater care than its three predecessors had been, opened on September 28 to the tune of action dispatches from the Meuse–Argonne, and closed October 19 with the loan again oversubscribed. There were war trophies now which were sent on tour to arouse enthusiasm, and American heroes, crippled in action. Charles Dana Gibson and Howard Chandler Christy and their coadjutors papered the land with flaming posters. Mary Pickford did her bit. And success was reached in spite of a handicap that would have obstructed politics as well as patriotism.

The 'Spanish flu' came to America. Whence the epidemic came, and how, was a matter for harassed doctors, ignorant of its pathology. It raised huge casualty lists and filled hospitals in France. It permeated the Army camps in the United States. It overspread the country until town councils forbade citizens to appear in public without the muslin masks that were designed to check infection. Theaters and schools were closed and the movie producers of Hollywood cut down on their release of films. Public meetings were ordered to the open air or banned. The desperate effort to check contagion by preventing crowds cut into the audiences that had been expected to listen to the orators on tour. The political meetings which might have given life to the campaign were curtailed. The President himself gave up the trip that might, if taken, have done more than float the loan. He gave it up on the ground of public business and forewent the last great stroke of political guidance that might have left him in November still the undisputed leader of his people.

He launched the loan, however, speaking in the Metropolitan Opera House in New York on the evening of September 27. Here he faced his three audiences in his three rôles, with a message for each. For his party, he had to stress the note taken in the reply to Austria. For his country, he had to stress the winning of the war. For the world, enemy or Allied, he had to restate the aims with which he had already gripped its masses and softened the allegiance of enemy peoples to their war Governments.

He repudiated compromise: 'no peace shall be obtained by any kind of compromise or abatement of the principles we have avowed.' He stressed a 'peoples' war' in which the 'common will of mankind has been substituted for the particular purposes of individual States'; in which 'the thought of the mass of men, whom statesmen are supposed to instruct and lead, has grown more and more unclouded, more and more certain of what it is that they are fighting for.' 'The German people,' he said, 'must by this time be fully aware that we cannot accept the word of those who forced this war upon us.' There must be, he declared, a league of nations; without which 'peace will rest in part upon the word of outlaws and only upon that word.' He challenged the leaders of the Allies to answer their people as to aims as explicitly as he had done it, and to criticize him should he be 'in any way mistaken' in his interpretation of the issues. He enumerated five 'particulars' in elaboration of his Fourteen Points:

> First. The impartial justice meted out must involve no discrimination between those to whom we wish to be just and those to whom we do not wish to be just. It must be a justice that plays no favorites and knows no standard but the equal rights of the several peoples concerned.
>
> Second. No special or separate interest of any single nation or any group of nations can be made the basis of any part of the settlement which is not consistent with the common interest of all.
>
> Third. There can be no leagues or alliances or special covenants and understandings within the general and common family of the league of nations.
>
> Fourth. And, more specifically, there can be no special, selfish, economic combinations within the league and no employment or any form of economic boycott or exclusion except as the power of economic penalty by exclusion from the markets of the world may be vested in the league of nations itself as a means of discipline and control.
>
> Fifth. All international agreements and treaties of every kind must be made known in their entirety to the rest of the world.

Wilson spoke for the loan on a Friday night, and before the weekend was over the whole two hundred miles of Western Front was again in motion, with American divisions fighting in each of the armies. As Americans read his words, they read, too, that Bulgarian envoys were seeking the headquarters of General Franchet d'Espérey, ready to accept peace without conditions. The Saloniki drive, started September 15, was already over. On Monday, September 30, Bulgaria laid down arms in unconditional surrender. The alliance of the Central Powers was broken and the uninterrupted line from the Baltic to Palestine was no longer intact. Damascus fell to Allenby the next day, his victory pointing to the near moment when Turkey, too, completely isolated, would leave the Central Powers to shift for themselves and abandon terms in search for peace.

At Berlin and at the German headquarters in the field the note had changed. Screened from Allied observation by the skill of the command, as the armies backed away from old positions, the note was now of despair. Memoirs reveal the conviction that the war began to be lost on July 18. By August 14 the leaders had given up hope of enforcing German will upon the Allies. They were now pressing upon the political government for immediate peace lest they be broken in the field and all be lost. They could not give guaranties of ability to hold together long enough for orderly retirement to the Rhine front. Behind the screen of the armies began a battle of the wits to win a promise that the peace should not be more bitter than the doctrine of the Fourteen Points, as now interpreted by the five 'particulars' of September 27. Woodrow Wilson had thus far been floating his doctrine upon the winds; he was now compelled to maneuver for it against the avidity of the enemy ready to accept what it must, and the reluctance of the Allies. The contest came to a focus on his desk, since he alone was in any way morally bound by the terms he had phrased, and since his country alone was completely free to discuss a peace.

Inside Germany, where never was the relentless one-minded *bund* that Allied imagery set up, the people were out of hand. The more liberal groups, not easy to control when battles were won, became unmanageable when battles were lost. There was validity in the picture of the German people as something different from the Government that ruled them. Death, hunger, and politics had for a year made it increasingly harder for the Imperial Government to carry on. Demands for parliamentary control of the Government and for electoral reform were impossible equally to talk down or to suppress. And as it became clear that Wilson would make no peace with military autocrats, the autocrats sought to disguise themselves as something else while their domestic enemies sought to abolish them in fact. At the end of September the resignation of the Imperial Chancellor, von Hertling, was in the hands of the Emperor; on October 2 a new Chancellor, Prince Maximilian of Baden, something of a liberal, was in office to discover on his doorstep the imperative demand of the army that he find peace now. Three days later Max announced to the Reichstag that he had made appeal to the President of the United States.

The first peace note, transmitted through the Swiss *chargé d'affaires*, did not reach Lansing until Monday morning, October 7; but already its substance had reached the headlines. And when the Senate convened on Monday the Republican leaders were convinced that the peace plot was at hand. McCumber was ready with a concurrent resolution, 'That there shall be no cessation of hostilities and no armistice until the Imperial German Government shall disband its armies and surrender its arms and munitions, together with the Navy, to the United States and her allies in this war.' Norris of Nebraska read into the *Congressional Record* the 'unconditional surrender' note of Grant to Buckner. Republican fears were voiced lest Wilson should allow himself to be hoodwinked. Democratic responses, not less insistent for complete victory, saw victory embraced within the terms stated by the President. What Germany asked (and what Austria-Hungary endorsed) was that the President should 'take steps for the restoration of peace,' invite the belligerents to name plenipotentiaries to discuss it, and bring about 'the immediate conclusion of a general armistice on land, on water, and in the air.' Prince Max avowed that his Government accepted, 'as a basis for the peace negotiations, the program laid down by the President of the United States' in his various utterances from the Fourteen Points to the five 'particulars.' There was no doubt then, nor is there now, that the overture was a desperate attempt to get better terms than would be possible should the war continue. To this extent — by the concealment of the German extremity — the overture was indeed a German trick.

While Senators safeguarded the constitutional right of their body to pass on treaties the President withdrew to his study. In Allied capitals the principals were nervous lest he, in his freedom of action, should involve them further than they cared to be involved. He summoned House to Washington and had him pack his trunks for Paris. House recommended as the response a colorless note announcing that the President would confer with the Allies. It could not be believed that Germany was really through; nor could there be thought of lessening ultimate victory by calling off the drive. The President took counsel, kept the discussion open since it might lead to peace, but conceded nothing. On Tuesday afternoon Lansing handed to the Swiss *chargé* and to the press a note that called the bluff.

Not showing a diplomatic hand, the President asked certain things and stated others. First, he inquired whether German acceptance of his terms was such that 'entering into discussions would be only to agree upon the practical details of their application'; second, he advised that he could not propose an armistice to his associates while the armies of the Central Powers were 'upon their soil'; third, he asked, what would have been grievously impertinent in normal times: 'whether the Imperial Chancellor is speaking merely for the constituted authorities of the Empire who have so far conducted the war.'

Each day was bringing a new battle-front in France and crowding it closer to the line of German communications. Foch was preparing to extend the front into Lorraine, and Liggett was on October 12 assigned to command the Second Army. The new Imperial Chancellor was himself discovering the degree of demoralization which the army folk had not uncovered to the political authorities. He had gained no relief by asking for a conference. He could neither draw back nor assert that he was not speaking for the old 'constituted authorities.' In his second note, October 12, meeting the inquiries of the President, he omitted the word 'Imperial' and described the 'present German Government' as having been 'formed by conferences and in agreement with the great majority of the Reichstag.' He declared his proposal to be supported by 'the will of the majority' and in 'the name of the German Government and of the German people.' In their name he avowed that his Government (he spoke also for Austria), 'for the purpose of bringing about an armistice, declares itself ready to comply with the propositions of the President in regard to evacuation.' He was categorical in asserting that the 'German Government has accepted the terms laid down by President Wilson.' Critics from all parties were quick to note that the Chancellor had stopped short of saying that his office was the political agent of the Reichstag majority.

The unofficial text of this second German note, broadcast instantly from Nauen, was before the President in advance of the arrival Monday morning, October 14, of the Swiss *chargé* carrying his decode of the original. House and Lansing were with the President as he considered which way to turn. Baker was just back from France and England with eye-witness reports of the Allied effort. The Republican Senators, assembling Monday morning, plunged immediately into discussion of the note in language that drew from Ashurst the hope that their speeches were 'not made for the purpose of securing any partisan advantage in the coming elections.' Interrupted for luncheon, the discussion ran through the afternoon, with Brandegee, McCumber, and the Democratic Reed leading in 'dolorous speeches' in criticism of the correspondence; and with Cummins of Iowa making a proposal for 'capital punishment for a nation.' They were not stopped when Ashurst, back from a visit to the White House, assured the Senate 'that when the President does speak ... it will be a speech ... which will not in any way relax the iron grip which our soldiers ... have in Flanders and in France.' Their uncertainty as to the answer was soon ended. Before the day's work ceased at half-past six, Hitchcock was able to read the Senate the text of the reply that had already gone forward. Even Lodge liked it: 'eminently satisfactory' he described it to the *Christian Science Monitor*.

In the light of the two notes already received, the President

was 'frank and direct.' Germany must clearly understand —
Austria would be considered separately — that evacuation and
armistice were matters to be determined, if at all, not by any
mixed commission, but by 'the military advisers'; and that the
United States would accept no arrangement 'which does not provide absolutely satisfactory safeguards and guaranties of the maintenance of the present military supremacy' of the Allied armies.
He assumed that the Allied Governments would agree with him
in this. No armistice could be considered while the German
armies persisted in their 'illegal and inhumane practices,' while
they devastated Flanders and France as they withdrew, or while
German submarines sunk 'passenger ships at sea.' And he quoted
his words, spoken at Mount Vernon on July 4, to the effect that at
the peace there must be destroyed 'every arbitrary power anywhere that can ... of its single choice disturb the peace of the
world or ... at least its reduction to virtual impotency.' The power
hitherto controlling the German people was of the sort he meant.
'It is indispensable that the Governments associated against
Germany should know beyond a peradventure with whom they
are dealing.' The conversation still lay open; but the war went
on.

The stage-settings of the negotiation were changing while the
actors spoke their lines. The Fourteen Points acquired new meaning and limitation as events developed, in spite of enemy effort
to make of them a specific contract to whose benefits Germany
and Austria were entitled whenever they should choose to claim
them. To Austria-Hungary Lansing indicated an altered attitude
on October 18, pointing out that the 'autonomous development'
of its peoples, demanded in the tenth point, must be considered
in the light of what its peoples had done for themselves. The
Jugo-Slavs had so defended their aspirations for freedom, not
autonomy, as to entitle them to recognition. The Czecho-Slovaks,
with enough of their people in the United States to make a nation,
had declared their independence and as early as September 3 the
United States had recognized their right to it and had conceded
military recognition to their belligerency. Hungary was declaring

its independence of the Dual Monarchy while the German Chancellor was brooding over his next reply.

It was no longer possible for Germany to acquire merit by offering a withdrawal from Belgium, one of the much-used baits for peace. Its army was being ejected thence. Albert entered his recaptured Channel towns in triumph and the French were ringing their own church bells in Lille and Laon. There was not much bargaining value even in the discontinuance of submarine activity, for the North Sea mine barrage was nearly tight.

Back to Berlin, as the note of October 14 was put upon the cables, the question of surrender came, and back to German army headquarters. In Berlin, Prince Max and his Foreign Secretary Solf could not let go of what they had begun. At headquarters the army leaders, who had forced Max to open the discussion, and who saw the United States still outside their trap, were prepared to argue that surrender in the field would be no worse than the acceptance of all that was stated or implied in the American notes. Much of what happened in the next six days was revealed by the German Republican Government, a few months later, when it published the documents to show how the army had let the people down. In *Vorgeschichte des Waffenstillstandes* (1919) — which the Carnegie Endowment translated in 1924 as *The Preliminary History of the Armistice* — it let the papers tell the story 'wie es eigentlich gewesen,' from the beginning at the council held at Spa on August 14. Back to Potsdam, too, went the question of surrender. Here it took the form of abdication, or something worse. The dynasty of William II was identified in the German mind, as in that of Woodrow Wilson, as chief among those masters who had betrayed the German people.

The answer of Germany, dated October 20, came through from London in informal shape in time to be carried in the morning papers of Tuesday, October 22. The official translation, released by the State Department that night, was printed the next morning by the side of the response of the President. Wilson was prompt; so prompt, indeed, that he missed the political advantage he might have picked from a delay dragging out the proceedings until after the elections which were only two weeks off. He was able now to take action, after more than a fortnight of inquiry designed to clear the air and to uncover traps.

Solf signed the German note of grieved submission; grieved because there was no room for negotiation concerning terms of armistice or of evacuation, but submissive in the hope that the President would 'approve of no demand which would be irreconcilable with the honor of the German people and with opening a way to a peace of justice.' Grieved, too, he was, because of the charge that retreating troops had done unwarrantable damage and that submarines had operated heartlessly as well as illegally. But his Government accepted what it must. He made specific admission that 'Hitherto the representation of the people in the German Empire has not been endowed with an influence on the formation of the Government.' But he pledged that the Government just formed was different, based on equal and universal franchise under a new constitutional scheme, and that now and in the future no Government could stay in office 'without possessing the confidence of the majority of the Reichstag.' Conceiving this to be a 'clear and unequivocal' response, Solf begged the President to 'bring about an opportunity for fixing the details' of armistice and evacuation.

Wilson had gone as far as he could go alone. The nerves of the Allied leaders, uneasy lest he should go too far, had been soothed by the stern caution of his notes. But it was beyond his power to grant an armistice on any terms. All he could do, he had done. His note of October 23 admitted that he could no longer 'decline to take up with the Governments with which the Government of the United States is associated the question of an armistice.' He had accordingly transmitted to them the correspondence, with the suggestion that if they were prepared to consider an armistice on the basis thus proposed they call upon their military advisers to draft terms to protect their interests and to 'ensure to the Associated Governments the unrestricted power to safeguard and enforce the details of the peace to which the German Government has agreed.' But he warned that Government that the only possible armistice would be one leaving the Associated Powers 'in a position to enforce any arrangements . . . and to make a renewal of hostilities on the part of Germany impossible.'

Candor forced him, in his concluding paragraph, to remind Solf that the German statements as to Reichstag control contained no guaranty that the control would last, or that it was even yet complete. It was not evident that the political government could control the military, or that the power of the King of Prussia in the Empire was impaired. The peace of the world called for plain speaking and he was harsh. The world could not trust 'those who have hitherto been the masters of German policy' and peace could be made only with 'veritable representatives of the German people who have been assured of a genuine constitutional standing.' If the Associated Powers must deal now with 'the military masters and the monarchical autocrats of Germany' they must demand 'not peace negotiations but surrender.'

In the covering note with which Lansing passed to the Allies the correspondence, it was stated that the President had 'endeavored to safeguard with the utmost care the interests of the peoples at war with Germany,' and the hope was expressed that each Ally 'will think he has succeeded and will be willing to co-operate in the steps which he has suggested.'

The matter of armistice and evacuation was thereafter in the hands of the Associated Powers, with every Cabinet debating the details, and with Foch, as chief of the military advisers, calling his generals into conference. The Supreme War Council, moribund since July, was called again to life as the clearing-house for Allied purpose. House, who had sailed after the drafting of the note of October 14, was in Paris by the twenty-sixth, bearing credentials from the President and empowered to engage with leaders there in conferences while the military advisers drafted the paragraphs of an armistice agreement. In the United States there was a lull while the Allies debated; a lull so far as diplomacy was concerned, but a vacuum to be abhorred by politics. The day that Colonel House reached France, October 25, the President did either too much or too little; but whatever its dimensions his act dug ground from beneath his feet so as to endanger his ability as President or as prophet to complete the work be had begun.

The lagging canvass had kept politics largely adjourned during the period of the loan drive, the flu epidemic, and the exciting days of conversations with Germany; adjourned, but not *sine die*. Each gain of the President as he crowded the German Government into its corner made it harder for Republican strategists to chart a battle or to make capital out of a claim to patriotism more stalwart than his. Sometimes the opposition leaders approved his steps, sometimes regretted them because they were so successful, and sometimes they deplored them.

The dilemma of the President was that of every President who believes in his mission. Confident in the soundness of his policy as a national policy, he must display it as national and invite public support regardless of party. Yet the mechanism for its accomplishment cannot be other than political, and the ability of any honest President to serve his people hangs on his ability as a partisan leader to secure enough votes to keep his party friends in office. When, however, he acts the party leader to defend his majority he invites the charge of political hypocrisy. Woodrow Wilson, the professor of government, would have had no difficulty in making a sound diagnosis of the party need. Woodrow Wilson, the politician, as he carried through the program of his first two years, would have known what to do and how to do it. The historian is driven to choose between a belief that the politician had lost his insight and a belief that the prophet was so wrapt in his prophecy that he lost touch with reality. For whatever reason, the grip on politics was lost.

As minority President, in his first Congress, Wilson had possessed a congressional majority bestowed upon him by the Republican schism of 1912, with freshmen Democrats sitting for constituencies unused to such representation. In 1914 the elections, reinforcing a little the Democrats in the Senate, had revealed the beginning of a recovery movement whereby Republicans, without acquiring a majority of the House had regained some sixty Representatives.

The elections in the presidential year two years later, 1916, installed a Congress that was Democratic only by courtesy. In the Senate a Democratic majority of under a dozen held on; but in the House there were more Republicans than Democrats, and the opposition might have organized the House for the war Congress had it been able to command the votes of a handful of independent Representatives. War or no war, the United States was settling back to its normal Republican control. If the Congress to be elected in 1918 was to be under Democratic control, permitting the United States to escape the sabotage inherent in a divided Congress, it was vital for Democrats to hold all of what they had, to pick up here and there a few more Representatives, and to defend in their seats the half-dozen Senators from normally Republican States who still held on. Except as death had thinned their number, the Senators precariously elected with Woodrow Wilson in 1912 must be re-elected or replaced by other Democrats. To crowd them out by any safe procedure was sound Republican politics; to save them for the party was Democratic necessity. And beneath the surface lull of politics pressure was turned on in those Republican constituencies where Democrats were still in Congress.

When Woodrow Wilson announced in May that 'politics is adjourned,' he had not yet forgotten his disaster in Wisconsin, where Paul O. Husting had in 1914 profited by Republican dissension to attain the Senate. Dead by his duck-gun in 1917, Husting was lost to the Administration. In the special election, in April, 1918, to choose his successor, Administration Democrats made every effort to retain the seat, although before Paul Husting there had been no Democratic Senator elected from Wisconsin since the Democratic interlude of 1891–93. A candidate was found in Joseph E. Davies. The Vice-President, Marshall, invaded Wisconsin, reinforcing J. Hamilton Lewis, and 'spilled the beans,' as he endorsed Davies against La Follette's old lieutenant Irvine L. Lenroot. The President did a damaging bit by calling the 'acid test' against Lenroot, who had voted against tabling the McLemore resolution. He helped elect Lenroot, and provided the caption, 'acid test,' for the National Security League to use in the autumn.

The honors were not uneven between May and October, as both parties avoided open political aggressives. The President proscribed Democrats in Democratic constituencies, but otherwise generally kept silent, save in Michigan. Here he invited Henry Ford, of no known politics, to enter the primaries as a Democrat. Ford entered both primaries, seeking also Republican endorsement for the seat which William Alden Smith had held since Russell A. Alger had vacated it. Against him in the Republican primary in August a former Republican Secretary of the Navy, Truman H. Newberry, was entered. Ford gained his Democratic nomination, but lost the other to Newberry whose overample financial backing made a national scandal out of the primary, and gave body to later Democratic gibes that the Republican majority of the Senate was 'out on bail.' Newberry was elected in November, not thereby changing the Republican strength in the Senate.

In Colorado, Delaware, Illinois, and Kansas Democratic Senators first elected in 1912 were under fire. In New Hampshire such a Democrat did not even seek renomination. In Missouri, normally Democratic, Republicans had hopes of ousting the temporary incumbent who had gone in on the death of William J. Stone. Should Democratic successors fail to get these seats, all of them, the Democratic majority was likely to be lost for the next two years, and Henry Cabot Lodge would certainly become chairman of the Senate Committee on Foreign Relations to receive whatever treaty the President of the United States should transmit for concurrence.

With the note of October 23 out of the way, the President yielded to nagging from within his party and to exasperation at the Republican roll-calling in which speakers asserting a Republican war loyalty recited the difficulties which the Administration had had with its own partisans: Champ Clark, and Claude Kitchin, and Stanley H. Dent (who had let the management of the Selective Service Act pass into the hands of the Republican Kahn of California), and Thomas S. Martin, the Democratic leader of the Senate, and Stone, chairman of the Foreign Relations Committee. On October 25 the White House issued a political manifesto addressed to 'My fellow countrymen,' and thereby brought politics fully back to life. If the people approved his leadership, Wilson urged them to permit him to continue it by 'returning a Democratic majority to both the Senate and the House of Representatives.' He paid tribute to the patriotism of the leaders of the minority, but spoke 'plain truth' in describing them as 'anti-Administration.' They had sought to take the conduct of the war out of his hands; and if they should be returned as leaders to the next Congress the world would interpret it 'as a repudiation of my leadership.' After his appeal he stayed out of the last days of the canvass; but he had done too little to arouse a non-partisan support for his Administration and too much to let it be hoped that the Republican tacticians would take it without rejoinder.

Hays, gloves off, was instantly in print describing the appeal as 'ungracious . . . wanton . . . mendacious.' Lodge and Smoot, Gillett and Fess, subscribed to a counter-manifesto. Republicans who had urged a party victory that they, better than Democrats, might support the war, denounced the President for asking that his own party might receive endorsement. Roosevelt, who had himself in 1898 demanded a Republican Congress so that William McKinley might complete his work, thundered defiance from Carnegie Hall. Having opposed a coalition Government in January, he now abused the President for not having formed one. He demanded war continuance until there should be an unconditional surrender, and a Republican Congress that might prevent the writing of the Fourteen Points into the agreements of the world. He foresaw in a league of nations a United States outvoted by Asiatics, an outside interference with American immigration policies, and, in point three, an abandonment of the principle of the protective tariff. For a full week the campaign raged in such a way as to unsettle every Democratic incumbent of a seat that he had gained with the help of Republican votes and to accelerate the re-establishment of the normal American equilibrium of Republican control. Moreover, on the morning, November 5, when the votes were cast, it was known that the need for war loyalty to an Administration had passed into history, for the Allied consent to accede to a request for armistice terms was on its way from Versailles, through Washington, to Germany. Should Germany accept the ultimatum, the acceptance would constitute complete surrender; should Germany reject, the victorious armies of the pursuit could write their own peace in a victory now within easy reach.

The votes reflected the national state of mind as well as the partisan emotion. The Democrats lost the House, with Republicans seating nearly twenty more Representatives than an absolute majority. They lost the pivotal Senators, not to be compensated for by taking a Massachusetts seat away from Republicans. They lost so many that by a majority of one the control of the Senate passed to those for whom a league of nations built by Woodrow Wilson had no charm. And while the people voted, the President relayed to Germany the word that 'Marshal Foch has been authorized by the Government of the United States and the Allied Governments to receive properly accredited representatives of the German Government, and to communicate to them the terms of an armistice.'

XX. VICTORY

THE real significance of the Democratic loss of Congress was
clouded for the laity. The Republican leaders knew what it
meant. In a parliamentary government it would have brought
about at once a new cabinet with a new prime minister. The
political leaders among the Allies had a glimpse of its meaning; a
glimpse brought into focus as private letters from Americans they
knew described the President as a leader without authority. But
the European peoples, seeing Wilson still in office, assumed that he
still possessed the power to lead. And Americans, wrapped up in
victory and peace, with another short session of the Democratic
Congress still ahead, generally forgot that it was only another
'lame-duck' session. The vision of a 'world safe for democracy,' to
be kept safe by a league of nations endorsed by the United States,
continued to have visibility clearer than that possessed by mere
realities of party politics.

The war continued, with an end in sight, but with no let-up.
There was still no certainty that Germany would accept the devastating terms laid down by the Allies. The War Department took a
chance, quietly stopping the sailing of more men and preparing
quickly to cancel unfilled war contracts. But with an enemy in
whose complete collapse it was impossible really to believe,
prudence required that pressure should not be relaxed until the
very end. The Italian armies had started back to Caporetto on
October 24 and Austrian elimination was now at hand.

Paris became the center of the negotiation after the President on
October 23 transmitted the German notes and his responses. And
on October 31 the Supreme War Council held formal session.

The meeting had been deferred until substantial agreement had been reached upon most of the matters at issue. So far as armistice terms were concerned, these were in the hands of Foch and there was no difference of opinion upon their complete, conclusive severity. They were to end the war beyond a possibility of reopening it. From Foch was expected, too, counsel in the matter of policy: should there be an armistice at all, or should the aggressive be continued until the enemy surrendered in the field?

Outside the possible competence of Foch was the question of larger policy, upon which the position of the United States was firm. The German notes had made desperate efforts to suggest that Germany was animated by a desire for peace on the Wilson basis rather than because of inability longer to resist the will of the victor. But by this time the Allies knew better, and before they pledged themselves in an armistice to any principles that should bind them in a subsequent peace, they could not escape the necessity to re-examine the Fourteen Points and the five 'particulars,' and to determine the extent to which they were willing to be bound. House put it bluntly to the Premiers that if they rejected the proposals the President would be forced to drop the negotiation. This, said House, 'would leave the President free... to determine whether the United States should continue to fight for the principles laid down by the Allies.' Anticipating, as Wilson blindly did, that Wilson would retain a majority and might be present in person at the peace conference backed by his authority over world idealism, the Allies were unwilling to permit a wedge to be driven between themselves and him. They might have been less unwilling had the decision been delayed until after the election. Wilson had for the moment a strong grip on their weary home constituencies. With victory at hand the world desired peace.

Hence arose the Allied discussions at home, the talks with House to get at the inner content of the mind of the President, and the decision that if Germany should accept the armistice they could afford to accept most of the Wilson doctrine.

On two points in variation or elaboration of the doctrine they were immovable. When they told the President they were ready

for Foch to receive the German envoys, they told him also of
amendments to his doctrine. These he transmitted to Germany on
November 5. His second point, they said, 'relating to what is
usually described as the freedom of the seas, is open to various
interpretations, some of which they could not accept. They must,
therefore, reserve to themselves complete freedom on this subject
when they enter the peace conference.' To this extent Wilson's
doctrinal contest with the Allies paused at less than victory for
him; and Germany received the armistice knowing this. In the
second place, and here the President agreed with the Allies as he
transmitted their decision to Germany, they expanded his declaration that 'invaded territories must be restored as well as evacuated
and freed.' The Associated Powers removed all doubts: 'they understand that compensation will be made by Germany for all
damage done to the civilian population of the Allies and to their
property by the aggression of Germany by land, by sea, and from
the air.'

Subject to these qualifications, and the acceptance of the
Armistice, they agreed to make peace on the terms laid down by
the President. They were well on the way to their agreement, after
private conference, when Foch advised the Supreme War Council
on October 31 that if necessary he could force the enemy to 'his
complete defeat.' In the discussions with his commanders which
he had begun five days before, Foch had found himself between
Haig and Pershing. The former believed an armistice to be
expedient and desired it not to be too harsh to be accepted. The
latter preferred no armistice at all. Foch asserted that such an
armistice as he would draft would accomplish the purposes of the
Allies, and that with these accomplished the war should stop.
Events in the field were making it each day easier to tighten the
demands. Turkey had signed a surrender on October 30, effective
the next day when the Council met. And the papers of November
3 carried in streamer headlines: 'Austria Quits.' The Austrian
surrender was effective at 3 P.M. on Monday, November 4, leaving
Germany in complete isolation before the American polls were
opened. That afternoon the Premiers signed the terms of the

Armistice, House cabled them in confidence to the President (for they were to be published only after Germany had asked for them), and victory hung upon the degree of the defeat of Germany. On election day the German fleet at Kiel was in the hands of mutineers, resisting an order to go to sea, and Germany had no longer any option. Ludendorff was already out of his command; and on the night of Saturday, November 9, the Emperor crossed the frontier of the Netherlands, an ex-Kaiser, seeking asylum.

Immediately on the receipt of the American note of November 5 the German envoys started for the frontier, guided by wireless from Foch who indicated the sector where fire would be stopped permitting them to cross the lines. French guides received them late on Thursday night, bringing them early Friday morning to the private train of Foch, parked in the Forest of Compiègne. Here, from the posture in which they awaited the offer of an armistice, they were driven to the humiliation of requesting terms. No proposal from them was entertained. No immediate cessation of hostilities was granted. They were given seventy-two hours in which to sign the memorandum; hours during which Foch continued his preparations for the extension of his active line into Lorraine. Hopeful, though without warrant for a hope, since all they had received was permission to ask for an armistice, the German delegates were halted by the severity of the military terms. Their powers to sign were insufficient to warrant them in signing the military memorandum; and although Foch was adamant upon the three-day limit, he permitted them to dispatch couriers to Germany for the additional authority.

The paper handed them by Foch and the British Admiral Wemyss, who had been delegated to act with him (since the terms were naval as well as military), called for a complete evacuation of the West within fourteen days and an occupation by the Associated armies step by step with the evacuation. It called for the evacuation of the left bank of the Rhine, the occupation by the victors of bridgeheads and sectors at Cologne, Coblenz, and Mainz, and the neutralization of a strip east of the Rhine from Switzerland to the Dutch border, forty kilometers wide at the western end, thirty

kilometers next to Switzerland. It called for immediate repatria-
tion of prisoners of war from German camps, without reciprocity,
and of inhabitants of occupied country who had been deported,
for a cessation of damage, a delivery of military establishments and
supplies and rolling stock for the railways, and a surrender of guns
and planes. It called also for the surrender of the German submarine fleet and the battle fleet, and carried detailed annexes
that stripped away all fighting power. It dealt in similar detail
with the various fronts on which Germany was fighting, and also
required the abandonment of the treaties of Brest-Litovsk and
Bucharest, extorted from Russia and Rumania as Germany had
put them out of the war. It reserved to the Allies and to the United
States full right to make claim for damage done, to requisition
property as needed in the German territory their armies should
occupy, and to maintain without relaxation the blockade conditions they had set up. It was to last for thirty-six days, with option
to extend, subject, however, to denunciation on forty-eight hours'
notice. Six hours after its signing the guns were to cease firing.

Harsh as the Armistice was, it must be signed; though by whom
was a matter of conjecture as revolution swept over Germany on
the day after its delivery. The Hohenzollern abdication ended the
Empire on Saturday. The Provisional Government of what was to
become the new Reich was set up on Sunday with Freidrich
Ebert, a Socialist, as first among the six commissaries. Early on
Monday morning, barely within the three-day limit, the envoys
with their full powers were back with Foch. At 5 A.M., Paris time,
Matthias Erzberger signed the first of the German signatures to the
Armistice, pursuant to which at 11 A.M., on the morning of Novem-
ber 11, the fighting stopped.

They signed in the Forest of Compiègne early enough for the
news to catch the morning papers of the United States, where
streaming headlines proclaimed that 'Germany Surrenders';
in time to make that day a holiday as riotous as though a 'false
armistice' had not preceded it; in time for the chaplain of the
Senate to thank God 'because Thy power has gotten us the victory'
and to pray for wisdom 'for the problems that confront us.' They

signed in time, too, for Woodrow Wilson to visit the Congress in joint session at 1 P.M. to read the terms of the Armistice:

> The war thus comes to an end [he said as he completed the reading of the terms]... it was the privilege of our own people to enter it at its most critical juncture in such fashion and in such force as to contribute in a way of which we are all deeply proud to the great result.... The arbitrary power of the military caste of Germany... is discredited and destroyed.... The great nations which associated themselves to destroy it have now definitely united in the common purpose to set up such a peace as will satisfy the longing of the whole world.... I, for one, do not doubt their purpose or their capacity.

He had forgotten himself as politician, forgotten it too wholly for his own success. But his words were consistent with his language as prophet. As President, he spoke of victory without undue elation, but with a 'humane temper and intention' which he ascribed to the Allied Governments as to his own. He said nothing of the *tour de force*, executed under his hand, which had for the first time mobilized for a common purpose the imagination, man-power, and material strength of American democracy.

THE END

INDEX

NC